SPORTS and ENTERTAINMENT MARKETING 4e

KEN KASER

DOTTY BOEN OELKERS

SOUTH-WESTERN
CENGAGE Learning·

Australia · Brazil · Mexico · Singapore · United Kingdom · United States

SOUTH-WESTERN
CENGAGE Learning·

**Sports and Entertainment Marketing,
Fourth Edition**
Ken Kaser, Dotty Boen Oelkers

SVP Global Product Management, Research,
School & Professional: Frank Menchaca

General Manager, K-12 School Group:
CarolAnn Shindelar

Publishing Director: Eve Lewis

Sr. Developmental Editor: Karen Caldwell

Marketing Manager: Kelsey Hagan

Sr. Content Project Manager: Martha Conway

Sr. Media Editor: Mike Jackson

Manufacturing Planner: Kevin Kluck

Consulting Editor: Peggy Shelton, LEAP
Publishing Services

Production Service: Integra

Sr. Art Director: Michelle Kunkler

Cover and Internal Designer: Tippy McIntosh

Intellectual Property Project Manager:
Michelle McKenna

Photo Researcher: Darren Wright

Permissions Research: Lumina Datamatics

Cover Images: Backstage Pass: © iStockphoto
.com/foto-ruhrgebiet; Biker: © iStockphoto
.com/chrisdeana; Football: © iStockphoto
.com/padnpen; Snowboard: © iStockphoto
.com/blublaf; Taking Photo: © iStockphoto
.com/maikid; Guitar: © iStockphoto.com/
AarStudio; Concert: © iStockphoto.com/Dirk
Freder; Basketball players: Vico Collective/
Alin Dragulin/Blend Images/getty images

Design Images: Banners: © iStockphoto.com/
PixelEmbargo; Arrow: © iStockphoto.com/
pagadesign; Popcorn: © iStockphoto.com/
xxmmxx; Orange background:
© iStockphoto.com/jxfzsy; Multi-ethnic:
© iStockphoto.com/philipdyer; Tickets:
© iStockphoto.com/AndrewJohnson; Bubbles:
© iStockphoto.com/esenkartal; Time:
© iStockphoto.com/hh5800;
Thumb up: © iStockphoto.com/_human;
Stars: © iStockphoto.com/OlgaMiltsova;
Baseball: © iStockphoto.com/beichh4046;
3d rendered: © iStockphoto.com/skvoor;
Concept: © Krasimira Nevenova/Shutterstock
.com; Icon: © file404/Shutterstock.com;
Arrow: © iStockphoto.com/pagadesign

Contents Images: Guitar: © Olga Miltsova/
Shutterstock.com; Basketball: © Aaron
Amat/Shutterstock.com; Baseball: © Dan
Thornberg/Shutterstock.com; Ticket:
© iStockphoto.com/zimmytws; Goggles:
© iStockphoto.com/klikk; Chronometer:
© iStockphoto.com/Instamatic

For product information and technology assistance, contact us at
Cengage Learning Customer & Sales Support, 1-800-354-9706
For permission to use material from this text or product,
submit all requests online at **www.cengage.com/permissions**
Further permissions questions can be emailed to
permissionrequest@cengage.com

ISBN: 978-1-133-60244-6

Cengage Learning
20 Channel Center Street
Boston, MA 02210
USA

Cengage Learning is a leading provider of customized learning solutions
with office locations around the globe, including Singapore, the United
Kingdom, Australia, Mexico, Brazil, and Japan. Locate your local office
at: **www.cengage.com/global**

Cengage Learning products are represented in Canada by
Nelson Education, Ltd.

For your course and learning solutions, visit
ngl.cengage.com

Visit our company website at **www.cengage.com**

Printed in the United States of America
Print Number: 07   Print Year: 2017

Reviewers

Amanda Coleman
Teacher, Business & Marketing Department
Elkins High School
Elkins, AR

Mark Drummond
Marketing Education Coordinator
West Deptford High School
West Deptford, NJ

Jacqueline N. Herrmann
Marketing Teacher, Coordinator
Deep Run High School
Glen Allen, VA

Janet Brown Jennings
Teacher, NBCT, Marketing
Eastern Montgomery High School
Elliston, VA

Barbara J. Lowery
Teacher, Business Department
Eastern Camden County High School
Voorhees, NJ

Matt Maw
Teacher, Business Department
Lincoln Southeast High School
Lincoln, NE

Debra M. Myers
Marketing Coordinator
Landstown High School: Governor's STEM &
   Technology Academy
Virginia Beach, VA

Rachel J. Schlachta, MSM
Business Teacher
Buena Regional High School
Buena, NJ

Daina M. Sisk
Teacher/CEIP Coordinator, Business Department
Shaker High School
Latham, NY

Belinda Speer
Teacher, Career & Technical Education
Ennis High School
Ennis, TX

Mark Steedly
Marketing Management & Research Instructor
Sycamore High School/Great Oaks Institute of
   Technology and Career Development
Cincinnati, OH

Christine Walker
Teacher, Business & Marketing Department
James E. Taylor High School
Katy, TX

About the Authors

Ken Kaser taught business and marketing courses in Nebraska and Texas high schools for 30 years. He currently serves as the Director for the Event Management and Sales Certificate program at Conrad Hilton College at the University of Houston. Ken has authored or co-authored seven books; written national, state, and local curriculum; served in many professional leadership roles; and earned numerous teaching awards at the national, state, and regional levels.

Dotty Boen Oelkers is a sports and entertainment author, educator, and enthusiast. Discovering, interviewing, and writing about the interesting people who market sports and entertainment is her passion. Dotty has written three books, co-authored one other, and contributed to numerous others. She began her career in retail management, is a former Marketing Education teacher and Career and Technical Education (CTE) Director, and has served as a consultant regarding CTE Administration in school districts across Texas.

SPORTS and ENTERTAINMENT MARKETING
Contents

Destination: Marketing Success

By incorporating feedback from instructors across the country, **SPORTS AND ENTERTAINMENT MARKETING, 4E** has expanded coverage, updated content, and exciting new features. Popular sports and entertainment topics continue to be the foundation for teaching marketing concepts. Throughout the text, each marketing function is highlighted with an icon to indicate how it is used in the marketing process.

Case Studies and Winning Edge activities for BPA, DECA, and FBLA are included in every chapter to prepare students for success in competitive events.

New Features

Social Media Marketing   Addresses current trends in social media as it relates to promotion and advertising.

Math in Marketing   Includes an application activity with critical-thinking questions, requiring students to estimate, calculate, and perform other math functions.

Communication Connection   Provides an opportunity for students to enhance their written communication skills by completing a brief writing application with a marketing spin.

National Marketing Standards—We've Got You Covered

Your planning and teaching just got easier. You can cover national marketing standards using an industry that brings relevance to learners. *Sports and Entertainment Marketing* follows the Marketing Cluster as outlined by the MBA Research & Curriculum Center. The following core standards have been developed:

Channel Management   Understand the concepts and processes needed to identify, select, monitor, and evaluate sales channels

Marketing-Information Management   Understand the concepts, systems, and tools needed to gather, access, synthesize, evaluate, and disseminate information for use in making business decisions

Market Planning   Understand the concepts and strategies utilized to determine and target marketing strategies to a select audience

Pricing   Understand concepts and strategies utilized in determining and adjusting prices to maximize return and meet customers' perceptions of value

Product/Service Management   Understand the concepts and processes needed to obtain, develop, maintain, and improve a product or service mix in response to market opportunities

Promotion   Understand the concepts and strategies needed to communicate information about products, services, images, and/or ideas to achieve a desired outcome

Selling   Understand the concepts and actions needed to determine client needs and wants and respond through planned, personalized communication that influences purchase decisions and enhances future business opportunities

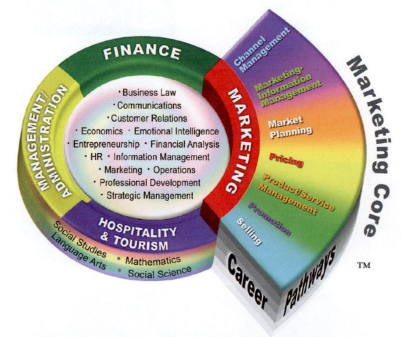

To the Student

Welcome to Sports and Entertainment Marketing

The field of sports and entertainment marketing is growing rapidly. Many colleges, universities, and high schools offer specializations in sports and entertainment marketing. In this text you will explore the intriguing world of sports and entertainment from the perspective of marketing.

The **core standards of marketing** are visually identified by icons throughout the text.

In addition to the seven core standards, the text also covers the important topic of finance.

MARKETING CORE STANDARDS

Channel Management · Pricing · Marketing-Information Management · Product/Service Management · Promotion · Selling · Market Planning

Winning Strategies presents real-world strategies used by successful sports and entertainment figures.

Winning Strategies

Opening Act begins each lesson and encourages you to explore the material in the upcoming lesson. Opening Act also gives you opportunities to collaborate with other students in your class.

Social Media Marketing discusses the emergence and use of social media strategies that help marketers work more effectively.

Judgment Call examines legal and ethical issues as they relate to the sports and entertainment industry.

JUDGMENT CALL

Math in Marketing includes an application activity with critical-thinking questions, requiring you to estimate, calculate, and perform other math functions.

MATH IN MARKETING

Intermission provides you with an opportunity to assess your comprehension at key points in each lesson. Ongoing review and assessment helps you understand the material.

 INTERMISSION

Time Out introduces you to interesting facts and statistics about sports and entertainment businesses.

Point Your Browser includes Internet activities and crossword puzzles for every chapter.

Virtual Business Sports & Entertainment presents suggestions for using this online simulation. To purchase the simulation, visit www.knowledgematters.com.

Communication Connection provides an opportunity for you to enhance your written communication skills by completing a brief writing application with a marketing spin.

COMMUNICATION CONNECTION

Extra Innings Project provides you with a group project in every chapter.

EXTRA INNINGS PROJECT

Take a Bow introduces you to people who have succeeded in sports and entertainment.

 *TAKE A BOW*

Encore provides you with an opportunity to assess your knowledge at the end of every lesson.

Winning Edge prepares you for BPA, DECA, and FBLA competitive events.

WHAT IS SPORTS AND ENTERTAINMENT MARKETING?

© iStockphoto.com/jodijacobson

POINT YOUR BROWSER

ngl.cengage.com/sports4e

Winning Strategies

Susan Boyle's Story

Susan Boyle was born in Scotland in 1961 into a musical family. Both of her parents sang, and her mother also played the piano. Despite having learning disabilities, the young Susan loved music and began performing in school musicals at the age of 12. Her teachers encouraged Susan to continue performing at school, but she did not attend beyond high school.

In 1995 Susan auditioned for *My Kind of People*, a televised talent show in the UK, but it ended in rejection. She didn't let it stop her, however. She continued to sing in her church choir and performed on karaoke nights at a local hotel.

In 1999 Susan used all of her personal savings to pay for a professionally produced demo tape that she sent to radio talent competitions, record companies, and local and national television stations. To improve her chances of success, Susan began taking singing lessons in 2002, and in 2009, Susan finally got her big break. The shy, unemployed 48-year-old was met by a doubtful, snickering audience on the competition show *Britain's Got Talent*. At the end of her performance, her rendition of "I Dreamed a Dream" from the musical *Les Miserables* was met with a standing ovation and more than 300 million hits on YouTube.

Social media has played a predominant role in Susan Boyle's success. Her video from *Britain's Got Talent* went viral. Her feel-good story emotionally connected with millions of people. Susan now has her own official website that includes up-to-date news releases about Susan's music, concerts, and special events. Susan Boyle showed how an underdog can beat the odds in the entertainment industry.

© iStockphoto.com/EdStock

Think Critically

1. What role did persistence play in the success of this story?

2. An entrepreneur is someone who takes risks to start a new business. How is Susan Boyle an entrepreneur?

3. How has marketing played a role in Susan Boyle's success?

1.1 Marketing Basics

The Essential Question

What are the core standards of marketing for a popular sports or entertainment event?

Learning Objectives

LO 1.1-1 Describe the basic concepts of marketing.

LO 1.1-2 Explain the marketing mix.

LO 1.1-3 Define the seven core standards of marketing and financing.

Key Terms

- marketing
- marketing mix
- product
- distribution
- price
- promotion
- discretionary income

OPENING ACT

Athletes and entertainers play a prominent role in marketing by endorsing products and services. After the legendary Shaquille O'Neal retired from playing NBA basketball, he put his other talents to work in television commercials. His endorsement of the Buick LaCrosse shows that the car has plenty of legroom, even for a giant like Shaq. Buick wanted to make a statement with the younger crowd and capture the attention of basketball fans by airing the commercial during televised NCAA weekend broadcasts. The commercial, titled "Oh Effect," has Shaq and his 325-pound frame showcasing what very few might know about the Buick LaCrosse, including attractive features such as the vehicle's 36 miles-per-gallon fuel-efficiency, luxurious interior, and roominess. Even Shaq, who is over 7 feet tall and 300 pounds, can comfortably fit behind the wheel.

Cooperative Learning Work with a group to identify four advertising campaigns that feature celebrities or athletes. How have the campaigns influenced your thoughts about the products? Would you buy the celebrity-endorsed brands? Why or why not?

LO 1.1-1 WHAT IS MARKETING?

According to the American Marketing Association, marketing is "the activity, set of institutions, and processes for creating, communicating, delivering, and exchanging offerings that have value for customers, clients, partners, and society at large."[1] Marketing is a highly visible business activity. Many individuals think of marketing as advertising. However, producing, distributing, pricing, and promoting are also essential marketing elements.

A simpler definition of **marketing** is the creation and maintenance of satisfying exchange relationships. This definition describes pieces of the entire marketing concept. *Creation* suggests that marketing involves product development. *Maintenance* indicates that marketing must continue as long as a business operates. *Satisfaction* implies that marketing must meet the needs of both businesses and customers when exchanging products or services. Finally, an *exchange relationship* occurs when the parties involved (business and customer) both give and receive something of value.

Satisfying Customer Needs

Customer needs should be the primary focus of marketing. This concept is not as easy as it might sound. To satisfy customers' needs, you need to perform three activities. First, you must identify your customer and the needs of that customer. Second, you need to develop products that customers consider better than other choices. And finally, you must operate your business profitably (revenues must exceed the costs of doing business). If you can do all of these activities well, you will be able to market your products or services successfully.

What customer needs will be satisfied by this entertainment venue?

Sports and Entertainment Marketing

Sports and entertainment marketing is a huge industry offering numerous products and services. Busy individuals and families must carefully choose which sports and entertainment activities and events they will enjoy with their limited time and financial resources. Marketers of sports and entertainment products and services must assess consumer demand, the competition, and the financial valuation of the goods and services they offer. When developing marketing plans for sports and entertainment products, marketers must consider the marketing mix and the core standards of marketing.

INTERMISSION

What is marketing?

LO 1.1-2   THE MARKETING MIX

To perform the tasks associated with marketing, marketers rely on a marketing mix. The **marketing mix** describes how a business blends the four marketing elements of product, distribution, price, and promotion.

A **product** is what a business offers customers to satisfy needs. *Production* is all of the activities involved in creating products for sale. Products include goods, such as athletic shoes, and services, such as movie tickets. Providing entertainment can also be considered providing a service. **Distribution** involves the locations and methods used to make products available to customers. **Price** is the amount that customers pay for products. **Promotion** describes ways to make customers aware of products and encourage them to buy.

Marketing Mix Considerations

Marketers must carefully consider the many factors that affect the marketing mix elements. Product offerings for sports and entertainment must be evaluated and updated constantly. Individuals have many entertainment options for their limited discretionary income. **Discretionary income** is the amount of money individuals have available to spend after paying for the necessities of life and other fixed expenses, such as housing and car payments. Entertainment options that are popular today may lose popularity next year. Choosing the right products to meet the needs and wants of the market is essential to the marketing mix. In addition, marketers must consider the quantities of the product to produce. Too much of a product could result in price markdowns. Too few of a product could result in lost sales.

Price influences the purchasing decisions made by consumers. A business must offer its customers products and services they need and want at prices they are able and willing to pay, while at the same time covering the costs of the business and making a profit. Prices charged for sports and entertainment events must be sensitive to consumer demand and the state of the economy. Championship teams will increase consumer demand and ticket prices. However, when the economy becomes questionable, consumers are likely to spend less money on sports and entertainment events.

Distribution involves transporting or delivering goods to final customers. Athletic uniforms arriving by UPS and turf for a football field arriving by semi-truck are both examples of the distribution function of marketing. Distribution of an event involves planning the location where the event will take place. A popular three-day outdoor concert event for country or rock music must be held at a location near the customer base and where nearby businesses, such as hotels and restaurants, can accommodate the needs of the fans.

Promotion is essential to inform prospective customers about sports and entertainment events and products. Forms of promotion can range from television commercials and newspaper advertisements to in-stadium advertising through special offers on the back of ticket stubs and on giant video screens. Promotion requires creativity to keep the attention of prospective customers. Promotion costs are high, making it important to create effective promotion plans that reach the largest audiences at the most cost-effective price.

Marketing Mix Examples in the Sports Industry

There are numerous examples throughout the sports industry of the marketing mix at work. You need only look as far as your favorite sporting event to see all of the marketing mix components—product, distribution, price, and promotion.

It's Kickoff Time The Super Bowl is the sports event of the year. This billion-dollar event generates large sums of money from sponsorships and ticket sales. The *product* offered by the Super Bowl is the game matching the best teams in the AFC and NFC. The Super Bowl is usually sold out before the professional football season begins. Actual ticket *prices* range from $500 to $2,600, but individuals may spend thousands of dollars more in travel and hotel

What is the marketing mix for this event?

costs to attend the game. Major cities compete to host the Super Bowl because of the great financial benefits for the local economy as fans utilize the area's hotels, restaurants, shopping malls, service stations, and the hosting stadium.

Distribution involves selecting a host city that is easily accessible by the fans. It must be near an airport and major highway and have sufficient nearby accommodations to meet the needs of the thousands of fans that will pour into the city for the game. Other distribution outlets for the Super Bowl include television and radio. Many Super Bowl parties are held in homes and sports bars throughout the United States. Distribution for the Super Bowl also involves ticket sales. Distribution methods for tickets include direct sales by NFL ticket offices, ticket retail outlets such as Ticketmaster, and online ticket distributors.

Promotion for the Super Bowl includes television commercials, newspapers, sports magazines, and related-product contests. For example, companies such as Coca-Cola and Doritos may conduct special Super Bowl promotional sweepstakes. Super Bowl sponsors spend large sums of money to air commercials during the big game. One 30-second commercial during the Super Bowl can cost nearly $4 million.

Start Your Engines NASCAR has 75 million loyal fans. The Daytona 500 is NASCAR's Super Bowl. This major sporting event takes place at the beginning of the racing season each February and is attended by approximately 200,000 fans. The 500-mile, 200-lap race is watched by 12.5 million households. The economic impact of the Daytona Speedway is huge—the state of Florida earns more than $1.6 billion each year and more than 18,000 permanent jobs have been created.[3]

The *product* offered to consumers is the race itself. Other products include the driver, car, and related merchandise. The average *price* to attend a NASCAR race is $88; it can cost more than $600 to attend Daytona. *Distribution* includes the location of the race such as Daytona or the other NASCAR tracks, media such as television and radio, and ticket sales through various outlets.

Promotion plays a big role in NASCAR. Promotions for NASCAR races can be seen on television and billboards, at sponsoring businesses, and at special events such as auto expos. Fans form a special bond with their favorite drivers, who often appear as advertising spokespeople. For example, although Danica Patrick is a popular NASCAR driver who has set many records, including the highest finish for a female driver at the Indianapolis 500, her career extends beyond auto racing as an advertising spokeswoman. Drivers often promote their own line of NASCAR apparel as well as products that appeal to the same target markets as their fan base. Among Danica Patrick's promotions are Coca-Cola and GoDaddy.com. Patrick's car itself is a promotion, with its many sponsors displayed across the car's exterior. The average annual amount a sponsor invests in a racing team is $15 million, money well spent because NASCAR fans are three times more likely to purchase sponsors' products than fans of other sports. Recent surveys conducted by NASCAR indicate that 40 percent of the fans are women, who spend $250 million annually on NASCAR-licensed products.[4]

Marketing Mix Examples in the Entertainment Industry

Many events take place in the entertainment industry. All of them benefit from the right marketing mix. A lineup of entertainment offered at the right location at the right price adds up to a successful event. The right promotion will make the event all the more successful.

Let's Go to the Fair State fairs are finding it increasingly difficult to compete with other sports and entertainment events. The *product* offered by a state fair must appeal to both rural and urban residents. State fairs offer livestock shows, domestic and commercial exhibits, rides, and a wide array of musical and other entertainment. State fair planners want to offer a product that draws the maximum attendance and profit.

Because state fairs are family entertainment events, admission *price* is an important factor to consider. State fairs must charge enough admission to remain financially sound while still attracting good attendance. The admission price must be sensitive to consumer demand. Many state fairs offer special admission prices to attract more attendance on weekdays. Frequently, price breaks are offered for advance purchases. Senior citizens and veterans may be offered reduced admission prices.

The success of entertainment events depends on *promotion* or communication to prospective customers. Advertisements on radio stations and in newspapers throughout the state are aimed at increasing state fair attendance. Television commercials are another option for promotion, but the cost in relation to the increased revenue they may generate might be cost-prohibitive.

Distribution involves location of the fair and the outlets where individuals can purchase admission tickets. Tickets can be purchased at the admission gate during the state fair or purchased in advance from the state fair business office or other ticket outlets.

The goal of the state fair's planners is to offer appealing entertainment at the right price to attract the maximum attendance. State fair boards must develop a marketing mix that will meet this goal.

A Celebration Mardi Gras takes place each year the Tuesday before Ash Wednesday. Although celebrated across the country, Mardi Gras is a major event in New Orleans, Louisiana, where Louisianans and their guests hit the streets for a day of fun and festivities. No two places celebrate Mardi Gras exactly the same way. In New Orleans, more than 60 parades roll during the two weeks before Fat Tuesday. Colorful boat parades and a wide array of family activities make Mardi Gras a popular event in the New Orleans area.

A wide array of entertainment *products* and *services* can be found during Mardi Gras, including parades, costumes, dancing, food, and music. New Orleans is the perfect location (*distribution*) for Mardi Gras activities for the whole family. *Promotions* for Mardi Gras can be seen in parades where cities advertise their upcoming events as well as on tourist websites. *Prices* for the various festivities will vary, but Mardi Gras can be an affordable event for the entire family.

INTERMISSION

What are the elements of the marketing mix?

LO 1.1-3 CORE STANDARDS OF MARKETING

The core standards of marketing are the basis of all marketing activities. There are seven core standards associated with marketing. They are channel management, pricing, marketing-information management, product/service management, promotion, selling, and market planning. In addition, financing plays a major role in marketing activities and is closely related to the core standards. Every marketing activity involves at least one core standard.

© MBA Research. Additional information regarding National Business Administration Standards: www.mbaresearch.org

Channel Management Determining the best way to get a company's products or services to customers is part of the *channel management* function. Television manufacturers such as Samsung sell their products through electronics retailers such as Best Buy. Samsung knows that shoppers go to Best Buy to purchase electronic goods and appliances. In sports and entertainment, channel management involves selecting the right location for an event and making tickets available through ticket sales outlets. For sporting goods, channel management involves getting merchandise to stores where customers can buy it.

 Pricing The process of establishing and communicating to customers the value or cost of goods and services is called *pricing*. Prices assigned to sports and entertainment events and goods are directly related to consumer demand. Prices may be set high if the seller knows people will buy at the high price. Super Bowl ticket prices go through the ceiling because there are a limited number of tickets and an enormous demand for them. Prices may be set lower if the seller needs to sell a large volume of a product. Pricing policies are also based on the cost of producing goods and sports and entertainment events. If costs of production are not covered, the business will not succeed.

 Marketing-Information Management Gathering and using information about customers to improve business decision making involves *marketing-information management*. Each month Apple surveys iPhone buyers throughout the world to determine why customers buy the Apple iPhone instead of competing Android products. The research is conducted to determine what features of the iPhone are used the most, the demographics of iPhone buyers, and the level of customer satisfaction. Successful marketing involves using marketing information to predict consumer demand, develop new products, and estimate the right quantities of merchandise to produce.

Product/Service Management Designing, developing, maintaining, improving, and acquiring products or services for the purpose of meeting customer needs and wants are all part of *product/service management*. Many of these activities occur during the production process, often beginning with an idea for a new or improved product. Concussions and traumatic brain injuries suffered by football players are a major concern for the NFL, NCAA, and the U.S. Congress. The National Operating Committee on Standards for Athletic Equipment has spent more than $3 million since 2000 to gain a better understanding of sports-related concussions. This research resulted in the development of materials for safer football helmets. Riddell (a major manufacturer of football equipment) is paying close attention to this research to help produce safer football helmets. Marketers must continually evaluate products to determine how well they meet customer needs.

Research conducted by Digital Insights indicates that there are more than 1.15 billion Facebook users, more than 500 million Twitter users, and more than 500 million Google+ users. There are more than 10 million Facebook apps, and the number continues to grow. The fastest-growing age demographic for Twitter is 55- to 64-year-olds. More than 400 million tweets are being sent every day. The Google+ platform has a customer base that is 67 percent male.[5]

All of these social media statistics provide marketers with valuable information. Marketers understand the need to keep up with the latest social media trends to communicate with current customers and to generate new customers. Nearly 75 percent of marketers believe that Facebook is important to generate new leads. Google+ is used by 40 percent of marketers and nearly 70 percent are planning to increase their Google+ activities.

Think Critically

Why do marketers need to understand how social media is being used by different consumer groups, such as males, females, teenagers, and adults? Give examples of three different social media strategies to reach three different target markets.

Promotion Using advertising and other forms of communication to distribute information about products and services to achieve a desired outcome is *promotion*. For example, sports fans often use coupons on the back of ticket stubs after they attend a ball game. The coupons are used to promote products or services and to entice fans into trying them at a discounted price.

Selling Any direct and personal communication with customers to assess and satisfy their needs is considered *selling*. Selling involves not only satisfying customers but also anticipating their future needs. Selling in today's world includes purchases made through the Internet with no face-to-face communication whatsoever.

Market Planning Analyzing markets that a company wants to serve and determining how to compete in those markets is the goal of *market planning*. The market planning process of a business typically results in a marketing strategy that can be used to enhance its sales. Sometimes professional sports teams make decisions to move to other cities. The decision to move to a different city is heavily influenced by financial benefits. In this case, the objective of market planning is to find the best location in which the target market has the financial resources to solidly support the team. Market planning will be influenced by the city or location that is willing to build a new facility with all of the latest technological advancements and required logistics to attract the target market.

Financing Without financing, the other core standards of marketing would not be as effective. *Financing* requires a company to budget for its own marketing activities and to provide customers with assistance in paying for the company's products or services. A company or organization can obtain financing from investors and sponsors. Sponsors spend large sums of money to promote their products during sports and entertainment events. Sponsorships range from millions of dollars for supporting college bowl games to as little as hundreds of dollars for sponsoring the local Little League baseball team. Customers receive financing in the form of different payment options, such as cash, credit, and installment payments. Customers are more likely to make purchases if they have payment options.

INTERMISSION

List and provide an example of each core standard of marketing for a sports and entertainment product or service.

ENCORE

Understand Marketing Concepts

Select the best answer for each question.

1. Which of the following core standards of marketing involves collecting and using data to make future business decisions?
   a. selling
   b. marketing-information management
   c. financing
   d. product/service management

2. Which of the following marketing mix elements makes consumers aware of products and events?
   a. promotion
   b. distribution
   c. price
   d. product

Think Critically

Answer the following questions as completely as possible.

3. When you think of the term *marketing*, what comes to mind? Based on what you have learned, write your own definition of marketing. Provide an example of marketing that illustrates your definition. (LO 1.1-1)

4. How would you incorporate all of the marketing mix elements, including product, distribution, price, and promotion, for an upcoming school concert? (LO 1.1-2)

5. List and describe how the seven core standards of marketing were involved in one of your recent sports or entertainment purchases. (LO 1.1-3)

1.2 Sets Marketing

The Essential Question

How is the economy affected by sports marketing?

Learning Objectives

LO 1.2-1   Define sports marketing.

LO 1.2-2   Explain the value of sports marketing to the economy.

Key Terms

- demographics
- sports marketing
- gross impression

OPENING ACT

Successful college athletic programs, particularly basketball programs, earn millions of dollars for their schools. Recently, a national champion University of Louisville basketball program earned more than $40 million in revenue with a net profit of $26.9 million. Top basketball programs reward their coaches with high salaries, partly because top coaches attract the best talent. Winning games and championships results in more television revenue, increased ticket sales, and increased alumni donations. Many college basketball coaches are paid higher salaries than professional basketball coaches earn. In a recent year, salaries for some of the top college basketball coaches were as follows:[6]

John Calipari	University of Kentucky	$5.4 million
Rick Pitino	University of Louisville	$4.8 million
Mike Krzyzewski	Duke University	$4.7 million
Billy Donovan	University of Florida	$3.6 million
Tom Izzo	Michigan State University	$3.6 million

Cooperative Learning   With a partner, discuss whether successful college coaches should earn such high salaries. What are the pros and cons of paying coaches high salaries?

LO 1.2-1   WHY SPORTS MARKETING?

Marketing-Information Management

Spectators of sporting events are the potential consumers of a wide array of products ranging from apparel and athletic equipment to food items and automobiles. Sports spectators sometimes have more in common than just a sport. Shared characteristics of a group, such as age, marital status, gender, ethnic background, income level, and education level, are known as **demographics**. Finding out a group of spectators' interests and planning a product or service that the spectators will buy is a function of sports marketing. **Sports marketing** involves using sports to market products.

History of Sports Marketing

Sports marketing is not new. The first known athletic event that required paid admission was a baseball game in Long Island, New York, in 1858, where spectators were charged 50 cents. Sports organizers soon realized the financial potential of sporting events and professional athletes. Golfer Gene Sarazen signed an endorsement deal with Wilson Sporting Goods in 1923 that, to this day, is the longest-running endorsement deal in the history of sports. The original agreement was for $6,000 a year plus an equal amount for travel expenses. Renewal took place every two years until Sarazen's death in May 1999. In 1949 Babe Didrikson Zaharias signed the first significant female endorsement with Wilson Sporting Goods for $100,000 a year. Coca-Cola partnered with the Summer Olympics in 1928 and remains a sponsor to this day.

The first pay-per-view athletic event was a boxing match, the "Thrilla in Manila," with Muhammad Ali taking on Joe Frazier in the Philippines in 1975. It was broadcast to 276 closed-circuit locations. Capitalizing on the popularity of sports, ESPN made its debut in 1979, offering advertisers a new way to reach their target markets. Today many high schools and colleges offer sports marketing programs—further proof of the impact of sports on today's society.

The Goal of Sports Marketing

The goal of sports marketing is to use the right marketing mix to meet customer needs while generating a profit. Sports marketers research the demographics and spending habits of fans in order to maximize profits on the items fans purchase in association with sporting events. The price that fans are willing to pay for a ticket depends on the interests of the market, the national importance of the event, the popularity of the participating athletes, and the rivalry associated with the contest. Fans are usually willing to pay for team- or celebrity-identified clothing or equipment and for the expenses of food and travel to and from a game. To find the right marketing mix that attracts customers, marketers must consider three factors—new opportunities, gross impression, and timing.

New Sports, New Opportunities Sports marketers must continually search for new ways to appeal to customers. New sports markets offer new opportunities for endorsement and marketing. Extreme sports, such as skateboarding and snowboarding, have captured a whole new audience. The Arena Football League (AFL), founded in 1987, offers football fans a more affordable way to attend a football game, with tickets selling for as low as $10 per game. The action is continuous because the clock doesn't stop, resulting in high scores, and the players meet fans and sign autographs after every game—all elements that add excitement and build interest.

Reinventing a product or service keeps consumers interested. The same is true of the sports industry. New sports must be invented and other sports must be reinvented or updated to maintain fan excitement. Hybrid sports

What strategy can be used to raise the visibility of this extreme sport?

have been invented to make traditional recreational activities more exciting. Skijoring is a sport that combines dog sledding and cross-country skiing. A dog or team of dogs pulls a rider on skis. There are no harnesses to steer the dogs, so participants must teach their dogs basic dog sledding voice commands. Skijoring participants must purchase cross country skis and cold-weather booties to keep the dog's paws warm.

You have probably heard of mountain climbing, but what about ice climbing? Ice climbing is a sport where climbers use axes and crampons to climb frozen waterfalls and other ice formations. Some of the other more innovative new sports include mega ramp skateboarding, ostrich racing, underwater golf, and flyboarding.

The onset of new sports brings new opportunities for cable and network stations as well as sponsors and advertisers. Networks increase their viewership as extreme sports enthusiasts tune in to watch their favorite new sporting events. Sponsors and advertisers will be quick to follow, hoping to increase their customer base among their target market.

Marketing-Information Management **Gross Impression** Gross impression is a commonly used practice in sports marketing. **Gross impression** is the number of times per advertisement, game, or show that a product or service is associated with an athlete, team, or entertainer. Often the message is a subtle one. Brands shown in movies, television shows, and televised sporting events all represent gross impressions. Every time you see a product or company logo on a pair of shoes, in a movie scene, or on a billboard, your brain records that image. Advertisers hope you will remember it when you are ready to buy such a product.

Many college and professional teams now have company or product logos on their uniforms. Marketers hope the spectators will see them, will want to be associated with the elite team or athlete, and will buy the sponsor's products. Every time the media mentions a player or team in association with a sponsor's product, there is one more gross impression made on a potential customer.

Timing Marketers are aware that the popularity of teams and sports figures is based on sustaining a winning record. A team or celebrity on a losing streak can lose more than just points in a game. Timing is extremely important when marketing sporting goods. Fans want products and services that identify them with a winner. Winning trends for athletes and teams must be monitored to determine when marketing strategies need to change. Similarly, marketers must be aware that success leads to increased competition. If one major athletic company has a successful marketing campaign, competitors are likely to increase their marketing efforts. Competition must be monitored so that a company's marketing remains fresh and unique.

INTERMISSION

Why are gross impression and timing important in sports marketing?

LO 1.2-2   THE VALUE OF SPORTS MARKETING

Sports marketing is a multibillion-dollar global industry that has a huge impact on the economy. The popularity of sporting events affects individual and family budgets. Whether it's the family vacation centered around a soccer tournament for the kids or the Orange Bowl for a national football championship, large sums of money are spent on sporting events and related products. The sports industry has far-reaching effects on the

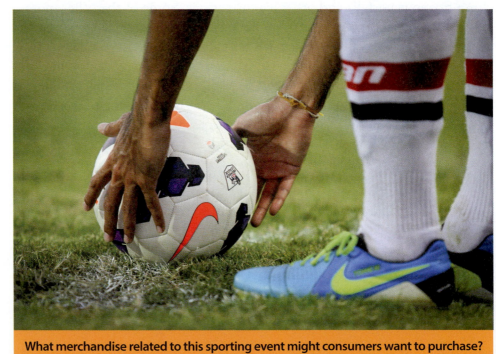

What merchandise related to this sporting event might consumers want to purchase?

© Chayatorn Laorattanavech/Shutterstock.com

NASCAR is no stranger to politics. The U.S. Department of Defense spends between $80 and $100 million on NASCAR sponsorships in an attempt to recruit young people for the military. The U.S. Army and The National Guard are two of the biggest NASCAR sponsors. Because of the downturn in the economy, the U.S. Congress must consider budget cuts. As a result, NASCAR sponsorships have come under much scrutiny. The NASCAR marketing strategy used by the Department of Defense seems logical because of the overlap between regions where NASCAR is popular and where military recruitment is successful.

Write Now

You are a marketer for the NASCAR organization. Conduct research about demographics for the military and demographics for NASCAR fans. Write a one-page paper explaining why the U.S. Department of Defense should continue funding NASCAR sponsorships.

automobile industry, as supportive parents buy and maintain minivans and SUVs large enough to transport families to various sporting activities and events. Think of the restaurants, hotels, and service stations that count on the business generated as a result of these events.

Sports marketing has created job opportunities ranging from parking lot attendants to marketing executives for professional sports teams. Stadiums and other entertainment venues must be built and maintained. Venues require building managers, lawn care professionals, security personnel, and maintenance crews. Athletes require trainers, handlers, and personal attendants. They also hire agents to handle publicity, personal appearances, and negotiation of contracts.

Emotional Value

Sports fans have emotional ties to their favorite high school, college, and professional teams. Many sports enthusiasts live for the weekend to see their favorite teams in action. Emotions such as affection and passion often compel fans to buy tickets and other sports-related merchandise. Fans will freely spend their discretionary income on sporting events that capture their hearts, so marketers try to appeal to the emotions of fans.

So Many Channels

Channel Management Marketers for the hundreds of television networks now available through cable and satellite systems must create marketing strategies to profitably capture the highest possible percentage of the viewing audience. Sitcoms that were once popular have taken a backseat to reality shows starring average, everyday people and costing little to produce. Shows like *The Voice, America's Got Talent, Survivor, Big Brother*, and *The Amazing Race* have taken the lead in television ratings. The networks must find the right mix of programming to reach audiences, attract sponsors, and maximize profits.

Sports programming has proven to be valuable. Sporting events such as the Super Bowl, college football playoffs, and March Madness attract the attention of large sports-minded audiences, which in turn, attract high-paying promoters. Television networks pay top dollar to obtain exclusive broadcasting rights for high-profile sporting events in hopes of reaping financial benefits. Advertising during some of these popular sporting events can cost a company millions of dollars.

Because today's consumers are watching more television than ever, it is important to understand what and how they're watching. The Nielsen Company uses expansive and representative panels of consumers to track their TV viewing behavior. This provides marketers with a detailed analysis of consumer viewing trends, habits, and demographic information. This wealth of knowledge allows companies to refine their marketing campaigns based on demographics and audience composition.

INTERMISSION

What is the value of sports marketing?

ENCORE

Understand Marketing Concepts

Select the best answer for each question.

1. Researching the demographics of a fan base for a particular sport would be most closely associated with which core standard of marketing?
   a. channel management
   b. pricing
   c. marketing-information management
   d. financing

2. Gross impression can
   a. include company logos on sports apparel
   b. take place on a television show
   c. involve the number of times a product is associated with an athlete
   d. all of the above

Think Critically

Answer the following questions as completely as possible.

3. What is a gross impression? Give two examples of how gross impressions are used at sporting events. (LO 1.2-1)

4. Give an example of how timing is essential to selling related merchandise for a popular sporting event. (LO 1.2-1)

5. Name a sport (amateur or professional) that is played in your city. Describe how this sport adds value to your city or community. What businesses or individuals are affected by the sport? Describe how. (LO 1.2-2)

1.3 Entertainment Marketing

The Essential Question

How has the delivery of entertainment evolved over the past ten years?

Learning Objectives

LO 1.3-1   Define entertainment.

LO 1.3-2   Describe the evolution of entertainment marketing.

Key Terms

- entertainment
- entertainment marketing
- ratings

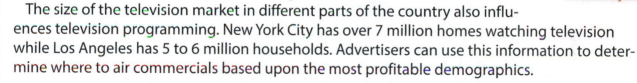

Television networks are very interested in the age and gender of the viewing audiences. While HGTV may be a major hit with women, ESPN may be the top choice for male viewers. The fate of television programs is based upon popularity, which is determined by the size of the viewing audience. Television networks typically want to attract viewers and consumers in the 18- to 49-year-old age group because this group is actively earning and spending money. However, an aging population has resulted in the median age of viewing audiences for major networks to rise to 51. Advertisers are interested in the demographics of viewing audiences because this information helps them determine if they want to air product advertisements during certain shows.

The size of the television market in different parts of the country also influences television programming. New York City has over 7 million homes watching television while Los Angeles has 5 to 6 million households. Advertisers can use this information to determine where to air commercials based upon the most profitable demographics.

Cooperative Learning   With a partner, identify three television shows and their target markets. Make a list of products or services that might be advertised during these shows. Discuss why the products' advertisers would be interested in sponsoring these programs.

LO 1.3-1   ENTERTAINMENT FOR SALE

Today's consumers are looking for fun-filled activities that capture their interest and hold their attention. Various forms of entertainment can fill this void. Although entertainment is thought of as a way to relax, have fun, and enjoy time spent alone or with others, it is actually much more. The entertainment industry has grown and evolved over the years into a profitable business. Various businesses operate in the entertainment industry and contribute billions of dollars annually to the U.S. economy. As the old saying goes, "There's no business like show business."

What kind of entertainment events do you think visitors might attend in Times Square?

What Exactly Is Entertainment?

Entertainment involves some type of performance that people are willing to spend their money and spare time watching. Entertainment can include sports or the arts and can be viewed in person or in broadcast or recorded form. A distinction often is made between sports and entertainment. The term *sports* is generally applied to games of athletic skill. Watching sports also can be entertaining, but the term *entertainment* is generally applied to movies, theater, music concerts, the circus, and so forth.

Sometimes what qualifies as sports and what qualifies as entertainment is a matter of opinion. For example, professional wrestling has little resemblance to the National Collegiate Athletic Association's sanctioned sport of wrestling. Professional wrestling is an exaggeration of a real sport, but is it really a sport or staged entertainment?

What Is Entertainment Marketing?

Because of commitments to work, school, home, family, and other activities, people have a limited amount of leisure time and money. Influencing how people choose to spend their time and money on entertainment is the purpose of **entertainment marketing**.

Entertainment marketing will be discussed in two ways. First, entertainment will be looked at as a product to be marketed. When trying to market entertainment as a product, marketers must convince consumers who have the financial resources how best to spend their free time. Second, marketing will be examined in light of how it uses entertainment to attract attention to other products. For example, a cookbook author may make a guest appearance as a judge at a cooking competition to promote her new book or a celebrity may appear on a TV talk show to discuss an upcoming movie.

INTERMISSION

What are the two ways of looking at entertainment marketing?

LO 1.3-2 EVOLUTION OF ENTERTAINMENT AND ENTERTAINMENT MARKETING

At the beginning of the twentieth century, the performing arts represented a major form of entertainment. Performing arts include live theater, ballet, opera, and concerts. Marketing was limited to posters, newspapers, magazines, and word of mouth. To enjoy any professional entertainment, people had to travel to the theater, concert hall, or arena where community entertainment was focused. The shows were live, and the entertainers received instant feedback from the audience in the form of applause, boos, and even ripe tomatoes tossed at the performers.

Moving pictures initiated the merger of technology and entertainment and added new dimension and depth to entertainment marketing. Technology distanced entertainers from their audience, first with movies and then with television. The Internet has increased the distribution of entertainment to the masses and has added an instant response element to the entertainment industry, which provides valuable marketing information. Facebook, Twitter, Google+, and other social media sites allow viewers to share their thoughts and opinions on television shows and other entertainment events instantly.

The Beginning of Change

Louis Le Prince made the first moving pictures in Britain in 1888. The Lumière brothers were the first to present a projected movie to a paying audience in a café in Paris in 1895. Promotion of films quickly followed with the construction of movie theaters.

The first movie with sound, *The Jazz Singer*, opened in the United States in 1927 in the few movie theaters that were equipped at that time to handle audio. Mickey Mouse arrived in 1928 in Walt Disney's *Steamboat Willie*. Ten years later, *Snow White and the Seven Dwarfs* became the first full-length animated film. In a masterful marketing move, Disneyland opened in Anaheim, California, in July 1955. A totally new approach to the marketing mix of entertainment was born with the opening of the theme park. The live arts and recorded arts were joined by an ever-evolving, technology-driven series of new media.

The Technology Revolution

When television began to arrive in great numbers of American homes, sports and entertainment marketers

How has the distribution of entertainment changed over time?

found a wide-open highway into the billfolds of consumers. As technology became more sophisticated, other forms of media helped the entertainment industry grow.

The Early Days of Television and Marketing Nine television stations and fewer than 7,000 working TV sets existed in the United States at the end of World War II. In October 1945, more than 25,000 people came to Gimbel's Department Store in Philadelphia to watch the first demonstration of TV. That same year, the American Association of Advertising Agencies encouraged the start of television advertising. TV changed the marketing of entertainment in a profound way. Far more than newspapers and magazines had ever been able to do, the audiovisual "life" of TV advertising hooked the imagination of the viewer.

In 1946, NBC and the Gillette Company staged the first televised sports spectacular—a heavyweight boxing match between Joe Louis and Billy Conn. The program was a viewing success with an estimated audience of 150,000 watching on 5,000 TV sets, or an average of 30 people watching the fight on each set.

Television's Increasing Influence Even in its simplicity, early television took promotion and advertising to a new level. Major national corporations lined up to buy time and produce advertisements. The price of commercial time slots was tied to the **ratings**, or the number of viewers the programming attracted. The nine TV stations of 1945 grew to 98 stations by 1949.

On September 9, 1956, 82 percent of all television sets in the United States were tuned to *The Ed Sullivan Show*, a weekly Sunday-evening

Why is TV an important marketing tool?

© Monkey Business Images/Shutterstock.com

variety show. The big attraction was the highly promoted appearance of the future "king" of rock and roll, Elvis Presley. Later, in 1964, more than 60 percent of all U.S. viewers watched the television debut of The Beatles on *The Ed Sullivan Show*. Ed Sullivan set the standard for marketing talent to an audience of millions by using technology (the TV) for distribution of the product. The show shattered ratings records by appealing to a mass audience rather than focusing on a single demographic group. Advertising fees charged for the show reflected the high audience ratings.

Today a wide range of TV programs, from reality shows to news programs, is drawing in advertisers and sponsors. CNBC is cashing in on the interest in the stock market by offering the humorous but smart *Squawk Box*. This daily TV show covers Wall Street news in a not-so-serious manner. During the show, sponsors promote their products, including sports and entertainment products, to busy, educated viewers who have money to spend.

Change Accelerated

Improvements in technology have changed the marketing of sports and entertainment dramatically by making distribution to the masses easier. What had been available to only a few is now available to many. The evolution of radio, moving pictures, TV, video recorders, CDs, DVDs, DVRs, and the Internet has made sports and entertainment products available to the world.

The Internet continues to evolve as a medium. Marketers are learning to use it for distribution as technology ownership by consumers catches up with the endless uses of the Internet. Television is considered a more mature distribution medium. However, it is taking on new twists, such as high-definition and 3D capabilities, that add to the viewer's pleasure and the marketer's opportunities.

Today consumers can download for free or purchase special apps (software applications) that perform useful tasks. Some apps allow users to get the latest sports or entertainment news or watch their favorite television show or team even when they are away from home. Many companies are creating their own apps that provide useful services to users while indirectly promoting the company and/or its products. For example, IBM created an app to be used at the Wimbledon tennis tournament that allowed fans to interact with their surroundings. They could get real-time scores and players' stats or find the shortest souvenir lines by pointing their mobile phone camera lens at various spots. Fans were impressed with the technology, which reinforced IBM's image as a cutting-edge innovator.

Technology and Customer Feedback

The use of television, the Internet, smartphones, and other forms of technology by entertainment marketers to get instant feedback from customers has evolved over time. Two-way

TAKE A BOW *Larry the Cable Guy*

Larry the Cable Guy (Daniel Lawrence Whitney) was born in 1963 in Pawnee City, Nebraska. Larry's blue collar comedy is based on 16 years of growing up on a family pig farm. The diverse backgrounds of Larry's parents also had an impact on his comedy. Larry's father was a preacher and a guitar player who performed with the Everly Brothers. His mother was an Elvis impersonator on the weekends. Larry the Cable Guy was introduced on the nationally syndicated *Bob and Tom Show* on radio. He ended the show with his popular "Git-R-Done" catchphrase. Regular appearances on comedian Jeff Foxworthy's *Country Countdown Show* resulted in a syndication deal to air his commentaries in radio markets throughout the United States. Larry's greatest success came when he joined comedians Foxworthy and Bill Engvall on the Blue Collar Comedy Tour. The show grossed $15 million in ticket sales and sold over 1 million DVDs. Larry shot to stardom and created a full-length CD called *Lord, I Apologize* that remained at the top of the charts for over two years.

In addition to making his fans laugh, Larry the Cable Guy started the Git-R-Done Foundation, which focuses on children's charities. He holds events that help support his charity. Proceeds from the sale of Larry the Cable Guy food products, such as spices, potato chips, nuts, salsas, and frozen burgers, also help fund his charity.

Think Critically

Conduct research online to learn more about the Git-R-Done Foundation. Why do some celebrities have charitable foundations and/or appear in public service commercials? Do you think this is a good idea? Why or why not?

communication allows the entertainment company to gather information from the customer and use it to refine and improve the product—the entertainment. If dissatisfied with the product, customers can instantly communicate through instant messages, texts, email, blogs, Facebook, Twitter, and other social media sites.

Reality TV shows allow viewers to create their own endings and select their new favorite entertainers. The marketing mix of reality shows is unique because the product is selected by the viewers using technology to communicate with the production company. Television shows such as *Dancing with the Stars* and *American Idol* allow audience members to vote for their favorite contestants. The final *American Idol* winners produce musical recordings that require little additional promotion to achieve record-breaking sales. The marketing mix has been fine-tuned based on customer input through social media.

INTERMISSION

Name two benefits marketers and advertisers gain from television.

ENCORE

Understand Marketing Concepts
Select the best answer for each question.

1. Which of the following can be considered entertainment?
   a. performing arts, such as theater, ballet, and symphony concerts
   b. participation in sports competitions
   c. whatever people are willing to spend their time and money watching
   d. both a and c

2. Which of the following statements is *not* true?
   a. Television is considered a mature distribution medium.
   b. The first televised sports spectacular was a baseball game.
   c. Technology enables marketers to receive instant customer feedback.
   d. all of the above are true

Think Critically
Answer the following questions as completely as possible.

3. Describe an activity that you find entertaining. How would you use entertainment marketing to promote the activity? (LO 1.3-1)

4. Explain how the Internet has affected entertainment marketing. Predict how the Internet and social media will change entertainment marketing in the future. (LO 1.3-2)

CHAPTER ASSESSMENT

Review Marketing Terms

Match the terms listed with the definitions.

1. Involves the locations and methods used to make products available to customers
2. The number of times per advertisement, game, or show that a product or service is associated with an athlete, team, or entertainer
3. Common characteristics of a group, such as age, marital status, gender, and income level
4. Ways to make customers aware of products and encourage them to buy
5. The creation and maintenance of satisfying exchange relationships
6. Some type of performance that people are willing to spend their money and spare time watching
7. What a business offers customers to satisfy needs
8. The number of viewers a program attracts
9. Describes how a business blends the four marketing elements of product, distribution, price, and promotion
10. Amount of money individuals have available to spend after paying for the necessities of life and other fixed expenses
11. Using sports to market products
12. Influencing how people choose to spend their time and money on entertainment
13. The amount that customers pay for products

a. demographics
b. discretionary income
c. distribution
d. entertainment
e. entertainment marketing
f. gross impression
g. marketing
h. marketing mix
i. price
j. product
k. promotion
l. ratings
m. sports marketing

Review Marketing Concepts

Select the best answer for each of the following questions.

14. Designing, developing, maintaining, improving, and acquiring products or services so they meet customer needs and wants is
    a. channel management
    b. selling
    c. financing
    d. product/service management
15. All of the following factors are important to the success of sports marketing *except*
    a. celebrities
    b. new opportunities
    c. timing
    d. gross impressions

16. The primary focus of marketing is
     a. maximizing profit
     b. satisfying customer needs
     c. promoting products and services
     d. improving brand recognition
17. Which of the following is an element of distribution?
     a. selecting a host city for a soccer tournament
     b. selling tickets to a concert online
     c. shipping TVs to an electronics retailer
     d. all of the above
18. A professional sports team decides to move to another city. This decision is part of
     a. product management
     b. channel management
     c. marketing-information management
     d. market planning
19. All of the following are demographics *except*
     a. marital status
     b. age
     c. price
     d. income
20. Which of the following does *not* demonstrate the emotional value of sports?
     a. buying season tickets each year to your college football games
     b. catching the latest baseball scores while watching the local news
     c. purchasing a jersey displaying your favorite team's mascot
     d. taking a vacation to go see the Olympics
21. Entertainment marketers can receive instant feedback through
     a. the Internet
     b. Twitter
     c. Facebook
     d. all of the above

Think Critically

22. Working with another student, discuss how entertainment marketing changed after television became popular. Make a list of at least five changes since 1945. Share the list with the class. (LO 1.3-2)
23. Select a product that you use frequently. Describe what you think is involved in the production of that product. (LO 1.1-3)
24. Using the Internet or sports magazines, find and briefly describe three popular new extreme sports. To whom and how are these sports being marketed? (LO 1.2-1)

25. Heavy Armour is a manufacturer of football cleats that wants to increase its market share. How can Heavy Armour market its products at sports camps to increase brand awareness and sales? (LO 1.2-1)

26. Compare the audience interaction of live theater to a reality TV show where messaging and voting can take place online or through text messages. (LO 1.3-2)

Make Academic Connections

27. **Math** You are a famous athlete whose image is on t-shirts produced by L&A Sports Products. You will receive 8 percent of the sales of these t-shirts. The t-shirts sell for $32 at a major department store. During the first quarter of the year, 8,200 shirts were sold. Calculate your share of the first quarter's sales. If the sales remain the same each quarter, what would be your annual share of sales? (LO 1.2-2)

28. **History** You are an entertainment marketer in 1950 America. Your job is to promote a new automobile from that time period. Research the types of television programs that were broadcast at that time. Write a one-page paper describing how you would use television to advertise your product. (LO 1.3-2)

29. **Technology** Go online to find the fan club of a favorite singer or band. Can you find examples of marketing and/or promotion on the website? Describe them. Are there ways you can provide feedback or talk to other fans? Explain how. As a marketer, what changes to the website would you suggest to make it more appealing to fans? (LO 1.1-1)

30. **Communication** Conduct research online about drive-in movie theaters. Your community has just opened a new, nostalgic drive-in movie theater. Prepare a sample billboard that advertises this new entertainment venue. Describe a special promotion to increase attendance at the drive-in movie theater. (LO 1.1-2)

31. **Geography** The Arena Football League (AFL) has become increasingly popular for cities with populations of 100,000 to 400,000. Average attendance at the AFL games has been around 9,000 people. Choose a college city where football is popular. Conduct research and describe the demographics for your chosen city. Provide ten good reasons for an AFL team to locate in this city. What type of sports venue would be the best suited for the 9,000 fans attending a game? (LO 1.1-3)

32. **Ethics** More than 100 lawsuits claiming negligence were filed by former NFL players, and additional lawsuits have been filed by former college football players These lawsuits claim that the NFL and NCAA failed to implement reasonable rules and regulations that would protect players from devastating head injuries resulting in concussions and traumatic brain injuries. While the lawsuits are not an immediate threat to the existence of the NFL or college football, it will make it more risky and expensive for NFL owners and colleges to operate. How do you think these stakeholders (NFL owners and colleges) should respond to the issues surrounding the lawsuits? (LO 1.1-3)

EXTRA INNINGS PROJECT

Males ages 12 to 18 often favor extreme sports over more traditional sports such as football. You have been hired by the NFL to develop a marketing campaign to increase the interest of males in this age group. The NFL wants to capture this market to assure high attendance at games in the future. You have been asked to choose NFL players who will be good spokespersons to promote the NFL to young males. You must decide on a major national retailer to distribute the NFL sports gear to young males. The NFL has asked you to plan activities for males ages 12 to 18 to get them more involved with the NFL. The NFL will hold sports camps in major cities throughout the United States with professional football players making guest appearances at the camps. You must organize the campaign to allow 500 young males to attend each NFL game throughout the nation during the next football season. You can use the Internet to conduct research for this project.

Work with a group and complete the following activities.

1. Which NFL football players will you use for your spokespersons for the campaign aimed at young males? Why? Write a half-page proposal you will present to each NFL player you have chosen to be a spokesperson.

2. Create a brochure that advertises a summer NFL sports camp in a major city for males ages 12 to 18. Be sure to include all of the details.

3. Each participant at the sports camp hosted by the NFL will receive a sports bag with NFL merchandise. What merchandise will you include in the sports bag? Who are the sponsors of this merchandise? Why?

4. Outline the guidelines for the distribution of 500 tickets to males ages 12 to 18 for every NFL game during the next season. Be specific about who receives the tickets and why.

5. Design an advertisement and contest that will encourage males ages 12 to 18 to get more involved with the NFL.

VIRTUAL BUSINESS *Sports & Entertainment*

Use the *Concessions* lesson to learn about satisfying customer needs, which is the primary focus of marketing. You will be able to carry up to six popular concession items at your concession stand. You will determine prices for the items and how much inventory to order. You will also determine how many concession stands to open and how to staff them. At the completion of this lesson, you will be able to provide an overview of how concessions contribute to the fan experience and thus satisfy customer needs.

For more information, go to **knowledgematters.com.**

Artwork courtesy of Knowledge Matters, Inc.

SHOULD COLLEGE ATHLETES BE PAID?

The NCAA is a multimillion-dollar industry that generated over $871.6 million in revenue in a recent year.[7] The top two revenue generators included the University of Texas at Austin with revenue exceeding $163 million and Ohio State University with revenue exceeding $142 million.[8]

Ticket sales and television, radio, and Internet rights agreements are some of the largest revenue generators for college athletics.

Athletic Scholarships

Full-ride scholarships earned by college athletes enable recipients to attend college at little or no cost. Tuition, room and board, books, and certain fees related to courses are covered. Full-ride scholarships are available to athletes who play head-count sports, sports considered to be revenue producers. Head-count sports for men include Division 1 football and basketball. Head-count sports for women include basketball, volleyball, tennis, and gymnastics. College athletes at major universities like Ohio State, Auburn, Georgia, Michigan, Texas, and Notre Dame enjoy the luxury of new student-athlete centers and facilities costing millions of dollars.

The NCAA created commercials to emphasize that most college athletes go pro in something other than sports. The message behind these commercials is that getting an education should be the number one priority.

Out of 20 million students who attend college annually, 60 percent must borrow money to attend. Most college graduates will leave college with a diploma and the financial burden of college loan debts. On the other hand, most college athletes, unless they receive only a partial scholarship or they have walk-on status, leave college with little or no debt. Unfortunately, many college athletes leave school without a degree. Even then they still might have an advantage. Big-name college athletes have the opportunity to network with high-level boosters. These networking opportunities often result in job offers or job assistance after graduation.

All Players United (APU) is a group of college athletes who believe that they should receive a stipend because their athletic performance produces large sums of revenue for their universities.

Think Critically

1. What is the difference between an amateur and professional athlete?
2. Should college athletes be paid? Why or why not?
3. Why do you think some people object to paying college athletes?
4. Although being a college athlete has its benefits, do you think it has any drawbacks? Explain your answer.

SPORTS AND ENTERTAINMENT MARKETING SERIES EVENT

The Sports and Entertainment Marketing Series Event consists of two major parts: a written cluster exam and a role-playing event. Participants are given a written scenario to review. They have ten minutes to review the situation and to develop a professional approach to solving the problem. Participants may use notes made during the preparation time during the presentation, but no note cards may be used. They are allowed ten minutes to present their plan of action to the judge. During or after the participant's explanation, the judge can ask questions related to the scenario.

You are the ticket manager for a major university that has sold out the 92,000-seat stadium every home game since 1963. There are an additional 20,000 fans who would like to attend each home game. Current season ticket holders get the first chance to buy season tickets that cost an average of $60 a game. Many fans will sell their tickets for higher prices to individuals who desperately want to attend a football game, even though ticket scalping is illegal. The athletic director (judge) wants the stadium to continue its sell-out status but has become increasingly concerned about ticket scalping. The director is interested in giving more fans the opportunity to attend the football games.

The athletic director has scheduled a meeting with you to hear your strategy for fairly distributing football tickets to fans and eliminating the illegal scalping of tickets. You must also present a plan to address the issue of high demand and low supply of tickets. You will present your plan to the athletic director in a role-play that will take place in the athletic director's office.

Performance Indicators Evaluated

- Explain the nature and scope of the pricing function.
- Explain the nature and scope of the selling function.
- Explain company selling policies.
- Discuss motivational theories that impact buying behavior.
- Demonstrate a customer-service mindset.

Think Critically

1. How is supply and demand involved in this case?
2. Is there any strategy to stop the ticket scalping? Explain.
3. What is a long-term solution the university should consider, since there are 20,000 additional fans wanting tickets?
4. Why should the university conduct marketing research? Who should be surveyed?

www.deca.org

CHAPTER

2

PUTTING THE CUSTOMER FIRST

Fort Worth Star-Telegram/McClatchy-Tribune/Getty Images

POINT YOUR BROWSER

ngl.cengage.com/sports4e

Winning Strategies

Making an Impact after a 12-Year Absence

The movie industry uses creativity, innovation, and exciting campaigns to market movies. Successful strategies can elevate a low-budget film into an unexpected hit.

The lovable puppet characters known as the Muppets have been featured in six theatrical films, the first of which, *The Muppet Movie*, was released in 1979. A new Muppet film was released every few years thereafter until 1999, when the sixth film, *Muppets from Space* was released. It took 12 long years until the furry creatures returned to the big screen in the film *The Muppets*. Although the Muppets were still highly recognized, some people wondered if they could capture the hearts of a new audience.

© Helga Esteb/Shutterstock.com

A viral marketing campaign ensued. Movie producers tried to win over fans with a massive Facebook Fan-A-Thon. Promoters released funny movie trailers and posters featuring the Muppets in spoofs of other movies due to hit the box office around the same time as *The Muppets* film. *Breaking Prawn (Twilight: Breaking Dawn)* and *The Pig with the Froggy Tattoo (The Girl with the Dragon Tattoo)* were just a couple of the movie spoofs used by *The Muppets'* marketing campaign. In addition, the actors in *The Muppets* had a presence on Google+, Twitter, and other mobile apps. The creative marketing strategy resulted in over $29 million in ticket sales during the opening weekend for *The Muppets* in the United States.

Think Critically

1. Why is the entertainment industry turning to social media to kick off marketing campaigns?

2. What can be learned from the marketing campaign used for *The Muppets*?

2.1 The Marketing Concept

The Essential Question

What is the marketing concept for sports and entertainment events?

Learning Objectives

LO 2.1-1 Explain the central focus of the marketing concept.

LO 2.1-2 Explain the reasons for increased sports and entertainment options.

Key Terms

- marketing concept
- productivity
- breakeven point
- opportunity cost

OPENING ACT

America's children are a popular target market for all types of food and beverages, with an estimated $10 billion spent each year on advertising to this group. In a recent year, The Federal Trade Commission reported that 44 major food and beverage marketers spent $1.6 billion to promote their products to children under 12 and adolescents ages 12 to 17 in the United States.[1]

Both traditional and nontraditional marketing channels, such as television, the Internet, product packaging, in-store advertising, and sweepstakes, are being used to reach children. Companies are now integrating traditional marketing campaigns with cross-promotional strategies that incorporate new movies or popular television shows. Fast-food restaurants often partner with movie studios. Restaurants offer action figures of movie characters in their children's meals. Both the restaurant and the movie benefit from the special promotion. Children learn about the special promotions in the more than 6,100 televised food advertisements they are exposed to each year.

Cooperative Learning Working in groups, discuss some of the cross-promotions you've seen. Who was the target market? Should restaurants and food companies be concerned about the obesity trend among youth and its possible relationship to their products?

LO 2.1-1 WHAT IS THE MARKETING CONCEPT?

Marketing is an important business function. You participate in the marketing process as a consumer of goods and services. About half of every dollar you spend pays for marketing costs. Marketing costs include product development, packaging, advertising, and sales expenses.

The most important aspect of marketing is satisfying customer needs. Customers' needs should be the primary focus during the planning, production, distribution, and promotion of a product or service. A business that keeps the focus on satisfying customer needs is said to be following the **marketing concept**.

Maintain Relationships

The marketing concept requires maintaining important relationships with customers. Successfully managing customer relationships involves listening to customers' needs and carefully monitoring the latest consumer trends. Maintaining a successful marketing relationship requires effort. Each customer is unique and has different buying habits, requiring a unique marketing strategy. While some customers demand lots of attention, others prefer to be left alone until they make the purchase.

Customer satisfaction is the bottom line for maintaining successful marketing relationships. Price, quality, service, and the amount of enjoyment gained from a sports and entertainment event are factors that influence customer satisfaction. Sports and entertainment event planners are challenged to organize events that customers want and can afford. When individuals purchase goods and services, they expect value for the money spent. Because there is so much competition in the sports and entertainment industry, marketing strategies must include a customer service component that stands apart from the others. Customers who have a satisfying experience are less likely to take their business elsewhere.

© JuliusKielaitis/Shutterstock.com

What type of customer service results in repeat business?

INTERMISSION

What is the most important aspect of marketing?

LO 2.1-2 INCREASED SPORTS AND ENTERTAINMENT OPTIONS

Over the years, the high standard of living in the United States has resulted in more discretionary income for consumers. During prosperous times, the average consumer has more money to spend on sports and entertainment events and related merchandise. Increased consumer demand for sports and entertainment events typically results in higher prices and more competition. Competition in the marketplace results in more options for consumers and improved events and merchandise.

Marketing strategies must include monitoring the competition and consumer trends and making improvements that meet the latest customer demands.

Celebrities are using social media to build their brand. When it comes to tweeting, celebrities are treating their fans like friends. Stars can talk to their fans in a relatively safe environment through the use of Twitter or Instagram. Fans love to communicate with their favorite stars, and when celebrities "keep in touch" through social media, they become even more beloved by their fan base. Fans like the authenticity of a tweet from their favorite celebrity; it makes them think the celebrity is just an ordinary person.

Social media interaction can be negative, however. Some stars participate in Twitter fights with distracters, or more vocal fans. Most stars do not engage in this, but those who do may have a marketing strategy in mind. Many celebrities believe that all publicity is good publicity, and a feud with a fan or fellow artist will get fans, magazines, and news shows talking.

Think Critically

Do you agree that all publicity is good publicity for celebrities? What might be the result when publicity comes from negative behavior?

In addition, marketers must be aware of the economy. When the economy is down, consumers have less discretionary income to spend on sports and entertainment events. During these times, it is more important than ever that businesses offer value for the money spent by consumers.

Customer Focus

Productivity is the rate at which companies produce goods or services in relation to the amount of materials and number of employees utilized. Productivity has made impressive strides in the United States as well as in many other developing nations. Whether it's the production of 5,000 concert T-shirts or 10,000 plastic promotional footballs for a professional football team, the product demands for sports and entertainment events can be filled quickly. But increased competition has forced businesses to focus beyond productivity to establish satisfying relationships with customers. Imagine being highly productive in manufacturing products that consumers do not need or want! Remember, the primary focus of the marketing concept is the satisfaction of customer needs.

Successful marketing strategies identify customer needs and ways to meet those needs by developing and marketing products that customers will view as being superior to other products. While it is important to maintain satisfying customer relationships, companies must also earn a profit. When marketing strategies do not focus on customer wants and needs, sports and entertainment events have disappointing attendance figures and stores have surplus merchandise, resulting in price cuts. The end result of not having a customer focus is a failed business.

Prospective customers must be offered the appropriate marketing mix—product, price, promotion, and location—to maintain satisfying relationships. Marketing success depends on offering the best product at a good price where demand exists. Customers learn about the products and services through promotion. Customers are the driving force behind the marketing concept.

Weekend Sports and Entertainment Choices

Every weekend, there are numerous entertainment choices, ranging from community celebrations and concerts to a wide array of sporting events. The organizers of all of these events realize the intense competition for consumer dollars. They develop promotional strategies to catch the attention of consumers as a way to increase attendance. The bottom line is that these events must earn a profit. Event planners need to know the **breakeven point**, or the minimum sales required to cover all of the expenses of organizing, promoting, and running the event. Revenue earned above the breakeven point is all profit.

Many young families use their entertainment dollars to attend sporting events for their children. Cities of all sizes want to capitalize by hosting sporting events, whether it is a soccer tournament, a track meet, or a cheerleading competition. Restaurants, hotels, motels, retail stores, and service stations all have an interest in locally hosted events.

Movie theaters are competing with businesses like Netflix, Hulu, and Amazon that offer streaming movies. DISH, DIRECTV, and other satellite and cable providers offer pay-per-view, high-definition movie channels that enable consumers to enjoy movies at home. Drive-in theaters that were popular in the 60s and 70s may be making a comeback in some cities. When traveling on Interstate 45 near Ennis, Texas, do not be surprised to see long lines of cars waiting to enter drive-in movie theaters where movies are projected on large outdoor movie screens.

Do you think drive-in movies can compete in the entertainment industry? Why or why not?

Concert events are another way consumers spend their leisure time. In the midst of all the entertainment choices, concert organizers are challenged to develop creative promotional strategies to attract fans willing to pay $25 to $100 or more to see their favorite performers.

Opportunity Cost

Car races, rodeos, craft fairs, and community celebrations are just a few of the additional sports and entertainment options for consumers. Factors that individuals consider when deciding to attend an entertainment event include convenience, enjoyment, price, and opportunity cost. **Opportunity cost** is the value of the next best alternative that you pass up when making a choice. The value is measured in terms of the benefits that you are giving up. For example, you may want to go to a car race and a music concert, but you cannot afford to do both. If you decide to go to the concert, the opportunity cost would be the car race. As a consumer, you must decide which opportunity you value the most. An increasing number of Americans are opting to stay at home during their free time due to high fuel costs, less discretionary income, and limited time to relax. Online and other forms of at-home entertainment will continue to grow because of these factors. The opportunity costs to these consumers include the value of the other entertainment options they are passing up to stay at home.

INTERMISSION

Explain the reasons for increased sports and entertainment options.

ENCORE

Understand Marketing Concepts

Select the best answer for each question.

1. Businesses that follow the marketing concept
   a. will face little competition
   b. will always be profitable
   c. will focus on satisfying customer needs
   d. will experience high productivity

2. Which of the following led to growth in the sports and entertainment industry?
   a. a higher standard of living and increased discretionary income among average consumers
   b. rising gasoline prices combined with periods of decreasing productivity in the U.S. economy
   c. less competition among sports and entertainment businesses
   d. none of the above

Think Critically

Answer the following questions as completely as possible.

3. Movie theaters face stiff competition from online subscription businesses and pay-per-view movie channels. How can a movie theater use the marketing concept to keep customers coming back? (LO 2.1-1)

4. Small, local sporting goods stores face stiff competition from large, national sporting goods chains and department stores. The competition makes it necessary to offer unique products and services. What could a sales associate at a local sporting goods store do to maintain positive relationships with the store's customers? (LO 2.1-2)

2.2 Discover What People Want

The Essential Question

Why must sports and entertainment venues conduct research to keep repeat customers?

Learning Objectives

LO 2.2-1   Explain the importance of understanding buyer behavior when making marketing decisions.

LO 2.2-2   List and describe means of collecting marketing information for use in decision making.

Key Terms

- economic market
- benefits derived
- comparative advantage
- emotional purchases
- rational purchases
- patronage purchases

The NFL draft and the search for corporate sponsorship have many similarities. Professional sports franchises scout college campuses to identify talented athletes and to determine if those athletes will be a good fit for the organization. Some questions that must be answered include the following: What is your performance history? Do you fill a team need? What values are important to you? Is there an opportunity to establish a mutually beneficial long-term relationship?

Sports organizations get quality corporate sponsors by evaluating the potential benefits of a partnership. Just like the relationship between the sports organization and a football player, the relationship between a sports organization and its corporate sponsor must be mutually beneficial for long-term survival. So, it is important to ensure that corporate sponsors are a good fit with the team!

Cooperative Learning   Work with a partner. Assume you are part of a sports organization in need of a sponsor. Discuss how you would research possible sponsors. What information would you need to ensure a mutually beneficial relationship?

LO 2.2-1   UNDERSTAND BUYER BEHAVIOR

The **economic market** includes all of the consumers who will purchase a product or service. Two of the major goals of marketing are to determine what consumers want and how much they are willing to pay. To achieve these goals, marketers must understand the actions of consumers, including their spending habits and buying motives. This information enables businesses to better assist consumers in satisfying their wants and needs. By knowing their customers, businesses are able to respond to their needs more quickly.

Consumers today are much more mobile than ever before. Apple Inc. recognized this and developed the iPod. Different variations of the iPod were created to serve different purposes. The iPod with video allows consumers to download episodes of their favorite TV shows. Customers can listen to iTunes Radio on their iPhone, iPad, and iPod Touch. To further meet the needs of consumers, Apple TV was introduced. It is a digital network media player that streams media, such as movies, music, and photos, from your computer to your television. Apple has partnered with other media companies, such as Netflix and Pandora, to allow streaming of their digital media. Consumers can enjoy a whole world of movies, television shows, sports, music, and more just by plugging in Apple TV.

Consumer Spending Habits

Pricing

It is important to research the spending habits of consumers to maximize profits on items they purchase at sporting and entertainment events. The price fans are willing to pay for a ticket depends on their degree of interest, which may be influenced by the national importance of the event, the popularity of the participating athletes or celebrities, and the rivalry associated with the sports contest. Fans' degree of enthusiasm will also influence their willingness to pay high prices for team- or celebrity-identified clothing and equipment.

If a business has a comparative advantage, how does that affect consumers?

xy/Fotolia LLC

The price fans are willing to pay is also related to their perception of the benefits derived. **Benefits derived** refers to the value people believe they receive from a product or service. In college sports, benefits derived may include the enjoyment received from a good game and the feeling of pride when wearing a sweatshirt that shows off the team logo.

The global market has intense competition. Organizations must determine where they have a **comparative advantage**—the capability to produce products or services more efficiently and economically than the competition. When a company can produce a product more efficiently and economically than others, it can pass along production cost savings to its customers in the form of lower prices. For example, a sports apparel manufacturer may have a comparative advantage because it produces its products in another country where labor costs are lower. This allows it to price its products lower than competitors do.

Consumer Wants and Needs

Marketing-Information Management

Abraham Maslow was an American psychologist who is noted for his theory of the *hierarchy of needs*, which identifies five human areas of needs. Maslow's hierarchy is referenced frequently by marketers when studying human behavior in relation to customer needs and wants. Maslow theorized that people's most basic needs must be satisfied first and then their focus will progress to higher-level needs.

The basic needs of food, water, sleep, and shelter are referred to as *physiological needs. Security* is the second level of the hierarchy—individuals want both physical safety and economic security. *Social needs* in the hierarchy include the desire for friends, family, and love. As individuals progress up the hierarchy, they focus on *self-esteem needs* to gain recognition and respect from others and feelings of adequacy and competence in themselves. The peak of the hierarchy pyramid represents *self-actualization,* or the realization of one's full potential and self-fulfillment. People are at different levels on the hierarchy at any given time, making it challenging to design effective marketing strategies.

When a major hurricane threatens a population, sports and entertainment events are not high on the consumer's priority list. The hurricane shifts attention to physiological and security needs. Games and sporting events are postponed while people take care of the more urgent issues presented by the storm. Lightning and severe storms will cause delay of games and evacuation of stadiums for safety reasons.

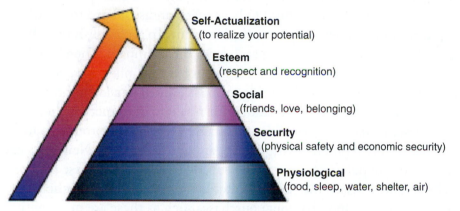

Maslow's Hierarchy of Needs Pyramid

Buying Motives Marketing research is conducted to determine why customers spend money on goods and services. Consumers make **emotional purchases** when they spend with little thought during emotional highs or lows. For example, when fans attend a concert of their favorite music star, they may be emotionally charged to pay top price for a T-shirt or the star's latest CD. When a team is on a winning streak and qualifies for a national or world championship game, fans are emotionally influenced to purchase high-priced tickets and merchandise with the team's logo.

Rational purchases take place when individuals recognize needs and wants, assess their priorities and budget, conduct research, compare alternatives, and then make purchases based on careful thought and sound reasoning. An avid runner makes a rational purchase when he or she shops around for the best shoes that provide support, shock absorption, flexibility, and durability. The ultimate goal of the purchase is to find comfortable shoes that will enhance the running experience and reduce the chance of injuries.

Patronage purchases are based on consumer loyalty to a particular brand or product. Tennis players may purchase Nike products due to endorsements by Maria Sharapova. Fans remain loyal to their favorite teams and players and purchase products directly related to them.

Positive experiences with a particular brand will reinforce the consumer's loyalty. The consumer will continue to buy the brand with confidence and will be less likely to try competing brands.

The Buying Plan

To increase sales, businesses must understand consumers' buying behavior. This knowledge is also used by businesses to develop buying plans. Retailers who sell popular athletic apparel have a limited budget. Sometimes they have to submit purchase orders for merchandise at least a year in advance. Thus, the retailer must develop a buying plan based on projected consumer behavior. Once the order has been processed and delivered, the retailer will receive invoices that must be paid. If a popular team goes on a losing streak, resulting in lower than expected related merchandise sales, the retailer will lose money on unsold inventory.

Projecting athletic merchandise sales and team success is a big risk that retailers must take. When the top two teams play for a championship, only one team will win. Retailers need to have merchandise related to the winning team ready immediately after the big event. To accomplish this, they may order merchandise declaring each team the champion. Then based on the outcome of the game, the merchandise for the winning team is sold while the merchandise for the losing team is counted as a loss for the retailer.

In addition to buying merchandise for resale to customers, businesses also buy merchandise for organizational use. College and professional sports teams must purchase athletic apparel for the players. New seats and scoreboards are purchased by stadiums. Movie theaters purchase popcorn machines and seats. Many theaters offer luxury seating for their deluxe screening rooms. Organizational purchases such as these are made with the customer in mind. Businesses want to make the customers' experience more enjoyable so that they become repeat customers.

INTERMISSION

What are the three buying motives and how are they different?

LO 2.2-2   GATHER INFORMATION

Most consumers use the decision-making process to decide how to spend their money. The first step of the decision-making process is to recognize a need or want and an opportunity to satisfy it. Conducting research to get more information on a product or service is the second step of the decision-making process. Information should be collected on all alternatives. After conducting research, individuals evaluate their choices and then make a decision to purchase. The final step of the decision-making process is the post-purchase evaluation in which purchasers assess their level of satisfaction and the possibility of future purchases.

When consumers save money for a well-earned vacation, they conduct research to determine the vacation options that meet their needs.

After thoroughly considering the alternatives, they purchase a vacation package. Post-evaluation of the vacation is important—consumers determine their satisfaction and adjust their strategies for planning future vacations.

Marketers must be aware of the consumer decision-making process. They often are involved in every step. A marketer can help a customer recognize a need for a product, provide information, assist with the purchase, and follow up with the customer after the sale to ensure satisfaction.

Information Needed for Marketing Decisions

Marketing decisions are based on consumers and the business environment. Important factors to consider about consumers include demographics and shopping behaviors. Marketing research looks at how consumers spend money, including product and brand preferences and the frequency by which products are purchased.

The business environment has an impact on consumer purchases. Economic conditions influence how individuals spend their discretionary income. Consumers are more cautious about spending and more likely to postpone making large purchases during periods of economic uncertainty. The amount and quality of competition in the marketplace determine the number of good options available to consumers. Government regulations, laws, and ethical issues also influence how consumers spend money. Additionally, advances in technology have broadened the flow of information and means of acquiring goods and services by consumers.

Once marketers have fully analyzed their potential customers and the business environment, they are better prepared to select the right marketing mix that will motivate customers to buy. Products offered must have features that meet consumers' needs and wants. They must be available at a price

Why do companies spend sizable amounts of money on marketing research?

customers are willing and able to pay. Offering solid product guarantees, special discounts, and a variety of credit choices helps entice consumers to make purchases. The location of products and the services offered by businesses will also influence consumer purchases. Promotional methods and choice of media must be selected carefully to reach potential customers.

Sources of Information for Businesses

To help customers with the decision-making process, it is essential to collect information about their needs and buying behaviors. Sources of information may be classified as internal or external. *Internal sources* of information about customer buying habits include a business's own customer records, sales records, production records, and operation records. Companies can look at their sales trends over past years as a starting point in determining future marketing strategies. *External sources* of information used by businesses can be obtained through government reports, trade and professional organizations, business publications, commercial data, information services, competitors' websites, and social media. Information from these sources gives decision makers a broader picture of what is happening in the industry and the marketplace.

Organizations often conduct research to learn more about consumer behavior. The data collected may be categorized as either primary data or secondary data. *Primary data* is obtained for the first time and specifically for the particular problem or issue being studied. Consumer surveys are frequently used to ask questions and obtain feedback on specific issues. Observing consumer behavior is another technique used to collect primary data. Security personnel may observe behavior of fans at a big sporting event to determine future security needs. Samples and simulations give prospective customers the opportunity to try something, such as a new soft drink or video game, and give feedback before it goes into full production.

Secondary data has already been collected for some other purpose but is found to be useful in the current study. Secondary data can include government statistics about population and other demographics that will provide valuable information to help make important marketing decisions.

Businesses often turn to research companies to obtain primary and secondary data. One of the goals of a business's marketing campaign is to determine what TV shows consumers are watching and how they are watching them. Nielsen Ratings uses representative television panels to track the detailed programming and commercial engagement by viewers. Nielsen analyzes viewing behavior and demographic information, such as education level, income level, and other household characteristics of television viewers. Businesses can use this data to refine their television marketing campaigns accordingly. Because there are multiple platforms by which entertainment is distributed, Nielsen conducts audience measurement across TVs, radios, mobile phones, and the Internet. Knowing what Americans are watching, reading, playing, browsing, and tweeting helps businesses create cross-platform marketing plans.

INTERMISSION

Explain the difference between primary and secondary data.

ENCORE

Understand Marketing Concepts

Select the best answer for each question.

1. The peak of Maslow's hierarchy of needs pyramid represents
   a. physiological needs
   b. self-actualization needs
   c. self-esteem needs
   d. rational purchases

2. Primary data may be collected through
   a. surveys and observation
   b. government reports
   c. business publications
   d. both b and c

Think Critically

Answer the following questions as completely as possible.

3. Define rational, emotional, and patronage purchases and give an example of each type of purchase at a sporting or entertainment event. (LO 2.2-1)

4. Sales of running shoes at your sporting goods store are declining. How would you go about gathering market information to determine the reasons for the decline and to decide what to do to attract more buyers? (LO 2-2.2)

2.3 Target Markets

The Essential Question

How do target markets and market segments affect a business's marketing efforts?

Learning Objectives

LO 2.3-1   Define target market and market segment.

LO 2.3-2   Describe how businesses use market segmentation.

Key Terms

- target market
- market segment
- mass marketing
- market share

OPENING ACT

College football players and fans sometimes take great pride in the school logos and mascots they wear on and off the field. Popular school logos and mascots can drive merchandise sales. Major universities earn large sums of money from such merchandise. On average, universities earn 12 percent of all sales from merchandise with their logo. The University of Texas topped the merchandise sales list representing $4.6 billion in annual college merchandise business. The teams in the SEC and Big Ten conferences commonly have the most popular university logos. These schools include Alabama, Florida, LSU, Michigan, and Ohio State, among others.[5] School logos and mascots are redesigned periodically to increase sales of merchandise among those fans who want the newest version of the logo.

Cooperative Learning   With a partner, select a college team that has successful merchandise sales. What sport(s) at this university have contributed to sales? Do you think the logo or mascot for your chosen school has an effect on the popularity of the merchandise?

LO 2.3-1   DETERMINE THE TARGET MARKET

Marketing-Information Management The first step in marketing a product is to determine who specifically "the customer" is for the product. A **target market** is a specific group of consumers a business wants to reach. To promote and sell products and services, a company must know the needs and wants of its target market.

Focus Marketing Efforts

Because it would be impossible to satisfy the needs of every consumer, businesses must narrow down the focus of their marketing efforts. Using different players or teams on the cover of the same magazine sold in different parts of the country illustrates this concept. A **market segment** is a group of consumers within a larger market who share one or more characteristics. Millions of people in the United States enjoy college basketball, but a smaller group specifically enjoys University of Kentucky basketball. Sports magazine covers featuring the Wildcats will sell well in Kentucky, but the same publication featuring the Indiana University Hoosiers might not sell well in Kentucky.

Snowbirds are a market segment of retirees who move to the South during the winter months and move back to their northern residences with the return of warm spring weather. Die-hard fans who follow the "Rolling Stones" concert tour are also a market segment. Everyone belongs to several different market segments. For example, rodeo fans may also enjoy attending country music concerts. Marketers must identify the market segment to which they want to sell.

Meet Target Market Needs

Businesses and entertainment organizations must analyze market segments to devise the most effective marketing strategies. Information that is important to prospective businesses includes the number of potential customers, their level of income, and the level of interest in the product or service. Market segmentation data can improve business decision making. Sodas used to be sold in collectible plastic souvenir cups at college games. Fans enjoyed collecting the cups, and universities made huge profits because fans were willing to pay higher prices for the cups. Sodas are now sold in plastic bottles with sealed caps for safety and health reasons. Although fans no longer get souvenir cups, marketing information indicated that safety and health standards were more important to consumers.

Mass Marketing

A business that uses market segmentation focuses its efforts on a specific group of consumers with unique needs. Some businesses choose to use **mass marketing**, which is an attempt to appeal to a large, general group

College football is becoming one of the most popular sports in the United States. According to a Harris Interactive poll, college football is the third most popular sport (11%), following professional football (34%) and baseball (16%).[6]

When might a business use mass marketing for certain products?

© Art Allianz/Shutterstock.com

of consumers. By using mass marketing, a business directs its efforts on the whole market to reach the largest number of consumers. One marketing mix is developed for all consumers. Businesses may choose to use mass marketing if they are unable or unwilling to spend the time or money needed to conduct research and analyze data to identify market segments. Mass marketing is used more commonly for products and services that everyone tends to buy, such as soap, snacks, and household cleaners.

There are some advantages of mass marketing. Businesses can reach a larger audience, gain wider exposure, increase sales volume, and lower marketing costs. Disadvantages involve the risk of using one marketing mix when trying to appeal to a diverse group of consumers with different needs. Also, mass marketing makes it more difficult for a business to succeed because there are numerous other businesses competing for the same consumers' dollars.

INTERMISSION

What is a target market? Provide an example of a company's target market.

LO 2.3-2   MARKET SEGMENTATION

Marketing-Information Management

Most businesses do not try to satisfy the needs of all possible customers. They recognize that individuals have different wants and needs and view product and service choices quite differently. For example, consumers purchase tickets to college football games for different reasons. The dedicated alumni who donate money to the athletic department may attend games due to school loyalty. College students may attend games as a social activity. A young family may attend the game as a family bonding event. Businesses try to narrow their marketing efforts to the specific market segments that they want to target. Markets can be segmented in many ways, such as by geographic location, demographics, psychographics, and behavior.

Geographic Segmentation

Geographic segmentation divides markets into physical locations, such as Eastern, Northern, Southern and Western regions of the United States or the urban and rural areas of a state. For example, a national clothing store chain may offer a different mix of clothing in northern states than in southern states because of the need for heavier clothing in the North during winter months. A sporting goods chain

How does geography affect a business's marketing strategy?

© Julie Keen/Shutterstock.com

in the South may stock a larger number and variety of water sports equipment. Also, sports fans are likely to be loyal to their own region when purchasing team-related products. Geographic segmentation even occurs within a single city. For example, a local newspaper publisher may segment markets by different areas of the city. Geographic segmentation also is commonly used in the travel and tourism industries.

Demographic Segmentation

Demographic segmentation focuses on information that can be measured, such as age, income, profession, gender, education, marital status, and size of household. Marketers might use income information to target advertising for upscale hotels to those who can afford them. Advertisements for animated films will target children. Promoters of college football and basketball camps focus their attention on high school athletes. An aging population may be more inclined to attend an entertainment event if it is promoted as a package deal that provides transportation and meals.

Psychographics Segmentation

Psychographics focus on characteristics that cannot be measured physically, such as values, interests, and lifestyle choices. For example, if a ballgame falls on a holy day of your faith, will you attend the game? Decisions like this are based on consumers' values. Consumers frequently make decisions based on their interests. Sports fans will buy more clothing bearing their team's logo.

Lifestyle choices also involve consumer interests. For example, bowling alleys meet the needs of a specific psychographic segment of consumers. Sports-themed restaurants and bars attract those who enjoy watching the games in a setting with other sports fans. Watching football games every Sunday on multiple big screen TVs at sports-themed restaurants has become a ritual for many.

Behavioral-Based Segmentation

Behavioral-based segmentation focuses on a customer's attitude toward products and services. Two categories of behavioral-based segmentation include product usage and product benefits. *Product usage* reflects what products you use and how often. For example, some individuals may visit amusement parks frequently while others visit them only occasionally. Frequency of use determines promotional strategies for a market segment. Marketers may want to develop separate promotions for different market segments. One promotion may encourage frequent visitors to continue to visit the park by purchasing a season pass. Another promotion may encourage infrequent visitors to visit the park more often.

© Joy Fera/Shutterstock.com

Why do marketers use behavioral-based segmentation to target consumers?

Marketers also group consumers based on the benefits derived from products or services. For example, individuals attend sporting events for different reasons. Benefits may include the satisfaction of spending time with the family or of showing team spirit. Marketers will examine the resulting benefits by different market segments and target their promotions based on this information. Competing sporting and entertainment events may use benefits-derived segmentation to encourage consumers to attend other similar events. During a major college football game, the announcer may advertise the university's upcoming basketball game. Fans that enjoy the school's football game also may be inclined to watch the school's basketball game. This strategy is aimed at gaining greater market share for one of the school's other sports team.

Capture a Market Share

Every business wants to sell its products to as many potential customers as possible. **Market share** is the percentage of total sales of a product or service that a company expects to capture in relation to its competitors. Businesses determine the most effective means of using their resources to reach a target market. Research is conducted to determine who is spending money and how much on different products and services.

An aging population opens up many opportunities for sports and entertainment businesses. Senior citizens are healthier today than ever before and are living longer, meaning they have more years to spend money on sports and entertainment events. Hotels, restaurants, and entertainment

COMMUNICATION CONNECTION

Garth Brooks surprised his large fan base when he left the music scene in 2001 to retire and spend more time with his family. At the time of his retirement, he was still touring and selling out live concert performances. He partially came out of retirement in 2009 and began performing regularly on weekends at the Wynn Las Vegas Resort.

After a long break, Brooks finally decided to start touring again. He announced his plans to kick off a global concert in 2014. After the announcement, Brooks spent three days talking with radio stations and *Country Aircheck* (a multifaceted media news source) about touring, producing new music, and selling music digitally. After being off of the radio airwaves for many years, Brooks realized that his success largely depended on these stations playing his songs as an introduction to his new tour. Brooks hinted that a new album was not out of the question; however, he continues to be outspoken against digital music sales by organizations like iTunes.

Write Now

Conduct research to learn the methods used by performance artists to communicate news about their concerts, new albums, and other noteworthy events. Why is it important for artists such as Garth Brooks to be open to using social media and other platforms (like iTunes) to distribute their music? Write a one-page paper in which you recommend communication techniques performance artists can use to successfully connect with fans.

destinations such as Branson, Missouri, are aware of the financial gains to be had by catering to a growing senior-citizen population. Marketing campaigns directed at senior citizens offer special discounts and vacation packages. Restaurants, movie theaters, and other businesses regularly offer senior citizens special prices. By targeting this demographic, businesses hope to gain a larger market share.

Teenagers spend billions of dollars each year on clothing, food, and numerous entertainment goods and services. Because of this, marketers are very interested in capturing a larger share of the teenage market. To compete for teen dollars, companies must conduct continuous research because this market segment has changing tastes and trends. The clothing industry provides a good example of how frequently teenager tastes in products change. To capture a bigger market share, businesses cannot rest on their past successes. They must keep up with target market trends.

INTERMISSION

List and describe four types of market segmentation.

ENCORE

Understand Marketing Concepts

Select the best answer for each question.

1. Demographics
   a. categorize market segments by age, gender, race, income, and educational level
   b. refer to the frequency of use of a product
   c. refer to interests, values, and emotional responses
   d. consider different parts of the country where market segments live

2. Market share
   a. is the total number of people in a particular age group
   b. refers to customers in a particular part of the country
   c. is a group of consumers within a larger market who share one or more characteristics
   d. is the percentage of total sales of a product or service that a company expects to capture in relation to the competition

Think Critically

Answer the following questions as completely as possible.

3. Give an example of a good market segment to target for state fairs during weekdays. Explain your answer. (LO 2.3-1)

4. Describe possible demographics, geographics, psychographics, and product usage for snowmobiles. (LO 2.3-2)

2.4 Customer Service

The Essential Question

What is an outstanding customer service culture, and why is it important at sports and entertainment events?

Learning Objectives

LO 2.4-1   Explain the importance of outstanding customer service.

LO 2.4-2   Explain what it means to establish a service culture.

Key Terms

• customer service gap
• values-based culture

OPENING ACT

When was the last time you received outstanding customer service? Good customer service is appreciated and keeps customers coming back. L.L. Bean sells clothing and camping and sporting gear. All of L.L. Bean's products have a lifetime guarantee. Its customer service representatives are known to be friendly and accommodating. They efficiently process orders and requests for refunds or replacements for those products that do not meet customer expectations. These factors have turned most L.L. Bean customers into repeat customers.

Good customer service must come from the heart of an organization and its employees. Customer service starts with people who genuinely care about other people and want to assist them with their needs. Unfortunately, good customer service has become a thing of the past for many businesses. Some reasons for the decline in customer service include low wages paid to sales associates, insufficient number of sales associates on the job, and high stress levels due to large crowds and demanding customers.

Cooperative Learning   As part of a group, discuss the last time you received good and bad customer service. Describe the situations and the end results.

LO 2.4-1   OUTSTANDING SERVICE EQUALS SUCCESS

Product/Service Management   Business success depends on excellent customer service. All customers expect to be treated with fairness and dignity. Customer expectations also include a safe, comfortable environment and value for the money spent. Customer relationships should continue after the sale of goods and services.

The best strategy for a business to rise above the competition is to provide uncompromising, outstanding customer service. Paying attention to customers and their needs is the first step in making customers happy. Successful sales personnel take time to get acquainted with customers. Many businesses establish customer databases that include home addresses, telephone numbers, email addresses, buying preferences, and customer birthdays. Businesses that take the time to send thank-you notes and birthday greetings with special coupons can strengthen their relationships with customers. It is also important to keep an eye on the competition and solicit customer feedback.

A Track Record for Great Customer Service

The **customer service gap** is the difference between customer expectations and the service that is actually received. Some examples of poor customer service include the following:

- Chatting on the phone or with others while customers are waiting to be served
- Dismissing a customer by saying, "It's not my department."
- Placing a calling customer on hold for long periods and transferring the customer from department to department
- Yelling at a customer who fails to understand company policies
- Failing to follow up with customers in a timely manner to ensure satisfaction

America's service economy fails when its members do not remember that customer service is everyone's department, from the parking lot attendant to the usher inside a stadium. Customers are more likely to try out the competition when they receive less than adequate service from a business. Further, while customers commonly do not talk about good customer service experiences, they are likely to tell others about their poor customer service experiences.

Training Programs That Make an Impact

It is important for businesses to train their employees on proper customer service before a problem occurs. But ensuring good customer service actually starts before the training ever takes place. First, the right employees

Customer service is so important to businesses that a whole week has been set aside to honor it and the people working in this field. Customer Service Week is an annual celebration during the first full week in October. CSWeek.com is a website that offers ideas for participation in Customer Service Week.

Why does customer service play such a big role in the success of a business?

must be hired. Individuals hired should have a positive attitude and look forward to meeting the public. Happy employees are more likely to treat customers well. Once the right employees are in place, they must be properly trained. Every company claims to have a training program for customer service. In many training programs, however, the focus is not on how to serve customers well. Instead, training mainly consists of how to deal with difficult customers or mistakes made by employees. Providing outstanding service does not come naturally, so it is necessary for leaders to explain what to do in various situations.

Employees hired by Nordstrom's shoe department are trained to bring out three pairs of shoes when a customer requests to try on a pair. The sales associate will bring out the requested pair, a second pair in the same style but a different color, and a third pair of that week's hottest-selling shoes. By having associates who go beyond customer expectations, Nordstrom hopes to maintain a competitive edge and keep customers returning.

Disneyland is advertised as the "Happiest Place on Earth." Customer service is a big reason for this. Disney provides all employees with customer service training. They are trained to be "assertively friendly" by actively seeking out contact with guests and making them feel important. Disney gives out name badges to people who are there for their first visit or for their birthday, so that employees can address the customer by name. Disney employees also are trained to be effective communicators. Because Disney takes great pride in running rides, shows, and trains on time, even a short delay is addressed. All Disney staff members are trained to answer common questions to avoid responses such as "It's not my job." Disney employees are aware of all show times and the length of each show in order to accommodate all questions asked by guests.

INTERMISSION

Why is outstanding customer service critical to a business in a highly competitive marketplace?

LO 2.4-2 CREATING A SERVICE CULTURE

Gallery Furniture is one of the biggest retail stores in America. Jim McIngvale (Mattress Mack), the owner, became well known in Houston, Texas, for his "Save You Money" advertising slogan. Mattress Mack's success at Gallery Furniture can be attributed to a strong work ethic, outstanding customer service, and principles that guide the business. Many of his principles can be applied to the sports and entertainment industries.

1. **Demonstrate a values-based culture, which is one that communicates values through high performance and excellent customer service.** Advertisements for Gallery Furniture consist of the word "TODAY." This means that customers will receive delivery of the furniture on the

day they purchase it. Delivery persons will make deliveries late into the night if necessary to keep the store's promise. This type of commitment results in repeat customers. To guide employees and build commitment to values, Mattress Mack believes that leaders have to practice them every single day and build a culture of trust. Customer service employees should go above and beyond customer expectations to show the customers they are valued by the organization.

2. **Follow the "FAST" (Focus, Action, Search, Tenacity) strategy.** Mattress Mack successfully focuses on such concepts as "promises made, promises kept," "being friendly," "providing top value to customers," "the customer is right," and "listen to what customers, employees, or suppliers are saying." A *focus* on these concepts gives sales associates a target. The next step is to turn the focus into *action*. Customer service employees must *search* for ways to increase customer satisfaction. *Tenacity* is a necessary element for survival in the highly competitive business world. Frustrated customers at crowded sports and entertainment events are not always pleasant, but good customer service agents will remain focused, take action, and persist until the customer is satisfied.

3. **Passion results in energy**. A successful business requires an enormous amount of energy. Energy is acquired by having a very strong interest in or a passion for what you do. This passion energizes people.

4. **Demonstrate pride in every sale**. Anyone working in the customer service field must be proud of what they do. That pride will swell over to customers who end up feeling good about attending an entertainment event. Ideally, the customer will come to identify all of the components of a sports or entertainment event as a brand. It is the customer service agent's job to sell the brand in a way that keeps customers coming back.

5. **Remember the value of long-term positive relationships**. Customers appreciate service representatives who answer their questions, give them guidance, and remember their first name. No question asked by a customer should be treated as a "dumb question." At sports and entertainment events, customer service agents can be the difference between a pleasant and an unpleasant experience.

Sports and entertainment businesses must recognize the importance of building a service culture. The number one goal of customer service is customer satisfaction. By identifying the wants and needs of customers,

Courtesy of Gallery Furniture

What steps can a business take to achieve a values-based culture , as exists at Gallery Furniture?

marketers can develop plans to achieve this goal. Those businesses that achieve this goal are much more likely to succeed.

How May I Help You?

When leaders overhear an employee telling customers any version of "It's not my department," they should intervene immediately. The customer must know that the organization will go to great lengths to ensure customer satisfaction. "It's not my department" should be replaced with "How may I help you?" Employees should observe the leader to learn how to assist customers properly.

Many sports and entertainment businesses are finding creative ways to ensure their customers are receiving the best service. Some businesses use mystery shopping programs to put their customer service to the test. For example, an amusement park may hire an outside marketing firm to send a mystery guest to the park to evaluate his or her experiences with the park's sales and service employees. The mystery guest can evaluate other

TAKE A BOW *Adolf Dassler*

Adolf (Adi) Dassler, the founder of Adidas, had a vision to provide all athletes with the best footwear for their sport when he made his first shoes in 1920. Dassler's quest for excellence resulted in 700 patents and other industrial rights worldwide.

Dassler's expertise was in track and field. He designed special shoes for athletes competing in the 1928 Olympic Games in Amsterdam. Adidas became the world's leading sports shoe manufacturer in less than two decades. In 1947 Dassler began using canvas and rubber from U.S. fuel tanks to produce his sports shoes. One year later, the company name Adidas (a combination of Adolf Dassler's first and last names) was introduced; the popular three-striped logo was registered the following year.

Dassler was the first entrepreneur to make the public aware of his innovations through the use of sports promotion. Popular athletes from a variety of sports, such as Jesse Owens and Muhammad Ali, advertised Adidas products. Adidas became known for using aggressive publicity strategies. New product innovations were developed for major sporting events to help promote the superiority of Adidas footwear.

After Dassler died in 1978, his son continued growing the company and expanded on his father's promotional strategies. Adidas was recognized globally for its innovations in sports marketing. Adidas acquired Reebok International Ltd. in 2006, helping to cement its global success with around $11.8 billion in athletic footwear and apparel sales.[7] Today Adidas is one of the fastest-growing sportswear brands in the United States.

Think Critically

What role do you think marketing played in the success of Adidas?

components of customer service as well, such as telephone and Internet interactions. A mystery guest might phone the amusement park to determine whether the phone is answered promptly, whether he or she is put on hold and for how long, and whether the customer service agents are friendly and knowledgeable. The mystery guest might also check the response time to questions emailed or posted on the park's website. The mystery shopping program can produce valuable marketing information that can be used to make improvements where needed. Positive feedback should be shared with employees to motivate them to continue their good performance. Employees who provide outstanding customer service should be recognized.

Some hotel training programs have hotel workers check into a top-rated hotel as customers to gain insight from the customer's point of view as to what characterizes exceptional service. Customer service employees benefit by understanding the customers' experience. This helps motivate them to offer the best service possible.

INTERMISSION

Explain what it means to have a values-based culture.

ENCORE

Understand Marketing Concepts

Select the best answer for each question.

1. The customer service gap
   a. is the first step toward quality customer service
   b. is not a major factor for businesses to consider
   c. indicates unmet customer service expectations
   d. must be established and maintained for continued success

2. Which element would *not* be part of a values-based culture?
   a. going beyond expectations
   b. explaining to customers that their problem is outside of your department
   c. providing top value
   d. keeping promises

Think Critically

Answer the following questions as completely as possible.

3. Make up an acronym for good customer service. List the word for each letter of your acronym and explain how it relates to outstanding customer service. (LO 2.4-1)

4. Use the Internet to find stories about outstanding customer service in the sports and entertainment industry. List the names of the organizations providing the services and explain what they do that qualifies as excellent service. (LO 2.4-2)

CHAPTER ASSESSMENT

Review Marketing Terms

Match the terms listed with the definitions.

1. A focus on satisfying customer needs
2. The value people believe they receive from a product or service
3. A specific group of consumers a business wants to reach
4. The value of the next best alternative that you pass up when making a choice
5. Purchases based on careful thought and sound reasoning
6. Point of sales at which all of the expenses are covered
7. Group of consumers within a larger market who share one or more characteristics
8. The percentage of total sales of a product or service that a company expects to capture in relation to its competitors
9. Purchases based on consumer loyalty to a particular brand or product
10. A business culture that communicates values through high performance and excellent customer service
11. Rate at which companies produce goods and services in relation to the amount of materials and number of employees utilized
12. The capability to produce products or services more efficiently and economically than the competition
13. Purchases made by consumers with little thought
14. Difference between customer expectations and actual service received
15. All of the consumers who will purchase a product or service
16. An attempt to appeal to a large, general group of consumers

a. benefits derived
b. breakeven point
c. comparative advantage
d. customer service gap
e. economic market
f. emotional purchases
g. market segment
h. market share
i. marketing concept
j. mass marketing
k. opportunity cost
l. patronage purchases
m. productivity
n. rational purchases
o. target market
p. values-based culture

Review Marketing Concepts

Select the best answer for each of the following questions.

17. An example of a specific market segment is
    a. females between the ages of 14 and 18
    b. the entire population of a country where the business is located
    c. all women worldwide
    d. none of the above

18. Which of the following is an example of secondary data?
- a. observation of consumer behavior
- b. government census figures
- c. telephone surveys from customers
- d. all of the above

19. The bottom line for maintaining successful marketing relationships is
- a. profit
- b. customer satisfaction
- c. increased market share
- d. product quality

20. When you and your friends decide to attend a concert instead of a football game, the football game becomes your
- a. economic alternative
- b. lost purchase
- c. opportunity cost
- d. economic gain

21. Purchasing a $30 T-shirt after your favorite college team wins the national championship is an example of a(n)
- a. emotional purchase
- b. rational purchase
- c. patronage purchase
- d. unsought purchase

22. College athletic conferences used to be based on states within close proximity for travel purposes. This type of grouping was based on
- a. demographic segmentation
- b. psychographic segmentation
- c. behavioral-based segmentation
- d. geographic segmentation

23. All of the following are examples of "customer service gaps," except
- a. chatting on the phone while customers are waiting to check out
- b. placing a customer on hold for an extended period of time
- c. following up with a customer to determine her level of satisfaction
- d. informing a customer that his question is outside your department

Think Critically

24. Use the Internet to conduct research about companies that offer the best customer service. You are the head of the customer service department at an entertainment venue. Based on your research, write five customer service rules that you would require all of your customer service associates to follow. (LO 2.4-2)

25. Determine three market segments for senior citizens. Explain what services you would offer to satisfy these three market segments. Choose three sports and entertainment events that senior citizens may be interested in attending. Explain how you will market each of these events to your senior citizen market segments. (LO 2.3-1, LO 2.3-2)

26. List the five levels for Maslow's hierarchy of needs. Describe how the levels of needs could be met at a sports or entertainment event. (LO 2.2-1)

27. Explain how competition among sports and entertainment businesses is good for consumers. Give an example of the last time you had to choose between two entertainment choices. Explain what factors determined your choice and explain the opportunity cost involved with your decision. (LO 2.1-2)

28. Define market share. Use the Internet to determine which sports apparel company is the leader (has the largest market share) in sales of running shoes. Explain why the company is the leader in the running shoe industry. (LO 2.3-2)

Make Academic Connections

29. **Marketing Math** You run a sporting goods store near a university in your town. This year's total sales of the university's flags totaled $1.2 million. Sales of the university flag at your sporting goods store totaled $400,000. What is your market share of university flag sales? The university receives 14 percent royalties for sales of all merchandise containing its logo and/or mascot. How much money will the university earn from the total sales of the university flags? (LO 2.3-2)

30. **Research** Price, quality, service, and level of enjoyment gained from a sports and entertainment event are factors that influence customer satisfaction. Write five customer survey questions to collect primary data about an outdoor music concert. Make sure the answers to your questions will be measurable and useful for future events. (LO 2.4-2)

31. **Communication** You are the manager of a water park. Customers have been complaining about the long lines and discourteous service they have been receiving from employees. To close the customer service gap, write a one-page report that explains how employees can offer better customer service. (LO 2.4-1)

32. **Economics** List all of your household's purchases during a two-week timeframe. Categorize each purchase as rational, emotional, or patronage. (LO 2.2-1)

33. **Language Arts** The NCAA has tried to shed a positive light on college athletics with its recent "more than dumb jocks" marketing campaign. Use the Internet to conduct research about this campaign and about the percentage of college athletes who actually graduate from college. The NCAA wants you to design a new campaign with a two-fold purpose: to shed a positive light on college athletes and to explain the role of the NCAA. Write a one-page description of your new campaign and describe a 30-second commercial that will air during televised college events. (LO 2.1-1, LO 2.2-2)

EXTRA INNINGS PROJECT

You want your family of four to attend the next basketball game at your favorite college within a half-day's drive. You need to know how much money to set aside for the trip. Because it is your idea, your family has put you in charge of the budget.

Work with a group and complete the following activities.

1. Using the Internet, find two hotels near the arena and two motels ten miles away from the arena. Assume your family will need one room for one night. How much will these rooms cost? Which will you choose?

2. How many gallons of gasoline will your car need to get you to your destination and back? How much will that cost?

3. Using the Internet, find ticket prices, parking prices, and if possible, the prices of snacks and souvenirs. Could you take public transportation from the motel and save a parking fee? How much would the fares be?

4. Plan to leave home early Saturday morning and return Sunday. Your parents want to eat at one nice restaurant, but the rest of the meals can be at fast-food or casual dining restaurants. Estimate the costs for four people for two breakfasts, two lunches, and one nice dinner. Don't forget taxes and tips.

5. Using spreadsheet software, show each itemized expense and its percentage of the total cost.

6. Create a pie chart or bar graph from your spreadsheet information.

7. Write a paragraph that justifies to your parents that this money is being well spent.

VIRTUAL BUSINESS *Sports & Entertainment*

Use the *Parking* lesson to understand why stadium parking is important to a positive fan experience. Satisfying customer needs through stadium parking can be a significant source of revenue. The *Parking* lesson will demonstrate that parking revenue can be profitable through increased demand. Note the drawbacks to stadium parking and other parking options. Observe how low demand and numerous complaints affect business. Learn how stadium owners can make stadium parking a convenient and worthwhile experience, thereby increasing customer satisfaction and revenue.

For more information, go to **knowledgematters.com**.

Artwork courtesy of Knowledge Matters, Inc.

ATHLETE-OWNED RESTAURANTS

Many gridiron and ballpark heroes are branching out to diversify their investment portfolios. Popular athletes open restaurants to create post-career business opportunities. It also gives them a way to show off their athletic victories in the form of jerseys, awards, photos, and other tokens from their glory days. The formula for athlete-owned restaurants is fairly standard: generic pub foods, lots of TVs, and memorabilia covering the walls. The only thing missing is the athlete. Don't expect to find Brett Favre greeting guests at his steakhouse in Green Bay, Wisconsin.

Sports stars have the name-brand recognition to pull in patrons, even after they are no longer living. Some of the country's most popular sports-themed restaurants are named after deceased sports heroes, including Yankee great Mickey Mantle, Green Bay Packer coach Vince Lombardi, and Chicago Cubs' announcer Harry Caray.

Some sports stars branch out beyond the restaurant business. NFL quarterback Vince Young has a steakhouse in Austin and also supplies his own brand of smoked meat to area grocery stores. Some of the most alluring restaurants don't even have the athlete's name on the door. Skateboarding champion Tony Hawk has invested in the Market Restaurant and Bar in California. Menu items that are prepared with organic ingredients, are popular with patrons.

Follow the Coach's Call
After his NFL football career ended, Dan Marino followed the lead of his Miami Dolphins coach by entering into the food business. Marino's former coach, Don Shula, owns Shula's Steakhouse. Taking advantage of his fan base, Marino has opened five restaurant establishments around Florida and one in Las Vegas. Chops and steaks are standard menu items. Because the restaurants in Florida are located near the ocean, fresh seafood options are always available. Dan Marino offers the recipes for his favorite menu items on his website.

Athletes of all kinds can raise our expectations, fulfill our dreams, and even dash our hopes. Many remain fan favorites long after their careers have ended on the field. The business-savvy athletes try to extend their careers off the field by starting new business ventures that play off of their popularity. Athletes at all levels of success can open restaurants, but only those with a winning formula will survive, no matter whose name is on the door.

Think Critically
1. Why do professional athletes open restaurants?
2. Why do you think restaurants owned by athletes often are successful initially but then fail?
3. List two celebrities who would be good candidates for theme restaurants. Explain your choices.
4. What personal characteristics do you think would make an athlete a good entrepreneur?

ENTREPRENEURSHIP PARTICIPATING EVENT: CREATING AN INDEPENDENT BUSINESS

The Entrepreneurship Participating Event includes the development and presentation of various aspects of a plan to form a business. You must develop and demonstrate mastery of essential skills that apply to the analysis of a business opportunity, the development of a marketing/promotion plan, and the development of a financial plan.

Performance Indicators Evaluated
- Communicate ideas clearly to the judge (potential investor).
- Analyze all relevant data for proposing a new celebrity theme restaurant.
- Demonstrate critical-thinking and problem-solving skills necessary to propose and operate a successful business.
- Interpret demographics and financial data for a proposed business.
- Understand consumer demand and the existing competition.

The body of the written entry must be limited to 11 numbered pages, not including the title page and the table of contents. You may use visual aids during the 15-minute oral presentation to the judge. Five additional minutes are allowed for the judge to ask questions about your business plan.

Your business plan must consist of the Executive Summary, Description and Analysis of the Business Situation (rationale and marketing research; introduction; self-analysis; analysis of the business opportunity, customer, and location; and proposed organization), Proposed Marketing/Promotion Plan, and Proposed Financing Plan.

Select a major city that has a professional sports team with a popular athlete (current or retired). Write a business plan for a theme restaurant that bears the athlete's name. The business plan must convince investors that the restaurant will be a profitable venture. Careful attention should be given to the demographics of the city, the competition, and consumer demand for the restaurant. The personality of the athlete should match the restaurant theme.

Think Critically

1. Why would a popular celebrity need a business plan to open a restaurant in a city where he or she is well liked?
2. Give three examples of successful athlete-owned theme restaurants and explain what makes them popular.
3. What would be a good grand opening event to attract the maximum amount of attention to the new restaurant?
4. What advantage does a professional athlete have over an average citizen when opening a restaurant?

www.deca.org

3 SPORTS AND ENTERTAINMENT MEANS BUSINESS

Photo Courtesy of the Dallas World Aquarium

POINT YOUR BROWSER

ngl.cengage.com/sports4e

Winning Strategies

Dallas World Aquarium

There is always something new at The Dallas World Aquarium (DWA). From its beginning, DWA has reflected the energy and imagination of its owner and creative genius, Daryl Richardson. Since its opening in 1992, the aquarium has grown into a dynamic entertainment and educational venue covering a full city block. DWA is so popular that it reaches the maximum occupancy of 800,000 visitors each year.

© tubuceo/Shutterstock.com

Daryl Richardson's inventiveness extends to his marketing innovations. Because DWA has become such a popular destination, visitors often have to wait to enter the facility. This might cause frustration at other attractions, but at DWA people are entertained while they are in line. Visitors begin on the winding path through the Wilds of Borneo, which features Australasian birds, fish, and mammals. This offers a glimpse into the facility prior to the admissions booth. The unique entrance is now being reproduced at other major aquariums.

Education about the ocean, forest creatures, and nature conservation is very important to Richardson. He supports efforts that help endangered birds and fresh water manatee.

Think Critically

1. Based on the information provided, why do you think so many people visit DWA?

2. Does DWA's focus on customers help reduce the risk of losing those who have to wait in line? Support your answer with facts from the DWA website.

3.1 Sports and Entertainment Economics

The Essential Question

Why do investors chance losing money, and what do they need to know to profit?

Learning Objectives

LO 3.1-1 Explain the importance of the profit motive in business.

LO 3.1-2 Summarize the impact of limited resources on businesses.

LO 3.1-3 Describe the types of economic utility.

Key Terms

- profit
- profit motive
- revenue stream
- economics
- economic impact
- loss
- scarcity
- economic utility

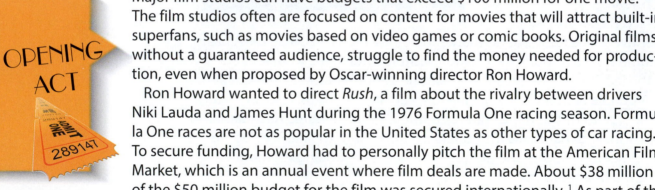

OPENING ACT

Major film studios can have budgets that exceed $100 million for one movie. The film studios often are focused on content for movies that will attract built-in superfans, such as movies based on video games or comic books. Original films, without a guaranteed audience, struggle to find the money needed for production, even when proposed by Oscar-winning director Ron Howard.

Ron Howard wanted to direct *Rush*, a film about the rivalry between drivers Niki Lauda and James Hunt during the 1976 Formula One racing season. Formula One races are not as popular in the United States as other types of car racing. To secure funding, Howard had to personally pitch the film at the American Film Market, which is an annual event where film deals are made. About $38 million of the $50 million budget for the film was secured internationally.[1] As part of the agreement, the film premiered in 16 foreign markets prior to its debut in the United States. Typically, major U.S. film studios debut films in the United States before moving to foreign markets.

Cooperative Learning Working with a partner, use the Internet to research the gross income made for the film *Rush* in U.S. domestic ticket sales and in worldwide ticket sales. Determine if the gross ticket sales exceeded the cost of the film's total budget.

LO 3.1-1   THE PROFIT MAKERS

Professional sports and entertainment events are expensive to produce. Investors and owners must use their own money to pay for production of a movie, which can cost hundreds of millions of dollars. The movie *Pirates of the Caribbean: At World's End* was reported to have cost $300 million, and *Avatar* has been widely reported as costing $237 million. They are two of the most expensive movies ever made.

Making Money

To entice investors to fund the making of expensive movies, there must be some assurance of a financial benefit for them. The financial benefit comes in the form of a **profit**—the amount of money remaining from income after all expenses are paid. When a business has a **profit motive**, it makes decisions on how to use resources in ways that result in the greatest profit. Having the potential to make a profit is a major reason why people are willing to risk their money and put time and effort into building a business. Making money is the goal. After spending money on producing the event, the owners and investors need a **revenue stream**—an activity (such as the sale of tickets) that will produce money. The revenue stream is used to pay all of the expenses. If there is money left, a profit is made.

According to Plunkett Research, the National Football League (NFL) has revenue in excess of $8.8 billion per year.[2] NFL football games are the most-watched TV shows, beginning in late August of each year and ending at the start of the following year with the Super Bowl. Revenue is earned from many sources, including ticket sales, licensed merchandise sales, and concession sales. In addition, revenue is generated through national sponsorship deals with partners such as Allstate Insurance, Nike, and Pepsi as well as local sponsorships. Under current agreements with the National Football League Players Association, owners must spend about 47 percent of all revenue on players' salaries. The balance is spent to cover business operation expenses, including costs of coaching, equipment, facilities, promotions, and taxes. The money that is left after all expenses are paid is profit.

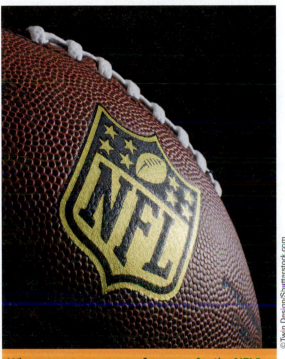

What are some sources of revenue for the NFL?

© Twin Design/Shutterstock.com

Making Business Decisions

Before they commit millions of dollars, sports and entertainment investors and owners need information for decision making. They need to know whether the opportunity to make a profit exists if enough paying fans or viewers are attracted to the event. Event-related merchandise, such as clothing, can be sold long after an event has taken place. If sales begin to decline, discounting the price of such merchandise can motivate people to buy late in the life of the product. But if people don't attend an event in the numbers needed to make a profit, then the money invested in the event and merchandise may be lost.

Ticket prices for the 2014 Super Bowl were projected to be the most expensive ever in Super Bowl history. That prediction proved to be wrong. Cold weather and travel concerns resulted in a drop in ticket prices for the game. It was played in New Jersey's MetLife Stadium, which is not domed.

Why does the profit motive drive business?

LO 3.1-2   ECONOMICS

Economics is the study of how goods and services are produced, distributed, and consumed. **Scarcity** occurs when there is a limited amount of resources needed to produce and distribute goods and services. Resources are required to produce a financially successful movie. It starts with a great story, which must be translated into a screenplay. A large budget is needed to pay for the director, cinematographer, actors, set designers, film editors, and many others who must be hired before the project even begins. The money, or funding, for filmmaking is a limited resource.

The Winners and the Losers

Investors who fund movies must make rational decisions to determine which movies to fund. An **economic impact** is the effect produced (such as jobs created or revenue generated) by decisions made by consumers and businesses. Many people make decisions about how to spend their time and money based on what will provide the highest level of satisfaction and the greatest benefits. Investors may decide to put millions of dollars into a movie proposed by an unknown writer. Or they may decide to take less of a risk by selecting a movie that can be made with a small budget. Some movies are never produced due to lack of resources. When businesses do not make enough revenue to cover expenses, they operate at a **loss**, instead of a profit. Profits are a clue that the consumers are happy with the product or service provided. Businesses that operate at a loss eventually go out of business, while businesses that are profitable continue to receive the resources they need to operate.

Sports and Entertainment Economics

Professional sporting and entertainment events are also a limited resource. They are available only at certain locations on certain dates and at certain times. When a team has the right mix of players and is winning, tickets

When Dwight Howard, who was one of the biggest names available in the National Basketball Association (NBA) free agent market, announced he would make his decision regarding his choice of a team via a tweet, he added 20,000 Twitter followers in one day. Howard, a seven-time NBA All-Star, chose the Houston Rockets. Los Angeles Lakers' player Kobe Bryant responded in his own way to Howard's decision to leave the Lakers—he stopped following Howard on Twitter.

Twitter has built-in systems that can determine how many people are following or liking a particular tweeter. Using Twitter is low cost for athletes and celebrities, but it demands their time and attention to make fans feel directly connected to them.

Think Critically

How do you think Twitter benefits from use by celebrities?

to the games become more difficult to obtain and usually sell out. In most years, tickets to the Super Bowl or World Cup are a scarce resource, making the demand for the tickets very high.

INTERMISSION 🍿 🍿

How does scarcity impact the economics of sports and entertainment?

LO 3.1-3   ECONOMIC UTILITY

Product/Service Management Consumers must make decisions on how to spend their limited resources (time and money) on sports and entertainment. Often, the decisions are based on the amount of satisfaction they believe they will receive. The amount of satisfaction a person receives from the consumption of a particular product or service is called **economic utility**. Consumers are more likely to purchase a product or service if it provides higher utility. For example, you might decide to attend a professional baseball game played by a team with a winning record rather than a team with a losing record. It is much more satisfactory to attend a game when your team is winning. A sports team or entertainment entity can make improvements in four different categories to increase the economic utility of its product. These four categories are form, time, place, and possession.

Types of Utility

Improving the physical characteristics of a product or service is called *form utility*. Watching a movie available on-demand is a form utility improvement over ordering a DVD of the movie online. The form utility of a boxing match that can be viewed only at the location where the event takes place can be improved by offering pay-per-view access to fans.

By using an online service such as Netflix, consumers can access a movie whenever they want to view it. *Time utility* is the result of making the product or service available *when* the consumer wants it. A movie theater can improve its time utility by offering a movie on multiple screens at multiple times of the day.

Place utility ensures that the product or service is available *where* the consumer wants it. Instead of attending the Super Bowl in person, a fan may want to watch the game on TV or listen to it on the radio in his or her home. Offering different places to watch or listen to the game improves place utility.

Even if form utility, time utility, and place utility requirements have all been met, the consumer still may not make the purchase unless possession utility is improved. *Possession utility* results from making the product or service available at an affordable price. Watching a boxing match on pay-per-view at home can

© Gustavo Fadel/Shutterstock.com

How does a live event compare to pay-per-view when it comes to possession utility?

be much less expensive than watching it live at the event location, which would require the purchase of a ticket and possibly travel expenses. Having multiple payment options is another way to improve possession utility. Paying with a credit card as opposed to paying cash can be more convenient.

Sports and Entertainment Utilities

Convenience is a major factor in the level of satisfaction consumers gain when spending their resources on sports and entertainment events. Ordering, paying for, and receiving refreshments from their seats while not missing any of the game or movie is a convenience fans will appreciate.

Catching game scores and highlights on a smartphone is much faster than waiting until a specified time for a TV sports program to report on your favorite teams. Additionally, the team and/or mobile content provider has an opportunity to make an immediate connection with fans while also opening the door for future interactions. Smartphone apps—mobile application software programs—bring economic utility to an amazingly high level by providing information at the right time, right form, right cost, and right place.

INTERMISSION

What are the four categories of economic utility?

ENCORE

Understand Marketing Concepts

Select the best answer for each question.

1. Economics is
   a. the study of sports and entertainment marketing
   b. the study of how goods are produced, distributed, and consumed
   c. the study of the relationships between goods and service providers
   d. none of the above

2. Having a profit motive means
   a. charging high prices
   b. increasing the number of products offered
   c. producing what consumers want
   d. making decisions to use resources in ways that result in the greatest profit

Think Critically

Answer the following questions as completely as possible.

3. Think of an event you would like to have attended. How could the form utility have been improved for you? (LO 3.1-3)

4. Why would a new, unknown musician start out by performing in small venues? How does the size of a venue change the potential profit for a game or concert? (LO 3.1-1)

3.2 Financial Analysis

The Essential Question

How do sports and entertainment businesses achieve profitability?

Learning Objectives

LO 3.2-1 Recognize sources of funding and revenue for sports and entertainment businesses.

LO 3.2-2 Explain how to manage financial resources through record keeping.

Key Terms

- return on investment
- venture capital
- forecast
- capital
- budget
- income statement
- balance sheet

Crowdfunding is a new way to fund the production of movies. It allows you to market your idea to millions of people. This funding model has been used successfully on the website Kickstarter. Project creators set a funding goal and deadline for reaching the total. If visitors to the website like a project, they can pledge money to make it happen. More than 2 million people a year make pledges from 177 different countries. Ten percent of the films shown at a recent Sundance Film Festival were funded through Kickstarter. More than 44 percent of the projects listed on the website have reached their goals, and over $100 million has been pledged to independent film productions. At least two Kickstarter-funded films have been nominated for an Oscar, and 63 films opened in theaters in one year.[3]

Cooperative Learning With a partner, outline how you think crowdfunding a film would differ from presenting a film idea to investors who typically fund movies. Present your ideas to the class.

LO 3.2-1 LOOKING FOR MONEY

Sports team owners and investors want to know what they will get in return for their investment in a team. They need to know if the return justifies the costs. If the return exceeds the costs, the owners can earn a profit. One way to measure this is called the **return on investment** (ROI), which calculates the business's return as a percentage of the money invested.

Finding Funding

Some entrepreneurs choose to start and fund a business with their own money. They may work out of home offices until they are able to afford office space. To save money, they choose not to hire employees and try to

© bikeriderlondon/Shutterstock.com

What are the benefits of funding and retaining ownership of your own business?

do all of the work themselves. Building a company without outside assistance is often referred to as *bootstrapping*. If the company is successful, the originators retain ownership of the business and will likely benefit the most if the company sells or continues to grow.

If the amount of money needed to start a business exceeds what an individual or partners can provide, then they must either borrow the money or find investors. Borrowed money must be paid back with interest. Finding investors involves creating a business plan and seeking sources of **venture capital**, which is financing provided to start a company in return for owning part of the company.

When sports or entertainment entrepreneurs start dreaming of a business, they must prepare data to show the costs for potential investors. The data includes *startup costs*, which are expenses that will occur only at the start of the business, or infrequently. These costs can include purchasing office furniture, business operating licenses, or signage. Next, the owners must determine the cost of ongoing monthly expenses, such as salaries for the owner and employees, utilities, taxes, and health insurance. Business owners should project these monthly costs for six months to one year. They must also estimate the amount of revenue earned during this time period. A report called a **forecast** predicts the expenses to be incurred and the revenues to be earned.

Money Sources

When a group of investors, including former basketball player Magic Johnson and global financial service firm Guggenheim Partners, purchased the Los Angeles Dodgers, they paid more than twice as much as other Major League Baseball (MLB) teams had recently cost. To get a return on their investment, the investors needed more than the standard sources of revenue, such as ticket sales. Los Angeles is the second-largest TV sports market in the United States behind New York City. The Dodgers are also one of the biggest sports brands. The new owners' financial plans included expanding the brand to earn more TV revenue.

The Dodgers' owners signed a contract with Time Warner Cable to create a new TV channel, SportsNet LA, which would provide the team with more than $7 billion in revenue over the next 25 years. Ownership of the new TV network was an important part of the financial plan. An MLB team must share its revenue with other MLB teams. Teams can reduce the amount they have to share by the cost of running their own TV network.

INTERMISSION

What are two sources of funding for businesses?

LO 3.2-2   MANAGING THE MONEY

Once an entrepreneur has the money to start a business, it is important that the money be managed well. Poor accounting and insufficient **capital**, which is a company's wealth in the form of money or property, are two reasons that almost 50 percent of all new small businesses fail. In the first years of a small business, instead of hiring an outside accounting firm, the owner should be the chief financial officer (CFO) in charge of the money. Later, a qualified CFO may be hired as an employee of the company.

Analyzing the Finances

A **budget**, which is a detailed projection of financial performance for a specific time period (usually one year or less), is a planning tool. The budget uses projections of revenue and expenses to help a business stay on track toward profitability. To keep track of money coming in and going out, a business prepares financial statements that summarize the performance of the business. One of the financial statements is the **income statement**, which shows all revenues received and all expenses incurred over a specific period of time. The income statement will reveal the company's profit or loss.

According to *TV Guide's* recent annual ranking of celebrity salaries, Judge Judy Sheindlin, from the TV show *Judge Judy*, was the highest-paid TV performer, earning $47 million. Her show cost about $10 million to produce in addition to her salary and brought in about $200 million in ad revenue.[4]

MATH IN MARKETING

When golfer Phil Mickelson won the Aberdeen Asset Management Scottish Open, he continued his winning streak the following week by winning the British Open Golf Championship. His last round was one for the history books. He birdied on four of the last six holes. Both tournaments were played in Scotland, and for this fantastic feat, his gross prize money totaled £1,445,000 (just over $2 million U.S. dollars). At that time, the United Kingdom (UK) set a 45 percent tax rate in Scotland on income over £150,000.[5]

Mickelson also earned $57 million in endorsements during one year. He had to pay the 45 percent tax rate for his endorsements earned during the 14 days he spent in Scotland. Assume that his endorsements are paid out at an even daily rate throughout the year. He paid his caddy 10 percent of his gross tournament winnings in Scotland, and his expenses were £10,586 for an airline ticket, hotel rooms, ground transportation, and meals. Assume that the conversion rate for British Pounds is 0.6264 for one U.S. dollar.

Do the Math

1. Use a calculator to figure the amount of UK taxes that Mickelson owed in British Pounds on all of his winnings and endorsement earnings in Scotland.

2. After paying taxes, his caddy, and all other expenses, determine how much money Mickelson had left (in British Pounds) to take home from his winnings and earnings.

Another financial statement prepared is the **balance sheet**, which shows the company's assets (items of value, including cash, property, and equipment) and its liabilities (amounts owed for purchases made on credit and loans) at a specific point in time. The difference between the assets and liabilities is the net worth of the business. The income statement and the balance sheet are used to financially analyze a business and determine if it is able to meet its long-term obligations and pay its debts.

The budget is evaluated monthly and yearly to see if changes to the budget are needed. The data on the income statement and balance sheet can be used to evaluate the budget to determine if the financial projections are accurate or need adjustments.

Inventory also affects the financial stability of a business. An inventory report, which lists each type of product that a company sells and how much of it is selling, is used by businesses to make buying decisions.

INTERMISSION

What are the two major reasons that half of all new businesses fail?

ENCORE

Understand Marketing Concepts

Select the best answer for each question.

1. Which of the following is an example of an ongoing financial cost to a business?
   a. salaries
   b. office furniture
   c. investors, networks, and revenue
   d. none of the above

2. Forecasting involves
   a. purchasing and promotion
   b. pricing and ticket sales
   c. predicting expenses and revenue
   d. planning, distribution, price, and advertising

Think Critically

Answer the following questions as completely as possible.

3. What do you think people would want to know before investing in a movie? Make a list of at least five items. (LO 3.2-1)

4. What information is provided by balance sheets and income statements that can be used to evaluate a budget? (LO 3.2-2)

3.3 Risk Management

The Essential Question

What are the sources and categories of business risk, and how are they managed?

Learning Objectives

LO 3.3-1 Categorize business risks.

LO 3.3-2 Explain methods a business uses to manage risks.

LO 3.3-3 Conduct a risk assessment and develop a contingency plan for safety and security.

Key Terms

- risk
- risk management
- liable
- contingency planning
- risk assessment

OPENING ACT

Media Rights Capital (MRC) is an independent film and television studio that produces creative premium entertainment content. MRC finances and produces films and TV series that some would consider risky. Its TV drama *House of Cards* was produced as original content for Netflix and starred Academy Award winners and nominees, but it was not a sure bet to be successful. Mordecai Wiczyk, MRC's co-founder, stated, "The only way to be successful is to be original. Playing it safe is the fastest way to ruin."[6] Wiczyk takes calculated chances and has a history of backing productions that more traditional film studio and TV networks reject.

Cooperative Learning Working in a group, research online what current films and TV shows MRC has financed and/or produced. How are the ratings of these shows? Are the films or TV shows attracting enough viewers to justify the money spent on the production?

LO 3.3-1 RISKY BUSINESS

When a sports or entertainment business opens, it is taking a **risk**—the possibility of financial gain or loss or personal injury. Financial loss occurs when revenue does not cover expenses, resulting in the loss of money needed by owners or investors to operate the business. Personal injury can occur if a business does not take the appropriate safety and security precautions. There are three sources of risk: natural risk, human risk, and economic risk.

Sources of Risk

Hurricanes cause incredible amounts of damage to sports and entertainment facilities. They also result in games and events being postponed or canceled. Hurricanes and other weather conditions are types of *natural risk* that cannot be avoided. Other less dangerous weather conditions may cause people to stay home instead of going out to spend money on sports and entertainment. The businesses that provide concessions for sports and entertainment events have already purchased the food and drinks to feed the estimated crowd. When fewer people attend, the sales may not cover the costs of the purchased food.

Human risk in business can result from customer dishonesty, employee theft, and employee incompetence. Theaters suffer a loss when people sneak into a second movie after paying for only one. Employees who steal are cheating the customers who must pay higher prices to cover the losses due to employee thefts. When employees steal, they can be charged with theft, in addition to losing their job and future job references. Employees who are not properly trained to perform their jobs, or who have a negative attitude about work, can create financial and safety risks. If food service employees at a game do not follow safety standards for washing their hands, many risks are involved. Fans may become ill, the reputation of the stadium and the team may suffer, and the business may have to pay for medical services for fans.

Economic risk faced by businesses is due to changes in the business environment. The economy affects a consumer's lifestyle, which plays an important role in what an individual purchases. When the economy is good, consumers have more discretionary income to spend on sports and entertainment. The opposite is true when the economy is bad.

The three sources of risk—natural, human, and economic—can be further categorized. Businesses should be aware of and develop plans for managing gain or loss risk, controllable risk, and insurable risk.

Gain or Loss Risk

Because of economic risks, there is no guarantee that consumer demand will remain consistent over any specific period of time. This means there is a chance that the demand will increase or decrease. If there is a chance to gain as well as lose when taking a risk, such as when investing money, investors are taking a *speculative risk* because the outcome is unknown. Playing professional football can be a risky career choice. If a football player is seriously injured and is cut from the team, he suffers a *pure loss risk* because there is no possibility of gain from the incident.

Controllable Risk

If a loss can be prevented or the likelihood of its occurrence reduced, it is called a *controllable risk*. If the NFL hires engineers to design football helmets that protect players from concussions, it is reducing the likelihood of injury. The NFL is also controlling the risk of injury when it establishes rules that prohibit players from head butting each other. If a tornado destroys the football stadium, that is an *uncontrollable risk*, because weather cannot be controlled.

Insurable Risk

If the chances of a loss are predictable and the amount of the loss can be estimated, it is an *insurable risk*. Fire insurance is available because the likelihood of a fire and the average dollar amount of the loss from the fire can be calculated using statistics of similar losses. Insurance can be purchased for insurable risks. If there is a chance that a loss could occur, but the dollar amount of the loss cannot be estimated, it is an *uninsurable risk*.

What are some ways employees pose financial and safety risks to a business?

LO 3.3-2 MANAGING RISK

Managing risk is an important financial consideration for sports and entertainment businesses. **Risk management** involves preventing, reducing, or lessening the negative impacts of risk. Risk management strategies include risk avoidance, risk transfer, and risk retention.

Risk Avoidance

Some risks are avoidable through careful planning, attention to details, and adherence to legal safety standards. Crowd control requires careful management of the flow of people into and out of an event. Those working the event must be prepared to handle various situations, from aggressive or unruly behavior by fans to medical emergencies. Extensive training in crowd control is an important step in avoiding potential risks. Well-trained employees help lessen the impact of unavoidable risks.

If a business does not take steps to ensure it is in compliance with safety laws, it could be held liable if an injury occurs. Being **liable** means the business is legally responsible for damages and possibly medical costs and other losses suffered by the injured person. If fire exits are blocked in a crowded arena or club, the danger of injury is higher. If reasonable steps have been taken to lessen the risk, such as making sure exits are clear of obstructions and well-marked and the security staff is well trained to handle emergencies, then some risks can be avoided.

Risk Transfer

Some risks can be transferred to another company or even to the consumer. One method of transferring risk is to purchase insurance, which transfers some or all of the financial loss for the insured risk to the insurance company. A park wanting to host a fireworks display may contract with a professional fireworks company for the show. In this way, most of the liability is transferred to the fireworks company. The park would still be responsible, however, for checking out the credentials and insurance of the fireworks company.

Multiple fans at baseball games have died from injuries caused by falling from the stands. The back of

© Keneva Photography/Shutterstock.com

How can an event organizer transfer risk to others?

a game ticket includes a statement that attempts to limit the liability of the team and the venue. When a fan buys a ticket and attends a game, he or she is accepting the risk of being at the game and cannot hold the team or the site responsible for certain risks. This does not relieve the facility or event management from providing a reasonably safe environment.

Risk Retention

Businesses that face uninsurable risks must assume the cost of the risk. This is referred to as risk retention. Investors in the production of a movie understand that they may not sell enough tickets to the movie to pay for the costs. A bad review may keep attendance low, and the company may suffer a loss that cannot be recovered through insurance. The investors retain the risk of the loss of sales. All businesses have some degree of risk because not all risks are predictable.

INTERMISSION

What are three ways to manage risks?

LO 3.3-3   CONTINGENCY PLANNING

When a crowd of enthusiastic fans gathers for an event, anything can happen. **Contingency planning** is the preparation for an unexpected emergency. It involves organizing the people and equipment needed to handle various situations, such as out-of-control fans, accidents, illness and injuries, and/or acts of violence. Everyone who works at an event, including the performers or athletes, event managers, promoters, facility staff, and the audience, is responsible for safety and security. They should understand the risks involved and take actions to limit damages.

What kind of safety precautions should be taken at an outdoor live event?

Safety

Jim Digby, the production manager for the rock group Linkin Park, has spent his career working with famous performers, including the Backstreet Boys and Bon Jovi. When he heard that people had died when an outdoor event stage collapsed at the Indiana State Fair, he knew the industry needed to develop safety standards and best practices for live outdoor events. Digby initiated the formation of The Event Safety Alliance (ESA), a nonprofit organization that promotes safety within the event industry. Members include tour managers, event producers, engineers, riggers, equipment owners, roadies, safety specialists, and others involved in the event production business. ESA has developed an operational guide of best practices that helps event professionals manage risk. Insurance companies expect event organizers to adhere to the ESA best practices for live events. By promoting awareness, preparation, and training, ESA is raising the bar when it comes to safety at live events.

Initial planning for an event starts with the hiring of an experienced, trained safety coordinator and an event safety team. To ensure they have resources available to handle a large event, the safety team should contact public service agencies, such as emergency management, law enforcement, fire and rescue, utility companies, and medical facilities. Working with these public agencies will also help ensure that all legal requirements for holding a large event, such as obtaining permits, are met. Safety strategies must be developed for transportation management, fire, first aid, major incidents, power outages, weather, and ending the event.

Security

The NFL always addresses security prior to the start of each season. After the Boston Marathon bombers were caught on various surveillance cameras carrying backpacks containing bombs, NFL fans faced a new policy about what they could carry into the stadium. The strict bag policy allows only small purses and handbags, clear plastic or vinyl bags, and one-gallon plastic freezer bags. Fans are observed by security staff while they are in the areas outside of the stadiums. They are reminded at that point that they are not allowed to approach the stadium if they are carrying items that are not permitted. The policy is intended to reduce the risk of threats to the fans and players. Overall, fans have accepted the league's effort to keep them secure. Other professional sports teams are also trying to limit risk.

Why do event production staff play an important role in safety at sports and entertainment events?

Event organizers want to prevent dangerous incidents from happening. Careful preparation for an emergency takes planning, training, and communication across all levels of staff involved. A **risk assessment** is a step-by-step process by which knowledgeable safety and security staff identify and prepare to manage risks. The steps may include the following:

- Identify potential hazards
- Determine who might be affected by the hazards
- Evaluate the options for managing the risk
- Implement the best option(s)
- Review the assessment to determine if improvements are needed

Taking simple steps can sometimes make a major difference in reducing risks. Cleaning up spills when they happen can keep people from slipping. Having safety and security personnel wear high-visibility clothing will help the public and other staff recognize those who can provide assistance during emergencies. Being proactive is the right way to manage risk.

INTERMISSION

Name three ways to make sports and entertainment events safer to attend.

ENCORE

Understand Marketing Concepts
Select the best answer for each question.

1. All of the following are examples of human risk *except*
   a. employee dishonesty
   b. thunderstorms
   c. poorly trained employees
   d. unskilled labor

2. The three ways to manage risk are
   a. gain or loss risks, insurable risks, and controllable risks
   b. financial loss, personal injury, and property loss
   c. risk transfer, risk retention, and risk avoidance
   d. fire, theft, and floods

Think Critically
Answer the following questions as completely as possible.

3. List four steps that a sports team could take to avoid risk of injury to fans attending games. (LO 3.3-2)

4. Write a letter to a state legislator about who should regulate the safety of rides at amusement parks. Should theme parks be self-regulating regarding the safety of their rides (as they currently are)? Or should local, state, or federal agencies be involved? (LO 3.3-3)

3.4 Business Ethics

The Essential Question

What does ethics mean in sports and entertainment marketing, and what impact does unethical behavior have?

Learning Objectives

LO 3.4-1   Interpret the meaning of ethics in sports and entertainment marketing.

LO 3.4-2   Analyze the impact of ethical and unethical behavior.

Key Terms

- ethics
- ethical dilemma
- principles
- integrity

OPENING ACT

Nielsen, a leading global research and information firm, recently ranked former New York Yankees pitcher Mariano Rivera as the second-most marketable player in baseball. A *New York Times* front-page headline called him "A Most Likable Yankee."[7] Rivera retired after a remarkable 19-year career and was rewarded for his personal character and other ethical attributes.

In Rivera's final season, at the final game played in each city, he asked to meet with the people who support baseball behind the scenes—secretaries, custodians, community-relations workers, and chefs. He talked with them about their jobs and lives and told them that he could not do his job without them. High-ranking team officials were not invited. Jerry Dipoto, general manager of the Anaheim Angels, asked to bring his 16-year-old son to the meeting so his son could be close to greatness. "It's who he is as a person, it's his work ethic," Dipoto said of Rivera.[8]

Cooperative Learning   As a group, discuss why Mariano Rivera has such an admirable reputation. Why is he so marketable and respected by fans and other players?

LO 3.4-1   ETHICS COUNT

There are many examples of sports and entertainment figures who act unethically, but their behavior is still rare enough that it receives lots of negative news coverage. The amount of news coverage leads many people to believe that sports and entertainment celebrities no longer value ethics, but the majority behave ethically. **Ethics** are a system for deciding between right and wrong in a reasoned and impartial manner.

Ethical Choices

An individual faces an **ethical dilemma** when he or she has to choose between two equal moral principles. The pressures of ethical dilemmas are rarely faced by people, including sports and entertainment celebrities and management. Most choices to be made are between what the right thing to do is and what a person would like to do, if there were no consequences.

More than 1,200 people stood in line on a brutally hot July weekend in Foxborough, Massachusetts, to exchange an Aaron Hernandez jersey for one of 11 other New England Patriots' jerseys after the player was arrested. Hernandez was also immediately cut from the team. The exchange of jerseys cost the Patriots an estimated $200,000.[9]

An attitude of "it's only cheating if you get caught" would free coaches and players of responsibility and place the emphasis on winning at any cost. There are athletes and coaches who think ethics do not apply to sports. But the majority believe that respectful and responsible behavior on and off the field bring victory with honor to the players and the team.

Football is the most-watched sport in the United States. The NFL would prefer to focus its marketing efforts on what is happening on the football field. Unfortunately, off-the-field negative publicity is a common occurrence. Players who are arrested for criminal acts make headline news, while examples of good ethical behavior are rarely reported. The NFL counters some of the negative news by citing Federal Bureau of Investigation (FBI) statistics—only about 2 percent of the league's approximately 3,000 players have been arrested compared with 10.8 percent of the general population of males ages 22 to 34.[10] The NFL is aware that the public does not want to pay to see immature, overconfident, criminals play professional sports. It stresses the importance of ethical behavior by all players.

Professional athletes and entertainers are prominent role models, so they should have high standards of behavior. The NFL makes a major effort to prevent behavior that could be damaging to the league. Each NFL team has an extensive process for assessing a player's history and background, including his social maturity level. The intent is to avoid signing players who could harm the team's reputation. Players who have a history of legal trouble may be passed over for players who have displayed more mature behavior.

In addition to players, the coaches, managers, and owners must make ethical choices. The enormous amount of money that is at stake in professional sports intensifies these ethical choices. For example, should a coach allow a superstar football player with a concussion to play, risking the health of the player in favor of keeping the team's winning streak alive?

Do you think athletes face more ethical dilemmas than the average person? Why or why not?

© Richard Paul Kane/Shutterstock.com

Building Character

Sports are a large part of education, and participation in sports is portrayed as a good way to build a young person's character. In the early stages of character development, a child learns that exhibiting bad behavior will result in punishment, while good behavior will result in rewards. As a child matures, the influence of others' expectations of him or her grows. Eventually, the child will reach a stage of maturity by which he or she acts on a set of **principles**, or the rules and codes of conduct on which ethical behavior is based. Lack of ethical adult role models makes it difficult for children to mature to this level. Constant exposure to news of unethical behavior by sports and entertainment figures may lead children to think that all talented, wealthy athletes behave that way. Just because "everybody is doing it" does not make it the principle by which to live, nor does it improve the marketability of a product. Negative behavior can result in publicity that will undo the best marketing plans.

INTERMISSION

What is meant by ethical behavior in sports?

LO 3.4-2   THE EFFECTS OF GOOD AND BAD BEHAVIOR

Integrity is a strong, voluntary adherence to honesty and morality. It is often linked to ethical behavior. People with integrity are trusted to bring honor to themselves, their family, and the business with which they are associated.

Sending a Message

The use of performance enhancing and other illegal drugs by famous athletes is an ongoing problem for sports teams. Many young athletes who are not prepared for sudden wealth and fame seem to forget the examples of those who have come before them and suffered because of their poor choices. They believe they are invincible and won't suffer any consequences. In doing so, they are risking their health, their reputation, and future earning power, as well as alienating their teammates and fans. They can lose it all. Athletes with integrity choose not to take this path.

Instant communication through social media breaks down the barriers between the general public and celebrities. It gives celebrities tremendous influence over fans. Many sports and entertainment celebrities choose to use their high level of influence in positive ways that improve the lives of other people. Bruce Springsteen is known for his extensive charitable work for people in need. He has received a great deal of positive publicity for his efforts. Other performance artists have a reputation for being less generous. Rapper Jay-Z was highly criticized (and even admitted to sounding arrogant) for implying that his rise to stardom offered hope to those who are less fortunate. When he stated "my presence is charity," he seemed to be saying that people in need should see him as an inspiration and fix their own problems instead of relying on him to offer a hand up.

Rapper Master P, who is also an entrepreneur, told the audience for a Black Entertainment Television (BET) seminar that many low-income people don't have the work ethic or financial literacy to handle the extreme wealth they acquire when they become super successful. "I want to show

TAKE A BOW   Charlie Hernandez

Charlie Hernandez is more than an excellent live concert production director; he is also an outstanding humanitarian with a generous heart. Hernandez knows how to run a music tour. His calm personality helps make even the most chaotic events run smoothly. He has toured around the world with Def Leppard and worked with Sting, David Bowie, Paul McCartney, The Rolling Stones, Prince, and many more artists. Hernandez is given credit for getting many U.S. bands into South America and opening a whole new fan base for live music.

Hernandez has received the Parnelli Lifetime Achievement Award, considered the "Oscar" of the live event industry. However, he considers his biggest achievement to be the founding of the charity Just a Bunch of Roadies (JABOR). The charity provides relief to major disasters around the world. Who knows better how to move needed supplies and equipment under stressful circumstances than a bunch of live concert roadies?

Think Critically

What characteristics do you think Hernandez and others have that make them charitable individuals? How do you think Hernandez's job as a worldwide concert production director has influenced his decision to start a charity?

the next generation how I did it" [made his wealth], stated Master P. He sees this as a way to give back to those who buy his albums and tickets. As a person with integrity, he believes in investing in young people who are eager for success, but need guidance about how to get there.

Effective and Ethical

Good decisions are both effective and ethical. Duke University basketball coach Mike Krzyzewski has been the U.S. men's national team coach for several years. He has worked alongside Jerry Colangelo, USA Basketball Chairman, to select and prepare teams for the summer Olympics. Both men insist that players must exhibit integrity and ethics on and off the court. Players whose attitude and demeanor do not represent a mature level of behavior will not make the Olympic team, even if they are NBA superstars.

In today's highly competitive market, organizations are under a great deal of pressure to achieve success. Customers appreciate and are more likely to support those organizations that base decisions on core values such as ethics and integrity.

INTERMISSION

Why is the behavior of athletes off the field important to a team?

ENCORE

Understand Marketing Concepts

Select the best answer for each question.

1. Ethics is
   a. doing what is easy
   b. not getting caught
   c. a system for deciding between right and wrong
   d. all of the above

2. Principles
   a. are applied to only certain people
   b. are rules and codes of conduct for ethical behavior
   c. have no effect on businesses
   d. none of the above

Think Critically

Answer the following questions as completely as possible.

3. Ultimate Fighting Championship (UFC) heavyweight fighter Cain Velasquez stated that he wanted to be a role model while doing what he loves. Research Cain Velasquez and write a paragraph about how he behaves as a role model. (LO 3.4-1)

4. Should the NFL hold players to a higher ethical standard, both on and off the field, than the general public? Why or why not? Name two or more NFL players who you think have integrity and explain why. (LO 3.4-2)

CHAPTER ASSESSMENT

Review Marketing Terms

Match the terms listed with the definitions.

1. The amount of money remaining from income after all expenses are paid
2. The study of how goods and services are produced, distributed, and consumed
3. The possibility of financial gain or loss or personal injury
4. A report that predicts the expenses to be incurred and revenues to be earned
5. The business is legally responsible for damages
6. Involves preventing, reducing, or lessening the negative impacts of risk
7. A measurement that calculates the business's return as a percentage of the money invested
8. A system of deciding between right and wrong in a reasoned and impartial manner
9. The amount of satisfaction a person receives from the consumption of a particular product or service
10. A financial statement that shows a company's assets, liabilities, and net worth at a specific point in time
11. An activity (such as ticket sales) that will produce money
12. A voluntary adherence to honesty and morality
13. Financing provided to start a company in return for owning part of it
14. Occurs when a limited amount of resources is available
15. A company's wealth in the form of money or property
16. The preparation for an unexpected emergency
17. Choosing between two equal moral principles
18. A financial statement that shows all revenues received and all expenses incurred over a specific period of time
19. The rules and codes of conduct on which ethical behavior is based
20. Making business decisions that result in the greatest profit
21. A step-by-step process by which knowledgeable safety and security staff identify and prepare to manage risks
22. Occurs when not enough revenue is made to cover expenses
23. The effect produced by decisions made by consumers and businesses

a. balance sheet
b. capital
c. contingency planning
d. economic impact
e. economic utility
f. economics
g. ethical dilemma
h. ethics
i. forecast
j. income statement
k. integrity
l. liable
m. loss
n. principles
o. profit
p. profit motive
q. return on investment
r. revenue stream
s. risk
t. risk assessment
u. risk management
v. scarcity
w. venture capital

Review Marketing Concepts

Select the best answer for each of the following questions.

24. Pure loss risks
    - a. involve the possibility for gain
    - b. involve no possibility for gain
    - c. are never insurable
    - d. are speculative in nature
25. Categories of economic utility include
    - a. place
    - b. possession
    - c. time
    - d. all of the above
26. Strategies for managing risk include
    - a. risk avoidance and risk acceptance
    - b. risk transfer and risk retention
    - c. risk acceptance and risk denial
    - d. both a and b
27. Sources of revenue for NFL teams include
    - a. budgets, editing, and talk shows
    - b. first downs, field goals, and passes completed
    - c. TV, partners, sponsorships, and ticket sales
    - d. all of the above
28. Some potential sources of funding a new movie include
    - a. the American Film Market
    - b. investors
    - c. major film studios
    - d. all of the above

Think Critically

29. Why do you think financial record keeping is essential to a business's success? (LO 3.2-2)
30. Why isn't ethical behavior commonly reported in the news? (LO 3.4-1)
31. List two human risks faced by businesses and describe strategies to overcome those risks. (LO 3.3-1)
32. Assess your school's fire safety practices. Make a list of signs, lighting, and other ways that the school tries to reduce the risk of injury to students. (LO 3.3-3)
33. Describe an example of unethical behavior in the sports and entertainment industry that has been reported in the media recently. Explain what effect this behavior had on the person(s) involved. (LO 3.4-2)

34. If your school cannot increase its seating capacity for basketball games, describe two other ways it can increase revenue from basketball. (LO 3.2-1)

35. Write a paragraph about how you would improve the economic utility of your favorite sports event. (LO 3.1-3)

36. With a partner, discuss whether you consider some professional sports more ethical than others. Explain your reasons. Do news accounts of unethical behavior influence your opinion? (LO 3.4-1)

37. How can a company's revenue stream have an economic impact? (LO 3.2-1)

Make Academic Connections

38. **Marketing Math** A movie costs $40 million to produce and $45 million to promote and distribute. The movie's total revenue from ticket sales is forecast to be 18 percent above costs, with 28 percent of revenue from U.S. sales and the balance from overseas. What is the total estimated revenue? How much of the total revenue will come from the United States? How much will come from overseas? (LO 3.2-2)

39. **Government** Use the Internet to learn about safety regulations for public entertainment complexes, such as theaters and sports arenas. What governmental agencies are responsible for ensuring that regulations are enforced? Write two paragraphs on your findings. Do you think that enough is being done to ensure public safety? Write an additional paragraph stating your position and describing any recommendations you would make. (LO 3.3-3)

40. **Ethics** Use the Internet to find guidelines that will help you determine whether something is ethical. What standards can you use in making a decision about whether an action is ethical? What if the action is legal—is that enough to decide if it is ethical? List at least two ways you can test a decision to determine if it is ethical. (LO 3.4-1)

41. **Geography** Research current facts about the United States and China. What is the geographic size of each country? What is the population of each country? If you were a movie producer, would you try to market your films in China? Why or why not? (LO 3.1-1)

42. **Finance** Research two NASCAR sponsors. Explain how they help finance NASCAR and how they benefit from the sponsorships. (LO 3.2-1)

43. **History** Use the Internet to research how the recording industry has changed over the last 100 years. Include information about the different media that have been used to record music and the improvements in form utility. (LO 3.1-3)

44. **Marketing Math** A local band with five members has the following expenses:

Renting a recording studio, $2,400
Creating a promotional website, $5,000
Arranging to sell downloads, $50,000
Advertising and distribution costs, $62,000
Agent and songwriter fees, 10% of revenues

If the downloads sell for $1.00 each, how many downloads will need to be sold to earn $10,000 for each band member? (LO 3.1-2)

EXTRA INNINGS PROJECT

Your school is concerned about safety at sports events in your school district. You have been asked to conduct a risk assessment for a sports event at your school. Work with your teacher and the school staff who are in charge of sporting events to identify which event you will assess.

Work with a group and complete the following activities.

1. Review the risk assessment information in this chapter and make a list of the steps that should be included in the assessment. Look at the risk assessment information at The Event Safety Alliance website and *Special Events Contingency Planning Job Aids Manual* published by the Federal Emergency Management Agency (FEMA) for samples of risk assessments. Find samples of risk assessment documents that are available online.

2. Work with your teacher to determine the school staff and departments that will be involved in this project. Develop a list of questions to ask the staff. Talk with the staff who are in charge of the sporting event to determine what risks they are aware of and what steps are currently taken to manage risks.

3. Make a list of public service entities that you should contact to help you conduct the assessment. Contact one or more of the public service entities in your community. Explain that you are learning about risk assessments and ask them what information is available locally.

4. Brainstorm with the group to outline the kinds of information that would be needed to complete the risk assessment for this event. Design a risk assessment document for this event.

5. Conduct the risk assessment and develop a report for the sports department.

VIRTUAL BUSINESS *Sports & Entertainment*

Use the *Player Management* lesson to understand the risk and reward of player selection. The goal of this lesson is to select a winning team while staying under a salary cap. Managing risk is an important financial consideration for sports and entertainment businesses such as a football team. Risk management involves preventing, reducing, or lessening the negative impacts of risk which occur due to injury and performance. Owners want a return on their investment, so you will have the opportunity to release players that are underperforming and/or have high salaries. You will gain an understanding of the importance of team building. If management reduces payroll and increases the number of wins during a season, more fans will attend games and spend money on concessions.

For more information, go to **knowledgematters.com**.

CASE STUDY

DO THE RIGHT THING

Professional sports teams face an ongoing battle between right and wrong. They frequently choose between fielding players who are cheaters or lawbreakers (or worse) or benching an excellent athlete who might help them win. Many professional teams publicly state that they do not tolerate lawbreakers but then look the other way at game time.

Mixed Messages

Some young, extremely talented athletes do not always have the integrity, character, and experience to avoid the use of illegal drugs or to avoid hanging out with the wrong crowd. They are suddenly propelled into a level of wealth that takes most people many years to earn, if ever. They also believe they are invincible and cannot be harmed—or that they won't get caught.

The harm done to athletes because of illegal behavior includes damaging their health and reputation and severely affecting their potential earning power from endorsements. Even if teams and some fans look the other way, few businesses want an athlete who generates negative publicity representing their product.

Professional sports teams have also sent the wrong message to players by allowing some to continue playing after drug use or conviction of criminal acts. Major League Baseball (MLB) has been accused of taking the sport's very severe steroid use problem too lightly. The MLB has repeatedly given players a slap on the wrist and

allowed them back in the game, missing out on opportunities to take a stand against drug use. In addition, steroids are extremely dangerous to players' health and tarnish the reputation of sports.

No Cheating Tolerated

Protecting the health of athletes and the integrity and fairness of sports for athletes worldwide is the intent of The World Anti-Doping Agency (WADA). WADA is in charge of drug testing worldwide in Olympic sports. The International Olympic Committee has consistently enforced anti-doping rules and banned violators as ineligible for participation, requiring them to forfeit all medals and points won.

The International Olympic Committee also has the authority to withhold some or all funding from National Olympic Committees that are not in compliance with the anti-doping rules.

Professional sports associations and players must decide if fans will continually forgive the drug-enhanced cheaters and criminal players or demand that highly paid athletes behave ethically and with integrity.

Think Critically

1. What can be done to influence young athletes to not cheat?
2. Why do professional teams tolerate cheaters?
3. Why do the Olympics have higher standards than pro teams?
4. Why is steroid use by professional athletes of particular concern in the sports industry?

SPORTS AND ENTERTAINMENT MARKETING SERIES EVENT

You are the athletic director for a major university that has a popular football team. Two of your job duties include stadium security and crowd control at the football games. The stadium always sells all 92,000 seats at home games. An avid fan (judge) has contributed large sums of money to the university's athletic department. He is very unhappy about the chain of events that evolved at last week's game and wants your explanation and reassurance to improve the circumstances for similar events in the future.

Weather forecasts during last week's game predicted storms with severe lightning. Your university has strict policies of suspending a game during a severe lightning storm and removing all people in the stadium from harm's way. During the second quarter of last week's game, weather forecasts predicted a severe storm entering the area within 30 minutes. You decided to suspend the game and empty the stadium before the storm struck. You realized that it would take considerable time to move 92,000 fans from the stadium.

The lightning storm did strike and fortunately most people had already exited the stadium. The avid fan (judge) is upset that there was not enough room in the stadium for all the fans to take shelter. Some of them had to go to their vehicles for shelter and missed a major portion of the third quarter while returning to the stadium. This fan has scheduled a meeting with you to learn more about the safety plan and evacuation process for the stadium. He is also interested in learning more about the stadium security policy and future strategies to ensure fans' safety during severe weather conditions.

You will present information about stadium safety procedures to the fan (judge) in a role-play to take place in your office. You are concerned about maintaining a strong relationship with such a major financial contributor. The fan will begin the role-play by greeting you and asking to hear your ideas. After you have presented your information and have answered the fan's questions, the fan will conclude the role-play by thanking you for your work.

> **Performance Indicators Evaluated**
> - Explain the nature of positive customer/client relations.
> - Demonstrate a customer service mindset.
> - Handle customer/client complaints.
> - Follow safety precautions.
> - Handle and report emergency situations.

Think Critically

1. What is an alternative for handling displaced fans during a suspended game due to bad weather?
2. How can stadium announcements be used to improve flow from the stadium during an emergency?
3. What strategy can be used in the future so all fans will receive the full value of their ticket during a suspended game due to bad weather?

www.deca.org

4 THE WIDE WORLD OF SPORTS AND ENTERTAINMENT

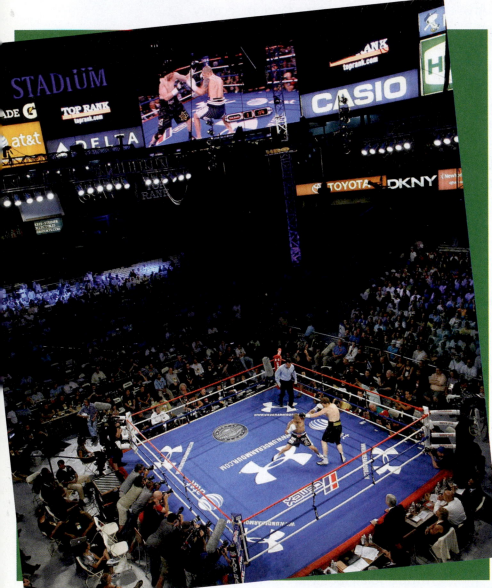

Photo Courtesy of Top Rank/Chris Farina

POINT YOUR BROWSER

ngl.cengage.com/sports4e

Winning Strategies

Top Rank

Top Rank has been the world's leading promoter of world championship boxing events for more than 40 years. It promotes world championship level boxers, including Tim Bradley and Manny Pacquiao. Very few of the live boxing events take place outside the United States, but they are viewed internationally. The rights to see live fights are sold in more than 150 countries. The number of international viewers can exceed the number of U.S. viewers.[1] Interest in live boxing is high in Japan, Europe, many South American countries, and Mexico. Top Rank has a separate division that caters to an international audience. It produces four to five events each week in Mexico alone. International distribution of the live events plays a major role in the financial success of each event.

Boxing from Top Rank is produced and distributed live online and in a pay-per-view (PPV) television format. PPV generates a large portion of the revenue for boxing and opens the fight to both die-hard and casual fans. The event is more than just a sporting match; it includes a great deal of in-arena activities and entertainment, such as a DJ, ongoing video of past fights, and appearances by celebrities to excite and engage the audience.

Think Critically

1. Why do you think live online and pay-per-view boxing matches are so successful on the international level?

2. How do you think boxing matches could be marketed successfully internationally?

4.1 Worldwide Sports and Entertainment Events

The Essential Question
What impacts do major international events and politics have on sports and entertainment?

Learning Objectives

LO 4.1-1 Discuss the effect of major international events on sports.

LO 4.1-2 Explain how politics affects sports and entertainment.

Key Terms

- International Olympic Committee (IOC)
- gender equity
- joint venture
- piracy
- censorship

OPENING ACT

Cuba's government has always promoted its amateur sports and victories in international competition as evidence of the success of the communist government system. Boxing was a popular sport in Cuba even before the Communist takeover in 1959, but it received special emphasis and support as an amateur program when professional boxing was banned in 1961 in Cuba. Cuban boxers have frequently dominated Olympic boxing, winning the most gold medals. Training for boxers, as with most Cuban sports, begins when the potential athletes enter a specialized school at age 12. Those who are the best advance through the highly technical training program.

In 2013 a major change was made in the status of boxers. For the first time in 52 years, Cuban boxers were allowed to box as professionals at the World Series of Boxing in Mexico City. Now, Cuban boxers are expected to move into the full realm of professional boxing, and the Cuban government is expected to benefit financially from the move. It is anticipated that Cuban boxers will become contenders in the world of professional boxing and attract new boxing fans.

Cooperative Learning In a group, discuss how the move to professional boxing in Cuba will change the sport both in Cuba and in the world. What are the advantages and disadvantages of this change?

LO 4.1-1 HOSTING THE WORLD

International sporting events help bring people around the world closer together. They give athletes a chance to compete on the same playing field and under the same rules agreed upon by all of the teams and players involved.

Every four years, the Mediterranean Games host athletes from 24 countries and regions, including France, Italy, Spain, Egypt, Albania, and Lebanon. Egyptian Mohamed Taher Pasha is called the father of the Mediterranean Games. He promoted sports as a way to achieve peace and brotherhood. The international, multisport games are recognized as a lead up to the Olympics. The host country often uses the event as a way to showcase its athletes and nation, as well as a platform for being considered as a future site for the Olympic Games.

In the United States, each sport goes through a series of qualifying events to determine the final competitors in the Olympics. These events are held across the country. Similar to international multisport events, they offer fans who are not going to the Olympic Games a chance to preview the best athletes in the United States.

The Olympics

The **International Olympic Committee (IOC)** is the governing authority of the Olympic Movement, which includes all of the National Olympic Committees (NOC), the International Sports Federations, Organizing Committees for the Olympic Games, athletes, sponsors, and broadcasting partners. All of these groups work together to produce the Olympic Games. Started in 1896, the modern Olympic Games are a revival of the original athletic competition which was held in Greece over 2,000 years ago.

© don Tran/Shutterstock.com

How do the Olympics affect national pride?

Host Cities
Every four years, athletes from around the world compete in the Olympics. The IOC selects which country will host the Olympics. The selection is made seven years before the event to provide the host country and cities time to prepare. The two-year host selection process has multiple steps, including the following:

- An extensive application process that provides details about the physical locations and facilities available for use in the cities
- An elaborate marketing campaign that includes presentations made by the top-ranking cities
- Site visits by the selection committee to view the city's infrastructure, such as roadways, which would be used by thousands of spectators and athletes

Financial, social, and political situations are also taken into account when deciding on the host city. Financial support for the Games by the host is critical. Russia invested $50 billion in the 2014 Winter Olympics, with intent to use the new infrastructure after the Games for tourism.[2]

Even current events in surrounding countries can affect the final selection of the host. When the IOC was determining the host city for the 2020 Olympics, Istanbul, Turkey, was making its fifth bid for the Olympic Games. It reached the final three candidate cities. Istanbul had a very vigorous economy, public support for the bid, and a young population. No predominantly Muslim country had ever been selected before. However, a civil war was taking place in Syria, a neighboring country to Turkey. Also, a recent scandal had surfaced regarding the ban of more than 30 Turkish athletes for testing positive for banned substances. In addition, the government had cracked down harshly on people who were protesting the environmental impact of the Olympics. Istanbul was not selected for the 2020 Olympics. The war nearby and political unrest in Turkey most likely influenced the decision.

Instead, Tokyo, Japan, was selected as the host city for the 2020 Olympic Games. It was considered a safer option than Istanbul and the other remaining finalist city, Madrid, Spain. Japan was considered better equipped to handle huge crowds and to meet the deadlines for facility renovations. Tokyo's mass transportation system is considered to be one of the world's best.

Broadcasting Rights   Being chosen to host the event can result in long-term benefits for the city if the event is well managed. One of the major benefits is the opportunity to promote the city and surrounding area to the world via broadcast television. The 1956 Olympic Games were held in Melbourne, Australia, and the organizers realized the value of providing TV coverage to the world. Even so, they refused to give away the rights to televise or film the games, insisting on payment for the rights. The major world media, including BBC, CBS, NBC, and Eurovision, argued that the event was a news event, and thus, they should be allowed to broadcast it free of charge. The organizers did not give in, and the 1956 games were not broadcast to the world. During the next Olympics, the European Broadcasting Union and CBS both paid for TV rights, and the games were seen in 21 countries. Since that time, the broadcast rights have turned into a major source of revenue for host cities. Broadcasts of the Olympics have also helped ensure the long-term financial stability of the Olympic Movement and have maximized exposure and support of the Games globally.

Olympic Sports   Each sport that is represented in the Olympic Games stands to win financially through global exposure to billions of television and online viewers. Marketing of the Olympics and participating sports is a fundamental part of the game. When a sport is selected as an Olympic sport, individuals and organizations provide financial support and promote youth leagues, because the national image is at stake. Seeing an athlete compete on the international level and win a medal inspires young people to play the sport. Growing a fan base ensures the sport's survival.

The IOC uses 39 criteria to decide which sports will be included in the Olympics. One of those criteria is **gender equity**, meaning the number of opportunities for men and women is roughly the same. As a result, women's ski jumping was added for the 2014 Winter Games. The list of sports changes from one Olympics to the next. Baseball was removed from the Olympic list in 2008 for various reasons, including illegal performance-enhancing drug scandals. Also, Major League Baseball refused to change its schedule so that players could participate in the Olympics.

Financial Support   The IOC organizes the Olympic marketing program. Its objective is to ensure the financial stability of the Olympic Movement. The sources of revenue include broadcast rights, sponsorships,

Athletes who are U.S. Olympic hopefuls are only partially funded by the U.S. Olympic Committee. They receive no U.S. government support. Many of the U.S. contenders have turned to fund-raising on the Internet to cover the costs of preparing for the Games.

ticketing, and licensing. Around 11 corporations participate in The Olympic Partner (TOP) program, which supports the Olympic Games. Coca-Cola Company, operating in over 200 countries worldwide, has been the longest continuous supporter of the Olympic Games since 1928.

International Professional Sports

Baseball, basketball, golf, tennis, auto racing, horseracing, and boxing are all international professional sports, but soccer might be the world's favorite sport. It is watched by millions of people on every continent.

The Premier League is the organizing body of the 20 football (the European term for soccer) clubs that make up the League in England. It is the dominant and top-performing soccer league in the world, much like the NFL is dominant in American football. The Premier League is part of the Union of European Football Associations (UEFA), which is responsible for the organization of competition and regulation of soccer across Europe. Europe is home to some of the world's best soccer players.

Recruitment of International Athletes

U.S. Major League Baseball (MLB) teams seek out international players. Prospects are sought by international scouts for each team. Many young men from other countries come to the United States while in high school, making them eligible for the professional player draft. The prospective international players who are not eligible for the professional draft are also a very important source of talent. Since the 1959 Revolution in Cuba, relations with the United States have been difficult, ranging from threats of war to discussions of possible renewed trade and tourism. Currently, only limited travel is allowed between the two countries, and Cubans are not freely allowed to visit the United States. Although Cuban baseball players are known for their talent, they are not observed over the years by recruiters, as are U.S. high school players. As it now stands, when a Cuban player defects (gives up allegiance to his country) and comes directly to the United States, he is eligible for the amateur draft. If he establishes residency in another country, such as Haiti, before coming to the United States, then he can petition the U.S. government to obtain approval to enter the country and become a free agent. Yasiel Puig, Yoenis Céspedes, and Aroldis Chapman are three former Cubans who are having successful careers in the MLB in the United States. This opportunity is not available under the current communist Cuban government.

Why do baseball players from other countries want to play in the United States?

© Photo Works/Shutterstock.com

Another example of a Latin American prospect who has succeeded in the United States is José Altuve. After being scouted from age 14 in his hometown of Maracay, Venezuela, Altuve was signed at age 16 by the Houston Astros for $15,000 during the international signing period. Altuve grew into his major league career at the age of 21 after playing with minor league teams across the country. He attracted attention in the major leagues by becoming an outstanding player who signed multimillion-dollar extensions to his contract and options through 2019.

Every year, each MLB team is allotted money to sign players from all over the world during the international signing period. Teams use this money to search for international prospects that could be the next big-name players in baseball. Those teams with the lowest winning percentage get more money. Teams must decide if they will sign only one or two very expensive prospects or several prospects who will sign for less money.

International Amateur Sports

Every August, thousands of people from around the world flock to Howard J. Lamade Stadium in South Williamsport, Pennsylvania, where the Little League World Series, an international tournament, has been held for more than 55 years. Little League Baseball players are usually between the ages of 11 and 12, and other divisions are set up for younger age groups and for players up to 18 years old. More than 2.7 million youths take part in Little League on six continents around the world, making it one of the world's largest organized youth sports programs.[3]

The Little League organization markets to parents, who must be convinced to allow their children to participate. According to Little League International, more than one million adults volunteer in local Little Leagues around the world each year. Local businesses are asked to sponsor Leagues as a way to give back to the community. In exchange for the sponsorships, the businesses receive advertising, publicity, and other benefits. The sponsorship funds are used to support the League operations. On a national level, Major League Baseball supports Little League. By doing so, it gains potential future players and fans.

INTERMISSION

How does being selected for Olympic competition benefit a sport?

LO 4.1-2 MONEY AND POLITICS IN SPORTS AND ENTERTAINMENT

All may seem peaceful and friendly at international sporting and entertainment events, but money and political considerations are always factors. When countries come together to work or play, there are rules and regulations that must be followed. Great emphasis is placed on international events because they can affect a nation's economy as well as its political relations.

The World Cup

The Fédération Internationale de Football Association (FIFA) is the international organizing and governing body of football, known in the United States as soccer. FIFA has 209 member associations, including the United States. FIFA sets the rules and establishes the competition for soccer on a worldwide level, including the World Cup, a tournament held every four years to determine a world championship team.

The 32 teams who earn their way into the World Cup represent their continent and their country. The teams compete within six geographic areas for a designated number of spots in the World Cup. The six geographic areas are Africa, Asia, Europe, North/Central America and the Caribbean, Oceania, and South America.

The FIFA Marketing team is based at FIFA headquarters in Zurich, Switzerland, and has four main departments: Sales and Licensing, Account Management and Operations, Strategy and Brand Management, and Ticketing and Hospitality. In addition, a fifth department is set up to support each site selected for the World Cup.

Playing in the World Cup can have a major financial impact on a nation's soccer industry. When Mexico's once-promising team was in doubt about qualifying for the World Cup, the financial devastation of failing to qualify was expected to cost the Mexican soccer industry as much as $600 million in lost TV, merchandise, sponsorships, and other revenue. TV in both Mexico and the United States also would have been major losers.[4] Fortunately, Mexico succeeded in qualifying for one of the 32 World Cup spots, giving sponsors and TV advertisers the potential for financial gain.

Tense Neighbors

When neighboring countries Afghanistan and Pakistan met on the soccer field for the first time in 37 years, it was hoped that the game would improve the relationship between the two countries, which had many long-running disputes. The match, played in Afghanistan and won by the Afghan team 3–0, was televised in both countries.

Later that same year, Afghanistan won the South Asian Football Federation Championship by beating India 2–0. The Afghani people's pride resulted in a national unity unseen in decades. The sports enthusiasm of the Afghani people had been held down for many years by wars and extremists, whose religious principles opposed having fun playing games of any kind. Soccer games, even for small children, were banned. The war-torn country was united behind the players who became national heroes.

Another rivalry example involves Russia and the United States. These two countries have clashed over politics for decades. Russia attempted to influence the U.S. public prior to the Winter Olympics in Sochi, Russia, by buying a series of eight-page advertising supplements to *The New York Times*.[5] The supplements had all the appearance of a regular news section, with only very small print indicating that it was an advertising supplement. Even though Russia was politically opposing U.S. action in the United Nations, it was attempting to attract U.S. Olympic fans.

Challenging China

China has the potential to become the world's largest consumer of sports and entertainment, but foreign businesses often don't do well under China's communist government. Government-run companies control the importation and distribution of foreign films in China. There is a strict quota on the number of films allowed into the country. A **joint venture** is an agreement between two or more companies to work together on a business project. Hollywood and Chinese companies form joint ventures to share the costs and profits of films. These films are not restricted by the quota limits on foreign films, but they must overcome other barriers. Chinese officials have been known to change the rules after foreign investors have spent time and money on co-production of a product.

Additionally, the Chinese movie theaters keep the largest share of the ticket sales, with the movie production studio receiving about 25 percent for movies

Why would U.S. film producers want to make films for the Chinese market?

© Lakeview Images/Shutterstock.com

shown is China.[6] In the United States, the share between the theater and studio is a 50/50 split. China believes that the potential profit from millions of Chinese consumers will convince Hollywood to abide by Chinese rules.

Piracy The theft of copyrighted material is called **piracy**. It is a problem for the film industry in China because the sale of illegal copies of DVDs affects the bottom line. *The Flowers of War*, a Chinese historical film starring Christian Bale, opened and grossed more than $95 million in China. However, U.S. film distributors were hesitant to handle the film, partially due to concern that the film would be pirated before it reached U.S. theaters. Because of Chinese piracy, U.S. filmmakers, theaters, and actors lose money.

Censorship When a U.S. company invests time and money into making a feature film, its major focus is to please the consumer. Making a film that appeals to Chinese movie fans is just one of the obstacles in China. Film companies that produce films in China or hope to distribute films in China operate under very strict government censorship rules. **Censorship** is the act of altering or editing media that is considered objectionable.

The Chinese State Administration of Radio, Film, and Television protects the Chinese film industry from competition. It is involved in the production process on all films shot in China. It guards against unwanted cultural or political influences by controlling the content of any film shown in China. Chinese filmmaker Jia Zhangke suspected the censors treated his film, *A Touch of Sin,* very lightly "because the news stories on which the film was based had already made the rounds on microblogs."[7] In other words, these stories had already been made public on the Twitter-like sites that many Chinese people read. The film was allowed to be shown in foreign film festivals and won best screenplay at the Cannes Film Festival. To date, the film still has not been seen in China. *A Touch of Sin* was considered a "strong contender" for an Oscar but was not submitted for consideration by China.[8]

The Chinese movie industry would like to have a worldwide audience. The Chinese government views a global audience for films as a way "to project influence through nonmilitary means."[9] A major obstacle in appealing to a U.S. audience is the Chinese government's tight control over content, which allows only positive—not necessarily true—images of China.

INTERMISSION

Who controls the content of films made or shown in China?

ENCORE

Understand Marketing Concepts
Select the best answer for each question.

1. Which of the following is not a source of revenue for the Olympics?
   a. broadcasting
   b. U.S. government funds
   c. ticketing
   d. merchandise

2. World Cup teams compete in which six geographic areas?
   a. North America, Mexico, Australia, England, Brazil, and Asia
   b. Brazil, the United States, Canada, China, Japan, and Mexico
   c. Africa, Asia, Europe, North/Central America and Caribbean, Oceania, and South America
   d. Africa, Asia, the United States, Brazil, Mexico, and Oceania

Think Critically
Answer the following questions as completely as possible.

3. How can international recruitment of athletes change a specific sport in the United States and in other countries? (LO 4.1-1)

4. Write a paragraph explaining why the content of a movie might be different in the United States than in China. (LO 4.1-2)

4.2 Global Sports and Entertainment Trends

The Essential Question

How have global trends and global communications changed the sports and entertainment industries?

Learning Objectives

LO 4.2-1   Assess global trends and opportunities in sports and entertainment.

LO 4.2-2   Identify the effects of global communications on sports and entertainment.

Key Terms

- international marketing
- differentiation
- globalization
- box office
- polyglots

OPENING ACT

Seven young men, future filmmakers from Iraq, participated in an International Film Exchange (IFE) workshop at the University of California, Los Angeles (UCLA) School of Theatre, Film, and Television. The IFE used funding from the American Embassy in Baghdad, Iraq, to help the filmmakers develop the technical and creative tools needed to document important social issues in their country. Including young women in the event was a cultural impossibility because young Iraqi women cannot travel with unrelated men.

The Iraqis received some California culture while learning how to make a film, including for some of them, seeing a film in a theater for the first time. The hope was that this could spark the beginning of a film industry in Iraq by teaching the participants to make movies that tell a story of interest to people.

Cooperative Learning   Form two teams to discuss how the film industry might be used to influence the culture of a developing nation.

LO 4.2-1   GLOBAL TRENDS

Market Planning   One of the best strategies for growing a sports or entertainment business is to consider **international marketing**—marketing a product in another country. Making the product or service desirable to international consumers takes knowledge of the cultural and language differences. It's also important to understand pricing based on the country's local currency.

Before creating international marketing strategies, businesses should assess the potential customers in the targeted countries. The assessment should include legal, political, and religious overviews of the target countries.

Sometimes a product or service can be marketed in multiple countries without making any modifications to it. Other products may require changes to be successful in a different market. For example, changes to flavors, sizes, color, or even electrical voltage may be required. Customizing a product to appeal to different markets is called **differentiation**.

Sports and entertainment are international products because people all over the world follow sports teams and watch films. The international economic relationships resulting from the integration of the world's markets is referred to as **globalization**. The U.S. film market's share of the **box office**—income from ticket sales—is often larger from outside the United States than from within it. In addition, there are many examples of the popularity of sports worldwide.

When Queen Elizabeth II's horse won the Royal Ascot Gold Cup in England, it was the first time a reigning monarch's entry had won in the 207-year history of the signature race.

Baseball

Baseball has been described as the game for **polyglots**, or people who speak many languages. Baseball may claim its origins in the United States, but it has been transported around the world. When the Pioniers, the local team in Hoofddorp, the Netherlands, had to move its baseball field, the town and team's management decided to build the new field based on Major League Baseball standards. By doing so, the team hoped to attract MLB exhibition games. Just as the National Football League (NFL) plays one or more regular-season games to a sell-out crowd from all over Europe in Wembley Stadium in London, England, MLB hopes to capitalize on the international draw of baseball.

Soccer

In the United States, soccer continues to grow in popularity. NBC has made a major commitment to cover world soccer games as U.S. interest increases, especially among the highly sought after U.S. fans between the ages of 12 and 24. Sold-out soccer games in this country are becoming a common occurrence, meaning the world has finally exported the "other" football to the United States.

© Larry St. Pierre/Shutterstock.com

Why do you think soccer is becoming more popular in the United States?

Go Mumbai Gladiators

Although professional football (NFL) is the most popular sport in the United States, it has been slow to catch on in other countries, despite the potential for millions of fans. Mumbai, India, is the most populous city in India with a total metropolitan population of 20.5 million and growing. The rivalry between India and Pakistan created a buzz when teams from the two nations played in the Elite Football League of India (EFLI). The fans had to be educated, because football is not a game with which the average Indian is familiar. Also, some U.S. traditions involving food and drink at games did not translate well in these countries. The use and sale of alcoholic beverages in India is banned in some Indian states, a major departure from the many beer producers who are football sponsors in the United States. Followers of the Hindu religion do not eat beef, and Muslims do not eat pork. So beef hamburgers or pork hot dogs, which are staples at U.S. football games, would not be on concession menus in predominantly Hindu or Muslim countries.

Chinese Power Swings

After the International Olympic Committee decided to reinstate golf in the 2016 Summer Olympics, China's interest in the game began to grow. Once considered "too extravagant," golf was banned in China from 1949 to the mid-1980s, but it has slowly re-emerged. Many young golfers are being trained privately through funding provided by their families. Most Chinese athletes in other sports are trained through state-run sports programs.

You cannot call Chinese golfer Xie (pronounced "shee-eh") Chengfeng a school dropout because he has never attended a traditional school. At eight years old, he has attended only golf academies and camps. Using a driver, he can hit the ball about 220 yards, about what an average adult hits. He is one of many very young Chinese golfers who are the beginning of a movement in China to win international golf tournaments and Olympic gold medals. The young golfers practice and maintain a full-time, rigorous golf training routine. Time will tell if the strenuous preparation pays off by producing high-quality players who can win. Or will it fail due to burnout by the young players or damage to young muscles and bodies?

Formula One

Formula One races are held all over the world. The logistics of moving a racing team from one location to the next is so vast that it requires a fleet of 747 aircraft and an official logistics partner. International shipping company DHL transports the racecars and team equipment between locations on as many as five continents. With its beginnings as a gentlemen racers' pastime, Formula One has grown into the ultimate test of drivers and cars. Formula One has been a global racing championship since its beginning and has one goal—speed.

INTERMISSION

What are some of the considerations and risks when doing business in a foreign country?

LINE is an instant messaging application for exchanging information and playing games. It has hundreds of millions of users in Asia, Europe, and Latin America and is owned by NHN Corporation of South Korea. LINE has an advantage over Facebook and Twitter because it was originally designed for use on smartphones, not computers, and does not collect users' data for use in advertising. LINE hopes to capitalize on growing concerns for privacy. It is known for its digital "sticker" cartoon images that help convey emotions. Users buy and send more than 1 billion stickers each day, earning about $10 million per month in revenue for LINE. Facebook took notice and also added a sticker function. LINE has negotiated with American pop stars who will be paid to use the product and to encourage others to do so.

Think Critically

Discuss with a partner how LINE should market its product in the United States. Whom should it target? What age groups might it target? Which U.S. pop stars would help attract the biggest market?

LO 4.2-2 THE WORLD ONLINE

The Internet gets much of the credit for connecting approximately 30,000 fans from around the world who flocked to Vladivostok, Russia, for a rock show. V-Rox is a showcase festival and international music conference. V-Rox was held at a formerly restricted Soviet military area. Almost 40 acts performed over four days, including artists from Japan, Singapore, and Korea. About 25,000 fans watched a live stream online. V-Rox demonstrates the power of the Internet.

Connecting Countries

Facebook worked for more than two years to provide Facebook for Every Phone—an app that offers access to the social media website for mobile phone users who have simple phones, not smartphones. The simple phones are no longer widely used in the United States and Europe but are still in wide use by millions of potential customers in developing nations such as India, Indonesia, Mexico, and Vietnam.

Facebook was hoping to win the loyalty of the billions of people globally who do not have Internet access by providing the service on their simple phones. As part of the effort, Facebook purchased an Israeli start-up company. The company pioneered data-compression technology that makes it possible to surf the Web even in areas without Internet access. With access to the Internet, a popular

How might Internet access via mobile phones change entertainment preferences globally?

musician in a socially and financially depressed area of the world can promote his or her music to the world. Opening up the Internet to people in developing countries provides opportunities for consumers and businesses. It can also have an effect on political and social change across the world.

Instant Communications

In the Fan and Media Engagement Center at NASCAR's headquarters in Charlotte, North Carolina, is a 47-inch flat screen monitor that shows a line graph labeled "social conversation." As events happen live and on TV, the graph indicates the response of fans from around the world on social media. The center is used to listen to the thousands of fans who are commenting during a race. The instant communication provides consumer feedback that can be used to adjust the live coverage and marketing strategies.

INTERMISSION

Name two ways the Internet has affected the sports and entertainment industries.

ENCORE

Understand Marketing Concepts

Select the best answer for each question.

1. Making a product or service desirable by international consumers requires knowledge of
   a. production challenges
   b. distribution channels
   c. the culture and language differences
   d. all of the above

2. The distribution of the Formula One vehicles to the races requires
   a. a political agreement between countries
   b. locations that are within close proximity
   c. detailed logistics
   d. all of the above

Think Critically

Answer the following questions as completely as possible.

3. How would you use the Internet to increase interest in American football in South America? In what countries would you start? What elements of culture in the chosen South American countries would you consider? (LO 4.2-1)

4. How would you help a musician in Nepal market her music to the world? (LO 4.2-2)

4.3 Diversity in the Sports and Entertainment Industry

The Essential Question

How do cultural and gender diversity relate to the popularity of sports and entertainment?

Learning Objectives

LO 4.3-1 Explain the impact of multiculturalism and diversity on sports and entertainment.

LO 4.3-2 Summarize the impact of women in sports and entertainment.

Key Terms

- culture
- prime time

OPENING ACT

The Rhythm Foundation brings culturally diverse live music experiences to South Florida. The Rhythm Foundation, founded in Miami Beach, Florida, is a nonprofit cultural organization that uses international music as a tool to promote cultural diversity. It works with similar groups in other cities to bring legendary musicians from Latin America, the Caribbean, Africa, Asia, Europe, and North America to Miami. These musicians bring their culture to the audience through their music. The Foundation staff also travel to find other diverse groups of unique, cutting-edge artists and help them make their U.S. debuts.

Brazilian singer Marisa Monte, who has the voice and training of an opera singer, combines diverse sounds into her extremely popular music. She sings only in Portuguese, the language of Brazil. The Rhythm Foundation featured Monte in one of her first U.S. appearances in front of a sell-out crowd of 430 people at the Colony Theater. Today Monte sings for sell-out crowds of 5,000 fans on multiple nights in Miami. The Rhythm Foundation helped Monte bring the sounds of Brazil to U.S. audiences.

Cooperative Learning Discuss with a partner why songs sung in one language are appealing to people who speak another language. Why would a nonprofit organization be interested in promoting diversity through music? Share your ideas with the class.

LO 4.3-1 MULTICULTURAL MARKETS

Culture is defined as the shared history, beliefs, customs, and traditions of a group of people that distinguish them from another group. Specific sports, music, dancing, entertainment, and celebrations can be considered part of the culture of a group of people. As travel and worldwide communication have become more accessible, people have had opportunities to see and hear the wealth of talent from around the globe. When exposed to the culture of others, culture-clash may sometimes occur because of differing beliefs and values. But frequently, parts of the culture are adopted. Mexico and the United States are close neighbors, and the Latino, or Hispanic, population is on the rise in the United States. Americans have embraced the Latino culture by enjoying its food, entertainment, and sports. Cinco de Mayo, a Mexican holiday celebrating Mexico's most famous military victory, is celebrated by some Americans. When the U.S. national soccer team defeated Mexico 2–0 and put Mexico's World Cup hopes in jeopardy, Mexico was dismayed. When the U.S. team beat Panama 3–2 and cleared the way for Mexico to enter the World Cup playoffs, newspaper headlines read "Thank You, USA." The two neighboring countries are somewhat like family members: they share history, customs, and traditions, but remain distinctly different.

Spanish-Language Sports and Entertainment

The population growth of the Latino market in the United States has opened opportunities for sports-related businesses, as well as entertainment. A survey by the National Association of Theater Owners found that Hispanics see more movies every year than any other ethnicity.[10] Boxing, soccer, and baseball are all popular sports with a large Latino following. Roughly 30 percent of Major League Baseball players are from Central and South America and the Caribbean. The audience for baseball is growing both in the United States and in the countries represented by the players. Offering game coverage in multiple languages rather than English-only broadcasts expands the audience and attracts a greater number of fans.

Univision is a Spanish-language broadcast television network headquartered in New York City. It reaches as large of a viewership as the five largest English-language television networks in the United States. The network is available on cable and satellite across the country. Univision is best known for offering *telenovelas*, a word created from *tele* for *televisión*, the Spanish word for television, and *novella*, the Spanish word for novel. Telenovelas are different from U.S. soap operas in that they have a limited number of episodes, while U.S. soap operas are ongoing series. Telenovelas also are shown during **prime time**, which is the block of time during the middle of the evening when the largest number of viewers is watching. Univision Communications Inc. joined with Disney/ABC to launch Fusion, a news, pop culture, satire TV, and digital network intended to appeal to an audience of younger Latinos who are English speakers or bilingual.

The Public Broadcasting Service's (PBS) three-part documentary called *Latino Americans* went a long way to help educate the general population about Latinos who have been war heroes and leaders in the United States. Latinos fought for Texas's independence from

Why are U.S. television networks interested in producing Spanish-language programs?

© Rob Marmion/Shutterstock.com

Mexico in the 1800s, were decorated heroes during World War II, and are still serving the United States today as educators, mayors, and U.S. Supreme Court Justices.

International Rhythm

The marketplace in North America has become very culturally diverse. Many ethnic markets offer potential for expansion by sports- and entertainment-related businesses. The music industry is one such example. Culture influences the types of music that people like. People also tend to be attracted to culturally familiar music. Experiencing music from other cultures can expand people's taste for the music and the culture.

South by Southwest (SXSW) Music Festival, a music business convention, started in 1987 as a showcase for U.S. regional and independent music. It is now a preview for every type of music originating from Mexico, Brazil, Australia, Spain, South Korea, China, and more. Although many big name stars such as Jay-Z and Kanye West perform at SXSW, the real experience is from hearing new groups who play music without borders.

Music is widely enjoyed around the world, but music censorship is practiced by some extremist groups, including the Taliban, which controlled Afghanistan in the late 1990s. Under the Taliban, all music, except certain types of religious songs and chants, was outlawed and became nearly extinct. The Afghanistan National Institute of Music was established in 2010 and strives to teach students both traditional Afghan music and classical Western music.

Photo Courtesy of the Rhythm Foundation

Why do you think so many different types of ethnic music can be heard in the United States?

Culturally Speaking

Marketing-Information Management If a U.S. sports and entertainment business wants to enter the global marketplace, it must have a website to reach potential customers and fans from around the world. Although English is the international language of business, providing information in the native language of website visitors can make a difference. Having the information available in multiple languages also makes it easier to find the site with a search engine. Good communication is key to a successful business. A business must design its website with its target market in mind.

INTERMISSION

How has growth of the Latino population in the United States influenced sports and entertainment?

JUDGMENT CALL

The International Olympic Committee (IOC) planned to conduct 2,457 drug tests just before and during the 2014 Winter Olympics in Sochi, Russia.[11] Less than three months before the opening ceremonies, the World Anti-Doping Agency (WADA) provisionally suspended the accreditation of the only anti-doping laboratory in Russia hired to do the drug screening for the Winter Games. WADA announced that the lab was unreliable based on the failure to identify banned drugs in blind samples. Additionally, the lab produced false-positive results, incorrectly finding drugs where none existed. The IOC guarantees the "integrity" of the drug-testing program. Under its agreement with the IOC, the host city has to cover the costs of flying samples to another accredited lab outside of the country if the drug lab's accreditation is revoked.

Think Critically

How do you think athletes would feel about having their drug tests conducted by an unreliable lab? Why is the IOC so concerned about the integrity of these tests?

LO 4.3-2 WOMEN IN SPORTS

Most girls growing up in the United States prior to 1972 rarely had opportunities to participate in organized competitive school sports. There were almost no college scholarships for female athletes. Many schools did not offer any sports for girls. Over the years, gender equality in sports has grown but is far from equal.

Title IX

In 1972 the passage of Title IX, an amendment to federal education law that prohibits discrimination against females in school sports, began to break down barriers for girls and women in sports. In 2002 the Title IX Amendment of the Higher Education Act was renamed the Patsy T. Mink Equal Opportunity in Education Act. Patsy Matsu Takemoto Mink, who co-authored the Title IX legislation, was the first woman from Hawaii elected to Congress as well as the first Asian-American woman elected to Congress.

Over the past four decades, Title IX has helped begin the slow equalization of access to sports for females. Under the law, schools must provide females with comparable opportunities to play sports currently offered to males. Since the implementation of Title IX, participation by females in high school sports has increased by more than 990 percent and female participation in college sports has increased by more than 560 percent.[12] Women's sports do not yet attract audiences equal to men's sports. They often face discrimination and less funding. But women's sports have gained momentum and will continue to strive for gender equity.

Fighting for Equality

Venus and Serena Williams are renowned women's professional tennis players who have changed the composition of the sport. They were not the first African-American women on tour, but they have endured, amazed, and inspired countless girls to play tennis. Minority women have faced a double jeopardy in sports—discrimination against their gender and their ethnicity or race. Venus Williams is credited with convincing the All England Lawn Tennis and Croquet Club, the venue for the Wimbledon Championship, to award female players equal payouts with male players.

The U.S. Open began paying equal prize money for men and women in 1973, due to efforts by legendary female tennis player Billie Jean King. She recruited Ban deodorant, a subsidiary of Bristol-Myers, to donate $55,000 to make the prizes equal.[13] That same year, King organized the Women's Tennis Association and famously beat Bobby Riggs in a tennis match known as the "Battle of the Sexes" held at the Houston Astrodome. Her win over a male opponent was a big boost for women's tennis. According to *Forbes*, seven of the ten highest-paid female athletes in the world are tennis players.[14]

At age 64, Diana Nyad was the first person to swim from Cuba to Florida without a cage to protect her from sharks. It took her nearly 53 hours to make the journey. Nyad had previously tried four times to complete the grueling feat.

INTERMISSION

Why was Title IX an important piece of legislation for women's sports?

ENCORE

Understand Marketing Concepts
Select the best answer for each question.

1. If a company wants to sponsor a sports team to reach Latino customers, which of the following sports might present the best opportunity?
   a. soccer
   b. boxing
   c. baseball
   d. all of the above

2. Which of the following statements is true?
   a. French is the international language of business.
   b. Providing information in a native language increases sales.
   c. A website is not a necessity for an international business.
   d. All of the above are true.

Think Critically
Answer the following questions as completely as possible.

3. Are there TV stations in your community or state that primarily use a language other than English? What languages are used? How can marketers use this information? (LO 4.3-1)

4. Conduct online research to develop a chart of the top-earning sportswomen and the top-earning sportsmen, using the most current information. Are there pay discrepancies? If so, do you think they are fair? Explain why or why not. (LO 4.3-2)

4.4 Destinations: Travel and Tourism

The Essential Question

What is the role of travel and tourism in sports and entertainment, and why is multigenerationalism a factor?

Learning Objectives

LO 4.4-1   Explain the role of travel and tourism in sports and entertainment.

LO 4.4-2   Discuss the roles of resorts and theme parks.

Key Terms

- direct economic impact
- indirect economic impact
- niche travel
- ecotourism
- multigenerationalism

OPENING ACT

ADMIT ONE
289147

Powder Mountain, a ski resort near East Eden, Utah, has a rich history, beginning as grazing land for sheep owned by Frederick James Cobabe. His son, Alvin F. Cobabe, who became a medical doctor while still working on the ranch, added acreage to the ranch. While horseback riding with friends, someone casually commented that the area would make a great ski resort. This caught Dr. Cobabe's attention, and he began working toward that objective. The mountain's current owners plan to keep the unique features of the pristine mountain resort. But they also want to add a maximum of 500 private homes, a sustainable mountain village with boutique hotels, and a members-only lodge and event center. Parcels of land in the development are rumored to have sold for $1 million. Member/owners will have access to year-round conferences, concerts, and speakers. The ski resort owners imagine a winter resort that is similar to a national park.

Cooperative Learning   With a partner, research what it might be like to live in a sustainable village. Discuss what conflicts might arise in building a sustainable village with 500 private homes on a mountainside. Present your thoughts to the rest of the class.

LO 4.4-1   TRAVELING

According to the World Travel and Tourism Council, 9 percent of the world's gross domestic product (GDP) is related to travel and tourism, which plays a very important role in the economic growth of many countries.[15] The travel and tourism industries are closely related to the sports and entertainment industries because many people travel to attend or participate in an event.

Travel destinations are endless. One person's dream destination might be the Accademia Gallery in Florence, Italy, to see Michelangelo's masterpiece sculpture *David*. A nature-loving person might want to hike through Big Bend National Park to see the Rio Grande River running through a

1,500-foot canyon. Still others may dream of swimming with manatees or attending the Super Bowl. Travel is often about creating family memories.

Wherever the destination may be, there is most likely a business or organization working to promote the travel spot. Attracting tourists and their money is vital to sustaining many destinations.

Attracting Tourists

Marketing-Information Management

Most people who attend a Super Bowl will have to travel to another location and spend one or more nights at a hotel.

A major reason for a city to want to host an event such as the Super Bowl is to attract out-of-town visitors. Visitors will purchase airline tickets, book hotel rooms, rent cars, visit local tourist attractions, and eat at local restaurants. The mission of the *travel trade*—a collective term for tour operators and travel agents—is to increase the volume of visitors and their spending.

The economic impacts to the surrounding area of an event such as the Super Bowl can be classified as either direct or indirect. The **direct economic impact** is the total amount of new spending resulting from an event or attraction. More than 100,000 people visit a Super Bowl city, and about one-third of the visitors are travel companions who do not attend the game. Additionally, as many as 5,200 members of the media will cover the event. When the Super Bowl was held in New Orleans, overnight visitors' average stay was 3.6 nights and average spending was $575 per day.[16] The **indirect economic impact** is determined by the multiplier effect, which is the portion of the money spent by visitors on local goods and services that is in turn spent by local employers and employees and re-circulated in the area.

Determining the direct and indirect impacts of a major event is not an exact science. One method is to examine the hotel occupancy rate from the same dates in previous years and consider the increase as a direct impact. Some tourism attractions in the host city will see a decrease in business because of the Super Bowl. This loss of business must be deducted from the revenue gains. In addition, not all of the increased revenue will be retained locally. Many nationally owned restaurant and hotel chains will send most of the money earned to their headquarters in other locations, but it can be assumed that at least some of the revenues will stay in the host city. Sales taxes on all of the extra

What are some examples of the direct economic impact for a city hosting a major event?

sales during the event will go to local governments that may use them to fund local public projects such as street repairs.

Although a city will benefit from hosting events such as the Super Bowl, there are costs involved. Costs to the host city include public funding of facilities; overtime pay for police, fire, and security forces; increased garbage cleanup; and increased traffic. All Super Bowl cities conduct research to assess the economic and financial impact of hosting the biggest game in town.

Tailor-Made Vacations

The word "vacation" may bring images of leisurely strolls through a tropical garden with a cool ocean breeze blowing through the palm trees. If beaches are not for you, travel marketers can repaint the picture. A wealth of travel opportunities exists and can be tailored to customers' vacation tastes and budgets. **Niche travel**, or recreational travel or tours planned around a special interest, are becoming popular. For example, a travel agency can design a niche travel package for a group of music enthusiasts who want to travel through Europe and listen to classical concerts.

Halls of Fame

Attracting visitors is critical to keeping a hall of fame alive. Motivating a traveler to exit the interstate requires the perfect marketing mix—the right theme for the site, a convenient location, an appealing promotion, and a fair price. Word of mouth is the best type of promotion for a hall of fame.

As a travel destination, a hall of fame can serve as a basis for promoting tourism. Sports halls of fame cover every recreation from lacrosse to jousting and from chess to marbles. While at the NASCAR Hall of Fame in Charlotte, North Carolina, you can learn about the history of NASCAR as shown in the High Octane Theater, get a behind-the-scenes look at a race day, and see actual racecars. Other halls include a multitude of entertainment interests, including the Rock and Roll Hall of Fame and Museum in Cleveland, Ohio, and the National Toy Hall of Fame located at the National Museum of Play in Rochester, New York.

Ecotourism

The International Ecotourism Society (TIES) defines **ecotourism** as "responsible travel to natural areas that conserves the environment and improves the well-being of local people."[17] International sports events attract hundreds of thousands of tourists from around the world and have a financial and environmental impact on the areas visited. Many international facilities, such as Wembley Stadium in London, where some NFL games are played, are built with the intent of reducing the environmental impact of events. Wembley Stadium is committed to, and has been recognized for, reducing the use of energy and carbon emissions; recycling and sending zero waste to landfills; and reducing the number of people traveling to the stadium by car in favor of using public transportation through its Green Travel Plan.

Rain forests and national parks are natural theme parks filled with the beautiful, natural wonders of the world. Ecotourism plays an important role in

How can the travel and tourism industry act to protect the environment and the local people?

preserving these destination spots. Most people would not think of Alaska as having a rain forest, but Tongass National Forest in Alaska has a glimmering rain forest that is home to many endangered species and rare plants. Tongass is the largest national forest in the United States with more than 17 million acres. Sustaining fragile areas while promoting tourism requires careful planning on the part of the American Indian nations that live in the area. In addition, organizations such as Sustainable Trip can direct you to hotels, tour operators, and other businesses that benefit communities by conserving natural resources and promoting the economic growth of the local people.

INTERMISSION

Why should the travel industry be concerned about the local people who live near tourist sites?

LO 4.4-2   RESORTS AND THEME PARKS

Product/Service Management

Resorts and theme parks are very popular tourist destinations. Theme parks are thought of as family-oriented destinations, while resorts are usually aimed at adults rather than children. Theme parks generally have activities, rides, and other attractions centered around movies, cartoon characters, or television shows that are well known to children. Resorts, on the other hand, frequently focus on a single recreational sport, such as golf, and other relaxing activities. Some include a celebrity connection. Many travel destinations have combined theme park and resort features—offering the best of both in an effort to attract a wide range of visitors and age groups.

Why is Orlando home to so many resorts and theme parks?

© Katherine Welles/Shutterstock.com

Creating a destination that is attractive to multiple generations of people can be a challenge. **Multigenerationalism** involves satisfying the needs of several generations of a family. Many resorts are changing their focus from adults to families. Some resorts are being made over as destinations that will please multiple generations with child-centered areas, zip lines, and bowling alleys. What Grandpa wants to see and do may not interest a high school student. But taking part in activities that showcase the regional culture is likely to appeal to all generations. Accommodating multiple generations is proving to be a successful business model.

Theme Park Central

Walt Disney theme parks are generally considered the world standard, ever since Disneyland opened in California in 1955. Hong Kong Disneyland opened in 2005, and Shanghai Disney Resort is scheduled to open

TAKE A BOW *Susan and Simon Veness*

Susan and Simon Veness are a successful writing team based in Orlando, Florida. Mr. Veness is from the United Kingdom (UK) and Mrs. Veness is from the Midwestern United States. Mr. Veness founded the Brit Guide travel book series while providing coverage of U.S. sports for UK media. Mrs. Veness used her knowledge of Disney to get a research position for the Brit Guide travel series and is now the author of a number of travel titles including *The Hidden Magic of Walt Disney World.*

Both are travelers, and their co-authored book *Brit Guide to Orlando and Walt Disney World 2013* is the 19th edition of Britain's bestselling travel guide. More than 800,000 people from the UK visit Orlando each year, and according to the Venesses, the appeal is the consistent value, sunshine, service, and variety for family vacations.[18]

Think Critically

Research other Brit Guide books. What other areas of the world are popular with people from the UK? Why do you think those areas are popular destinations?

in 2015. Both of these locations provide Disney a way to introduce new films and characters to Chinese customers.

Orlando, Florida, has been home to Walt Disney World and seven other major theme parks since 1971. The city is an extremely popular vacation site with more than 100 attractions that bring over 55 million visitors a year (for business and pleasure) to the city. There are many restaurants and lodging options that can be included as part of a central Florida vacation package. Tickets to the theme parks can also be customized; the per-day ticket price drops as additional days are added. When tickets are packaged with a Disney property lodging stay, visitors can access the park after closing hours, when fewer people are there. To maximize the revenue per guest, Disney wants to provide all of the products and services that visitors may want and need during their stay.

Chengdu, China, boasts the world's largest single building with about 19 million square feet of floor space—or about the size of 329 football fields. The New Century Global Center has shops, hotels, offices, and a water park with beaches under a gigantic glass dome that will accommodate up to 6,000 visitors.

INTERMISSION

Why might a theme park add restaurants and lodging to its site?

ENCORE

Understand Marketing Concepts

Select the best answer for each question.

1. Travel and Tourism
   a. is equal to 9 percent of the world's gross domestic product
   b. is the world's ninth largest industry
   c. has little impact on the world's economy
   d. none of the above

2. The indirect economic impact of a tourist event or attraction to the local economy is
   a. the total of new spending that is a direct result of the attraction or event
   b. the cost of operating the event or attraction
   c. determined by the multiplier effect
   d. all of the above

Think Critically

Answer the following questions as completely as possible.

3. Conduct research online to determine how Super Bowl cities are selected. List four characteristics of the winning cities. (LO 4.4-1)

4. You work for the convention and visitors bureau in your state. You want a theme park to be built in your state. Recommend a specific location and write a one-page explanation of why investors should choose your state. Specify what your state has to offer. (LO 4.4-2)

CHAPTER ASSESSMENT

Review Marketing Terms

Match the terms listed with the definitions.

1. An agreement between two or more companies to work together on a project
2. The governing authority of the Olympic Movement
3. The international economic relationships resulting from the integration of world markets
4. The portion of money spent by local employers and employees that came from money collected from tourists
5. The shared history, beliefs, customs, and traditions of a group of people
6. Recreational travel or tours planned around a special interest
7. Theft of copyrighted material
8. When opportunities for men and women are roughly equal
9. The total amount of new spending resulting from an event or attraction
10. Marketing a product in another country
11. People who speak many languages
12. Income from ticket sales
13. Customizing a product to appeal to different markets
14. Block of time when the largest number of viewers are watching TV
15. Responsible travel that conserves the environment and improves the well-being of local people
16. Satisfying the needs of several generations of a family
17. The act of altering or editing media considered objectionable

a. box office
b. censorship
c. culture
d. differentiation
e. direct economic impact
f. ecotourism
g. gender equity
h. globalization
i. indirect economic impact
j. international marketing
k. International Olympic Committee
l. joint venture
m. multigenerationalism
n. niche travel
o. piracy
p. polyglots
q. prime time

Review Marketing Concepts

Select the best answer for each of the following questions.

18. The basic structural foundations of a city, such as roads are called
    a. an industry
    b. infrastructure
    c. travel trade
    d. industry standards
19. The longest continuous supporter of the Olympic Games is
    a. the United States Government
    b. Frito-Lay
    c. Coca-Cola
    d. NBC

20. The Premier League is
   a. the National Football League
   b. an athletic club
   c. a Cuban boxing team
   d. the organizing body for soccer in England
21. The travel trade is
   a. a type of transportation
   b. a movie theater
   c. collective term for tour operators and travel agents
   d. a type of market
22. Making and showing films in China is challenging because of
   a. Chinese rules and regulations
   b. piracy
   c. censorship
   d. all of the above

Think Critically

23. Research how many countries currently play Little League baseball. What does this number indicate to you? (LO 4.1-1)
24. Why do you think Chinese movies are not popular in the United States? What strategy would you recommend to a Chinese movie producer to help the movie succeed? (LO 4.1-2)
25. How has global communication increased the popularity of sports and entertainment around the world? (LO 4.2-2)
26. Use the Internet or your library to research a Convention and Visitors Bureau (CVB) in your state. How are CVBs funded? What is the purpose of a CVB? (LO 4.4-1)
27. Explain how an entertainment or sports event, such as the MLB World Series, has a direct economic impact on the city that hosts the event. Provide specific examples. (LO 4.1-1)
28. Research the changes that have occurred in women's sports since the passage of Title IX. Write a one-page report explaining the positive changes for women and address what still needs to happen to achieve full gender equity in sports. (LO 4.3-2)
29. Give an example of how politics affects entertainment, such as movies. (LO 4.1-2)
30. Explain what piracy means in the movie industry. How does piracy affect the money earned by the industry? Do you think piracy is unethical? Why or why not? (LO 4.1-2)
31. Baseball is not an Olympic sport. U.S. Major League Baseball has chosen not to change its game schedule to allow time for players to compete in the Olympics. Do you agree with this decision? Why or why not? Will not competing in the Olympics have a long-term impact on world interest in baseball? Explain your answer. (LO 4.1-1)

Make Academic Connections

32. **History** You are a sports marketer in the early 1900s and want to attract international fans to the Olympics being held in the United States. Select a U.S. city and create a one-page brochure to attract sports fans from around the world to that city during that era. (LO 4.1-1)

33. **Geography** As a promotion, Hong Kong Disneyland offered Hong Kong residents a two-day pass for the price of a one-day pass, which is about $65 U.S. dollars. At the same time, it offered Mainland Chinese and international visitors a free photo or a souvenir lunch box with the purchase of a one-day ticket. On a map, look at the location of Hong Kong and Mainland China. Why would the offers be significantly better to Hong Kong residents than to others? (LO 4.4-2)

34. **Government** Use the Internet to determine if the film *A Touch of Sin*, directed by Jia Zhangke, was ever released in China. The film about contemporary China received approval from the Chinese film bureau's censors and was scheduled to be released in China, but the film's fate was unknown months later. Determine where the film has been seen. (LO 4.1-2)

35. **Geography** Use the Internet or your library to research information about Kanyakumari, India. What are some of the cultural features of that region? What cultural features make it attractive to tourists? How can tourists travel to Kanyakumari? (LO 4.3-1)

36. **Finance** You plan to operate a basketball sports camp during the summer at Duke University. The total number of participants for the camp is 200. Camp participants will stay three nights in the university dormitories, and each room will house two camp participants. Duke charges you $40 per room each night. Liability insurance for the camp will cost $3,000. Meals for the three-day camp will cost $6,000. Duke University will not charge you for the use of the basketball facility. Nike will provide sporting goods to be used by, and given to, participants. You and your partner each want to clear $8,000 profit from this camp. How much will you have to charge each camp participant to meet this goal? (LO 4.4-1)

37. **Technology** How could you use social media to increase the interest in ecotourism? (LO 4.4-1)

38. **Government** Work with a partner to list reasons why the United States does not provide taxpayer funding to support the U.S. Olympic teams. Research what other countries do to support their Olympic teams. Should the United States be concerned about the image portrayed when other countries win more medals at the Olympics? Why or why not? Do you think U.S. support of Olympic teams would improve the USA teams' winning record? Explain your answer. (LO 4.1-1)

39. **Marketing** Create a fund-raising plan to raise support and obtain donations from high school students for Olympic athletes. (LO 4.1-1)

EXTRA INNINGS PROJECT

The executive committee of The Fédération Internationale de Football Association (FIFA) oversees soccer, the most popular sport in the world. FIFA's mission includes building a better world by using "the power of football as a tool for social and human development, by strengthening the work of dozens of initiatives around the globe to support local communities."[20] Individuals have a responsibility to act in ways that are sensitive to other people and the environment. Likewise, sports and entertainment entities such as FIFA seek ways to improve the social conditions of areas where major events are held, including the World Cup. The selection of the tiny, gas-rich Arab state of Qatar for the 2022 World Cup raised many questions about the selection process. Human Rights Watch, an international organization dedicated to defending human rights, called attention to the *kafala* system of sponsorship-based employment in Qatar. The system allows construction employers to confiscate passports from immigrant workers and force them to work under extremely high temperatures while building facilities for the World Cup. Worker safety and rights became a significant issue for FIFA after these conditions came to light.

Work with a group and complete the following activities.

1. Conduct online research to find ESPN or *Sports Illustrated* stories regarding the social responsibility issues faced by FIFA and the International Olympic Committee (IOC). Read how issues such as facility construction, worker safety, or human rights are being handled. Find two or three examples of coverage. Summarize your findings in writing.

2. Conduct online research about FIFA's and IOC's commitment to social responsibility. List the commitments made by each organization.

3. Use the summary and list created above to brainstorm with the group ways you think the international athletic associations should address safety and human rights issues.

4. Select one idea from your brainstorming session. Based on your idea, write a plan for FIFA and the IOC that outlines ways to support human rights and social issues while governing international sporting events.

5. Create a brochure to persuade FIFA and the IOC to adopt your ideas.

VIRTUAL BUSINESS *Sports & Entertainment*

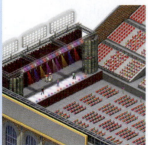

Use the *Picking and Promoting a Band* lesson to learn more about the economics of stadium shows. Identify reasons large acts might consider an arena rather than a stadium venue. Conduct market research to determine the most popular type of music in your city. Book a band, set ticket prices, advertise, and see how the choices you make affect your profits.

For more information, go to knowledgematters.com.

Artwork courtesy of Knowledge Matters, Inc.

SAVING THE MANATEES

Manatees are gentle, slow-moving giants that are an endangered species. They live in warm water and can be found in areas from Florida to Brazil, in the Amazon River, and on the west coast of Africa. Manatees are mammals that never leave the water but must surface to breathe. They spend their day feeding on sea plants and resting. The average adult manatee weighs 1,500 to 1,800 pounds and measures ten to twelve feet in length. They are thought to be related to modern day elephants. The decline of the world's manatee population is attributed to hunting for their meat, destruction of their habitats, being struck by boats, and pollution.

Rescued Orphans

The Dallas World Aquarium (DWA) is strongly committed to conservation and is one of more than 250 member zoos and aquariums linked by the World Association of Zoos and Aquariums (WAZA).

DWA owner, Daryl Richardson, has always been involved with global conservation of endangered animals and has worked to rescue manatees. In 1999 the first pair of manatees arrived at DWA after being rescued from hunters and fishermen in Venezuela. Manati and Ayurami were accompanied by Venezuelan Luis Sandoval, who is their main caretaker and friend. He hand fed them and even taught them to swim when they first arrived at DWA.

Ayurami and Manati can be viewed on the animal cam at the DWA website.

They live among the many other animals at DWA, the majority of which have been rescued and are threatened or endangered in their natural habitats. DWA works with conservation and breeding programs and with government and nongovernmental organizations in Brazil, Costa Rica, Mexico, Panama, Peru, and Venezuela.

When DWA was first contacted requesting assistance with four orphaned Amazonian manatees in Iquitos, Peru, the response was immediate. DWA sent powdered milk, medical supplies, and funding. DWA is instrumental in the Amazon Rescue Center, which provides environmental education to help the native people understand why each species plays a role on the earth. Each year on Earth Day, in Iquitos, Peru, the rescued manatees that are ready and able to live on their own are returned to the wild. (See the release photo on p. 115.)

Think Critically

1. Why should you be concerned about endangered species?
2. How can travel and tourism help improve the plight of endangered animals and the natural environments where they struggle to survive?
3. What would you include in a plan for increasing awareness and preventing destruction of endangered animals and their environments? How would you promote your plan?
4. What would you include in a newspaper article about your plan?

SPORTS AND ENTERTAINMENT MARKETING TEAM DECISION MAKING EVENT

Soccer (football) is the most popular sport in the world. The sport has become increasingly popular in the United States due to a highly diversified population. Many young children play on soccer leagues in cities of all sizes in the United States.

Professional soccer has successfully made its way to the U.S. sports scene. A growing Hispanic population fuels the excitement for soccer. Oklahoma City's United Soccer Leagues' Professional Division soccer team—the Oklahoma City Energy FC—will debut in the 2014 season.

At first, the team will use a high school stadium for its games. The Energy then plans to build a state-of-the-art stadium in the greater Oklahoma City area to call its own. Oklahoma City is prepared to pass bond issues to pay for a new facility.

Many of the growing Oklahoma City suburbs are also very interested in hosting the Oklahoma City Energy FC. You are the city planner for Norman, Oklahoma, a suburb of Oklahoma City where the University of Oklahoma is located. Your city wants to be the home for the Oklahoma City Energy FC. You understand the economic benefits of having the team locate in your city. Norman has a growing population of

115,562, and Oklahoma City has a population of 599,199. Norman is located 25 minutes from downtown Oklahoma City, and the freeways provide an excellent connection between the two cities. The population of Norman, Oklahoma, is projected to grow 9.4 percent next year. Venture capitalists in Norman have raised enough funds to build state-of-the-art facilities for the professional soccer team.

You will meet with the general manager (judge) for the Oklahoma City Energy FC to convince him to locate the team in Norman. The meeting will take place in the general manager's office. You have 10 minutes to explain the rationale for locating in Norman, and the general manager has an additional 5 minutes to ask questions about your plan.

Performance Indicators Evaluated

- Pitch a marketing communication idea to the client.
- Demonstrate negotiation skills.
- Participate as a team member.
- Make a client presentation.
- Gain a commitment from the client.
- Identify the product's/service's competitive advantage.
- Demonstrate an understanding of entertainment distribution.

Think Critically

1. Why would a city want a professional soccer team?
2. What are two advantages for Norman of being the host city for the team?
3. Why should the team locate in a suburb?
4. How might the soccer team play a role in diversifying the sports fans in Norman, Oklahoma?

www.deca.org

MARKETING-INFORMATION MANAGEMENT

POINT YOUR BROWSER

ngl.cengage.com/sports4e

Winning Strategies

The Nielsen Company

Nielsen is a global information company that focuses on consumers in over 100 countries. It measures what people watch and buy. Nielsen relies on panels of people to provide accurate feedback on their shopping and media consumption. Instead of simply tracking computer and television usage, Nielsen interacts with the panel members. According to its website, Nielsen's audience measurement standards "measure people instead of cookies." A cookie is a small data file stored on a computer that is used to collect data about the user's online history.

© Jason Stitt/Shutterstock.com

Nielsen is well respected for its research. It spots marketing trends such as those used by the French music duo Daft Punk. The musical pair skipped traditional marketing and began promoting their new release several months before the album was available. They created a buzz by targeting music fans with a TV promotion during *Saturday Night Live*. Nielsen spotted Daft Punk's marketing efforts and documented their moves.

Nielsen has about 35,000 employees around the world. It plays a key role in providing marketing information to a wide variety of businesses that are connected to sports and entertainment. Nielsen is quick to point out that word-of-mouth recommendations from friends and family are still the most trusted sources of information about products and services.

Think Critically

1. Visit the Nielsen website and look at examples of data collected about entertainment. Name two kinds of data that are collected. How does Nielsen collect this data?

2. How can data collected about the viewership of a TV show be used by a potential advertiser?

5.1 Marketing-Information Systems

The Essential Question

What are the characteristics and purposes of marketing-information systems, and what role do ethics play?

Learning Objectives

LO 5.1-1   Explain the characteristics and purposes of marketing-information systems.

LO 5.1-2   Describe the role of ethics in marketing-information management.

Key Terms

- marketing-information system
- marketing research
- syndicated research
- client-side researchers
- soft data
- hard data

OPENING ACT

Most theater productions on Broadway in New York City begin with several weeks of preview performances in theaters outside of New York. This provides an opportunity to fine-tune the production and determine what changes need to be made to attract the largest possible audience. Producers used to rely on their own instincts and information they picked up from watching the audience's reaction during the play. Now, productions aiming for Broadway use additional tools to determine what will please an audience. The tools include handheld dials that chart the reaction of selected audience members. During the production of *Somewhere in Time* in Portland, Oregon, producer Ken Davenport had 60 audience members make one of three choices: "Love this part," "Neutral about this part," and "Hate this part." The reactions were charted on a computer. According to Davenport, the charted dials matched his instincts.[1] This was the first time the dials had been used for feedback on a play that had its sights set on Broadway.

Cooperative Learning   Share with a partner how you would react if asked to use a device to provide feedback while watching live entertainment. How is the feedback valuable to a producer?

LO 5.1-1   FINDING MARKETING SOLUTIONS

When a theater sells out every performance of a play, the producers consider this a form of positive feedback from customers. If customers keep buying, that means they are happy. Successful businesses continuously consider how to keep current customers and find new customers. Businesses need to know what is and what is not working. Marketing information collected from customers can be used by businesses to help make needed improvements. A **marketing-information system** (MIS) is a set of procedures and methods used to systematically collect, analyze, distribute, and store information needed by business managers to make decisions, including decisions about how to please customers.

Seeking Information

A live theater performance in Portland, Oregon, may cost about $1 million to produce, but moving the play to a theater located on Broadway in New York will cost in excess of $10 million.[2] Making sure the play will please the audience is critical to the financial success of the venture. Theater producer Ken Davenport wanted to obtain feedback from a preview audience for one of his plays to help him improve the play before moving it to Broadway and incurring higher expenses. He collected marketing information through a simple form of **marketing research**—a process designed to provide solutions to marketing problems through the use of a scientific problem-solving system.

When research is conducted by an independent company and then offered for sale to all businesses in the industry, it is referred to as **syndicated research**. Data is collected, analyzed, sorted, and displayed in charts and graphs so that it can be used to make decisions on how to improve the product or service.

Some large companies have a marketing research department within the firm but also work with outside marketing research firms. In-house staff researchers who also work with external research agencies are referred to as **client-side researchers**, because they are employees of the client (the company that hired the outside marketing research firm). Client-side researchers communicate with other internal staff to identify research needs. Then they work with the external research agency to develop a plan for collecting the marketing information needed to aid in decision making. After the research is conducted, client-side researchers deliver the findings to the internal staff.

Benefits and Limitations of Marketing Research

Marketing research is limited by two things: (1) the humans involved in the design of the research and (2) the humans who provide the information that is collected. When research is professionally designed and conducted, the

While Netflix claims to have over 40 million subscribers, Netflix does not sell advertising and does not release any viewership data. This leaves the public to guess about the actual number of viewers for its "smash" hits.

What is the role of a client-side researcher at a business?

© iStockphoto.com/DragonImages

Passing themselves off as human has been the goal of robotic Internet programs almost since the start of the Internet. Socialbots are automated programs that tweet and retweet messages. They piece together phrases that are relevant to the target audience by using built-in databases of current events. According to Ian Urbina, an investigative reporter for *The New York Times*, "some researchers estimate that only 35 percent of the average Twitter user's followers are real people."[3] Marketers are using socialbots to send out messages hoping to influence people's behavior and buying habits based on automated "likes" that socialbots post while pretending to be real people.

Think Critically

How do you feel about the use of socialbots to influence people? Will it lead to a distrust of social media? Why or why not?

results can provide effective solutions to business problems. The solutions may help the business survive and grow.

Gallup is an international marketing research firm focused on growing businesses by measuring and improving employees' performance. Gallup helps businesses select the right employees, develop their strengths, and increase the employees' engagement with the company. An engaged employee is one who feels his or her work contributes to the success of the company. Gallup's research has proven that engaged employees feel a connection to the company, which has a positive effect on the level and quality of their work. By improving employee engagement, businesses hope to do two things: (1) increase the emotional connection between employees and customers and (2) empower employees, or give them the authority, to "do what is right in their customers' eyes." When organizations engage both their customers and their employees, they experience a 240 percent boost in performance-related business outcomes.[4]

INTERMISSION

Explain the characteristics and purposes of marketing research.

LO 5.1-2   RESEARCH ETHICS

It often is easy to deceive people when conducting marketing research or when reporting the findings, but it is not an ethical business practice. Customers eventually learn of the deceit. Unethical behavior can damage the public's opinion about a business. Remember, keeping customers is much less expensive than finding new ones, and treating people ethically is one step that businesses can take to retain customers.

Trusting the Data

Multinational research firm Nielsen works hard to make sure its data collection practices meet its high ethical standards. In the past, Nielsen

registered as an individual user on websites and then collected publicly available data. It has ended this practice if the website does not give prior consent to the collection of data.

A Little Privacy, Please

Marketing-information systems contain personal data about the people who participate in the research. People have the right to keep their personal information from being misused. They also have the right to be excluded when they choose not to be involved with research. Ethical marketing researchers take great care to protect the personal information of marketing research participants by not revealing any identifiable information. They also include only those people who choose to be involved.

Ethical Conflicts

Ethical conflicts arise when someone has to choose between going against or standing by one of his or her moral principles when neither choice is an easy one. A marketing researcher has an ethical duty to the client or business that is paying for the research to gather reliable and accurate data. The marketing researcher also has an ethical duty to the research respondents to allow them to choose whether to participate, to not invade their privacy, and to treat them with consideration. Top management at the client company must enforce ethical behavior.

A major ethical issue marketing researchers face is the integrity of the research. Research is not valid if results are altered, misinterpreted, ignored, or withheld. Such occurrences will reflect badly on the researcher.

A client may ask a researcher to estimate the number of people who will attend a musical festival. An estimate is considered **soft data**, which is data based on an educated guess. **Hard data** includes statistics gathered through valid research. If management is planning to use the research results to show that it has made a good decision, the researcher may feel pressured to falsify the results. A client may even request that a specific research

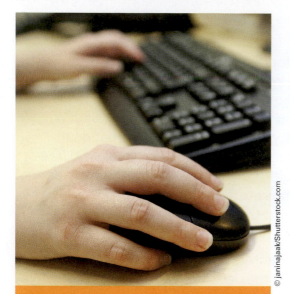

When people provide information to businesses, should the businesses be legally required to keep it confidential? Why or why not?

method be used, knowing that it will more likely result in the answers the client wants. Ethical researchers will not provide false data.

Other major ethical issues researchers face include privacy and confidentiality. A marketing research firm may have access to confidential information such as a client's marketing plan or credit history. If the researcher goes to work for a competitor, he or she has an ethical obligation to maintain the confidential information, even if it would help the new client.

Today, data is collected everywhere. Every click of a computer mouse on the Internet can be recorded, people's movements are captured on security cameras, and credit card transactions are monitored and analyzed. The rules related to the ethical treatment and management of information are still under development and will continue to be debated for many years.

INTERMISSION

Describe the role of ethics in marketing-information management.

ENCORE

Understand Marketing Concepts
Select the best answer for each question.

1. Syndicated research is
   a. conducted by client-side researchers
   b. conducted by independent companies
   c. conducted for one specific client
   d. none of the above

2. Ethical research involves
   a. gathering and reporting data that the paying client wants to hear
   b. gathering consumers' private and personal information for other uses
   c. reporting all information accurately and objectively
   d. all of the above

Think Critically
Answer the following questions as completely as possible.

3. How does a marketing-information system relate to marketing research? (LO 5.1-1)

4. Why are ethics so important to marketing-information management? (LO 5.1-2)

5.2 The Marketing Research Process

The Essential Question

What are the steps in marketing research, and how is data collected and managed?

Learning Objectives

LO 5.2-1 Summarize the steps in marketing research.

LO 5.2-2 Discuss technology used to collect and manage marketing-information data.

Key Terms

- market research
- sample
- price points
- analytics
- algorithm
- data interpretation
- frequency table
- focus groups

Many marketing research firms specialize in a specific industry. Screen Engine specializes in the entertainment industry. With big budget movies costing in excess of $400 million, producers want all of the information they can get. During the opening weeks of a movie, producers need to know what the audiences thought and what brought them to the movie. Companies such as Screen Engine specialize in providing that information. Screen Engine and Retrak jointly developed a product called PostTrak that provides data about a film as it moves from its release in movie theaters to its release in various forms of media that can be viewed at home and on mobile devices. PostTrak polls audiences as they exit a movie theater and asks them to participate in electronic surveys. PostTrak helps predict future ticket sales, DVD sales and rentals, and video on-demand profits. Data can be provided in categories based on gender, ethnicity, age, and overall reaction to the movie.

Cooperative Learning With a partner, discuss how data can be used to improve the revenue earned by a future movie. Select four ideas to share with the class.

LO 5.2-1 MARKETING INFORMATION THROUGH RESEARCH

Research conducted by Nielsen has shown that the quality of a TV advertisement is directly connected with how memorable the ad is to viewers. An ad aired during a popular TV show can boost the ad's effectiveness. People more often respond to, or act on, ads that are more memorable. The data for this study was collected over a three-year period using 70,696 ads that were shown on English- and Spanish-language shows.[5] A network known for its popular programming may use this research to show companies why they should advertise on the network or during a specific program.

When information that is specifically focused on a single target market is gathered, it is referred to as **market research**, rather than the broader topic—*marketing research*. Marketing research may involve market research, but it is a process that can be applied to a number of marketing problems.

The Steps

Marketing research is a problem-solving tool that helps focus decision making. The process, which must be ongoing, repeated frequently, and revised often, involves seven steps.

1. Discover and define the problem
2. Analyze current conditions
3. Develop the process for data collection
4. Collect the data
5. Analyze and report the data
6. Determine a solution to the problem
7. Implement and evaluate the results

1. Discover and Define the Problem

Albert Einstein is quoted as saying, "The formulation of the problem is often more essential than its solution." The goal of marketing research is to solve the problem. Once the problem has been identified, it can be translated into a set of research objectives. Researchers need to interview the decision makers at a business to identify and clarify the problem and its symptoms.

In *Exploring Marketing Research*, Zikmund and Babin state, "All problems have symptoms just as human disease is diagnosed through symptoms."[6]

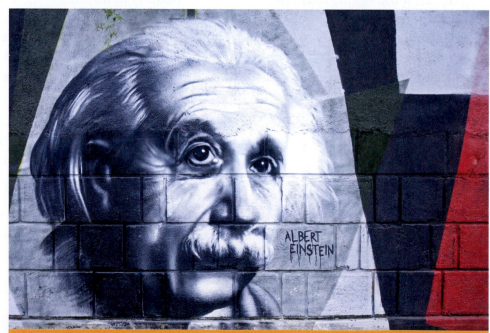

As Albert Einstein pointed out, the formulation of the problem is essential to its solution. Why is this true in marketing research?

© Bokic Bojan/Shutterstock.com

By observing the symptoms, researchers can design the research to effectively address the problem that is causing the symptoms. For example, a drop in a business's projected sales may be a symptom. Talking with the decision makers about the drop in sales will help shed more light on the problem that is causing the drop in sales.

2. Analyze Current Conditions

Analysis might include examining sales volume and customer data to understand current business conditions. If sales of merchandise related to team uniforms and logos have slowed while season ticket sales have remained high, more information is needed about the reasons for low sales. Determining what has changed may provide that information. Current conditions can be uncovered by reviewing sales reports. It is helpful to know how the sales data is collected. In addition, information about recent changes in the quality, price, or selection of merchandise is also valuable.

3. Develop the Process for Data Collection

There are a number of ways to conduct marketing research, including observing the test market and conducting a survey. When trying to decide whether to switch team uniforms, the marketers could have the team wear each of the uniforms for one-half of a game and observe the fans' reactions. Another method would be to develop a brief survey and ask fans to respond on their smartphones.

When a sports team needs to make a decision, such as how to update team uniforms, it makes good sense to ask the fans for their opinions. The most effective way to gather information about current and potential customers is through personal interviews. For example, fans can be shown samples of the new uniforms or merchandise and provide their feedback. However, this is a very expensive and slow process. The Internet can be a more efficient way to conduct a survey. Marketers can reach out to more fans and show them photographs of players wearing the new selection of uniforms. No matter how the survey is conducted, questions must be carefully worded to assure that the answers will be valid and will provide the needed information.

4. Collect the Data

Using technology to contact season ticket holders to obtain their opinions about the uniforms could be an effective method of collecting data. Because it is often impossible to contact every member of the potential market, a **sample**, or a small number of people representative of the large group, is contacted during the data-collection phase. Ideally, the questions asked will be carefully worded to clearly define the problem. They should be easy for the respondent to answer in a short time and formatted so that responses can be electronically compiled as they are submitted.

5. Analyze and Report the Data

After the responses are electronically gathered, researchers will look for patterns in the data and draw conclusions based on those patterns. For example, the data could reveal that 75 percent of respondents chose uniform number two over uniform number one. Most research is more complex and may involve thousands of bits of information. Tracking sales of team-related merchandise can involve more than just determining how many T-shirts are sold. Sales data

The arrival of Twitter had a dramatic impact on the marketing research industry. Social-data firms now specialize in the collection of information from the constant stream of tweets. Venture capital has been used to start hundreds of companies that are paid to spot trends using social media that would take months for researchers to identify on their own.

may be analyzed at the end of the season or after each game. Important data can include which styles, sizes, and colors sold best and at which **price points**—the range of prices charged for a category of merchandise. For example, the highest-quality jerseys may sell for $250 while those of lesser quality may sell for $20, with a variety of other choices in between. Tracking which price points sell best will provide insight into what customers want and how much they are willing to spend to get it. Another factor to consider is the effect on sales when the team is winning or losing. All of this data can be used to determine what types of merchandise to offer in the future.

Sorting thousands of bits of data and making sense of them can be tedious and time-consuming. Spreadsheet and database programs allow marketers to sort data and place it into graphic representations that busy executives can quickly analyze. For example, a dashboard format, as shown at the left, can be used to present the data around gauges and dials resembling those found on automobiles. The definition of *dashboards* has broadened over time to include most charts and graphs that visually represent data. The intent is to provide the report in a reader-friendly format.

Customer Satisfaction Survey

82%

© iStockphoto.com/hh5800

A chart, such as the one shown below, is a common way to represent data graphically. The graphs and charts can be updated automatically as new data is collected. With the capabilities of today's software, many different formats for displaying data are available. The chosen report format must be meaningful to the client who needs the data to solve the identified problem.

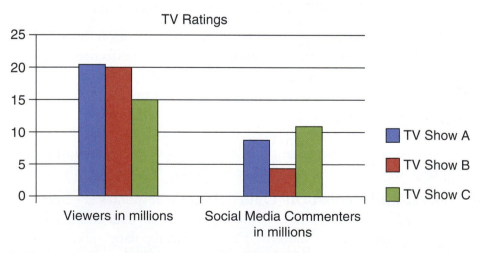

TV Ratings

TV Show A
TV Show B
TV Show C

Viewers in millions

Social Media Commenters in millions

6. Determine a Solution to the Problem
Based on the conclusions from the data, recommendations will be made to change the current conditions, such as the style of uniforms, the price of the merchandise, or the distribution channels used for merchandise sales.

MATH IN MARKETING

The growth rate of digital delivery of movies is expected to rival the North American motion picture theater box office, which is not increasing. Moviemakers are very interested in receiving information from the digital providers about what viewers are watching and when. However, the information is being closely guarded by the digital service providers. It is widely assumed that digital distributors know much more about their customers than film studios can determine from box office analysis, focus groups, exit polls, and social media. Making digital data more readily available is expected to be a high priority in financial negotiations in the future. Revenue from digital delivery of films and television shows has been increasing by almost 25 percent every six months.

Do the Math

Assume that the revenue from digitally delivered films for the first six months of this year is $3.2 billion. Also assume that the rate of increase in revenue from digitally delivered films is 25 percent every six months for last year, this year, and the upcoming year. Calculate the estimated total yearly revenue for each of the three years. Use spreadsheet software to create a line graph (or draw a line graph by hand) that shows the estimated total yearly revenue over the three-year period: last year, this year, and next year.

7. Implement and Evaluate the Results   Finally, the company must implement the changes and determine whether they result in an effective solution to the problem. If the problem continues, marketers may need to revisit some steps in the marketing research process.

 INTERMISSION

List the steps of marketing research.

LO 5.2-2   COLLECTING AND MANAGING DATA

Marketing- Information Management   Marketing research firms are continually developing ways to collect data to learn how people consume media. Nielsen gathers data about TV ratings, Google does Web traffic analysis, and Gallup conducts public opinion polls. Collecting information, compiling it, and recognizing the patterns that emerge are all part of managing data.

Research Sophistication

In some businesses, gut feelings and intuition are used in decision making. In others, scientifically based research is valued and actively used as a decision-making tool. Most companies fall somewhere between these extremes. Marketing research can never completely remove uncertainty about the success or failure of a new product or service, but decisions based on sound information can greatly improve the odds of success.

Marketing researchers use **analytics**—the process of using computer programming and incorporating statistics to organize data into meaningful patterns. The data is then presented in reports. When preparing the reports, the computer software uses an **algorithm**, which is a detailed set of instructions on how to sort data. If 500 people participate in an electronic survey to give their opinion on the ending of a movie, the software can organize the results and display the data in charts or graphs. Imagine the time it would take to read each individual response from the 500 participants as compared to the time needed to view the chart or graph.

Revealing patterns and measuring data are part of **data interpretation**, or finding meaning in the data. Based on how the data is visually displayed, certain patterns can be revealed or hidden. For example, the number of people attending a sporting event each week can be organized into a graph or displayed in a **frequency table**, which shows how often each numerical value, response, item, or range of numbers in a set of data occurs. The frequency table below contains attendance data for a baseball game. The number of times the attendance falls within various ranges is tracked. When this data is viewed in conjunction with other factors, such as the day the game is held or special promotions are offered, marketers can draw conclusions and modify marketing plans as needed.

Baseball Game Attendance		
Date of Game	**Special Promotion**	**Attendance**
May 4 (Monday)	None	12,555
May 10 (Sunday)	Free Bobbleheads	15,778
May 16 (Saturday)	None	16,334
May 20 (Wednesday)	Free T-shirts	14,998
May 29 (Friday)	After-game concert	15,233

Attendance Range	**Frequency**
12,001 to 13,000	1
13,001 to 14,000	0
14,001 to 15,000	1
15,001 or more	3

Making Media Work for Marketers

Marketers often track the number of people who have seen an advertisement. To collect this kind of data, a market researcher may use focus groups. **Focus groups** consist of a panel of people who answer market research questions related to their observations or opinions about a product or service. When Google wanted to know more about how people use the Internet, it formed a panel called Screenwise Trends. The panel members were provided gift cards for allowing Google to monitor their Internet use. Focus groups sometimes meet in person or stay in contact through the use of media, such as smartphones.

When the National Broadcast Company Universal (NBCU) outbid Fox and ESPN for the television rights to the Olympic Games through 2020, it paid over $4.3 billion. By making that kind of financial commitment, NBCU needed the support of advertisers. To convince advertisers to spend large sums of money, NBCU needed to collect and share information about who would watch the Olympics and how they would watch it. Advertisers will be able to profit from their support of the Olympics only if they have an understanding of consumer behavior and the best way to reach consumers. The Olympics lasts about 18 days and can capture massive audiences while being broadcast internationally on multiple platforms, including TV, cable, satellite, mobile devices, and online media. Advertisers want to reach consumers across all of these platforms. NBCU plans to provide live coverage on every platform currently in use or still to be invented.

© Monkey Business Images/Shutterstock.com

Why are focus groups a good way to conduct market research?

INTERMISSION

Why are charts and graphs used to display data?

ENCORE

Understand Marketing Concepts
Select the best answer for each question.

1. An algorithm
   a. is confusing data
   b. is used to determine cause-and-effect relationships
   c. is a detailed set of instructions for sorting data
   d. is a type of response

2. Price points are
   a. the highest price
   b. a range of prices
   c. the lowest price
   d. the sale price

Think Critically
Answer the following questions as completely as possible.

3. Write a brief example of the steps of marketing research a sports team might conduct. (LO 5.2-1)

4. How has the collection of marketing information changed with the use of technology? (LO 5.2-2)

5.3 Turning Information into Action

The Essential Question

What factors should be considered when interpreting marketing information and making decisions based on data?

Learning Objectives

LO 5.3-1   Describe how to interpret marketing information.

LO 5.3-2   Discuss the concept of data-driven decisions.

Key Terms

- data mining
- big data
- convergence analytics

- customer's lifetime value
- data-driven decisions
- cohort

- shopping cart abandoners
- cart-reminder email

OPENING ACT

Jack Welch, who was the CEO of General Electric (GE) for more than 20 years, is credited with growing GE by more than 4,000 percent and is thought of as a very knowledgeable businessperson. One of his famous quotes is "An organization's ability to learn, and translate that learning into action rapidly, is the ultimate competitive advantage."[7] Businesses learn from listening to customers, creating plans based on what customers are saying, and then acting on the plans.

Cooperative Learning   Discuss with a partner what Jack Welch meant by the above quote. Share your ideas with another pair of students.

LO 5.3-1   WHAT IT MEANS

In the past, when trying to determine which TV programs potential viewers would watch, advertisers sometimes relied on what had succeeded previously. Today, they rely heavily on data to make decisions. Data from companies such as Nielsen can provide details about who is watching a TV show and how many people are watching it, as well as how many are tweeting about it. The two points of data (TV viewers and Twitter users) are not necessarily the same, because Twitter's users are more likely to be young, urban dwellers than TV viewers are as a whole.

Using technology to "dig up" data is called **data mining**. Digging up data about the age, gender, income level, geographic location, and email address of all one million people who have viewed a TV show can be worthless unless the marketers understand the meaning of the data and how to act on it. To interpret data, marketers must have the knowledge to see patterns and understand what those patterns mean. Then marketers will make decisions based on their interpretations of the data.

The Buzz about Big Data

Big data is a term used to describe the extraordinary amount of data that is being collected and stored for marketing purposes. Sports and entertainment businesses have vast amounts of information available to them, including information collected from credit card and communication companies, smartphone GPS devices, social media sites, clicks made on websites, and other customer contacts.

Having access to so many sources of data can become confusing, but new analytical tools can help simplify the information. **Convergence analytics** is the process of organizing data from multiple sources into usable information. Complex data is turned into a dashboard-like report to make it easier for marketers to interpret the data. Convergence analytics makes it easy to track a customer's first contact with a business and predict the **customer's lifetime value** (CLV), which is a calculation of the estimated profit the business will earn from the customer. CLV predictions help businesses focus on their most valuable customers. If Super Bowl commercials can reach those customers who buy a product and who are predicted to have a high CLV, then the price of the Super Bowl commercial is worth it. A company can use low and high CLV predictions to make changes to its marketing plans to ensure it is focusing its efforts in the right direction.

© Micimakin/Shutterstock.com

What kind of data can be collected when consumers use credit cards?

INTERMISSION

How can data from many sources be simplified for use in decision making?

LO 5.3-2   APPLYING THE INFORMATION

Marketing-Information Management

Because the convergence analytics process draws information from many sources, it provides insights into consumers' actions. When a once popular TV show, such as *American Idol*, loses viewers, the TV network or cable company must determine why viewers have stopped watching. The TV executives can speculate, but what they need is factual data. They need to know whether the former viewers are watching something on another channel, viewing a show online or on a digital video recorder (DVR), or enjoying other activities. By accessing data from multiple sources, the decision makers will begin to see patterns that show who is not watching and why.

When popular shows such as *The Big Bang Theory* begin showing reruns during the regular season, people turn to other shows. According to Jay Sures of United Talent Agency, his company's research found that "the disruption of the ordered pattern of episodes is a big issue."[8] Because viewers don't know when another new episode of a TV show is scheduled, they may not return. In the TV industry, advertising revenue is based on viewers, and lost viewers means lost revenue. Showing reruns may not be the only reason for a decline in ratings. The show's decision makers need a wide array of information to improve the situation. **Data-driven decisions** are based on data and analysis rather than experience and intuition. However, data must be balanced with common sense and ethics.

Finding Patterns

A **cohort** consists of a group of people who share certain characteristics. The characteristics of the people in a cohort may include income or spending levels, age, ethnicity, geographic location, credit rating, or any combination of these. Data shows that a cohort generally behaves in a specific way. By finding patterns in a cohort's behavior, marketers can create more effective marketing plans. For example, young people between the ages of 13 and 19 may watch certain TV shows. Based on this data, certain companies may want to advertise during these shows.

Deeper Data Analysis

Once information is presented in reports with graphs and charts, points of interest to the reader will start to appear. Data on movie ticket sales outside of the United States may show that there is more growth in movie attendance in China than in the United States. A movie marketer would

TAKE A BOW *Charlie Colon*

Charlie Colon's dynamic career in marketing research began during a summer internship at Gallup, a worldwide research firm that provides information, analytics, and advice to private and public sector organizations. Colon is currently the Global Channel Manager for the Employee Engagement Suite for Gallup.

Gallup's primary customers have been businesses with more than 5,000 employees. Under Colon's leadership, Gallup launched a new product for small businesses that allows online access and use of Gallup's signature product called Q12®. Q12 is a survey that measures employee engagement based on the employee's responses to 12 workplace elements. Businesses that can increase an employee's motivation and enthusiasm are more likely to succeed and grow. Colon's work at Gallup helps companies turn the data obtained through the Q12 surveys into key performance action. As a result, businesses benefit through increased levels of employee productivity.

Think Critically

What do you think is the connection between employee engagement and a customer's perception of a business? Why do you think companies would want to use programs such as Q12?

want to dig deeper to determine which movies had the highest attendance in China. Then that data can be broken down further based on other demographics, such as the ages of those attending the movies. After doing so, additional charts and graphs can be created to provide more insight into the Chinese market. Because the vast majority of growth in media consumption is expected to take place outside of the United States, marketers need data to determine what these customers will pay to view.

Potential Buyers

One of the data measurements used to determine the effectiveness of online stores is the number of **shopping cart abandoners**—people who start to make an online purchase, but leave the website without completing it. Website marketers for a sports store may consider a high number of shopping cart abandoners as lost sales, but in fact, they could present opportunities. A closer look at the data collected about shopping cart abandoners generally reveals that they have a high potential to become buyers if they are sent a **cart-reminder email**—an email reminding a customer of his or her incomplete purchase left in an online shopping cart.

INTERMISSION

How do marketers use data to make decisions?

ENCORE

Understand Marketing Concepts

Select the best answer for each question.

1. Data mining is
   a. compiling a report
   b. digging up data
   c. defining a problem
   d. none of the above

2. A customer's lifetime value is
   a. how often the customer makes a purchase
   b. the frequency of visits to a company's website
   c. the predicted profit earned from the customer
   d. both a and b

Think Critically

Answer the following questions as completely as possible.

3. What data would be needed to determine how and where to advertise products developed primarily for high school students? (LO 5.3-1)

4. Which is more accurate—measuring a distance or guessing the distance? How does this relate to making data-driven decisions? (LO 5.3-2)

CHAPTER ASSESSMENT

Review Marketing Terms

Match the terms listed with the definitions.

1. A set of procedures and methods used to collect, analyze, distribute, and store information
2. A small number representative of a large group
3. In-house staff researchers who work with external research agencies
4. The range of prices charged for a category of merchandise
5. Gathering information specifically focused on a single target market
6. A process to solve marketing problems using a scientific problem-solving system
7. An estimate or an educated guess
8. Statistics collected through valid research
9. The process of applying computer programming and statistics to data
10. Research conducted by an independent company offered for sale to businesses in an industry
11. A detailed set of computer software instructions on how to sort data
12. Finding meaning in data
13. Showing how often each value in a set of data occurs
14. A panel of people who answer market research questions
15. An extraordinary amount of data
16. The process of organizing data from multiple sources
17. A calculation of the estimated profit earned from a customer
18. Decisions based on data and analysis
19. People who start to make an online purchase but don't complete it
20. A reminder of an incomplete online purchase
21. Using technology to "dig up" data
22. A group of people who share certain characteristics

a. algorithm
b. analytics
c. big data
d. cart-reminder email
e. client-side researchers
f. cohort
g. convergence analytics
h. customer's lifetime value
i. data interpretation
j. data mining
k. data-driven decisions
l. focus groups
m. frequency table
n. hard data
o. market research
p. marketing research
q. marketing-information system
r. price points
s. sample
t. shopping cart abandoners
u. soft data
v. syndicated research

Review Marketing Concepts

Select the best answer for each of the following questions.

23. When changes in a product are being considered, a business might
    a. contact a sample of customers
    b. contact people who are current customers
    c. summarize suggestions from customers
    d. all of the above

24. The first step in marketing research involves
   a. defining the problem
   b. analyzing current conditions
   c. collecting data
   d. none of the above
25. The difference between marketing research and market research includes
   a. marketing research is focused on a very specific target market
   b. marketing research involves a much broader scope
   c. market research can be applied to a number of marketing problems
   d. all of the above
26. An ethical conflict in marketing research could involve
   a. how a computer is used to record visits to websites
   b. having to choose between the research client and the research re-
      spondents' privacy
   c. giving clients the answers they want
   d. all of the above

Think Critically

27. Why would a sports team that has client-side researchers on staff need or want to hire an external firm to conduct research? (LO 5.1-1)
28. Why do companies need to gather and manage marketing information? Describe some of the ways the information might be used. (LO 5.1-1)
29. If you could create a student-operated marketing research firm for your school, what steps would you take to produce research that would solve an important problem at your school? (LO 5.2-1)
30. If you were an event manager, how would you determine what to charge for tickets to an event? What kinds of information would you need to know about the people who might attend the event? (LO 5.3-1)
31. Professional sports teams are concerned about the decline in youth attendance at games. Develop a five-question survey for youth that would help a sports team design marketing strategies aimed at increasing youth attendance at games. (LO 5.2-2)
32. When businesses collect data about your purchases, how can that affect you? Provide examples of how that data can have positive and negative effects on you. (LO 5.2-2)
33. What are the ethical issues and privacy concerns when collecting data? What boundaries do you believe should be set? (LO 5.1-2)
34. Advertising tobacco products on television is prohibited. Given this, why would market researchers want to collect data about the televised sports that smokers watch? (LO 5.3-2)
35. What might it mean if the last three movies made by the same producer were not profitable? What data would you need to substantiate your interpretation? How would you display that information? (LO 5.3-1)

Make Academic Connections

36. Language Arts Review the definition of *market research* on p. 132. Assume you are a concert promoter. Write a clearly defined problem you are having for which you think research can help solve. (LO 5.2-1)

37. Ethics Your sports team is considering building a new stadium, and several locations are under consideration. You prefer a location on the edge of the city that is less expensive and has better parking. Other staff members prefer a location with nearby public transportation, restaurants, and other attractions. You decide to hire a firm to conduct research. Research Firm A has a spotless reputation and has never had a customer question the validity of its work. It has been in business for about 10 years, and most of the employees have worked there from 3 to 10 years. The cost of its research is $500,000. Research Firm B also has a good reputation and has been in business about 12 years. Its researchers meet with you privately and indicate they are in agreement with you and their research can provide the answer you want. Write a paragraph about which firm you will hire and why. (LO 5.1-2)

38. Government Using the Internet, conduct research to learn how the European Union (EU) is trying to protect the personal data that is collected from its citizens without their knowledge. Write a brief summary of actions taken by the EU. (LO 5.1-2)

39. Math You placed different ads on two search engine sites. When certain key words are used at each site, your ad comes up on the search-results page. Both ads link visitors to your website. Search engine site A reported that in the past month, your ad was displayed 56,690 times, 8,503 visitors clicked on your ad, and 103 made a purchase. Search engine site B reported that your ad was displayed 66,500 times, 8,910 visitors clicked on your ad, and 50 made a purchase. Based on this data, which ad was the most effective? How can you use this data to create future Internet ads? (LO 5.3-1)

40. Geography Find a map of New York City (NYC) online or in your school library. There are five boroughs that make up NYC. NYC has two baseball teams and two stadiums. Name the teams and the stadiums. Determine the location of each of the stadiums. Does a person's residency make a difference in which of the two baseball teams he or she supports? How does each team know which residents are their fans? (LO 5.3-1)

41. History Select a major league sports team and use the Internet to learn about its fans. How have their demographics changed in the past 25 years? How are sales of team merchandise affected by the fan's demographics? (LO 5.3-2)

42. Language Arts Movie theaters often charge more for popcorn and a drink than they charge for a movie ticket. Is there a point at which moviegoers will not buy refreshments because of the price? How can theaters know the price point at which demand is the highest? Write a paragraph describing how the price point may be determined. (LO 5.2-1)

EXTRA INNINGS PROJECT

The National Basketball Association (NBA) was formed in 1946 with 11 teams. Today, there are 30 NBA teams (29 in the United States and one in Canada) that are divided into the Eastern Conference and the Western Conference. Most of the teams are located in the eastern half of the country, reflecting the population distribution of the United States.

New York City is made up of five boroughs: Brooklyn, Bronx, Manhattan, Queens, and Staten Island. Two of the boroughs are home to NBA teams: the Brooklyn Nets and the New York Knicks, who play in Manhattan. The Nets had previously played in New Jersey and were considered a second-tier franchise, but the move to Brooklyn has provided new opportunities. When both teams are struggling to earn wins, they also fight for fans and battle to win the hearts of New Yorkers. Both teams want to increase their attendance records.

You have been hired by one of these two teams to research how to increase attendance at home games by 15 percent a year.

Work with a group and complete the following activities.

1. Choose one of the teams. Write a description of the problem.
2. Use ESPN, *Sports Illustrated*, the NBA website, the team's website, or some other sports-related media to research the team you have chosen. Write a description of the situation, including the current attendance. Estimate the time needed to research the goal.
3. Use software to make a bar graph, or draw one by hand, showing the attendance and number of season ticketholders for the past three years.
4. Determine what additional data you need and how you will collect the data, analyze it, and report it. Write at least three paragraphs to describe the data collection, analysis, and reporting process.
5. Write a description to explain how you will know you have solved the problem (met the research objective).

CRUNCHING THE NUMBERS

The movie industry is a complex business. Thousands of people are competing to produce films that people will pay to see at a theater, on a mobile device, or at home. The total worldwide box office number for a film is readily available after the film has been distributed. The box office information is often published in the media. But before a movie can ever be made and hit the big screen, filmmakers and investors need information to determine if a movie will be profitable. Marketing information can help determine which key players (cast and crew members) will attract the largest audience.

Finding the Value

The film industry data-crunching firm Nash Information Services, LLC (NIS), provides marketing information and research to potential investors and entertainment industry companies. NIS uses many different metrics to provide information, depending on what data is needed.

NIS devised a complex process to determine the value that a cast or crew member might bring to a particular movie. When two movie industry cast or crew members have worked together on a film, NIS assigns an economic value to this relationship. NIS does not reveal the exact method of assigning the value between two people, but it does provide an example. It starts by ranking the people based on their billing, or the order in which their names appear in the film credits. For example, the lead actor might be assigned a value of 1, the supporting actress a value of 2, and the director a value of 3. To determine the relationship value between the lead actor and director, a formula is applied to arrive at a score: $1/(1+3)$, or $1/4$. The lead actor and actress would be assigned a score of $1/(1+2)$, or $1/3$. These values are combined for all of the films in which the two people have worked together, no matter what role or job they had in that movie. The relationship value for all of their joint films is then multiplied by the amount the film made to provide a "worldwide box office relationship value" for the two people, which is displayed as part of the Hollywood Creative Graph.[9]

NIS also developed The Numbers Bankability Index, which estimates how much someone adds in value to the film industry each year based on analysis of the Hollywood Creative Graph. A monthly report of the Bankability Index is for sale and lists the 250 most valuable people in the film industry based on NIS metrics.

Think Critically

1. Who might want to buy the information contained in a report like the Bankability Index? Why?
2. How would this process affect actors and movie production crew members who are just entering the movie industry?
3. How could this type of marketing information be used in sports?

TRAVEL AND TOURISM TEAM DECISION MAKING EVENT

Branson, Missouri is noted for being a country music entertainment attraction for senior citizens. The city, located in central Missouri, attracts guests from all over the country. Many senior citizen groups from surrounding states take charter bus tours to see their favorite country music performers and enjoy gambling provided by local casinos. Outlet malls located near Branson are an additional attraction for tourists. Most tourists stay an average of two nights in the local hotels.

Fall foliage turns bright red and yellow in Branson during the months of September and October. The climate is nearly perfect during these two months with cool mornings and mild afternoons. The president of Branson Entertainment Incorporated believes that the beautiful foliage each year is an additional attraction for Branson tourists. The president has hired your advertising team to develop a marketing strategy that highlights the red and yellow leaves of fall in Branson during the months of September and October. All of the other reasons for visiting Branson should also be incorporated in your marketing plan. The president is counting on your creativity to incorporate red and yellow leaves in the advertising campaign. Your team must describe marketing strategies that target senior citizen groups. You should highlight the special services offered to this age group that will make the trip to Branson even more appealing.

Your team will meet the president of Branson Entertainment Incorporated in her office to explain your marketing strategy for attracting tourists during the beautiful fall season in Branson, Missouri. Your promotion/advertising plan must make a positive impact on senior citizens.

Performance Indicators Evaluated
- Explain the nature and scope of the product/service management function.
- Identify the impact of product life cycles on marketing decisions.
- Generate product ideas.
- Plan the product mix.
- Evaluate the customer experience.

Think Critically

1. Why is fall a better time than winter for senior citizens to travel?
2. Why should Branson hotels and restaurants consider offering senior citizen discounts?
3. What type of marketing research would you conduct to determine how to best meet the needs of senior citizens?
4. What type of family reunion packages could Branson advertise to increase the number of tourists? What other ways could Branson increase tourism?

www.deca.org

6

THE PRODUCT IS SPORTS AND ENTERTAINMENT

Jack Hollingsworth/Digital Vision/Getty Images

POINT YOUR BROWSER

ngl.cengage.com/sports4e

148

Winning Strategies

Fame and Fortune Used to Benefit Others

Ellen DeGeneres is a popular comedian who got her start in stand-up comedy clubs. She began touring nationally in the 1980s and won the title of "Funniest Person in America" in a competition sponsored by the cable network Showtime. She can now be seen hosting *The Ellen DeGeneres Show*.

© Helga Esteb/Shutterstock.com

Ellen is also well recognized for her charitable work. In recent years, many charities have benefited from Ellen's generosity of time, effort, and money. To help fund animal welfare charities, she hosted a 24-day charity auction on eBay with all proceeds going to the Humane Society. She also supports many other pet rescue and animal organizations through her charity work. In another effort to raise money, Ellen auctioned off clothing that she wore on her show and award shows.

Ellen also works with other celebrities to promote charities. She joined actor Ben Affleck to launch a "Small Change Campaign." The campaign encouraged people to collect loose change, which would then be donated to Second Harvest hunger charity (now called Feeding America). The goal of Feeding America is to distribute food and other grocery products to millions of people who go hungry each day, while raising the public awareness of domestic hunger.

As part of her TV show, Ellen works with sponsoring organizations regularly to reward deserving viewers with donations to help pay for needed items such as school supplies and uniforms, college education, and cars. Fans of Ellen's TV show can visit the show's website to view "Ellen's Organizations," a listing of charities and organizations that Ellen supports. You can also follow Ellen on Twitter to learn more about her charity work.[1]

Think Critically

1. Why do you think celebrities such as Ellen DeGeneres feel the need to support charitable causes?

2. If you were to contact Ellen about a cause you'd like her to support, what would it be and why?

6.1 The Product Mix

The Essential Question

What are the components of the product mix for a sports or entertainment event, and how can the product for that event be enhanced?

Learning Objectives

LO 6.1-1   Define product mix, product extension, and product enhancement.

LO 6.1-2   List and describe the components of the product mix.

Key Terms

- product mix
- product extensions
- product enhancements
- product line
- brand
- trademark
- licensed brand

OPENING ACT

While prize winnings at major golf tournaments continue to rise, the vast majority of money in the sport is still made off the course. In a recent year, the top 20 golfers made $400 million through endorsements, licensing fees, and appearances. Many golfers made more money off the course than on it.

In a recent year, Yani Tseng earned $3.5 million off the golf course and $1.5 million on the course. Sponsors for Yani include Acer, Audi Taiwan, and Titleist. Phil Mickelson earned $40 million off the course and $5.3 million on the course. Phil's sponsors include Barclays, Callaway, and KPMG. The biggest winner was Tiger Woods, who earned $9.1 million playing golf but earned $77 million in his ventures off the course. Tiger's sponsors include Nike and Rolex. Female golfers also did well. Ai Miyazato earned $4 million off the course and $1.4 million on the course, with Oakley and Bridgestone as sponsors. Golf equipment manufacturers know the importance of associating products with popular golfers.[2]

Cooperative Learning   Do you think there should be restrictions for golfers or other athletes who earn money from corporate sponsors? Why are companies willing to spend big money on athletic sponsorships? Discuss your answers with a partner.

LO 6.1-1   WHAT IS A PRODUCT MIX?

Every product is a complex blending of tangible and intangible parts. *Tangible* parts are physical features that can be seen and felt. On an athletic shoe, tangible parts include the rubber sole, the shoelaces, and the color of the shoe. *Intangible* parts are the nonphysical features associated with services. For example, the features offered by an Internet service provider are intangible. When making a new product, decisions must be made about its **product mix**, which includes the product's final form and its assorted features. The brand name, the various products offered under the brand, and the packaging are also part of the product mix.

Product Extensions

Product extensions are items offered in addition to the product to make it more attractive to the target market. Product extensions may be in the form of guarantees, warranties, instructional videos, and even additional related products. Automobiles that come with 100,000-mile warranties appeal to consumers. They like the idea of not having to worry about unexpected major expenses should repairs become necessary. Instructional videos that are easy to follow and 24-hour toll-free help lines are other product extensions that are attractive to consumers. When a customer buys a new baseball bat from a sporting goods store, the sales associate might also suggest related products such as batting gloves and a baseball cap. These types of product extensions can improve the use of the original product, helping the customer get more value from his or her purchase.

© iStockphoto.com/svetikd

What types of product extensions might be added to help sell a car?

Basic vs. Enhanced Product

A *basic product* is one that meets the needs of a target market. **Product enhancements** are features added to the basic product to satisfy additional needs and wants with a single purchase. An automobile is a basic product that consumers need as a mode of transportation. But some consumers want more than just a basic automobile. They may want enhancements such as dual comfort controls, leather seats, cruise control, a power convertible roof, a GPS navigation system, and a more powerful engine.

Athletic shoes are a basic product constructed for support and safety to avoid injuries while playing sports. Nike has created specialized running shoes with air-cushioned soles and lightweight fabric. The added features to its running shoes increase the comfort and performance of runners. Some target markets want athletic shoes that serve multiple purposes. Cross-trainer shoes are enhanced running shoes that are good for walking, hiking, running, biking, and other amateur sports. The cross-trainer shoes satisfy several needs with one purchase.

Another example of product enhancement can be seen in a football stadium or basketball arena. The basic seating at a football game may be the bleacher seats in the end zone without back supports. Product enhancements would include individual seats with back supports located on the 50-yard

Although the base price for a luxury car may be advertised as $38,000, this is unlikely the final price. Typically the car will sell for $42,000 to $46,000 due to the costs of enhanced features. For those customers who desire luxury, the extra costs may be worth it.

line or seats located in a climate-controlled suite. Fans who watch the games from suites can also enjoy personalized food service and other special comforts. All of these product enhancements help the stadium satisfy those fans who have additional wants and needs. For example, companies that want to entertain business clients may be the target market for stadium suites.

Consumers are now starting to see product enhancements at movie theaters. At newer theaters, families can go to a restaurant and see a movie all under one roof. Many theaters offer seat-side food and beverage service.

Product enhancements may be viewed as important by some but unnecessary by others. Although product enhancements add value to a product, they usually increase the price. However, in today's competitive market, it is important to give consumers options.

INTERMISSION

Provide three examples of a product enhancement.

LO 6.1-2 PRODUCT MIX COMPONENTS

Product/Service Management

In an attempt to satisfy customer needs, marketers must make many decisions about their product and product mix. Product mix includes the product line, packaging, and brand development.

Product Line

A **product line** is a group of similar products with slight variations to satisfy the different needs of consumers. The goal of the product line is to achieve the greatest amount of sales possible by satisfying the needs of a diverse target market. The addition of items to a product line increases the satisfaction of individual customers. However, adding items to the product line increases the cost of manufacturing, distribution, inventory control, and other marketing activities. Retailers who sell extended product lines need more display space.

Soft drinks are a perfect example of a product line. There are several choices to meet the needs of different consumer tastes and diets. The Coca-Cola Company offers Coca-Cola Classic; Diet Coke; Caffeine-Free Diet Coke; Coke Zero with no

Why would a company offer a line of products to its customers?

© ValeStock/Shutterstock.com

carbohydrates; and varieties of Coke with added flavorings, such as vanilla, lime, and cherry. A product line can also include a variety of product sizes. TV sets come in sizes ranging from 5-inch screens to 60-inch and larger screens.

Product lines for travel can range from short weekend getaways to vacations lasting a week or longer. Central themes for vacations may include skiing, snorkeling, golf, and other related activities. Popular tourist resorts offer a product line with a wide array of activities, lengths of stay, and prices.

Product lines can also involve variation in the quality of goods sold. Airlines, for example, offer first-class and economy flights with a variation in quality. First-class passengers receive extra leg space, food service, boarding preference, and other benefits not experienced by economy passengers. For this reason, the price for first-class airline tickets is much higher than the price for economy tickets.

Packaging

Packaging is important. Ease of use, safety, security, attractiveness, accessibility, and the environmental friendliness of the package influence sales. Today's consumers are environmentally conscious and often prefer packaging that is recyclable. The package must also be convenient for consumers to handle. For example, some manufacturers of snack foods and beverages package their products in individual serving sizes. This makes a convenient snack or drink at sporting events such as a child's soccer game or Little League baseball game.

© iStockphoto.com/jfmdesign

Why is packaging an important component of the product mix?

Brand

Brand is the name, symbol, logo, word, or design (or a combination of these elements) that identifies a product, service, or company. The brand represents the company's reputation for quality, reliability, and status in the marketplace. Target markets often associate brands with successful athletes and celebrities. For example, the company that makes Bounty paper towels has teamed up with Olympic stars to promote its product.

Trademarks and Licenses A **trademark** is the legal protection of words and symbols used by a company. A trademark makes it illegal for other companies to use a secured brand name. This extends to personal names as well. Colleges and college coaches are reaping additional financial benefits by trademarking their own slogans, names, or images on merchandise. The Ohio State University is making sure it benefits from

Social media has made it easier for coaches at top athletic schools to communicate with high prospect players. The National Collegiate Athletic Association (NCAA) has set restrictions on the frequency and modes of electronic communications coaches can have with recruits. The NCAA currently allows basketball coaches to send unlimited texts and other forms of electronic communications, but texting has been banned in football recruiting since 2007. Unlimited texting could be coming back to college football recruiting. According to a recent ESPN.com survey of more than 700 high school football recruits in the classes of 2014 and 2015, more than 91 percent of the athletes believed they should be able to text with college coaches.[3]

Write Now

Conduct online research and report on how social media is used to recruit high school athletes. How could aggressive recruitment strategies used by major colleges distract students from successfully graduating from high school? Would some colleges have an unfair advantage if the social media restrictions on college football recruiting were lifted? Write a one-page paper giving your opinion on these issues and others regarding the use of social media to recruit college athletes.

---

the popularity of its football coach by trademarking the phrase "Urban Meyer Knows." Coach Dabo Swiney at Clemson University has trademarked his name, and Kansas State University has a detailed licensing agreement to use the name and likeness of football Coach Bill Snyder. USC Coach Steve Sarkisian has negotiated the right to approve all uses of his name, voice, signature, or likenesses. College athletes, however, cannot profit from the use of their names or likenesses on merchandise, such as jerseys or game programs, due to NCAA rules. All student-athletes must sign forms authorizing the NCAA to use their name or picture to promote NCAA events.

A **licensed brand** is a well-known name and/or symbol established by one company and sold for use by another company to promote its products. Organizations such as The Walt Disney Company sell licenses to other companies that allow them to use character names and images on clothing and toys. Licensed products from popular children's movies are sold in department stores and fast-food restaurants. The organization that sells the license receives a percentage of the sales—usually 8 to 12 percent—of the merchandise bearing the licensed name or image. College and professional teams also license their names and mascot images for products.

Levels of Brand Recognition

There are generally five stages of brand recognition. These include nonrecognition, rejection, recognition, preference, and insistence. During the *nonrecognition stage*, consumers are unable to identify brands. Although a new brand of athletic gear may be nice, it may not sell well because consumers do not know or trust the brand. *Rejection* occurs when a customer will not purchase a product because of the brand. Consumers may reject sporting goods bearing brands known for poor quality or that have had recalls due to safety issues.

During the brand *recognition stage*, consumers know of the brand, but the brand has little influence on their purchases. Consumers view brands as valuable during the *preference stage*. They will purchase a preferred brand if it is readily available but may purchase another brand if it is not. *Insistence* occurs when consumers value a brand to the extent that they reject other brands even when the preferred brand is not readily available. They will go to great lengths to purchase the desired brand or will do without rather than buy a competing brand. Most consumers who drink cola insist on one brand over another—for example, Coca-Cola or Pepsi. Some athletes will wear only Nike shoes. Companies strive to reach the insistence level of brand recognition to develop consumer loyalty.

Many popular brand restaurants, gas stations, and hotels have highly recognizable logos. Individuals traveling on busy highways look for signs displaying these well-known logos. Travelers might drive a little farther knowing their favorite restaurant is located only a few exits away.

INTERMISSION

What are the components of the product mix?

ENCORE

Understand Marketing Concepts

Select the best answer for each question.

1. Which of the following is not a stage of brand recognition?
   a. preference
   b. introduction
   c. recognition
   d. rejection

2. Product extensions include
   a. warranties
   b. related products
   c. instructional videos
   d. all of the above

Think Critically

Answer the following questions as completely as possible.

3. Athletic shoes produced by Nike and Adidas are popular with runners. What product enhancements could these companies make to their running shoes to better satisfy runners and nonrunners? (LO 6.1-1)

4. List three brands that you like to purchase. Why are you loyal to these brands? (LO 6.1-2)

6.2 People Are the Product

The Essential Question

What is the bottom line for sporting events, and why are the costs so high?

Learning Objectives

LO 6.2-1   Define the bottom line for sports.

LO 6.2-2   Explain the high cost of sports and entertainment events.

Key Terms

- blue-chip athletes
- NCAA
- fringe benefits

OPENING ACT

Look through any sports magazine, shop at any athletic store, or turn on any sports television channel and you will see the immense power of advertising in the sports world. Whether you see a tennis star wearing a sports company's products and logos or a racecar covered with multiple company names, you will understand that advertising is the fuel on which professional sports run. Millions of advertising dollars are spent every day by companies that want people to buy their products and to use their services.

Cooperative Learning   Why are companies turning to the world of sports to help meet their promotional needs? How do companies decide which teams or individual athletes to sponsor? Work with a partner to create a list of ideas.

LO 6.2-1   THE BOTTOM LINE FOR SPORTS

Millions of dollars are spent on sports and entertainment events each year. Marketing strategies must attract the best blue-chip athletes for college and professional sports. **Blue-chip athletes** are high-prospect athletes who have exceptional athletic ability and who demonstrate good character and leadership qualities on and off the field.

The bottom line for sports is winning. The bottom line for business is profit. Winning teams generate profit for team owners, sports venues, and related businesses. Successful athletic teams depend on high-caliber athletes who can deliver top-notch performances.

Recruiting athletes is the most important element for the future success of college and professional teams. The recruiting process for college athletics is highly competitive. Coaches at major universities host football and basketball camps to attract the best high school junior and senior athletes. Athletes who attend these camps and make a positive impression on coaches have the inside track to athletic scholarship offers from universities.

NCAA Regulations

The National Collegiate Athletic Association **(NCAA)** is a voluntary organization through which the nation's colleges and universities govern their athletics programs. It regulates the college recruitment process and comprises more than 1,250 institutions, conferences, organizations, and individuals committed to the best interests, education, and athletics participation of student-athletes. The NCAA has four major goals: (1) to advance academics, (2) to provide opportunities, (3) to develop life skills, and (4) to enhance communities.

High school athletes can be offered athletic scholarships from major universities, but currently, they cannot be offered any additional financial rewards or other benefits to attend a university. Alumni and coaches who become overzealous in the recruitment process jeopardize the integrity of their university. Athletic teams are penalized and even placed on probation for recruitment violations. Recruitment violations may involve paying bribes to recruits, giving incentives to the families of recruits, and altering grade transcripts to make athletes eligible to play. NCAA punishments for recruitment violations can include the following:

- Limiting the number of scholarships offered
- Prohibiting post-season play
- Suspending players
- Forfeiting games
- Shutting down the school's athletic programs

Compensation for Athletes?

Since its inception, the NCAA has operated under the rule that student-athletes are amateurs and should not be paid for performing in their sports. The NCAA has punished teams that have illegally paid players and has suspended the players. At other times, it has taken away wins from the programs that have violated the rules.

Photodisc/Getty Images

Why do some people think that an athlete who signs with a college team should get paid to play?

Collegiate athletics has not always been a multimillion-dollar industry. Even today, most college sports programs lose money. NCAA Division I football and basketball, however, generate huge revenues. According to a *USA TODAY* report, the top 25 most prosperous college athletic programs had revenue ranging from $82 million to $164 million a year.[4]

Currently, athletes receive scholarships and grants for their college education but do not get paid to play. Between classes, practices, traveling, and games, they do not have enough time to work part-time jobs to earn additional income. Some of the best college athletes are tempted to sign multimillion-dollar contracts with professional sports organizations before graduating from college, making them ineligible to play college sports. In some states, proposals to pay college athletes have been brought before the state legislature.

A recent study by the Associated Press indicates that universities in six major athletic conferences spend $100,000 per scholarship athlete each year.[5] This amount is 6 to 12 times the amount spent on students who are not athletes. The National College Players Association and the Department of Sports Management at the University of Drexel study shows that the average football or basketball player who has an all-expenses-paid scholarship has $3,000–$3,222 in expenses for necessities not covered by the scholarship. In August 2014, the NCAA voted to allow colleges in the top five conferences (ACC, Big Ten, Big 12, Pac-12, and SEC) to pay players' cost-of-attendance (living) expenses. Some believe this extra perk is reasonable when you consider that the market value or revenue generated by each basketball and football player is calculated to be worth $120,000.[6]

INTERMISSION

Why don't college athletes get paid for playing sports?

LO 6.2-2 THE COST OF SUCCESS

Major universities count on knowledgeable, skilled coaches to lead their teams to success. They also expect top-notch players to score victories for their school and attract fans and sponsors. Event managers book popular entertainers to attract visitors to an event. The cost of attracting and keeping top performers in sports and entertainment can be very high.

Attracting and Keeping Coaches

Elite college football coaches have difficult, stressful jobs and are highly compensated for their work. The University of Alabama head coach Nick Saban will likely be remembered as one of the highest-paid NCAA football coaches in the country, with a contract that guaranteed over $5 million a year before additional bonuses. When Alabama finished first in the Associated Press Top 25 poll in 2013, Saban was paid a $200,000 bonus plus $110,000 for making the BCS title game. Ohio State finished the 2012 season undefeated but was barred from participating in bowl games for breaking NCAA rules during the previous season. This did not stop Ohio State's coach, Urban Meyer, from receiving a $150,000 bonus for finishing third in the Associated Press Top 25.[8] **Fringe benefits** are incentives received in addition to a base salary. They may include bonuses for special accomplishments, medical insurance, a company car, and paid travel. In addition, top coaches may receive opportunities for endorsements, TV and radio shows, and other income-producing ventures.

Attracting and Keeping Star Athletes

Coaches are responsible for recruiting top athletes. Recruiting involves knowledge of personal selling, financing, and marketing-information management. Coaching staffs must have charismatic recruiters who can convince young athletes, and their parents, to commit to a university that may be located far from home. Honesty and integrity are two characteristics necessary to be a successful recruiter. College recruiters who emphasize the importance of the athlete's education gain the attention and support of parents. Athletes and their families like those coaches who take a personal interest in the well-being of their recruits. The recruitment process itself is expensive, and signing blue-chip athletes is hard work. Recruiters fly all over the country to market their universities to top prospects. They must maintain careful records on all of the prospective athletes and determine specific needs that must be met to close the deal.

The National Football League (NFL) requires players to wait three years after graduating from high school before they can apply to professional drafts. The National Basketball Association (NBA) requires players to be at least 19 years old and one year out of high school before going professional. Some college athletic conference leaders, however, are now saying that it does not make sense to force teens who don't want an education to go to college.

Jim Delany, Commissioner of the Big Ten Conference, does not believe that college athletics should be "minor league" testing grounds for professional sports. Professional teams are now aggressively recruiting a handful

In the United States, 45 million children ages 6 through 16 participate in youth sports. Of those participants, 20 million are involved in organized out-of-school sports and 25 million are involved in competitive school sports. On average, parents spend $671 per child for sports participation. Twenty percent spend over $1,000 per child for sports.[7]

of the top high school athletes. LeBron James was selected directly out of high school at the age of 18 by the Cleveland Cavaliers as part of the first overall pick in the 2003 NBA Draft. The current eligibility rules were put in place in 2005. NBA teams and major sporting goods companies are anxious to offer million-dollar contracts to young athletes. So when it comes to getting the best athletes, college coaches realize that they are competing not only against college rivals but also against professional teams. Recruiting top athletes is closely related to the economic concept of supply and demand. The supply of top-performing athletes is limited while the demand for those athletes is very high.

The likelihood of high school athletes making it to the college or professional level of play, however, is very small. Even though 58 percent of high school football and basketball players believe that they will get a college scholarship, 98 out of 100 high school athletes will never play collegiate sports of any kind. Less than one out of every 100 high school athletes receives a scholarship of any kind to a Division I school. Only 1 in 16,000 high school athletes attains a professional career in sports.[9] For the 15,999 high school athletes who will never play pro sports, careers in related fields such as sports marketing are an option.

Paying the Price for Top Entertainers

Concerts, rodeos, state and county fairs, and seasonal celebrations often feature top entertainers as a way to increase attendance at the events. Popular performers may charge organizations $50,000 to $100,000 for one performance. Event planners must determine whether the audience will be large

How does the cost of entertainers affect the bottom line for an event?

enough to cover the costs of the event. In small venues, it may be necessary to charge $50 to $150 per ticket in order to make a profit. Concerts held in large stadiums allow costs to be spread among a greater number of attendees, and thus ticket prices may be lower. Seats located near the stage are an option for those willing to pay higher ticket prices.

Like musical entertainers, celebrities starring in highly rated sitcoms demand large salaries. The sponsors of the shows pay the television networks to air advertisements, hoping to reach the large number of fans that tune in to see their favorite shows. The stars of the popular sitcom *The Big Bang Theory* were each earning $350,000 per episode when, going into the eighth season, they began negotiations for $500,000 an episode. These negotiations were similar to the demands of the actors starring in the popular 1990s sitcom *Friends*. The cast members wanted (and received) $1 million per episode.

Marketing Women's Sports

Until recently, sports marketing had significantly neglected the women's sports industry. While many fans would tune in twice a year to watch events such as women's figure skating and women's gymnastics, these competitions were mostly amateur, with limited marketing appeal.

Social media is used by many celebrities for self-promotion. Celebrities enhance their presence by providing daily tweets, status updates, and posted photos. They keep fans up to date by sharing activities, plans, and information about upcoming performances. Fans access information in different ways. For example, some may use Instagram while others use Twitter. Thus, market-savvy celebrities use multiple platforms to reach all of their fans.

Lady Gaga knows how to use social media effectively. She tweets hints, teasers, and riddles about upcoming albums, tours, and videos, all to keep her fans guessing. Some tweets include information about the music creation process or offer photos of her personal life. When Lady Gaga tweets or posts a photo, she makes instant music news. Social media has significantly contributed to Lady Gaga's megastar status. Her concerts sell out as soon as tickets go on sale.

Think Critically

Go online to find out how celebrities are using social media sites. What kind of information do fans like to get? How can celebrities use social media to strengthen their popularity?

When the U.S. Women's Soccer Team won the World Cup Soccer Championship in 1991, it barely made the sports pages. Now the women on the U.S. national team are some of the world's most talented athletes, having won four gold medals at the Olympic Games. The goalkeeper for the 2012 Olympic team, Hope Solo, is one of the most recognizable and talented soccer players in the world. Solo's skills on the field have earned her major endorsements from Gatorade and Nike, as well as a competitor's spot on TV's *Dancing with the Stars*.

Women's National Basketball Association (WNBA) is drawing fans to arena seats and WNBA telecasts. The Chicago Sky saw a 17 percent increase in attendance, and the Phoenix Mercury experienced a 9 percent bump compared to the previous year's average attendance. Two of Phoenix's home playoff games averaged 9,560 fans, including 11,110 in attendance against the Los Angeles Sparks, for the team's best-attended first-round home playoff game in 15 seasons. In an attempt to increase attendance even more, Phoenix used unique marketing—it offered its male fans free tickets to home games. Excitement about the Phoenix Mercury also led to attendance records on the road. Opposing teams added courtside seats and increased ticket prices when the Mercury were in town. Due to this upswing in popularity, ABC Sports and ESPN agreed to televise WNBA regular-season and playoff games until 2022.

Salary Inequities Although women's professional sports are becoming increasingly popular, salaries are grossly unequal in comparison to male professional athletes' pay. The average annual salary of a WNBA player is $75,000 to $80,000, with top salaries around $107,000. Rookie salaries start at $37,950 for the four-month season, while the minimum salary for veterans with three or more years of experience is $55,000.[10] The salaries for the top 40 NBA players range from $3.5 million to $12.4 million per year.[11]

Women's professional football attracts players from all walks of life. The 11-team Women's Professional Football League (WPFL) pays players only $100 per game for the ten-game season that runs from October to early February. Each team roster has 40 players plus ten members on the practice squad. Unfortunately, only two of the original teams are still in existence and the continuation of the WPFL seams highly unlikely.

A Marketing Frontier   The growing popularity of women's sports is adding new female fans, many of whom have been uninterested in traditional men's games. Marketers are taking notice of this growing fan base. Women have different interests than men. Creative marketers must come up with ideas for sports-related merchandise that will appeal to this category of fans. Those who do are sure to find this target market lucrative.

INTERMISSION

Why is the role of a recruiter so important to a team?

ENCORE

Understand Marketing Concepts
Select the best answer for each question.

1. Amateur athletes
   a. are now being paid to play college games
   b. perform on college teams
   c. are represented by agents
   d. can endorse products and businesses

2. The recruitment process to get top high school athletes to play at colleges
   a. is highly competitive
   b. is regulated by the NCAA
   c. cannot include additional financial rewards
   d. all of the above

Think Critically
Answer the following questions as completely as possible.

3. Do you think universities should pay their athletes? Why or why not? Do you think student-athletes should receive benefits (or perks) that are not offered to other college students? Explain your answer. (LO 6.2-1)

4. Choose a major university that is successful in football or basketball. Play the role of a coach recruiting a blue-chip athlete and compose a letter to encourage that athlete to attend your university. (LO 6.2-2)

6.3 Product Marketing Strategies

The Essential Question

Why are marketing strategies adjusted for different stages of the product life cycle?

Learning Objectives

LO 6.3-1 List and describe the stages of the product life cycle.

LO 6.3-2 Explain how products are positioned in the marketplace.

Key Terms

- product life cycle
- skimming price strategy
- penetration price strategy
- positioning

OPENING ACT

A recent ESPN poll indicated that soccer is the second most popular sport among Americans between the ages of 12 and 24 and the most popular sport among Hispanics. Soccer in the United States has 33 million devoted fans. The same study indicated that a record 7.2 million Americans ages 12 and over are Major League Soccer (MLS) fans. MLS has grown tremendously since 2000, when the league classified only 2.8 percent of Americans as fans and recorded the lowest attendance record in history, averaging about 13,700 fans per match.[12]

The United States has more soccer players than any other country. Currently, there are nearly 18 million official U.S. soccer players. Fourteen million (or 78 percent) of U.S. soccer players are under the age of 18. Recent data indicates that 284,000 boys and 209,000 girls are competing in high school soccer. The odds of a high school soccer player receiving a full scholarship to a Division I or II school is 1 in 90.[13]

Cooperative Learning   Work with a partner and list three marketing strategies that could increase the popularity of soccer in the United States. What cities would be good locations to test the marketing strategies? Why?

LO 6.3-1   THE PRODUCT LIFE CYCLE

Product/Service Management

Every product has a life cycle. There are four stages in the **product life cycle**, including introduction, growth, maturity, and decline. Marketing strategies for a product will differ at the various stages of the life cycle.

Introduction Stage

Because consumer interest in products often declines over time, businesses must introduce new products to the marketplace. During the *introduction stage*, the product is somewhat unique in the marketplace and only one brand of the new product is available.

New product development begins by finding ideas for new products. The ideas are screened to select the one with the greatest chance of success. Research is conducted to identify a target market and product mix. A financial analysis is completed to project production and marketing costs as well as potential sales and profits. The product is then developed and tested. Finally, the new product is introduced to the market. This involves coordinating and scheduling the activities of manufacturers, transportation companies, warehouses, retailers, and marketers.

To encourage customers to try a new product, businesses may use a price strategy. Common price strategies implemented during the introduction stage include skimming and penetration.

The **skimming price strategy** introduces new products at a very high price. Quality and uniqueness of the product are emphasized to justify the high price. Skimming results in higher profits for the company, but it encourages other companies that want a share of the profits to enter the market. Price skimming was used when flat-screen and plasma televisions first entered the market. Most of the flat-screen televisions could not be purchased for less than $1,000. Increased competition from television manufacturers has resulted in much lower prices. A 32-inch flat screen television that once sold for more than $1,000 can now be purchased for less than $200.

The **penetration price strategy** uses low pricing to help capture a large market share early. A company may offer low introductory prices on a new product or service to help establish a customer base. Although this pricing strategy may result in lower profits, it discourages competition. A sport that is new to a city, such as ice hockey or roller derby, may offer low ticket prices as a way to draw in fans and compete with other attractions.

Growth Stage

The *growth stage* is the second part of the product life cycle. During this stage, sales of a product and profits increase. The target market knows about and regularly purchases the product. Advertising during the growth stage focuses attention on customer satisfaction. Products in the growth stage may need to be modified and new models offered to maintain customer loyalty. Product extensions and enhancements are used to meet changing customer needs. In the growth stage, competition increases as competitors begin offering alternative products. During the growth stage of the reality show *American Idol*, numerous other similar shows popped up,

© iStockphoto.com/phildate

What can a company expect to occur when a product is in the growth stage?

such as *America's Got Talent.* The success of *American Idol* made the talent show format appealing to television networks that wanted a share of the market.

The Maturity Stage

The *maturity stage* is the third phase of the product life cycle. Sales level off or slow down, and most of the target market has already purchased the product at one time or another. Price is an important factor during this stage because of increased competition. Sales prices may be offered. Marketing costs rise as promotions increase to fight off the competition and maintain market share. TV and radio commercials for products during this stage may actually make comparisons to the competition. For example, The Mall of America in Minnesota may run advertisements comparing its amusement park to traditional amusement parks. The mall may point out the advantages of visiting its year-round amusement park that also provides access to stores and restaurants under the same roof.

The Decline Stage

The final stage of the product life cycle is the *decline stage*. During this stage, sales decrease and may not generate enough revenue to justify continued marketing of the product. Companies have several choices during the decline stage. They may drop the product, sell or license the product to another company, discount the product, regionalize the product, modernize/alter the product, or recommit the product. During the decline stage of the product life cycle, marketers are forced to make tough decisions that will have a major impact on the future of the product and company.

Drop a Product   To cut company losses, marketers may choose to drop a product entirely. Amusement parks are always under pressure to offer the most thrilling rides. Rides that were once standard at every amusement park, such as the giant slide, are often torn down to make room for rides that are more appealing to thrill seekers.

Sell/License   Some companies choose to minimize losses during the decline stage of a product life cycle by selling or licensing the product to another company. The other company assumes the risk of marketing the product, but a license agreement allows the originating company to continue to receive a percentage of the sales. Clothing designers Missoni, Jason Wu, and Phillip Lim have made the bold decision to license lines of designer clothing for Target. This strategy of offering designer clothes at reasonable prices has been very successful. It also helps the designers reach a new target market.

Discount   In the decline stage, companies often reduce prices so that the merchandise sells faster. The costs of developing the product have been recovered at this point, and promotional budgets will be reduced to keep costs down. The discounted price alone hopefully will encourage more consumers to buy the company's product instead of its competitors' product. The higher volume of sales

`Pricing`

Why are discounts offered during the decline stage of a product's life cycle?

may earn the company enough profit to continue offering the product.

Electronic gadgets come and go. New technology or new uses for technology can change the popularity of current products. When stand-alone GPS navigation devices hit the market, they were a must-have for many drivers. At that time, a GPS device could cost you a few hundred dollars. Today, most smartphones have built-in navigation systems, reducing the need for stand-alone units. Thus, some GPS manufacturers now sell their devices for under $100.

Regionalize   A business may choose to regionalize by committing its product to a geographic location where it is the most popular and profitable. Manufacturers of ski equipment and clothing may commit their merchandise to Colorado and other popular ski markets to move merchandise during the decline stage.

Modernize/Alter   The enthusiasm of consumers for a product may be re-ignited by modernizing or altering the product in some way. Products that are marketed as "new and improved" or "more effective" are examples of this strategy. Companies must project what alterations or modernizations will increase sales. Many new sports stadiums have been built in recent years to reignite fans' enthusiasm for attending a game. The new stadiums include amenities that are more appealing to fans, such as high-definition scoreboards, spacious luxury suites, and more restrooms. Added attractions such as live music, restaurants, and hall of fame museums are also being offered as a way to bring in more fans.

Recommit   A product originally may have been developed and promoted for a specific purpose. As sales decline, the product is *recommitted* when other purposes for the product are discovered. Aspirin was originally promoted as a pain reliever. Now it is promoted as a measure to prevent heart attacks. A bottled drink originally developed to recharge athletes on the playing field can also be promoted as a refreshing beverage for health-conscious consumers.

As another example, Facebook was originally marketed to college students. Teenagers in the 13- to 18-year-old age group recently accounted for only 10 percent of the Facebook population. Instead, teenagers and college students are now using Twitter, Instagram, and Snapchat to communicate with friends. Now that young people are using other forms of social media, Facebook may need to recommit its product to other age groups.

Facebook's largest customer base is now 18- to 29-year-olds. Because users in this age group grew 74 percent in just one year, its members are referred to as Facebook super users. They use Facebook for networking, chatting, and meeting other people as well as for posting text, images, music, and videos. Dedicated super users check their Facebook pages multiple times each day and frequently make posts using mobile devices.

Facebook users between the ages of 30 and 49 make up an interesting market segment within an aging population. Individuals in this age group keep in touch with their family members and friends through photos and social communication posted on Facebook. Statistics show that users in this age group are less likely to check their Facebook pages as frequently as those in their twenties.

Facebook is the third most popular site for individuals who are 65 and older. Those between the ages of 45 and 54 make up 12 percent of the Facebook population; individuals aged 55 to 65 make up another 7 percent.[14] Both of these age groups provide growth opportunities for Facebook. Social media websites such as Facebook must monitor trends and recommit their product to different market segments when new products are introduced in the marketplace.

© iStockphoto.com/pressureUA

Why would Facebook want to change the focus of its target market?

INTERMISSION

What are the steps in new product development?

LO 6.3-2   POSITIONING A PRODUCT

Product/Service Management

Companies must decide how they will position their products in the marketplace. **Positioning** is a strategy used by a company to differentiate its products or services from its competitors' products or services. Companies can use various positioning strategies. Some companies position their products using price and quality. Other companies position their products based on features and benefits. Comparing a product to the competition's product to point out differences is another way to position a product in the marketplace. A company may decide to group its products together and promote the product line. The entire product line can be positioned by quality, price, and product features.

Company Positioning Strategies

Nike positions its products using brand recognition and status. Because of its many celebrity endorsements, Nike is associated with status. This helps create high consumer demand for its products. When a popular basketball star endorses Nike basketball shoes, it fuels consumer demand and drives up the price. Fans who want to imitate their favorite player have been known to pay over a $1,000 for a pair of Nike shoes that are in low supply because of high demand.

Luxury hotels position their products in the marketplace based on price and related services. Walt Disney World and Universal Studios sell family season passes to their parks in Orlando, emphasizing entertainment and price savings. Other sports and entertainment organizations may try to position themselves based on their safety record. A statement on the official website for Riddell, a U.S. sports equipment manufacturer, indicates that the company is committed to designing and manufacturing the most protective helmets for all football players. This positioning strategy can have a big influence on parents who need to buy football helmets for their children.

Universities may position their brand through involvement in sports. While all schools hope to win a national championship, only one team ends up with the number one ranking. Some universities are associated with athletic conferences that are noted for top football, basketball, and baseball programs. Other schools promote their academic accomplishments, integrity, and long-standing history. Prospective students may look at these factors favorably when choosing which university to attend.

TAKE A BOW Maria Sharapova

Maria Sharapova is a professional tennis player from Russia. Her career was thrust into the spotlight when, at age 17, she defeated Serena Williams in the 2004 Wimbledon final. Her successful tennis career has led to modeling assignments and endorsement deals. Well-known brands such as Nike, Porsche, and Canon understand the value of sponsoring the tennis star. She also has her own line of perfume and her own line of candy called "Sugarpova." Because of her worldwide popularity, Sharapova was hired by NBC as a correspondent for the 2014 Olympic Games. With all of her success on and off the court, it was important to Sharapova to help those less fortunate. In 2007 she founded the Maria Sharapova Foundation, which includes a scholarship program for students affected by the Chernobyl nuclear accident in parts of Belarus, an area bordering Russia where she has family roots. A portion of the sales from her Sugarpova candy is also donated to her foundation.

Talent on the tennis court and business savvy have resulted in Maria Sharapova being one of the richest international athletes, earning $29 million in a recent year from endorsements, winnings, bonuses, and appearance fees.[15]

Think Critically

To help raise money for the Maria Sharapova Foundation, create a television commercial (or other type of advertisement) to promote Sugarpova candy, featuring Maria Sharapova and another popular celebrity.

Individual Positioning Strategies

In today's competitive workplace, it is important to stand out from the crowd. One way to do this is to build your own personal brand that can help you position yourself in the workplace. Students can start doing this while in school. They can position their personal brands through their actions, accomplishments, and association with sports and student organizations. Students who participate in sports acquire many transferable skills. They learn to work as part of a team, develop leadership skills, and gain a sense of discipline. Feelings of competency and self-worth also grow. Students who join student organizations such as DECA, FBLA, and BPA position themselves as young professional adults who are learning about successful business strategies. This positioning strategy helps young people get noticed by prospective colleges and employers. Business leaders are aware of the objectives for DECA, FBLA, and BPA, and they are more likely to hire individuals who have demonstrated leadership skills in these professional organizations.

INTERMISSION

List three ways a product may be positioned in the marketplace.

ENCORE

Understand Marketing Concepts
Select the best answer for each question.

1. Penetration pricing is
   a. used to attract a large share of the market early
   b. used to discourage competition
   c. a low-price strategy
   d. all of the above

2. At which stage of the product life cycle do sales level off?
   a. introductory stage
   b. growth stage
   c. maturity stage
   d. decline stage

Think Critically
Answer the following questions as completely as possible.

3. Where would be a good place to regionalize the sale of cross-country skis that are in the decline stage? Explain your answer (LO 6.3-1)

4. How would you position a designer brand polo shirt at a university bookstore? (LO 6.3-2)

CHAPTER ASSESSMENT

Review Marketing Terms

Match the terms listed with the definitions.

1. A product's final form and assorted features
2. Incentives received in addition to a base salary
3. The legal protection of words and symbols used by a company
4. Items offered in addition to the product to make it more attractive to the target market
5. The introduction, growth, maturity, and decline stages of a product
6. Introducing a new product at a very high price, emphasizing quality and uniqueness of the product
7. A group of similar products with slight variations to satisfy the different needs of consumers
8. Features added to the basic product that satisfy additional needs and wants
9. A voluntary organization through which the nation's colleges and universities govern their athletics programs
10. High-prospect athletes who have exceptional athletic ability and who demonstrate good character and leadership qualities on and off the field
11. Using low pricing to help capture a large market share
12. The name, symbol, logo, word, or design that identifies a product, service, or company
13. A well-known name and/or symbol established by one company and sold for use by another company to promote its products
14. A strategy used by a company to differentiate its products or services from its competitors' products or services

a. blue-chip athletes
b. brand
c. fringe benefits
d. licensed brand
e. NCAA
f. penetration price strategy
g. positioning
h. product enhancements
i. product extensions
j. product life cycle
k. product line
l. product mix
m. skimming price strategy
n. trademark

Review Marketing Concepts

Select the best answer for each of the following questions.

15. During the decline stage of the product life cycle, all of the following are options except
    a. regionalizing
    b. recommitting
    c. raising prices
    d. discounting

16. Which of the following is not a component of the product mix?
    a. product line
    b. packaging
    c. brand
    d. distribution channels
17. When consumers value a brand to the extent that they reject other brands even when the preferred brand is unavailable, which level of brand recognition has been reached?
    a. nonrecognition
    b. rejection
    c. preference
    d. insistence
18. Which of the following is *not* a goal of the NCAA?
    a. to advance academics
    b. to develop life skills
    c. to provide financial rewards to athletes
    d. to enhance communities
19. Which of the following strategies is not appropriate during the decline stage of a product?
    a. drop the product
    b. sell the product or license to another company
    c. implement a skimming price strategy
    d. discount the price of the merchandise
20. Clothing designer Ralph Lauren wants his merchandise to be sold only in upscale department stores. This strategy is part of
    a. positioning the brand
    b. skimming the market
    c. penetrating the market
    d. regionalizing the product

Think Critically

21. Select four sports and/or entertainment products and indicate the stage of the product life cycle for each product. What marketing strategy would you use for each product? Explain your answers. (LO 6.3-1)
22. Why would a company choose to license the marketing of its product that is in the decline stage to another company? (LO 6.3-2)
23. What is the difference between tangible and intangible features of products? Provide two examples of each. (LO 6.1-1)
24. What is the difference between a basic product and an enhanced product? (LO 6.1-1)
25. How do the salaries for professional female athletes compare to salaries for professional male athletes? Why does a difference exist? What do you think it would take to bridge the gap? (LO 6.2-2)

Make Academic Connections

26. **Research** Select a specific type of sports equipment and a specific brand for that equipment. Use the Internet to research the complete product line offered by the brand. What items are included in the product line? What are the price points? Describe the target markets for each item in the product line. (LO 6.1-2)

27. **Advertising** Think of a new purpose for a common product. Assume the product is in the decline stage of its product life cycle. Create an advertisement that recommits the product to the market. (LO 6.3-1)

28. **Marketing Math** Six celebrities starring in a popular sitcom that has a 12-show season are each paid $350,000 per episode. Additional costs of producing the sitcom total $200,000 per episode. A 12-show reality series costs $250,000 to produce each episode. What is the difference between the total cost to produce the sitcom and the reality series? How might this affect the television network's decision about producing shows? (LO 6.2-2)

29. **Geography** You are in charge of recruitment for a major college football program. Eight coaches will visit recruits throughout the United States. Print a map of the United States and divide it into eight recruitment regions. Use the Internet to record the estimated population in each region. (*Hint:* The U.S. Census Bureau lists population estimates for each state.) (LO 6.2-1)

30. **Economics** Your company has developed a unique product that no competitor can currently match. The CEO of the company is very concerned about using the proper pricing strategy when the product is introduced to the market. Prepare a short report for the CEO that describes alternative pricing strategies and the advantages and disadvantages of each. Which strategy would you recommend? Why? Include any assumptions you make about the product. (LO 6.3-2)

31. **History** Use the Internet to conduct research on the history of women's sports. Who were some of the groundbreakers who helped surge the popularity of women's athletics? Create a timeline that shows important dates and events for women's sports throughout history. (LO 6.2-2)

32. **Psychology** Give three examples of sports products that are associated with status. Use the Internet to determine why these selected products are popular. Also explain the psychological advantages that consumers associate with the purchase of these products. (LO 6.3-2)

33. **Math** A popular fast-food restaurant sells chicken sandwiches at local college football games. The restaurant expects to sell sandwiches to 10 percent of the fans that attend each game. During each home game, the 96,000-seat stadium sells out. The price charged for a chicken sandwich is $5, and the owner of the restaurant earns 15 percent from each sale. How much money can the owner hope to make at one home game? (LO 6.3-2)

EXTRA INNINGS PROJECT

A college recruiter is responsible for identifying prospective athletes and convincing them to play for his or her school. In addition to traveling to high schools to visit with students, a recruiter also hosts recruitment events at the college. These events include fun activities and campus tours as a way to promote the college and surrounding community.

You are the recruitment coordinator for a major university that is highly recognized for success in football. The school is located in a sparsely populated U.S. city that has cold winters.

Work with a group and complete the following activities.

1. Use the Internet to research a university with the characteristics listed above. What are the major attractions for the university and the city where it is located?
2. What special events could be scheduled for prospective football players coming from high schools located throughout the United States?
3. What are three things that you want prospective athletes to learn about your school after visiting it?
4. Create a brochure to give to prospective athletes that highlights the benefits of attending your selected university. Include a description of the product and service lines your university offers to athletes.
5. Create a multimedia presentation to convince prospective athletes to attend your selected university. The presentation should highlight the university and city and address education and other major concerns of the athletes' parents.
6. Conduct research about the NCAA to learn what guidelines recruiters must follow when recruiting prospective high school athletes. Design a brochure that explains legal and illegal recruitment strategies. This brochure will be given to coaches, players, athletes, and parents to ensure that no NCAA rules are broken during the recruitment process.
7. Develop a list of things that your selected university will do to attract the best football athletes.

CROSSFIT—THE LATEST TREND

The latest exercise trends tend to come and go like diet fads. The popularity of aerobics, jazzercise, yoga, and Pilates has been surpassed by the popularity of CrossFit. A recent survey by the Los Angeles *Examiner* classifies exercise trends as:

- a general development or change in the way that people are exercising
- a temporary fad that is only popular for a short period of time

CrossFit involves using the top nine exercise trends in continuously varied workouts. High-intensity interval training associated with CrossFit includes:

- body weight training
- strength training
- exercise and weight loss
- functional fitness
- group fitness training

CrossFit is rapidly gaining followers. Participants are led through exercises by experienced fitness professionals. Personal training fitness programs are available for older adults.

Higher Risk=Higher Reward

CrossFit progams include short bursts of high-intensity exercises followed by short periods of rest for recovery. Many CrossFit participants prefer the varied workouts to those workouts devoted to a single activity, such as walking on a treadmill or running. A major drawback for the CrossFit program is the high possibility of injury due to the fast-paced, high-intensity nature of it.

Fading Fast

Zumba is a Latin dance workout that includes interval-type exercise and resistance training. Zumba experienced rapid growth from 2010 to 2013. Because of its declining popularity, Zumba is now considered an exercise fad rather than a trend. Spinning was ranked in the Top 20 exercise programs in 2013 but has now dropped out of the rankings. Popular exercise boot camps also have dropped out of the Top 20 in less than two years. Exercise fads will continue to grow as more Americans look for ways to lose weight.

Think Critically

1. What makes CrossFit an appealing workout? (Conduct online research to learn more about CrossFit.)
2. Why are some exercise programs just a fad while others remain popular over time?
3. When promoting a new exercise trend, what would you emphasize to attract followers?
4. Are exercise clubs/gyms on the rise or decline in the United States? (Conduct online research to find statistics.) What do you think contributes to this trend?

DESKTOP PUBLISHING EVENT

Many aspects of today's visual business publications require desktop publishing. This event challenges participants to demonstrate skills in the areas of desktop publishing, creativity, and decision making.

You have been hired by the manager of the state fair to develop a desktop publishing document to advertise this year's fair and the activities it offers. Your publication will be included in community newspapers throughout the state.

The state fair is concerned about the declining attendance during the past five years. New exciting concerts and other activities have been scheduled as a way to revive interest. In addition, new rides have been added this year. The state fair manager wants to increase publicity to make state residents aware of the annual event. Corporate sponsors also want to see an increase in attendance.

Performance Indicators Evaluated
- Prepare an attractive newsletter that incorporates the latest desktop publishing technology.
- Create a newsletter that will meet the goals of the project: to increase awareness and attendance at the state fair.
- Select graphics and fonts that appeal to the intended audience.
- Produce a final product that indicates a clear thought process and an intended, planned direction with formulation and execution of a firm idea.

You must research this year's state fair to determine the dates, admission prices, entertainment, sponsors, and special promotions. You and a partner may use two computers, a scanner, and clipart to complete this project within a two-hour deadline. Your final product should showcase your graphic and text design skills. Layout creativity and appropriate use of fonts and type size are also an important component in your final product.

Think Critically

1. What promotional item could be included in your desktop publishing document to help increase the attendance at the state fair? Why do you think it would be effective?
2. How can the state fair measure the effectiveness of your publication?
3. What types of graphics would be appropriate for this publication? Why?
4. Do you think the state fair could benefit from multiple forms of publicity? Explain your answer.

www.fbla.org

7

MANAGING THE CHANNELS

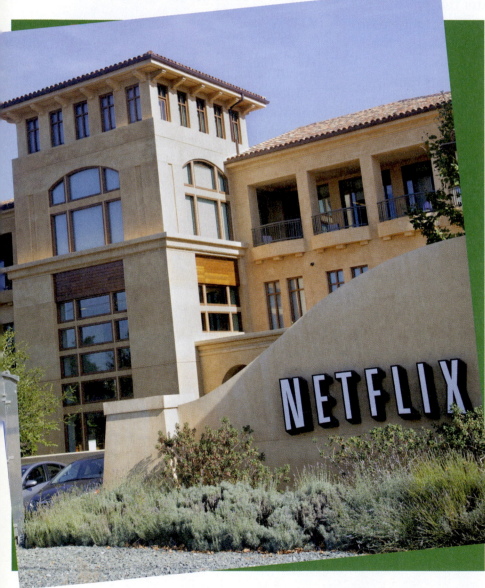

© iStockphoto.com/JasonDoiy

7.1 Channels of Distribution

7.2 Social Media and Technology Channel Management

7.3 Entertainment Distribution

7.4 Sports Distribution

POINT YOUR BROWSER

ngl.cengage.com/sports4e

Winning Strategies

Netflix

Netflix was founded in 1997 when it began offering unlimited movie rentals for one low monthly subscription rate and no late fees. By 2007, movies and television shows were instantly available through online streaming. Netflix soon became available on a wide variety of devices including personal computers, TVs, Wii, Playstation, and iPhones. By 2010, Netflix became available internationally. New members were added around the globe. Netflix is currently the world's leading Internet television network. In a recent year, there were over 30 million subscribers spanning over 40 countries.[1]

Netflix recently partnered with DreamWorks to offer subscribers original content. Investors were delighted, and the stock of both companies rose. DreamWorks agreed to provide over 300 hours of new programming inspired by the characters from DreamWorks hit feature films, such as *Shrek* and *Turbo*. The DreamWorks Animation shows are to be offered in all of the countries in which Netflix operates.

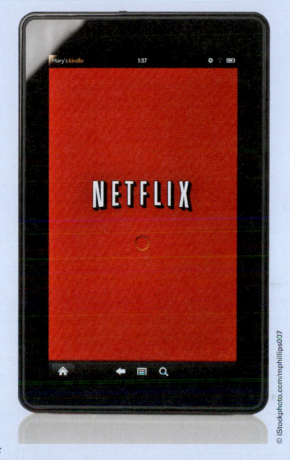

© iStockphoto.com/mphillips007

Offering original programming has given Netflix a new surge of subscribers, and the partnership with DreamWorks Animation is helping the company attract new customers, especially families with young children. Competitors such as Amazon and Google are racing to narrow Netflix's lead as an online distribution channel.

Think Critically

1. How does Netflix compare in format, product, cost, availability, and ease of use to other similar services, such as Amazon or Hulu?

2. In what ways has Netflix continued to evolve its distribution strategies since it was founded? Which strategies do you think have provided the most growth in membership?

7.1 Channels of Distribution

The Essential Question

What legal and ethical issues have an impact on the role of channel management and global distribution?

Learning Objectives

LO 7.1-1   Explore the role of channel management in sports and entertainment marketing.

LO 7.1-2   Investigate global distribution channels for sports and entertainment.

LO 7.1-3   Classify legal and ethical considerations in channel management.

Key Terms

- channels of distribution
- intermediaries
- logistics
- amphitheaters
- venue
- mass media
- disruptive technologies

OPENING ACT

The off-Broadway production *Sleep No More* offers a distinctly different experience to each patron. The traditional stage that separates the actors and the audience has been removed. Instead of assigning the audience members a seat, each person is given a mask, which designates his or her role as an audience member. The silent, masked audience roams through the spaces and discovers the unknown. In this immersive theater production, the audience experiences emotional storytelling inside a sensory set design where lighting and sound create drama, even when no actors are present. Each individual sees the action from a different angle, meaning he or she sees a scene by chance. The experience is similar to walking down a street and viewing life as it takes place. What to watch and where to go are individual choices, as each person experiences this unique theatrical production.

Cooperative Learning   Working with a partner, list why you would or would not like an immersive production. Then list why you think someone who is your grandparents' age would or would not like an immersive production. Share your ideas with the class.

LO 7.1-1   CHANNEL MANAGEMENT

Channel Management   Determining the best ways to make a product or service available to consumers requires knowledge of distribution channels. If it is an event, the organizers must choose the most effective location, date, and time. If it is a product, a company must choose the best method of getting it in the hands of customers. *Distribution* is one of the four elements of the marketing mix. It involves the locations and methods used to make products available to customers.

The **channels of distribution** include all of the businesses through which products or services pass on the way to the consumer. The businesses, or channel members, involved in making the product or service available are called **intermediaries**. Selecting and managing the intermediaries is an important part of the marketing process.

Establishing the Channels

The channels of distribution may be very simple or complex. Arranging for a local singer to perform at a restaurant is an example of a simple distribution channel. The restaurant owner may contact the singer directly to make the arrangements and then pay the musician for the performance. Because entertainment can be offered through multiple distribution channels (as shown in the illustration), and people have limited time and money to spend, distribution channels must compete for consumers' attention. Consumers decide which is the most satisfactory distribution channel for the cost. They may decide to stay home and watch TV instead of going out to hear live music.

Channels of entertainment distribution compete for a consumer's attention.

female: © iStockphoto.com/alejandrophotography; tv: © iStockphoto.com/adventtr; smartphone: © dencg/Shutterstock.com; mp4: © StockPhotosArt/Shutterstock.com; tablet: © Oleksiy Mark/Shutterstock.com

Very complex channels of distribution have a large number of channel members. For example, the distribution of a live boxing match produced in Macau, China, by a U.S. company is complex. The originators of the event must conduct research to collect data about the target audience for the live event. Before they become involved, distribution channel members, such as ESPN, want to know that the audience is large enough to produce a profit.

Each channel member has a specific role to play in moving the product or service from the originator to the consumer. The number and types of intermediary channel members will vary in every situation. For a concert or sporting event, intermediaries could include the event originator, the event facility, the media, and transportation companies.

- The event originator's role:
  - produce and oversee the entire event
  - manage the career of the talent or athlete
  - estimate costs and revenue and set pricing
  - arrange for promotion of the event
  - hire security
  - negotiate contracts with channel members
  - schedule the media, facility, special equipment, and more
- The event facility's role:
  - provide the space
  - set up some equipment such as chairs, tables, and sound system
  - provide for concessions and other audience services

- The media's role:
  - establish and manage communications across various platforms such as satellite, cable, broadcast, the Internet, and pay-per-view
  - transmit the event

- The transportation companies' role:
  - deliver sound, lighting, and other equipment
  - transport the cast and crew

It would be poor channel management to organize an event that costs more to produce than the expected revenue. Working with the most efficient channel members at an affordable price is good channel management.

Efficient Channels

Selling a product directly to the consumer is an example of a simple channel to manage, but it can also be an inefficient channel. Compare the process of managing the career of a musician who performs in small restaurants to producing a successful live concert. Although performing at a restaurant is a simple way to reach an audience and involves few channel members, it is an inefficient way to widely distribute the musician's talent.

Logistics is the process of planning, organizing, and managing the distribution of products and services. It is a way to help assure that the right products or services are in the right place at the right time. Logistics is one component of channel management. The logistics of the Internet make distribution of content an extremely efficient process. The Internet has forever changed the music and television industries. Consumers can now access music and TV shows online when and where they want.

When cable networks first contracted with television networks to distribute TV shows, the cable company made all of the programming decisions, controlling what consumers could watch and when. Cable networks, once the biggest revenue generators for media, are forecast to be on the way out as a distribution model. Technology, especially the Internet, has provided channels for more efficient distribution of products and services and will continue to evolve in the future. The logistics of the Internet are allowing consumers to be in control.

INTERMISSION

What is meant by channels of distribution?

LO 7.1-2   THE GLOBAL CHANNELS

Moving a sports or entertainment product around the world from the producers to consumers is a challenge. Customers want the product to be available when and where they want it. Currently, there are only two major channels of distribution for sports and entertainment events—live or via media. Within these two channels, choices of location and the types of media and media devices continue to evolve and grow.

Live Events

Historically, the only option for delivering sports and entertainment events was to present them live. Only those people who could travel to an event and pay to enter could view it. Early in the 1st Century A.D., the Romans built a number of amphitheaters across the vast Roman Empire. **Amphitheaters** are oval-shaped outdoor theaters with tiered seating around a central staging area. The Colosseum in Rome, Italy, (shown in the photo as it stands today) was built almost 2,000 years ago. It was an amphitheater that held about 70,000 spectators. Deadly fights between humans (often slaves) or between humans and wild animals were staged as gory entertainment for the Roman emperors, the rich and famous, and common citizens.

Audiences for live performances in the Colosseum were limited. The size of the **venue** (the facility where an event is held) limits how many can attend. In addition, live events are expensive to produce and generate a limited amount of revenue. Live performances continue to be an appealing form of entertainment. A well-produced, live, broadway-style performance can pack Broadway theaters for weeks. It is more fun to cheer your favorite team to victory in person, or to hear your favorite group perform, than to experience it through any type of media.

Photo Courtesy of Dotty Oelkers

How does the distribution of live shows today differ from the past?

Media Events

When distance, price, or limited availability prevents fans from attending a live event, media can provide the next-best option. Advancements in technology have produced user-friendly media that distribute events to audiences. **Mass media** is a term used to describe a method of distributing an event to a large volume of people—the masses. Examples of mass media include radio, television, and the Internet. Distributing an event through mass media to millions of fans can provide substantial marketing opportunities far beyond what is available with a live audience. Marketers can also reach smaller, more targeted audiences for live events via pay-per-view channels.

Often mass media is used to distribute a live event internationally. The logistics of delivering such an event to audiences is an important factor. The location of the live event can greatly affect costs and timing. For example, an event produced in China by a U.S. business would involve many distribution channel members and high transportation costs. If the main audience is in the United States, the time of the event would be a logistical factor. The time zone on the east coast of China is 12 to 13 hours later than on the east coast of the United States. Because a U.S. audience would prefer viewing a live event during prime time, the event would need to be produced in the morning in China.

Radio Once thought to be on its way out of use, radio has carved a unique place in the minds and hearts of sports fans and music lovers. Radio is unique because it requires inexpensive equipment and is readily available where other media is not. People can listen while they drive, work, or visit remote areas, where cell phones may not have reception.

Radio is an audio medium, meaning the action must be described to create a picture in the listeners' minds. Good radio sportscasters form a bond with their listeners that has never been matched by TV sportscasters. Regardless of whether the fans have ever been in the ballpark, a good sportscaster's play-by-play can make fans feel as if they are there. Radio is an effective delivery system for sports and entertainment. Internet and satellite technologies have added new dimensions to the availability of radio. Internet-based Pandora Radio allows users to select playlists based on personal preference. Fans believe Pandora helps expose listeners to new music and music artists that they may not have discovered on their own.

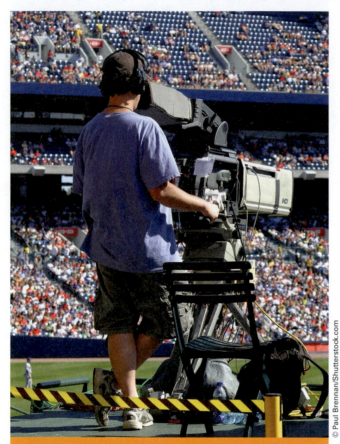

Since the onset of television, what has changed about when and where TV shows are watched?

© Paul Brennan/Shutterstock.com

Television What was once the dominant media device in hundreds of millions of homes is now losing consumers to newer media devices. An increasing number of viewers are turning away from TVs to smartphones, tablets, and other Internet-connected devices.

Connected TV, also known as Smart TV, is one way that TV is staying relevant. A Smart TV is equipped with the technology needed to connect to the Internet for web browsing, social networking, or for streaming video. Watching a game on a big screen with a room full of friends still has an attraction that a smaller device can't offer.

Sports are particularly attractive and profitable to television networks. Sports are more easily broadcast than entertainment shows that require sets, scripts, and paid actors. Sporting events have the following advantages:

- An existing venue is available
- Areas are well lit, making them sufficient for television cameras
- An existing fan base is in place

U.S. football is especially well suited for broadcast over a visual medium such as television. Each football play lasts for a short period of time, allowing enough time in between plays for the camera to refocus on the area of the field where the players regroup to start a new play. Sports such as soccer and hockey have continuous activity, and cameras sometimes have a hard time following and catching all of the action on the small screen. The NFL has grown into a driving force for TV, delivering tens of millions of viewers who watch live games.

Television content producers are also helping the medium stay relevant. A number of companies that have been successful in the film industry have ventured into production of content for TV. Weinstein Company, a movie industry business, added a number of scripted TV series and unscripted reality projects for TV to its list of productions. Weinstein believes that TV offers the potential for long-running hits as opposed to films that have shorter lives. Although TV is considered a more stable channel of distribution, it is not one without risk. Not all TV shows are a hit with viewers.

The Internet   The tremendous impact of the Internet on distribution cannot be overstated. Older channels of distribution for sports and entertainment have been enhanced as a result of the Internet. Cable and broadcast TV have traditionally controlled the distribution of media by offering bundled and scheduled programming. They now face stiff competition from Internet-based providers such as Netflix and Amazon that allow consumers to watch what they choose, when they choose. Stay tuned—new ways to distribute sports and entertainment are evolving.

The Future

Today, visual media involves some type of screen, whether it is a movie screen or a smartphone screen. When film director Steven Spielberg spoke to a group at the University of Southern California film school, he told the audience that he envisioned a future without on-screen entertainment. He predicted the onset of an *immersive* form of entertainment—one in which the viewer is surrounded by a three-dimensional environment that will actively engage the individual.

A low-tech way to implement Spielberg's future vision is through immersive theatrical productions. Virtual reality simulations with goggles and earphones are a step toward three-dimensional immersion, but they still involve a screen as the channel of distribution. The future may surround and engage people with screen-free entertainment.

INTERMISSION

What are two current major distribution channels for entertainment?

LO 7.1-3   LEGAL AND ETHICAL ISSUES IN CHANNEL MANAGEMENT

Traditionally, TV viewers watched what the networks produced, when the networks scheduled the show. If a viewer missed a show, he or she would have to wait and catch it as a rerun. New technology allows consumers to have more control over when they watch shows, but in some cases, this technology is being legally challenged by traditional services.

Whose Content Is It?

Cable, satellite, and Internet services pay television networks a retransmission fee to show content owned by the network. Retransmission fees, along with advertising revenues, pay for the costs of producing television content.

Cable, satellite, and Internet service providers earn their revenue by charging a subscription fee to consumers. All of these distribution channels are facing competition from new technology for sports and entertainment content distribution.

Some of the new distribution channels are called **disruptive technologies**—new technologies that change existing forms of communication channels. The new technologies are being challenged legally by the traditional media distributors because they disrupt the current distribution model. With these technologies, payment of retransmission fees to the content owners and to traditional distributors can be avoided. Viewers tune in to watch TV shows that are expensive to create. Content creators (writers, producers, directors, actors, and so forth) cannot be expected to work for free. The new technologies must find a fair way to pay for TV content creation; otherwise, distributors eventually will be left without content to distribute.

Media distribution companies such as Aereo enable users to receive broadcast television shows through antennas. A DISH Network service called Hopper allows TV viewers to skip commercials. Major networks view both of these services as a way to use network-created or network-owned content without paying for it. As far back as 1984, a landmark Supreme Court case held that taping and replaying shows for personal use was legal. Companies such as Aereo or DISH have been judged by some courts as an extension of personal recording by viewers. However, a recent U.S. Supreme Court decision ruled in favor of the networks, stating that Aereo violated copyright law by retransmitting content without permission from or payment to the content owners. Deciding who is going to pay for (and make a profit from) the content will continue to be a legal issue. The NFL and MLB threatened to stop airing sports on free broadcast TV if companies

© bikeriderlondon/Shutterstock.com

What legal issues are related to the new media distribution strategies?

like Aereo continue not to pay for content. If this model of distribution continues, either advertisers or subscribers will have to provide the steady stream of revenue needed to produce original content.

Fighting the Pirates   Production of mobile phone applications (apps) for sports and entertainment is a growing business. The primary distributors of apps in the United States are official outlets such as Apple's App Store. However, in China the major distributors are alternative app stores that offer unauthorized knockoffs—pirated, illegal copies. As many as one-third of Chinese iPhone owners "jailbreak" their phones, which involves hacking into the phones to give them nearly unlimited access to apps not authorized or offered by Apple. Jailbreaking is discouraged because it can damage or disable the phone. Once this happens, you may not be able to rely on Apple to fix the problem. Apple is working with Chinese companies to create clean and legal app distribution channels. Chinese piracy of original content and software continues to be an ongoing problem.

INTERMISSION

How do traditional TV broadcasters pay for the production of content?

ENCORE

Understand Marketing Concepts
Select the best answer for each question.

1. Distribution
   a. is a core marketing standard
   b. includes the activities involved in delivering products to consumers
   c. is a type of promotion
   d. all of the above

2. Sporting events are particularly attractive to television networks because
   a. they have an existing fan base
   b. they take place in an existing venue
   c. they are played in well-lit areas
   d. all of the above

Think Critically
Answer the following questions as completely as possible.

3. If you were trying to increase interest in soccer in the United States, describe the channels of distribution you would use and why. (LO 7.1-1)

4. What types of sports and entertainment are best distributed on the Internet? What trends do you expect in the future? (LO 7.1-2)

7.2 Social Media and Technology Channel Management

Learning Objectives

LO 7.2-1   Describe the use of technology in the channel management function.

LO 7.2-2   Compare the efficiency of using social media and technology to the physical distribution of products or services.

Key Terms

- predictive search
- broadband
- podcasts

OPENING ACT

Some people get an uneasy feeling the first time they experience new technology. New phone apps seem to know a lot about you, where you are, and what you are doing. Claire Cain Miller, a technology reporter for *The New York Times,* described first using Google Now, a personal assistant application for smartphones. Her phone buzzed to tell her she needed to leave in 15 minutes for a restaurant reservation because of traffic conditions. However, she had not told her phone that she had a reservation or where she was or the route she planned to take. Google Now had spotted the OpenTable reservation in her Gmail in-box, knew her location based on her phone's GPS, and checked Google Maps for traffic conditions. "I was creeped out," stated Ms. Miller.[3] Miller now trusts the app to provide her useful information. She has moved from a state of "distrust to dependence."

Google and other tech companies know that people quickly adapt to, and learn to like, the way these devices anticipate their every move.

Cooperative Learning   Form two teams. Debate whether there should be restrictions on the collection and storage of information about individuals. What are the downsides to this type of technology? Are the benefits worth it? Why or why not?

LO 7.2-1   MANAGING THE CHANNELS WITH TECHNOLOGY

Channel Management   Technology apps, such as Google Now, use a feature known as **predictive search** that reviews your private data to provide you with answers to questions it predicts you might ask. It searches your calendar entries, social network activity, email, and the location of your smartphone to gather information. The predictive search tool can act as a distribution channel for sports and entertainment. If tickets to a sold-out Broadway show become available, you may be offered the tickets immediately based on your preferences as identified by a predictive search. This is just one example of how the channels of distribution are changing. Companies continue to look for ways to improve how consumers receive products and services.

Cutting the Cable: Streaming Media

New technology has dramatically changed the landscape of managing entertainment distribution channels. In the past, a show might be broadcast on TV once, rerun a few times, and then disappear. Today, a show can be distributed at any time almost instantly via streaming media. In many cases, cable networks are being replaced by streaming online subscription services.

The number of households subscribing to cable is on the decline. Satellite TV has lost customers at an even faster rate than cable. Broadcast TV networks base the price of contracts with cable and satellite networks on the distributors' subscriber numbers. Because of the falling number of subscribers, TV networks are now interested in partnering with online video services. Cable and telecom providers are being forced to become more reliant on their Internet offerings for growth.

How can a company use predictive search technology as part of its distribution strategy?

On-Demand Programming

The competition between the TV networks, cable, and Internet providers has greatly increased. To win over viewers, web-based services such as Netflix are investing in the production of original programming. In 2013 Netflix released its own series—*House of Cards*. It was a huge success, and Netflix subscriptions surged. As a result, Netflix planned to double its offerings of original programming.

Viacom Media Networks has the largest share of ad-supported cable networks in the United States. The brands include MTV, Comedy Central, BET, and Nickelodeon. Each of the Viacom brands develops original content based on its audience. Viacom has broadened its distribution channels by reaching an agreement with a new online TV service created by Sony. The new service allows paying subscribers to receive cable channels online. It is similar to on-demand media libraries such as Netflix or Hulu. Sony, Intel, and Google were all pursuing the top content producers (including Disney and Warner Bros.), hoping to be the service provider to offer their programming via the Internet.

Does It Come at a Cost?

To watch content over the Internet, consumers are required to have **broadband**—high-speed Internet service. Broadband Internet service providers have battled the Federal Communications Commission (FCC) in court over who controls the Internet. The broadband providers want to charge more for faster, express service to major online customers such as Netflix. Consumer advocates fear that Internet service providers (ISPs) will partner with content creators and block content that is not part of the partnership. Or, the ISP could make the delivery

You are a journalist for your local newspaper covering stories about the entertainment industry. Recently, you have focused on the entertainment industry's use of technology as a distribution channel. You have been assigned to write an article about the entertainment distribution channels most commonly used by high school students in your community. Based on current trends, you want to report on possible future trends related to entertainment distribution channels.

Write Now

Write a newspaper article that is approximately 400 to 600 words. You will need to interview at least three people to collect quotes that reflect their views on the topic. The parts of the article should include a headline, byline (your name), lead-in (preview of the story), and the story.

of media so slow that content creators and consumers would be forced to join the partnership. Regardless of the outcome, the cost of Internet service is expected to grow as the demand for broadband services grows.

Unexpected Markets   The new online services were not expected to target older Americans as consumers. However, the user-friendliness of online services and the low cost has made them extremely attractive to all age groups, including those over 65. Older viewers who have lower incomes often are looking for ways to reduce the cost of TV service. Additionally, according to a Nielsen survey, people over age 65 watch more than seven hours of TV a day. Many older viewers already have a high-speed Internet connection needed for streaming TV.

Audio Revival

Talk radio is alive and well, but it is changing its channel of distribution. **Podcasts** are a way of distributing multimedia files over the Internet for later playback. The podcasts, which are primarily audio, consist of prerecorded radio talk shows. Podcasts have become a very personalized form of entertainment and information. They are designed to be downloaded from the Internet for offline listening. The audience is free to listen to what they want, when they want. Busy people find podcasts a great way to catch up on the latest news about their favorite sports team or to listen to a celebrity interview they have missed. One of the distribution channels for podcasting is an iTunes app, which has more than one billion subscriptions for podcasts. A number of comedians use podcasts as a marketing tool. Comedians can expand their fan base through the podcasts' connection to the digital world. Top podcasts have millions of downloads. Radio talk shows attracted new, younger listeners when podcasts were made available for download to mobile devices.

INTERMISSION

How has technology changed the distribution of TV shows and talk radio?

LO 7.2-2 TECHNOLOGY EFFICIENCY

Distribution technology "flew" into the future when Amazon founder Jeff Bezos announced the potential use of drones to provide package delivery to homes. However, the delivery service is waiting for Federal Aviation Administration (FAA) approval of civilian drone use and faces many other hurdles. Film directors are also waiting for approval to use drones for aerial shots.

Technology that makes the channels of distribution more efficient is an exciting area for businesses and consumers. The potential for new innovations and continuous improvements is endless. Some of the latest uses of technology to deliver media to fans are already underway.

Engaging the Consumer

Early Romans communicated with letters and news written on scrolls. They were shared with many people and even posted on walls in public locations. Thus, in a sense, social media has been around for thousands of years, but the distribution channels have changed. People use technology to communicate instantly, instead of actually posting written messages on walls. Now, marketers who chat via social media have easy access to consumers. With the right marketing tools, they can create solid, engaged relationships with customers by delivering product information and other valuable messages, such as helpful product hints. Engaged consumers tend to be repeat customers. However, pointless exchanges with customers can damage the relationship or result in loss of customers altogether. So marketers must carefully plan how to use social media as a distribution tool.

NASCAR Digital

Dale Earnhardt Jr., one of NASCAR's most popular drivers, reaches out to fans from Hendrick Motorsports' social media command center—Digital Dashboard. Earnhardt is able to connect with fans who want exclusive access to the sport's celebrities. NASCAR sees the Digital Dashboard as an efficient key selling point to use in gaining sponsorships. The sponsors see the addition of social media as a way to engage fans.

Video Gaming

The 20 top-selling video games account for more than 40 percent of total U.S. game sales.[4] The number of games being released is shrinking, which is a risky distribution strategy for the long term. This means that the revenue from fewer game titles must cover all game development costs. By using this strategy, game producers must count on loyal consumers to continue to play and purchase newer versions of the games.

Console-based games, which generally are expensive, are losing customers to inexpensive online games, which can be played on small mobile devices such as smartphones. The growth of online, multiplayer games has a network effect because people are attracted to what others are playing. Extra features purchased online, such as more lives for a character, are a source of additional revenue for the game producers. These low-budget games, created for less than $1 million in production costs, are finding their way

Danny Lewin was a math genius who cofounded Akamai Technologies. Before his death in an airplane crash, Akamai pioneered a way to deliver web pages at a very high speed. His innovations allowed web pages to handle massive traffic in almost real time. Because of Lewin's innovations, Akamai continues to make the Internet fast, reliable, and secure for businesses and consumers.

to consumers. By obtaining financing through crowdfunding (numerous investors) and distributing games digitally, video game producers are able to expand the number and variety of games available to consumers.

Pay What You Can for Music

In the movie *Inside Llewyn Davis*, a guitar-toting, 1960s folk singer struggles to get his music heard. After performing one of his songs, Davis is told by a music promoter, "I don't see a lot of money here," meaning he didn't think Llewyn would become a financial success. After the music CD business crashed due to the rise in Internet downloads, musicians have sought new distribution models. The band Rabbit Rabbit has found one solution to the problem. It uses a subscription website, called Rabbit Rabbit Radio, to distribute music. The band releases a new song online for subscribers on the first day of every month. It also posts video clips, slide shows, information about other musicians they admire, and notes about restaurants they have discovered on tour. Subscriptions cost $2 to $5 a month, allowing fans to pay what they can. The band gained over 900 subscribers in the first 18 months.[5]

INTERMISSION

Give an example of how technology has made distribution more efficient.

ENCORE

Understand Marketing Concepts

Select the best answer for each question.

1. New technology has made TV shows
   a. more available
   b. less available
   c. illegal to access
   d. none of the above

2. Social media can be used to
   a. engage customers
   b. connect the consumer with the product
   c. provide access to an athlete or celebrity
   d. all of the above

Think Critically

Answer the following questions as completely as possible.

3. Find an adult who subscribes to an online service such as Netflix. Ask what he or she likes and dislikes about it. (LO 7.2-1)

4. Describe how social media influences the entertainment people choose. (LO 7.2-2)

7.3 Entertainment Distribution

The Essential Question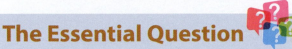

How can channel management strategies and costs be managed?

Learning Objectives

LO 7.3-1 Classify the channel management strategies used in entertainment distribution.

LO 7.3-2 Describe how to manage channels to minimize costs.

Key Terms

- in-concert movie
- platforms
- wide release
- art-house movies

In the movie *Star Trek: The Next Generation,* the first officer of the Starship Enterprise steps into a "holodeck." The holodeck is a chamber in which a range of entertainment for the crew is available. Matter replicators could transform energy into furniture, food, or drink. The participant could enjoy a simulated ride on a train or fight in a famous battle from history. Energy matter converters are, at this writing, still in the future. But consumers are seeking more engagement in their entertainment. Passive viewing is no longer enough for members of a generation that have grown up with video games and digital simulations.

Cooperative Learning   With a partner, list your ideas for distributing entertainment in the future. Share your ideas with the class.

OPENING ACT

ADMIT ONE

289147

LO 7.3-1   IT'S ENTERTAINMENT

Channel Management   The best entertainment in the world is worthless unless customers can have access to it where they want it and are willing to pay enough to make it profitable. Katy Perry rocked the film box office with *Katy Perry: Part of Me*, which cost about $12 million to produce and took in almost $33 million worldwide.[6] The movie was a combination of a documentary and **in-concert movie**, which contains film of actual concert performances. It is an example of a film with a built-in audience, relatively low production costs, and potential for profits.

It's Live

Distribution of live theatrical performances on TV was a major strategy in the 1950s but had rarely been done in the past 60 years until recently, when NBC produced *The Sound of Music*, based on the stage play. Although not popular with critics, the ratings results gave NBC 18.6 million viewers, one of its highest viewer ratings in years.[7] Shortly afterward, NBC announced that it would produce *Peter Pan*, beginning a tradition of new live TV productions. A live performance is always a risky and expensive venture. There are no "do-overs" as there are with prerecorded TV shows.

It's Recorded

Although consumers may prefer to attend a live performance, they may not be able to for various reasons, such as the cost or the location. Katy Perry's in-concert film gave fans who could not attend a live concert the chance to see her perform on screen. Distributing the concert via film proved to be successful. It gave consumers the product they wanted in the right place and at the right price, resulting in huge profits.

As technology continues to advance, the **platforms**—types of delivery systems—used for recorded sports and entertainment events will continue to expand and improve. Consumers' level of satisfaction with the platforms (or their economic utility) will help determine which platforms become popular and gain wide acceptance. Creative inventors and marketers will continue to search for ways to satisfy customers.

INTERMISSION

Why do you think people prefer live events instead of recorded events?

LO 7.3-2   WHICH CHANNEL?

Channel Management
Moving entertainment from the producer to the consumer involves various channel members. Movie producers must work with the traditional distribution channels or find other means of distribution. *Some Girl(s)* was a relatively low-budget movie. The movie producers turned down an offer from a traditional distributor. Instead, they opted for distribution on Vimeo On Demand, a direct-to-fan online distribution service that streams independent films for a fee. The producers decided to charge Vimeo members $5 to rent the movie, which could be viewed on a variety of devices. For films with smaller markets, it is important to find ways to control distribution costs.

Following the unexpectedly large audience for the live TV production of *The Sound of Music*, NBC Executive Producer Craig Zadan said, "Social media played a pivotal role in the success of the show." Twitter and Facebook traffic "lasted the entire performance and beyond."[8] Even though many of the social media comments were critical, the audience was deeply engaged.

Think Critically

Discuss with a partner why social media can have such an impact on the success of an entertainment event or show. Why are critical comments not necessarily viewed as a negative thing?

Making It Pay

Advertising, production, and distribution costs are major expenses for movie studios. One way to cut costs is to regulate the release of movies. A **wide release** involves distributing a movie nationally to a thousand or more theaters at the same time. **Art-house movies**, which are typically independent films that are outside the commercial mainstream of blockbuster films, draw smaller audiences. Because they are not designed for mass appeal, they have a limited release, which lowers the distribution costs.

Until the late 1990s, movies were distributed to theaters on giant reels of 35-millimeter film. The cost of transportation was about $1,200 to $3,000 for each reel. Digital distribution and satellite distribution cost much less than shipping reels to theaters. However, digital distribution requires newer, digital projection equipment, which can be very expensive. The costs of the new distribution technology exceeded the potential for profit for many small theaters and forced them to close, leaving some towns without a theater.

Regal, AMC, and Cinemark theaters partnered with Digital Cinema Distribution Coalition (DCDC) to receive films, promotional materials, and more via satellite. Universal Pictures and Warner Bros. helped form DCDC, and other studios are expected to join.

INTERMISSION

What happens when distribution costs exceed what is reasonable to pay?

ENCORE

Understand Marketing Concepts

Select the best answer for each question.

1. Why would making an in-concert film be a good distribution strategy?
   a. built-in audience
   b. low production costs
   c. potential for profits
   d. all of the above

2. What are some alternatives to traditional movie distribution?
   a. digital and satellite
   b. theaters
   c. reels
   d. trade shows

Think Critically

Answer the following questions as completely as possible.

3. What factors would influence your decision to attend a live concert starring your favorite musician? (LO 7.3-1)

4. How can costs of entertainment be minimized through distribution channel management? (LO 7.3-2)

7.4 Sports Distribution

The Essential Question

What strategies are used for sports distribution?

Learning Objectives

LO 7.4-1   Select distribution strategies for amateur sports and recreation.

LO 7.4-2   Explain considerations in distribution of college sports.

LO 7.4-3   Discuss channel strategies for professional sports.

Key Terms

- nonrevenue sports
- cable bundle
- cartel
- league agreement
- multichannel video programming distributor

OPENING ACT

ADMIT ONE
289147

Dorothy Kelly Boen, an octogenarian (a person age 80–89), defies the rocking-chair image associated with her age group. She walks and weight-trains at one health club and participates in water aerobics at another club. "I belong to two different health clubs. I like the people at one and the equipment at the other," she stated. She frequently invites her water aerobics class to her home for lunch and a swim in her pool.

By 2050, a U.S. federal report projects that there will be 19 million people in the United States age 85 and over, one of the fastest-growing markets in the United States.[9] Remaining active has been directly linked to remaining healthy.

Cooperative Learning   With a partner, make a list of products and services that would appeal to an active octogenarian who wants to stay fit. What channels of distribution would be best to reach this demographic?

LO 7.4-1   AMATEUR SPORTS AND RECREATION

Health, leisure time, and money all drive the recreation industry. People are interested in staying active and healthy. Research has shown that there is a positive correlation between participation of youth in physical activities and their emotional well-being. Continued participation in recreational sports into adulthood provides health benefits throughout life.

Fitness and Fun

Product/Service Management   Each year the Sports and Fitness Industry Association produces a report on sports participation in the United States. Results from a recent study are listed on the following page. For the first time, Generation Z, those born in the year 2000 or after, was tracked.

How can communities support healthy recreational activities?

- Thirty-three percent of Americans are active to a healthy level.
- Swimming for fitness is the top aspirational activity for six of the eight age categories.
- The top cities for group-based fitness programs are Salt Lake City, Atlanta, and Washington D.C.
- Spending has increased on team sports play.[10]

One challenge of recreational marketing is to motivate people to actively participate in the sports and activities that interest them. Over the long term, high costs may reduce people's interest, but smart marketers will fill this gap with recreational activities to help people stay active and fit.

Facilities versus Wilderness

Making sports facilities available where they are needed is a continuing challenge for amateur sports marketers and community leaders. Access to good recreational sports facilities may prevent some people from participating in sports. The recreational needs of people and the environmental impact of recreation must be considered in regional planning. Outdoor experiences such as backpacking, off-road driving, and rock climbing can be potentially destructive to wilderness areas. Somehow, leaders and citizens must balance the two needs and help educate outdoor enthusiasts about how to enjoy and protect the wilderness.

INTERMISSION

What factors affect the development of recreational sports facilities?

LO 7.4-2 COLLEGIATE SPORTS

Product/Service Management

A winning college team has economic implications for its school and for the community, region, and state. The exceptions are the **nonrevenue sports**—those sports that are funded by schools but do not provide a return on investment. Examples of nonrevenue sports include soccer, tennis, softball, track & field, and swimming. In an increasing trend, sports such as rowing or men's gymnastics are being cut from university varsity rosters. Some universities have tried to link the cuts to the need to increase athletic participation and scholarships for women. Gender equity in athletics is mandated by the 1972 law Title IX. However, despite the claims of some universities, there is no evidence of a relationship between this law and the varsity sports cuts. In fact, women participate in college rowing to a greater degree than men, so making cuts in rowing programs is a step in the wrong direction. On the other hand, collegiate football and basketball are stronger than ever and are not in danger of any cuts.

Football Rules

In the mid-2000s, ESPN, a Disney affiliate, owned the rights to more college football games than it could show on ESPN and ESPN2. If ESPN did not show a college game, the college was prohibited by exclusive contracts from reselling the game to other national networks. College Sports Television (CSTV) accused ESPN of having a monopoly, leading CSTV to ask the U.S. Justice Department to investigate. Colleges felt that ESPN was buying up rights to college games and warehousing them to prevent other networks from airing them. No charges were filed against ESPN, but CSTV credited the government inquiry for a change in ESPN's policy. ESPN now shares college games with other networks. ESPN also started a new channel, ESPNU, to focus exclusively on college sports. ESPNU is now a prominent part of the Disney **cable bundle**—a group of TV channels sold as a package for one monthly price by TV subscription services.

How do federal laws affect the varsity sports offered at universities?

© John Kropewnicki/Shutterstock.com

College Team Rankings

Preseason rankings of college football teams influence which games are shown on television. Televised games bring greater revenue to the team and its university. Rankings influence advertisers and bowl game sponsors. When an organization applies to sponsor an NCAA-licensed bowl game, at a minimum, it must pay for both of the participating teams' travel and participation expenses. Sponsors want to attract a sell-out crowd and a large TV audience to obtain maximum revenue from ticket sales, merchandise sales, and related events. The addition of newer distribution channels, such as computers, tablets, and smartphones, offers even more opportunities to attract viewers to see the top teams play.

ESPN wanted to deliver the final college bowl game of the year in a way that would appeal to every type of football fan. To do so, it began distributing the game six ways. It expected most people to watch the game on ESPN but supplemented it across ESPN's family of networks, as shown in the chart below.[11]

ESPN	ESPN2	ESPNews	ESPN Goal Line	ESPN Classic	ESPN3
Normal football game coverage	Title Talk, featuring analysts and coaches	In-depth, play-by-play with non-traditional camera angles	Split screen with live action and replays and live statistics	Viewer control of audio, allowing viewers to eliminate play-by-play calls in favor of sounds on the field	Online service of each team's radio coverage and live fan reactions

INTERMISSION

How do contracts with TV networks affect the distribution of college games?

LO 7.4-3 PROFESSIONAL SPORTS

About half of all live athletic events televised in the United States are produced by ESPN. ESPN receives more than $6 billion each year in cable fees from almost 100 million homes.[12] Despite its dominance, ESPN has seen viewers move away from cable. ESPN considers this a real challenge to its business model and is looking for different ways to connect with new fans.

Worldwide Coverage

ESPN kicked off its 2014 FIFA World Cup coverage six months before the games with a two-minute video intended to attract new fans. The World Cup soccer tournaments match up teams from around the world. The games are played to worldwide audiences with viewership numbers greater than those for a Super Bowl. Soccer is the most popular game worldwide, while U.S. football is ranked as the thirteenth most popular.[13]

JUDGMENT CALL

Frontline, a Public Broadcast Service (PBS) public affairs program, is known for covering tough, controversial issues that advertisers might not want to sponsor. PBS is funded by viewers and donors, not advertisers. For more than a year, ESPN collaborated with PBS's *Frontline* on the production of a two-part program titled *League of Denial: The NFL's Concussion Crisis*. The program was based on a book written by two of ESPN's investigative reporters. ESPN suddenly ended its affiliation with *Frontline*, less than two months before the program was scheduled to be shown and a week after a lunch meeting between the NFL Commissioner and ESPN executives. ESPN has a $15.2 billion contract with the NFL and has been accused multiple times of allowing its sports interests to take precedence over its news division.

Think Critically

Discuss with a partner reasons why ESPN might have a conflict of interest between sports news journalism and sports broadcasting. Conduct an online search to learn whether *Frontline* and ESPN have journalistic guidelines they follow. If so, describe them.

Political Football   Hosting the Super Bowl is a great accomplishment (and undertaking) for any U.S. city. Hosting it in the largest metropolitan area in the United States means everything is super-sized. Super Bowl XLVIII was played at MetLife Stadium in New Jersey, about nine miles from Times Square in New York City. The price of hotels and TV advertisements during the game were at record high costs.

When the stadium was selected as the Super Bowl site, controversy and questions surrounded it, including the construction of an entertainment mall, American Dream, located across the highway from the stadium. The American Dream was to include a 12-story-high indoor ski slope, an indoor water park, an amusement park, stores, and restaurants. Construction on the mall began in 2004. Repeated delays kept the mall from opening, despite a promise to be open for the Super Bowl. NFL's New York Giants and New York Jets, who both play at the MetLife Stadium, sued the mall. Both teams want to avoid traffic problems by keeping parts of the mall closed on game days, if and when it does finally open.

The Super Bowl site selection also renewed scrutiny over the funding of the New Jersey stadium. The stadium was built with private funds from the Jets' and Giants' owners, without state government funds. During negotiations with New Jersey for the stadium, the NFL owners demanded, and won, a prohibition on a tax on luxury suites, ticket sales, or any other revenue generators. The Jets and the Giants now pay the New Jersey Sports Authority about $6.3 million a year in rent. They will not have to share revenue from parking, premium seats, or about $100 million a year from concerts and sponsorships.[14]

While some don't view this as a good deal for New Jersey and its citizens, the owners believe everyone in the region benefits from the distribution of sports and entertainment in the stadium, especially when hosting the Super Bowl.

Distributing the Game

There are more U.S. cities that want professional sports teams than there are teams available. The various leagues control the number of teams and the location of the teams based on the benefits to the leagues' owners. Individual teams within a league are separately operated businesses, but they are not in competition with each other as they would be in a free market. Instead, each team is a member of a cartel. A **cartel** is an organization of independent businesses formed to control production, pricing, and marketing of a product. In the case of professional sports, the cartel is a number of independent sports teams grouped together and governed by a league agreement. A **league agreement** controls the marketing mix and governs the distribution of professional sports games, including the locations of the teams and the number of teams allowed in the league. Because teams must have other teams to play, they must stay in the league or start a new league. Federal antitrust law prohibits cartels in most businesses, but special legislation excludes the professional sports leagues from those laws.

How Distribution Is Decided   Comcast's NBC Sports and ESPN were outbid by 21st Century Fox for the right to televise the U.S. Golf Association (USGA) tournaments. The financial terms of the agreement, which runs through 2026, weren't disclosed. However, it is known that the agreement resulted in a significant increase in the $40 million rights fees that the USGA had been receiving. Fox is making a major run at becoming a destination for sports coverage. It launched Fox Sports 2, a 24-hour national sports network. The USGA indicated that its decision

Each NFL team has 12 to 20 footballs that have been precisely prepared for the starting quarterbacks. Equipment directors spend hours preparing the balls by removing the wax, wetting the ball, brushing the ball while it is wet, and scrubbing it with a high-speed buffer. Eli Manning of the New York Giants makes sure to practice with every ball before using it in a game.

How does a league agreement affect the distribution of sporting events?

© Rob Marmion/Shutterstock.com

to change the long-standing relationship it had with NBC and ESPN was partly because of the increased rights fees. Additionally, it was because Fox reaches a younger demographic group.

It Takes Money   The Houston Rockets basketball team and Houston Astros baseball team expected to benefit financially by establishing their own TV distribution system. The teams contracted with NBC Universal to launch Comcast SportsNet Houston (CSN Houston). CSN Houston was available only to about 40 percent of the 2.2 million people in the local TV viewing market. About 60 percent of the area's viewers were not able to receive the games. Viewers in other parts of Texas and surrounding states who had previously received the games could not under the new system. Wider distribution was hampered by at least three key elements:

- The Astros had a weak winning record, thus viewer interest was low.
- CSN Houston wanted to charge other distributors, such as DirecTV and DISH Network, a high price. With such low demand, other carriers refused to distribute the games at the high price being asked.
- The territorial restrictions on the distribution of Rockets' games prevented them from being shown in other major city markets in Texas. In comparison, the viewing areas of NBA basketball teams Dallas Mavericks and San Antonio Spurs are vast.[15]

TAKE A BOW   Richie Parker

When Hendrick Motorsports, the most winning team in NASCAR, hired Richie Parker, some people asked, "What can he do?" Eight years and five championships later, the question now is, "What can't he do?" As a vehicle engineer, Parker uses a computer to design auto chassis and body components for Jimmie Johnson, Kasey Kahne, Jeff Gordon, and Dale Earnhardt Jr.

Richie Parker's whole life has been a study in engineering, as he has successfully conquered every hurdle life has thrown his way. He was born without arms but turned a love of cars, his problem-solving ability, and his design talent into a remarkable career. As Parker stated, "I don't know there's a lot in life … that I'd say I can't do. Just things I haven't done yet."[16]

Think Critically

Conduct online research and find additional information and video about Richie Parker. Why is Richie Parker such an amazing inspiration and role model for both abled and disabled people?

CSN Houston filed for Chapter 11 bankruptcy protection when it was unable to gain widespread distribution of the games. Many believed that Comcast, the nation's largest cable network, overpriced the shares of the CSN Houston network sold to the Astros and the Rockets and did not fully develop the distribution coverage strategy.

Nonstop Distribution

Channel Management

For the fan that can never get enough of the NFL, the NFL Network is available through a **multichannel video programming distributor** (a cable or satellite distributor) and even through some local phone companies on a 24/7 basis. The network offers television and radio programming that covers professional football from every angle, including an inside view of professional football training camps, highlights of the previous season's best games, and even tips on how to become an NFL cheerleader.

INTERMISSION

Why would a TV network, such as ESPN, use multiple distribution channels for coverage of a single game?

ENCORE

Understand Marketing Concepts

Select the best answer for each question.

1. To gain the rights to show a professional game on TV, the media must
   a. be skilled at playing the professional sport
   b. participate in sports competitions
   c. outbid competitors
   d. both a and c

2. Which of the following statements is true?
   a. Universities financially support all sports.
   b. Nonrevenue college sports are being cut by some colleges.
   c. Basketball and football are not financially supported in colleges.
   d. All of the above are true.

Think Critically

Answer the following questions as completely as possible.

3. Write a paragraph about the positive impact of recreational sports on the health and economy of a community. (LO 7.4-1)

4. What factors influence which collegiate sports are offered at a university? (LO 7.4-2)

CHAPTER ASSESSMENT

Review Marketing Terms

Match the terms listed with the definitions.

1. Distributing a movie nationally to a thousand or more theaters at the same time
2. Independent films outside the commercial mainstream of blockbuster films
3. All of the businesses through which products or services pass on the way to the consumer
4. A way of distributing multimedia files over the Internet for later playback
5. Oval-shaped outdoor theaters with tiered seating around a central staging area
6. A cable or satellite distributor
7. High-speed Internet service
8. A group of TV channels sold as a package for one monthly price by TV subscription services
9. Businesses involved in making the product or service available to consumers
10. New technologies that change existing forms of communication channels
11. Types of delivery systems
12. The process of planning, organizing, and managing the distribution of products and services
13. A method of distributing an event to a large volume of people
14. Controls the marketing mix and governs the distribution of professional sports games, including the location and number of teams
15. An app feature that reviews private data to provide answers to questions it predicts you might ask
16. The facility where an event is held
17. An organization of independent businesses formed to control production, pricing, and marketing of a product
18. Contains film of actual concert performances
19. College sports that do not provide a return on investment

a. amphitheaters
b. art-house movies
c. broadband
d. cable bundle
e. cartel
f. channels of distribution
g. disruptive technologies
h. in-concert movies
i. intermediaries
j. league agreement
k. logistics
l. mass media
m. multichannel video programming distributor
n. nonrevenue sports
o. platforms
p. podcasts
q. predictive search
r. venue
s. wide release

Review Marketing Concepts

Select the best answer for each of the following questions.

20. The location of a pro sports team is determined by
    a. the fans
    b. the league
    c. the FCC
    d. the NCAA

21. Television transmission of sporting events is
   a. not attractive to TV networks
   b. difficult because there is no existing fan base
   c. set in an existing venue
   d. illegal
22. Channels of distribution members could include
   a. event promoters
   b. facilities
   c. media
   d. all of the above
23. The term "knockoff" can be used to describe
   a. a boxing match
   b. a pirated, illegal copy
   c. a form of entertainment
   d. none of the above
24. Which of the following is a true statement regarding technology?
   a. It gives customers more control of distribution of entertainment.
   b. It always increases the costs of distribution.
   c. It makes distribution more difficult.
   d. None of the above are true.

Think Critically

25. Write two paragraphs explaining how the media selected for use in the global distribution of sports and entertainment can affect the success of an entertainment product. (LO 7.1-2)
26. Why do some college sports receive more support than others? How does television affect the marketing of college sports? (LO 7.4-2)
27. Why do you think musicians and creators of original entertainment content are concerned about piracy? Why is piracy so prevalent in China? (LO 7.1-3)
28. Listen to a talk radio show about sports. How do the hosts engage the listeners? (LO 7.2-1)
29. Conduct research to learn how social media is being used to distribute marketing information about entertainment. Make a chart illustrating the process. (LO 7.2-2)
30. Why do you think the economic utility of live entertainment makes it worth the cost and trouble of traveling to the location of the event? (LO 7.3-1)
31. Do you think people will tire of using social media? Will it become a thing of the past? What might take its place? Describe what you see as the future of global distribution channels for sports and entertainment. (LO 7.1-2)
32. How do professional sports teams differ from other businesses that compete in a free-market system? What keeps businesses from using the same system used by sports teams? (LO 7.4-3)

Make Academic Connections

33. **Careers** Many people play a role in distributing a TV show or sports game to fans. Conduct research on a specific channel member role or a related group of roles that interest you. What about the role interests you? What level of education is required to fulfill the position? What kinds of prior work experience or internships would be most beneficial to people in this role? What are some of the tasks these people complete? What is the salary range for this career area? Write a paragraph or more to summarize this information. (LO 7.1-1)

34. **Technology** You are an electronics retailer who wants to target both boys and girls ages 10 to 13. You sell video games, movie videos, and other forms of entertainment technology. You are considering using the Internet for product distribution. Develop a plan for starting your business online. (LO 7.3-2)

35. **Geography** On a map, mark the locations of the professional football teams across the United States. What do you believe were some of the geographic considerations in the placement of these teams? (LO 7.4-3)

36. **Ethics** In the interest of a free-enterprise system, antitrust laws in the United States prohibit cartels in most industries. Special legislation makes professional sports leagues exempt from antitrust laws. Why do you think this exception is made? Do you believe that allowing the control of the leagues by cartels is ethical? Justify your answer. (LO 7.4-3)

37. **Research** Select a college and use the Internet to research the ranking of its basketball team. Explain how the team's ranking and contracts with TV networks might affect the distribution of its games and the amount of revenue it generates. (LO 7.4-2)

38. **Finance** The TV industry uses advertising and retransmission fees to pay for operations and production of original content. How has the use of the Internet changed the sources of revenue? (LO 7.2-1)

39. **Communication** Your city wants to improve its recreational facilities and will need to increase taxes to get the funds. Write a persuasive letter to your mayor outlining why you think this is a good idea and what types of facilities you believe are most needed in your city. (LO 7.4-1)

40. **History** Research the history of the Internet. How and why did it start? When did it become available to consumers? In your opinion, what types of sports and entertainment are best suited for this mode of distribution? What trends do you expect in the future? (LO 7.2-1)

41. **Marketing Math** To host the Super Bowl, a city must spend $17 million to update the city's infrastructure and meet NFL requirements. Overtime pay for police officers will cost $5,236,000, and extra garbage collection will cost $1,240,000. There will be 80,000 fans in attendance for 3 days that will spend $700 a day that is taxable at 14 percent. Another 25,000 people will attend related events for 2 days and spend $300 a day that is taxable at 8 percent. After paying all expenses, how much net revenue will the city earn? (LO 7.4-3)

EXTRA INNINGS PROJECT

Because of continuous advances in technology, the media used to distribute sports and entertainment is expected to change at an accelerated pace. Marketers must anticipate this change. Your marketing firm wants to be on top of any new technologies currently in development that might become the next big trend.

Work with a group and complete the following activities.

1. Use the Internet or library to research ESPN, *Sports Illustrated*, *Variety*, or other sports and entertainment media to determine current technology trends.
2. Based on your research, brainstorm with your group to create a list of ideas about the direction of media.
3. Write a one-page summary describing your projections about the new media and explaining how it will be different from current media. What improvements will it bring? In the summary, include your group's opinion on the future of technology media.
4. Present your group's opinion and supporting evidence to the class.

VIRTUAL BUSINESS *Sports & Entertainment*

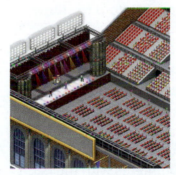

Use the *Promotion with Social Media* lesson to explore how social media is used in marketing. Social media use is growing across all age groups. Reaching ticket buyers of all ages is becoming easier with mobile devices. Gain an understanding of social media marketing by managing a concert with no promotion and observe the attendance. Then, use social media and see the impact on concert attendance. Recognize the importance of distribution channels such as Twitter, Facebook, Pinterest, Instagram, and Google+. After the completion of using social media to promote this concert, you will be challenged to promote another concert with a smaller audience and a limited budget.

*For more information, go to **knowledgematters.com**.*

TO DISTRIBUTE OR NOT TO DISTRIBUTE— THAT IS THE QUESTION

For over 40 years, the Federal Communications Commission (FCC) required multichannel video programming distributors (MVPD), such as cable or satellite providers, to black out retransmission of live sporting events if the event was not available for local broadcast. The rule was intended to support the leagues, colleges, and even high schools by protecting ticket sales revenue. Without TV coverage, people would be more likely to attend the game in person. It was also assumed that if sports leagues lost revenue, they might refuse to sell broadcast rights to distant stations. This goes against the intention of the rule to ensure the availability of sports to the public. Forty years later, the FCC proposed eliminating the rule and leaving the distribution up to the interested parties.

Targeted Blackouts

Sports leagues' blackout policies determine which games are blacked out locally. The league policies are put into effect through contracts between the leagues that hold the rights to the games and the entities to which they sell distribution rights.

The National Football League (NFL) has followed a league rule that blacks out games in the team's home area if less than 85 percent of the seats are sold 72 hours before kickoff. The FCC proposed eliminating its rule that supported the NFL blackout, but the NFL objected to the change and threatened to move games from free broadcast stations to cable or pay-TV platforms. The FCC made it clear that it was not proposing to eliminate the sports leagues' blackout policies, but only wanted to remove FCC support for the policies.

The FCC was motivated to eliminate the sports blackout rule by groups such as the Sports Fan Coalition, Inc., National Consumers League, Public Knowledge, League of Fans, and Media Access Project. These groups had filed a joint petition urging the FCC to act. They believed the following:

- Ticket prices for sports events were at historic highs
- The rule was anti-fan
- Fewer people could afford to attend local sports events

The rule elimination also had support from a number of sports economists and thousands of individuals. The NFL, Baseball Commissioner, National Association of Broadcasters, and a group of network television affiliates filed comments with the FCC opposing the rule elimination.

Think Critically

1. Why would the sports leagues strongly oppose dropping the FCC rule if the fans wanted it dropped?
2. Why would fans be in support of dropping the FCC support?
3. Do you think sports leagues should be able to control who gets to view the games on free TV? Why or why not?
4. Do you think stopping the blackouts would have an economic effect on communities? Explain your answer.

MARKETING MANAGEMENT SERIES EVENT

Participants of the Marketing Management Series Event are given a written scenario to review. They have ten minutes to review it and to develop a professional approach to solving the problem. They are allowed ten minutes to present their plan of action to the judge. Five additional minutes are available for judges to ask questions about the proposal.

The Houston Livestock Show and Rodeo is the world's largest indoor rodeo. Each year, almost 3 million people attend the event. The NRG Center, NRG Stadium, and NRG Park are transformed into a gigantic, one-of-a-kind Western shopping mall.

A small western wear store has met the qualifications to be a retail vendor during the show, which lasts 18 days. There will be about 35 other retailers selling clothing and shoes. You have been asked by the western wear store's owner to develop plans for operation during this event. Specifically, the storeowner needs to know what products to sell during the show. It is important to her that the products sold are made in the United States.

Performance Indicators Evaluated
- Identify the product's/service's competitive advantage.
- Communicate the core values of the product/service.
- Explain the importance of company involvement in community activities.
- Create written briefs for outside agencies/consultants.

To ensure the store has enough products at the show during the 18 days, the plan should address the best methods of communicating with product suppliers and store employees. The storeowner also wants you to develop a news release to announce the introduction of the store at the show. It should emphasize the store's support of the show.

The event judge will be role-playing the storeowner. You must present your plans describing how you would select products, work with product suppliers and store employees, and promote the store in the midst of other competition.

Think Critically

1. What would you need to know before meeting with the owner?
2. What factors would you consider in choosing the products to sell?
3. What information do you need to know to talk to the product suppliers?
4. What specifics would you include in a news release?

www.deca.org

THE ECONOMICS OF SUPPLY AND DEMAND

© Chiyacat/Shutterstock.com

POINT YOUR BROWSER

ngl.cengage.com/sports4e

Winning Strategies

Cereal Stars

Marketers have long known that celebrity endorsements help sell products. Wheaties® cereal provides a classic example of the successful use of this marketing strategy. Wheaties came into existence by accident in 1921. A man was fixing his breakfast and dropped an oatmeal-like wheat bran mix on a hot stove, and the splat cooked into a crispy flake. The man ate it, loved it, and recommended it to the Washburn Crosby Company. Washburn Crosby marketed the discovery as Gold Medal Whole Wheat Flakes. Later, the name was changed to Wheaties, and General Mills took over Washburn Crosby.

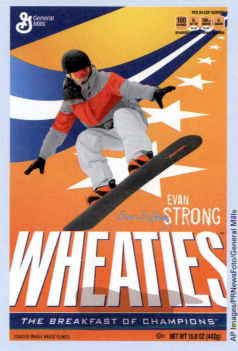

AP Images/PRNewsFoto/General Mills

The first star that Wheaties featured was a fictitious character from radio—Jack Armstrong, All-American Boy. Lou Gehrig was featured on the box in 1934, and from that point on, athletes became a permanent fixture on the box. Stars from baseball, aviation, tennis, skating, NASCAR, basketball, swimming, track, gymnastics, hockey, and golf have appeared on the boxes of cereal. Being featured on a box of Wheaties is a career goal for many athletes. It is an honor and looked upon as a sign of success.

In 1999 Wheaties launched a five-box series of packages devoted to women in sports. The featured athletes were members of the U.S. Women's Soccer Team, including Mia Hamm and Brandi Chastain. This was General Mills' way of permanently honoring them and recognizing their achievements.

Think Critically

1. How does displaying the image of a star athlete on its cereal boxes benefit Wheaties? How does it benefit the athlete?

2. What are the possible risks to Wheaties of featuring real people on its cereal boxes?

3. What types of nontraditional athletes and sports figures could be represented by Wheaties on its cereal boxes?

8.1 Supply and Demand

Learning Objectives

LO 8.1-1   Explain the relationships among supply, demand, and price.

LO 8.1-2   Discuss the government's influence on pricing.

Key Terms

- law of demand
- law of supply
- scarcity
- equilibrium
- price fixing
- bait and switch
- price discrimination

OPENING ACT

Economists believe the economic value of a professional sports team does not measure up to the social and psychological significance of the team. Most team owners and sports fans would disagree. For an existing team to move to a city or for expansion teams to be approved, there must be financial benefits to the league's member owners, to related businesses, and to the cities in which the team will locate. Success cannot occur if one makes a profit and the others lose money.

Cooperative Learning   In a group, brainstorm the benefits, other than financial gain, that might come to a community acquiring a professional sports team. Exchange and discuss the lists with other groups.

LO 8.1-1   THE LAWS OF SUPPLY AND DEMAND

Pricing   Consumers purchase products to satisfy their needs and wants. Concerts, sporting events, air flights, and hotel rooms satisfy certain consumer needs and wants. Thus, they are in demand by consumers. *Demand* is the relationship between the quantity of a product that consumers are willing and able to purchase and the price. Consumers often conduct research and talk to friends and family to select goods and services to satisfy their needs.

Producers are businesses that use resources to develop products and services. Producers also conduct research to gather information about the types of goods and services that customers are likely to purchase. *Supply* is the relationship between the quantity of a product that producers are willing and able to provide and the price. Ballparks, special-event centers, and surrounding restaurants and hotels are built based on consumer demand for sports and entertainment events.

Price–Demand Relationships

Finding a balance between what companies are willing to produce and what customers are willing to buy is a major challenge for marketers. Many factors must be considered when trying to determine the marketing mix—the right blend of products, pricing, promotion, and distribution.

If consumers know about a desirable product and it is readily available, they may be willing to buy more of it when the price is low. But they will buy less of it when the price is high. This inverse relationship between price and demand is known as the **law of demand**—when the price goes up, demand goes down; when the price goes down, demand goes up.

Redbox provides consumers with a good alternative to watching movies at the theater. Instead of paying high ticket prices at a movie theater or paying a membership fee to join an online rental service, consumers can pick up a movie at a Redbox kiosk while at the grocery store or other location and watch it in the comfort of their homes. This relatively inexpensive, convenient service has resulted in an increased demand for movie rentals.

Price–Supply Relationships

The producers of a product, whether it is a sports event or a movie, are in business to make a profit. They are willing to invest their resources—time, money, and materials—if making a profit is possible.

Smartphones have risen in popularity since they were first introduced on the market. The invention of various smartphone applications that allow consumers to view movies and play games made the smartphones even more popular. The price for smartphones remains relatively high, making them profitable. Because of this, many more smartphone manufacturers have entered the market. The producers of smartphones will continue to invest millions of dollars in their products in an attempt to get a bigger share of the market. In addition, ever-changing technological advances give smartphone manufacturers the opportunity to introduce newer, better

Redbox has become the popular choice for consumers who want to rent movies and video games. It has over 35,000 locations in the United States with more than 3 billion rentals since its inception. Redbox is a fully automated video rental store that takes up only 12 square feet of retail space.[1]

© iStockphoto.com/georgeclerk

How does consumer demand affect product manufacturers?

smartphones to the market, keeping consumer demand high. As long as smartphones are in high demand, they can be sold for higher prices. The relationship between price and supply is known as the **law of supply**—when the price goes up, the supply produced goes up; when the price goes down, the supply produced goes down.

Marketers help balance the effect of the laws of supply and demand by providing consumers with information about new products, often through advertising. Consumers then decide how to use their limited resources to purchase products that will meet their wants and needs. Producers must be aware of consumer buying habits and adjust their production accordingly.

Scarcity

Consumers have limited time and money to spend on sports and entertainment products and events. Producers also have limited resources to use in the production of products and events. The lack of resources is referred to as **scarcity**. Consumers and producers must decide how to use their limited resources to meet unlimited wants and needs.

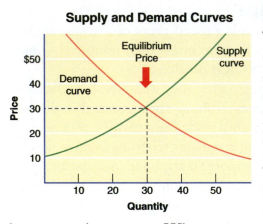

Supply and Demand Curves

Equilibrium

The economics of supply and demand can be illustrated by curves on a graph. The supply curve indicates how much product will be provided at different prices. When prices for the goods rise, producers are encouraged to produce more. The demand curve shows how much consumers will buy at different prices. Consumers generally will buy more at lower prices. When prices are too high, consumers will choose other alternatives or do without the goods. **Equilibrium** is the point at which the supply and demand curves intersect. Equilibrium indicates the best quantity and price for goods and services.

Concerts in the Spotlight

Popular concerts sell out in a few hours, sometimes months before the actual event, due to high consumer demand. Fans will form lines at the ticket outlets several hours before tickets go on sale. Extreme loyalists may even camp outside overnight to ensure they are first in line to purchase tickets. Because of the high demand and limited supply of available seating, ticket prices may be high. If demand is high enough, event planners may increase supply by adding a second show.

Environmental Influence on Supply and Demand

In today's eco-friendly world, companies are finding that environmentally sound practices and products are affecting consumer demand. In an effort to protect and preserve the environment, many consumers will pay more for products that are eco-friendly, or "green." Senda Athletics is a sports ball provider with a social conscience. It works with manufacturers to provide soccer balls made from sustainably harvested rubber. Brooks, a sports apparel company, manufactures running shoes made from recycled materials. The shoes also have biodegradable mid-soles. As consumer demand for these types of products increases, companies will continue to supply them.

The Internet and Supply and Demand

The Internet has had a major impact on the supply and demand of products. Consumers now have easy access to products for sale all around the world. The sale of sports memorabilia has increased due to sites such as eBay, an online marketplace that allows individuals to buy and sell merchandise. Individuals interested in purchasing retro sports jerseys, for example, can locate the rare or hard-to-find merchandise online. Consumer demand for retro sports jerseys will influence the price charged. If the jerseys are selling for a high price, others might be motivated to sell their retro sports jerseys, thus increasing the supply.

INTERMISSION

How does price affect demand?

LO 8.1-2 GOVERNMENT INFLUENCE ON PRICING

Pricing The United States has a free-enterprise system, also called a *private-enterprise system*, based on independent decisions made by consumers and businesses. The government plays a limited role, but even a private-enterprise system calls for some government involvement. The government influences prices charged for merchandise directly and indirectly through antitrust laws, taxation, and various consumer protection laws.

How does competition benefit the consumer?

Ian Dagnall/Alamy

MATH IN MARKETING

A popular college football stadium accommodates 92,000 fans. Ten percent of the highest-priced seats are available in the suites at the stadium. A suite seat sells for $200 per game, while the other 90 percent of seats sell for $60 each per game. The stadium sells out for each home game. A small nonconference team has agreed to play two years consecutively as the opposing team at the large stadium if the home team will pay the smaller nonconference school $1.5 million each year.

Do the Math

How many seats in the stadium are classified as suite seats? How many seats in the stadium are not suite seats? What is the revenue earned at one sold-out game? What is the net revenue of a game in which the nonconference team plays at the big stadium?

Benefits of Competition

Antitrust laws serve to encourage competition and to avoid *monopolies* in which one business controls the entire market. Increased competition is beneficial to businesses and consumers alike. Competition in a free market allows the laws of supply and demand to set the prices. Innovative businesses stay ahead of the competition by improving their products and services. Competition also encourages businesses to develop new products and services to meet the changing needs of consumers.

Taxation

Taxation is another strategy used by the government to encourage or discourage economic activity. Increasing taxes on products, such as alcoholic beverages or cigarettes, results in higher prices for those items. The higher prices will discourage sales as well as provide needed revenues to the government. Taxes imposed on gasoline help states pay for highway repairs. Cities use hotel taxes to fund new sports venues.

On the other hand, tax reductions encourage production and sales. Tax breaks for companies manufacturing ethanol help encourage production of an alternative fuel source. Tax breaks are also given to manufacturers of more fuel-efficient cars. Some cities even offer tax credits to entice professional sports teams to locate in that city. Film companies are given tax credits by cities and states to encourage them to produce movies there.

Illegal Pricing

Price fixing occurs when related businesses conspire to charge high prices. Suppose that all competing fast-food restaurants formed a *cartel* (an agreement between businesses not to compete) that decided to charge $20 for all hamburgers. Consumers would have no choice but to pay the

$20 if they wanted to buy a hamburger at a restaurant. Price fixing is an illegal practice in the United States.

Bait and switch is another illegal practice. **Bait and switch** occurs when a product that is advertised at a low price is "out of stock," so the salesperson tries to sell customers a higher-priced alternative. For example, a sportswear store may advertise popular running shoes for a great sales price (the bait). However, when customers try to buy them, they are told that all of those shoes are sold out and are persuaded to buy a "higher-quality," more expensive pair of shoes (the switch). Prices that are advertised cannot be deceptive or misleading.

Price discrimination occurs when an individual, group, or business is charged a higher price than others purchasing the same product or service. There must be a valid reason for price variances, such as the difference in distribution costs for various locations, the volume (or quantity) of sales, or changing market conditions.

INTERMISSION

List three ways the government influences pricing.

ENCORE

Understand Marketing Concepts

Select the best answer for each question.

1. Which of the following is *not* an accurate statement based on the laws of supply and demand?
   a. When demand for a product goes up, prices can be set higher.
   b. When demand for a service goes down, a business will increase prices to make up for the loss of sales.
   c. When the supply of a product increases, prices tend to fall.
   d. The price point at which supply and demand are equal is said to be the equilibrium point.

2. Advertising a product for a great price and then not having it available for consumers to purchase is part of which practice?
   a. bait and switch
   b. price discrimination
   c. price fixing
   d. none of the above

Think Critically

Answer the following questions as completely as possible.

3. Based on the laws of supply and demand, explain why a baseball signed by Babe Ruth commands a high price. (LO 8.1-1)

4. Why do governmental laws seek to restrict monopolies and cartels? How does this benefit consumers and businesses? (LO 8.1-2)

8.2 Pricing Strategies

The Essential Question

What factors help determine the price for a sports or entertainment event?

Learning Objectives

LO 8.2-1 Discuss pricing strategies used by businesses to increase sales.

LO 8.2-2 List five steps for determining price.

Key Terms

- operating expenses
- markup
- price lines
- loss-leader pricing

OPENING ACT

Kid Rock introduced a fan-friendly concert tour with unconventional pricing for the summer of 2013. The "$20 Best Night Ever" tour priced the majority of tickets at $20, enabling more fans to attend his concerts. Kid Rock decided that he would take a pay cut to fight high ticket prices. If fans purchased their concert tickets at Walmart, they didn't have to pay parking and ticket service charges. Those attending the "$20 Best Night Ever" concert could also purchase reasonably priced food and T-shirts. One thousand platinum tickets ranging in price from $60 to $350 were also sold for each of Kid Rock's concerts. Kid Rock received a percentage of ticket, merchandise, and food sales instead of a large upfront fee for each show.[2]

Collaborative Learning   With a partner, identify financial and nonfinancial benefits to Kid Rock as a result of his "$20 Best Night Ever" tour. Why might this be a risky strategy?

LO 8.2-1   PRICING CONSIDERATIONS

Pricing

Price is the amount that customers pay for products and services. *Pricing* is the process of establishing and communicating the value of goods and services to customers. When determining the price to charge for goods and services, businesses must take into consideration the cost of merchandise, the operating expenses, and the desired amount of profit. In the case of a retailer, the cost of merchandise includes what is paid to manufacturers for the products that the retailer offers for sale. **Operating expenses** are all of the costs associated with running a business in addition to the cost of the merchandise. Examples of operating expenses include utilities, salaries, unemployment taxes, and payroll taxes (Medicare and Social Security taxes). The amount that is added to the cost of a product or service to cover operating expenses and to allow for a profit is the **markup**.

Remember that pricing is also determined according to the rules of supply and demand. In a monopoly situation, where there is only one company offering a product or service, the company can set high prices if consumer demand for the product is strong. When there is competition, it is important for a company to differentiate its product or service to ensure sales. In situations of *pure competition*, there are many companies offering the same product and customers do not recognize major differences among the brands. This type of market drives the prices lower as companies compete for consumers' business. If the *market price*, as determined by the laws of supply and demand, is not sufficient to cover a business's product costs and operating expenses and allow for a profit, then the business will stop offering the product.

How does pure competition affect prices?

© Pavel L. Photo and Video/Shutterstock.com

Pricing Policies

A *one-price policy* means that all customers pay the same price for a product, such as a concert, football game, or running shoes. A *flexible pricing policy* allows customers to negotiate prices within a price range. Automobile dealerships typically allow room for customers to negotiate better prices. Sports equipment manufacturers typically allow room for customers to negotiate prices based on the volume purchased.

JUDGMENT CALL

Tim Tebow was acquired by the New York Jets in 2012 for a salary of $2.53 million. Many people did not understand the selection of Tebow, because he rarely played in games during the previous season. Because Tebow is a popular player, some fans believe the Jets acquired him to sell jerseys and gain positive exposure for the team. Tebow's jersey ranked eighth in overall NFL merchandise sales, and his jersey was the highest-selling Jets jersey.

The sale of Tebow-related merchandise would have needed to generate nearly $81 million to pay his salary because NFL merchandise revenue is shared evenly among the 32 NFL teams. By all accounts, this sales goal was not realistic. In addition, the signing of Tebow did not result in more ticket sales or corporate sponsorships for the Jets.[3]

Think Critically

Why do so many fans like Tim Tebow? Why do you think the Jets invested millions of dollars in him for one year? Was this a good or bad business decision? Explain your answer.

Price lines are distinct categories of merchandise based on price, quality, and features. Ralph Lauren has its Polo brand as its high-end price line and its Chaps brand as the next-best, lower-priced alternative.

Geographic pricing allows pricing variations based on geographic location. Factors influencing geographic pricing include distribution costs, local competition, and local taxes and/or restrictions. Generally, when manufacturers are located closer to retailers, distribution costs are lower, which helps keep prices down for consumers.

A Variety of Pricing Strategies

Retailers use a wide variety of pricing strategies in an effort to increase total sales. Marketers must choose the right strategy to motivate customers to buy.

Psychological Pricing
When retailers use *psychological pricing*, they are creating an illusion for customers. Odd-even pricing is an example of psychological pricing. Prices ending in odd numbers, such as $.95 or $.99, are used to give customers the illusion of spending less than the next higher even dollar amount. For example, when Netflix offers unlimited DVD rentals for $7.99 a month, customers view this as being less expensive than $8.00, even though there is only a difference of one cent.

Prestige Pricing
When retailers charge higher-than-average prices for merchandise and target customers who are seeking status and high quality, they are using the *prestige pricing* strategy. Sportswear manufacturers such as Nike and Under Armour charge higher prices for their merchandise, suggesting superior quality.

Volume Pricing
Stores such as Walmart advertise everyday low prices. Walmart pays lower prices for its merchandise due to the *volume pricing* it receives from its suppliers. Walmart passes these savings on to customers. In turn, the high volume of sales Walmart experiences allows it to continue to offer low prices.

How do retailers use pricing strategies to increase sales?

© Barry Blackburn/Shutterstock.com

An increasing number of businesses are counting on social media marketing companies to help sell the businesses' goods and services. Using Twitter and Facebook to communicate with customers costs a lot of money. To launch and manage a new Twitter account, complete with consumer interaction (140 characters at a time), a social media marketing company may charge its client $2,000–$4,000 a month. This charge includes content creation. Clients that want a new Facebook account may be charged $2,500–$5,000 a month for setup and management. A social media marketing strategy, including a plan and goals, likely will cost even more.[4]

Think Critically

Why are businesses turning to social media marketing companies to help sell their goods and services? What should businesses consider before paying high prices for the set up and management of social media sites such as Twitter and Facebook?

Some sports teams give fans better ticket prices when they buy a season ticket package. The sale of season tickets benefits the team because sold-out games are more likely. Fans benefit because the cost of buying season tickets is lower than the cost of buying the same game tickets individually.

Promotions   To get more customers in the store, retailers may use *special event promotions* that associate sales with major events, such as Christmas or March Madness. Many businesses use *promotional pricing* strategies. Examples of promotional strategies may include the 50-percent-off sale, the buy-one-get-one-half-price sale, and the no-interest-for-12-months-credit sale. Some businesses use **loss-leader pricing**, which involves reducing the price of a product below the store's cost to create more customer traffic. Although the store may lose money on the sale of the product, customers who are attracted by the loss leader likely will purchase additional merchandise with a much higher markup. The revenues generated by the additional sales will make up for the losses from the loss leader.

Some stores attract repeat business with coupons and rebates. For purchases made in December, a retailer may give customers a coupon for 25 percent off any purchases made in January. This type of promotion will encourage customers to come back the following month, when business is typically slow, to buy more merchandise. *Rebates* are offers on products that customers can mail in for a refund. Some manufacturers offer instant rebates on products.

Quantity Discounts   Power bars may sell for $2 each or have *multiple-unit pricing* of three bars for $5. Customers save money by buying a larger quantity of power bars. Theme parks may charge visitors $60 for a single day's admission or $120 for a three-day pass, reducing the cost per day to $40. When the park offers a season pass for $160, visitors score even bigger savings.

Trade-In Allowances　Customers may be given a *trade-in allowance* for old merchandise when making a new purchase. The trade-in allowance helps reduce the cost of the new item. Some sporting goods stores give trade-in allowances for used sports equipment, such as golf clubs, that can be refurbished and resold. As athletes excel at a sport, they may trade in old equipment that they used as a beginner for more advanced equipment. The trade-in allowance is a cost-efficient way to buy newer or higher-quality equipment.

INTERMISSION

List and describe five pricing strategies to increase sales.

LO 8.2-2　DETERMINING THE PRICE

Pricing

There are five steps for determining the price to charge for a good or service.

1. **Establish price objectives.** You must first decide the amount or percentage of profit you want to earn.

2. **Determine the cost of the product or service.** A hot dog with bun and toppings costs an average of 50 cents. An average vendor resells the hot dog for $2.50. If you sell 100 hot dogs a day, you will earn a profit of $73,000 a year. If you sell 250 hot dogs a day, you will earn $182,500 a year. The average gross income for a hot dog vendor, working year round is about $100,000 a year; however, that figure becomes much smaller after the costs of food handler license fees, equipment, rent, utilities, and spoilage of product are calculated into the equation. Hot dog revenue can be increased by charging extra for toppings, such as chili, sauerkraut, and cheese. For example, vendors may charge 50 cents each for additional toppings.

What factors should a business consider when pricing its products and services?

3. **Estimate consumer demand for your product or service.** Will demand for the product be high enough to command a high price? Will setting the price low generate enough additional demand to both move the merchandise and make a comfortable profit? Many hot dog vendors work during special events such as sporting games, parades, and carnivals when demand is higher. The earning potential for a single highly successful event can be $500–$5,000 a day.

4. **Study the competition.** Consumers must be able to distinguish your goods and services from those offered by the competition. Higher prices can be charged for better merchandise or better service.

5. **Decide on a pricing strategy.** Carefully evaluate your product or service to determine an appropriate price that will result in sales. Smart pricing decisions are based on good marketing information, including an assessment of the competition and consumer trends.

INTERMISSION

List the five steps for determining price.

ENCORE

Understand Marketing Concepts

Select the best answer for each question.

1. Which of the following allows consumers to negotiate prices?
   a. one-price policy
   b. flexible pricing policy
   c. psychological pricing
   d. promotional pricing

2. Which of the following statements is true regarding markup?
   a. Markup does not take into account the profit you want to make.
   b. Markup is not affected by operating expenses.
   c. Markup must be sufficient to cover operating expenses and allow for a profit.
   d. none of the above

Think Critically

Answer the following questions as completely as possible.

3. Why do so many price tags end in .95 or .99? What is this pricing strategy called and why is it effective? (LO 8.2-1)

4. The owner of a sporting goods store has decided on a 250 percent markup on all apparel. How much will the store charge for bicycle shorts it purchased from the wholesaler for $10 each? What did the store pay for running shoes that it is selling for $70? (LO 8.2-2)

8.3 Market Conditions

The Essential Question

What are the business cycles and how do they affect consumer spending on sports and entertainment events?

Learning Objectives

LO 8.3-1 Define the business cycle and describe its effect on the sports and entertainment industries.

LO 8.3-2 Discuss the importance of monitoring consumer trends.

Key Terms

- business cycle
- inflation
- shoulder period

OPENING ACT

There is some truth to the saying, "What goes around, comes around." The clothing industry is a prime example of how popular styles make a comeback 15 to 30 years later. Similarly, the sports and entertainment industries also experience swings in business based on consumer trends. Although boxing is still popular, it is losing fans to mixed martial arts fighting, which many people find more entertaining. Generations ago, college students faithfully attended their school's football games. Today, students are less inclined to do so because there are many other entertainment options. Drive-in movie theaters that were once on the brink of extinction are making a comeback across the country. Sports and entertainment marketers are well aware that competing for consumers' dollars is increasingly tough in today's "trendy" marketplace.

Collaborative Learning Discuss with a partner what sports and entertainment marketers can do to make their offerings more appealing to consumers in order to remain profitable as trends come and go.

LO 8.3-1 IMPACT OF THE BUSINESS CYCLE

Marketing-Information Management

The **business cycle**, also known as the *economic cycle*, refers to the ups and downs of the economy. While referred to as a cycle, there is not a well-defined pattern. The length and severity of each up and down swing can vary significantly. Sports and entertainment planners should be aware of the market conditions they are facing as they make their plans.

Expansion

The upside of the business cycle is referred to as *expansion*. During the expansion phase, there is a growing demand for goods and services. It is a growth period that has great potential for profit, which encourages competition to enter the market. The *peak* is the highest point of growth in the economy.

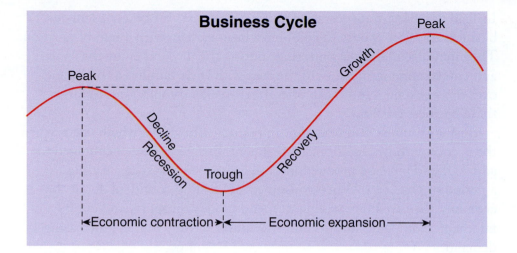

Contraction

The downside of the business cycle is referred to as *contraction*. During this time, the economy is in a decline, unemployment goes up, and consumer demand lessens. The lowest point of a contraction period is called a *trough*. Depending on the severity of the contraction, it may be referred to as a *recession* or a *depression*.

Inflation occurs when prices for goods and services rise faster than consumer income. The combination of inflation and growing unemployment can mean less discretionary income available for spending on sports and entertainment. How customers feel about the economy and their economic security influences the money they spend on sports and entertainment. Even consumers who remain actively employed may become more cautious about spending money and will tighten their budgets. Spending will be reserved for necessities. Individuals may opt to watch the big game on television instead of spending large sums of money to attend the event in person.

Business Reaction

Whether the business cycle is in a period of decline or growth, sports and entertainment businesses must react to changing consumer demand caused by the business cycle. Sports and entertainment businesses are usually hit hard during a recession. When consumers cut back on spending but still want to enjoy some form of sports and entertainment, competing attractions vie for consumer dollars. Businesses must tighten their budgets, reduce production and supply, and/or offer low-cost alternatives to the budget-conscious consumers.

The travel and tourism industry takes a hit when fuel and airline prices go up. Rising prices can rapidly change an expanding economy into a contracting economy. Hotels must create strategies to maintain occupancy rates during downturns in the economy. When increasing energy prices hit, consumers still may travel and take vacations, but destinations and spending may be less extravagant. Astute travelers look for the best deals.

Instead of paying transportation and lodging costs for two trips, many business travelers choose to combine a business trip with a family vacation. They may attend business meetings during the day and enjoy the sports and entertainment offerings of the area with their families at night and over the weekend. Hotels can offer great weekend room rates to target these business travelers.

Businesses must also react during periods of *recovery*, which occur when the economy shows signs of improvement. Businesses are encouraged to add staff and increase production during the recovery stage, leading to a period of *prosperity*. When consumers are feeling confident about the economy, they are more willing to spend money on sports and entertainment. Companies in this industry must be ready to meet increasing demand.

Seasonal Cycles

For some businesses, the demand for products and services fluctuates with the seasons. A ski resort's *high season*, for example, would typically be the winter, while for an amusement park, winter is typically the *off-season*. A period of moderate demand is called a **shoulder period**.

Why do businesses need to be aware of seasonal cycles?

©Tatiana Popova/Shutterstock.com

Orlando, Florida, relies heavily on travel and tourism. The hotels and amusement parks such as Universal Studios and Walt Disney World need to attract business year-round. Marketers are challenged to create strategies to attract tourists during the traditional shoulder and off-season periods, such as during the school year. Special promotions for Halloween, prom, senior days, Mardi Gras, and other occasions help keep amusement parks and hotels profitable. Organizations with large memberships, such as DECA with more than 190,000 members, are an attractive target market for convention cities and nearby amusement parks. The New York Experience and the Sports and Entertainment Management Conference hosted by National DECA are popular events that bring business to tourist destinations such as New York City and Orlando. Cheerleading and music camps are other examples of special events that generate business during traditionally slow periods. Sports and entertainment marketers must develop creative plans to help even out the fluctuations created by changing seasonal demands.

INTERMISSION

What is inflation and how does it contribute to a recession?

LO 8.3-2 IMPACT OF CONSUMER TRENDS

Marketing-Information Management

Successful sports and entertainment marketing firms need to be aware of the latest consumer trends and attitudes. Baseball stadiums that added roofs for protection from the weather are now making the roofs retractable to bring the outdoors back to the game, as preferred by fans. Reality programming is currently very popular with viewers and is much less costly to produce than sitcoms. But how long will this trend continue before audiences long for the return of more traditional programming like *The Big Bang Theory* or *NCIS*? Trends in the world of sports and entertainment are dictated by consumer demand.

Retro Television

Retro is in style, even in the world of television. There are cable channels dedicated solely to old sitcom television shows such as *Leave It to Beaver*, *The Andy Griffith Show*, *The Golden Girls*, *Everybody Loves Raymond*, and *Friends*. Fans of retro shows like to relive the "good old days" and recall positive memories of growing up watching the stars in those sitcoms. Showing popular reruns is less costly to television networks.

Game Shows

Even game shows from the past are making a great comeback. There are now game show channels that rerun old favorites. The major television networks dedicate entire television specials to game shows such as *Let's Make a Deal*, *The Newlywed Game*, *Hollywood Squares*, and numerous other hit game shows of the past. Game shows such as *The Price Is Right* and *Wheel of Fortune* have survived over the years due to broad viewer appeal. *The Price Is Right* is the highest-rated game show for young people, middle-aged fans, and senior citizens alike. Bob Barker successfully hosted the show for 35 years before comedian Drew Carey took over as host in 2007. The likability of both hosts has helped make the show a success. New game shows are being produced to meet consumer demand.

Reality Television

Over the past decade, an increasing number of viewers have become hooked on reality television shows. Reality television frequently features unknown cast members in unscripted situations. Reality television has an expansive range of topics, from talent shows to house flippers. The expansive nature of reality television makes it attractive to a wide range of socioeconomic groups and age groups of all education levels. The endurance of reality shows can be attributed to the wide assortment of interesting topics that appeal to viewers and the low cost of production for TV networks.

Audience Ratings Speak

New television shows are introduced with great expectations for success. However, some series do not last for more than six airings due to flat ratings. Shows that appear to be early failures are pulled from the network schedule quickly to cut losses. Television networks cannot afford to risk losing viewers to other networks airing more exciting or appealing shows.

Sweeps Week runs four times a year. TV networks pull out all the stops to attract audiences during this time period because the rates that they charge advertisers are based on the viewership numbers collected during Sweeps Week.

Even local television station newscasts change during Sweeps Week, when viewer ratings are measured. Oftentimes, newscasts will save the spiciest consumer watchdog stories for Sweeps Week. The Nielsen ratings have a definite impact on strategies pursued by television networks.

Socio-Culture Issues

Socio-culture issues include trends in customer attitudes, lifestyles, opinions, and demographics. Lifestyles that include eating out frequently may result in obesity, which opens up a new market for businesses to serve. For example, the demand for weight loss products has increased due to the growing obesity epidemic. Businesses must be aware of lifestyle

TAKE A BOW S. Truett Cathy

S. Truett Cathy was the founder and chairman of Chick-fil-A, Inc. Truett and his brother Ben opened The Dwarf Grill (later renamed The Dwarf House) in 1946. The successful Atlanta, Georgia, diner led Cathy to open his first Chick-fil-A restaurant in an Atlanta shopping center. Today, there are more than 1,700 Chick-fil-A restaurants in 39 states and Washington, D.C. Due to Truett's leadership, Chick-fil-A has had an unmatched record of more than 40 consecutive years of annual sales increases.

In addition to founding a successful business, Cathy also had a strong sense of obligation to the community and its young people. Cathy started WinShape Foundation in 1984, which provides scholarships and other youth-support programs. It also provides students at Berry College near Rome, Georgia, with experiential training in leadership and community involvement. Helping care for foster children is another way the foundation gives back to the community. WinShape-operated foster homes that provide long-term care in a positive family environment have been established in several states.

Cathy's business success was based on hard work, humility, and family principles. All Chick-fil-A restaurants are closed on Sunday, without exception, to allow employees time to spend with their families. The cost to start a Chick-fil-A restaurant is $5,000, which is much lower than the franchise fees for other fast-food restaurants. However, candidates interested in operating a Chick-fil-A restaurant must make it through a rigorous screening process.

Think Critically

Why is Chick-fil-A such a successful restaurant? Why do you think Chick-fil-A has a rigorous selection process for prospective operators of its new restaurants? Do you think Truett Cathy's charity work benefited his restaurant business? Why or why not?

choices to determine such things as the best hours of operation for a store or restaurant, the best airtime for a televised ball game, and the best time for special sales.

Businesses must also pay special attention to changing demographics, whether it's the growth of the senior population or greater ethnic diversity. Sports and entertainment businesses cannot assume that past successes will mean future profits. Today's young consumers (sometimes labeled as Generation Z) cannot be taken for granted. They are not as loyal to entertainment venues as individuals who are part of the Baby Boomers, Generation X, or Generation Y (Millennials).

Sports and entertainment businesses must follow the socio-culture trends closely and invest their money wisely. Trends are important factors when designing goods and services. Assessing customers' ever-changing needs and wants is the bottom line when it comes to the success or failure of a product or service.

 *INTERMISSION*

Why must sports and entertainment marketers pay careful attention to consumer trends?

 *ENCORE*

Understand Marketing Concepts

Select the best answer for each question.

1. The business cycle
   a. is a well-defined, predictable pattern in the U.S. economy
   b. refers to the ups and downs of the economy
   c. does not greatly affect sports and entertainment businesses
   d. all of the above

2. Which of the following is characteristic of the expansion phase of the business cycle?
   a. growing unemployment
   b. less discretionary income
   c. increased consumer demand
   d. decreased competition

Think Critically

Answer the following questions as completely as possible.

3. What impact does the price of fuel have on family vacations? How can tourism and hospitality businesses respond? (LO 8.3-1)

4. Explain how consumer lifestyle choices can influence a business's operation. (LO 8.3-2)

Review Marketing Concepts

Match the terms listed with the definitions.

1. Occurs when related businesses conspire to charge high prices
2. The lack of resources
3. The inverse relationship between price and demand—when the price goes up, demand goes down; when the price goes down, demand goes up
4. The ups and downs of the economy
5. The point at which supply and demand are the same
6. A period of moderate demand
7. Occurs when prices for goods and services rise faster than consumer income
8. All of the costs associated with running a business in addition to the cost of the merchandise
9. The amount that is added to the cost of a product or service to cover operating expenses and to allow for a profit
10. A strategy whereby the price of a product is reduced below the store's cost to create more customer traffic
11. Occurs when a product that is advertised at a low price is "out of stock," so the salesperson tries to sell customers a higher-priced alternative
12. Distinct categories of merchandise based on price, quality, and features
13. Occurs when an individual, group, or business is charged a higher price than others purchasing the same product or service
14. The relationship between price and supply—when the price goes up, the supply produced goes up; when the price goes down, the supply produced goes down

a. bait and switch
b. business cycle
c. equilibrium
d. inflation
e. law of demand
f. law of supply
g. loss-leader pricing
h. markup
i. operating expenses
j. price discrimination
k. price fixing
l. price lines
m. scarcity
n. shoulder period

Review Marketing Concepts

Select the best answer for each of the following questions.

15. Which of the following is an example of prestige pricing?
    a. selling a football jersey for $9.99
    b. negotiating prices at a swap meet
    c. charging high prices for status products
    d. charging wealthy customers higher prices than other customers
16. Which of the following practices is restricted by law?
    a. bait and switch
    b. price fixing
    c. price discrimination
    d. all of the above

17. At the point where supply of a product is the same as demand
    a. the market for the item is said to be in equilibrium
    b. the price is set at its optimum point
    c. inflation will occur
    d. both a and b
18. Polo and Chaps, which are Ralph Lauren brands, are examples of
    a. prestige pricing
    b. price lines
    c. psychological pricing
    d. promotional pricing
19. Which of the following is an example of psychological pricing?
    a. charging wealthy customers higher prices than other customers
    b. charging high prices for status products
    c. using bait-and-switch pricing tactics
    d. pricing merchandise at $49.99 instead of $50
20. The downside of the business cycle, when the economy slows down and
    unemployment goes up, is called
    a. contraction
    b. inflation
    c. expansion
    d. peak

Think Critically

21. Explain how the prices charged for tickets to sports and entertainment events have been influenced by the free-enterprise system. (LO 8.1-1)
22. How can cities take advantage of rising gasoline prices to increase revenue from sporting events, travel, and tourism? (LO 8.3-1)
23. You are the marketer for a resort in the Rocky Mountains. Your high season is in the winter because of ski enthusiasts. In the past, the resort has closed for the summer. The owners have decided to keep the resort open all year. How can you attract summer business? (LO 8.3-1)
24. Why would a store be willing to lose money on a loss-leader item? (LO 8.2-1)
25. Describe how marketers can help balance the relationship between the supply that producers are willing to make available and the demand that consumers have for a product. (LO 8.1-1)
26. Describe current U.S. economic conditions. Explain how these economic conditions impact the sports and entertainment industry. (LO 8.3-1)
27. A cable TV network that shows old television sitcoms wants to generate a larger audience. It has asked you to plan a contest using social media that will increase the network's ratings. Describe the contest and explain how it will generate more viewers. (LO 8.3-2)

Make Academic Connections

28. Communication Using the Internet, conduct research to determine the best U.S. cities to host large student leadership conferences such as DECA, FBLA, and BPA. The cities must have hotel rooms and convention facilities to accommodate 15,000 participants. The selected cities must also have additional attractions for conference participants when they are not competing or attending meetings. Prepare an electronic presentation that promotes three different cities for your student conference. (LO 8.3-1)

29. Math Your favorite college team has just won a national championship. You operate a screen-printing company that has the exclusive rights to manufacture and sell the championship T-shirts. The plain cotton shirts cost $3. Supplies, labor, and marketing costs for each shirt average $4. All research that you have conducted has indicated that a 300 percent markup on championship merchandise is the industry norm. How much would you charge for a championship T-shirt if you add a 300 percent markup? (LO 8.2-2)

30. Government Explain the government's role in the U.S. free-enterprise system. What are its goals? How does this affect the sports and entertainment industries? (LO 8.1-2)

31. Ethics Describe some pricing policies that you have encountered that you think were unfair to consumers. Were the business's pricing policies illegal? If not, do you believe such policies should be made illegal? Explain why. (LO 8.1-2)

32. Finance Your grandmother has always dreamed of being on *The Price Is Right* show. You would like to surprise her with a trip to California to be on the show. Use the Internet to conduct research about obtaining tickets for the show, the price of flights to California, the price of nearby hotels, and other miscellaneous expenses associated with attending the show. Prepare a budget for you and your grandmother based on your research. Explain how current market conditions might affect your planning. (LO 8.3-1)

33. Economics Draw a supply and demand graph for gym shoes. Set the equilibrium price point at $50 and the equilibrium quantity sold at 600. Show on the graph what would happen if the price of the gym shoes rose to $60. (LO 8.1-1)

34. History Conduct research using the Internet and other resources to determine the history of television game shows. Prepare a presentation that compares and contrasts the earliest game shows to the current game shows. Explain how the content for the game shows has changed over time. (LO 8.3-2)

35. Psychology Check out the prices of menu items at restaurants such as Chick-fil-A. Do the restaurants use psychological pricing strategies? Explain your answer. (LO 8.2-1)

EXTRA INNINGS PROJECT

Supply and demand, pricing strategies, and current market conditions can all have an impact on major entertainment events. Promoters for state fairs, vacation destinations, professional and college sports, and concerts must be aware of these issues in their business planning.

Work with a group and complete the following activities.

1. Use the Internet to locate websites for your state fair, a popular vacation destination, and your favorite college team. What special promotions are being advertised by these entertainment venues to attract attendance?

2. Why should college and professional football teams, some of which are building new stadiums, be concerned about the declining interest and demand of young people (Generation Z)? Describe in detail five promotional strategies to attract a younger target market to college and professional football games.

3. Why is it important for new stadiums to serve as venues for multiple entertainment events?

4. Explain the concept of inflation when considering ticket prices for the Super Bowl or college football's BCS Championship.

5. Why must the sports and entertainment industries be sensitive to economic conditions when setting ticket prices?

6. How can social media be used to increase the demand for sports and entertainment events?

VIRTUAL BUSINESS *Sports & Entertainment*

Use the *Ticket Pricing* lesson to change prices and observe the effect on revenue and ticket sales. A major challenge for marketers is finding the right balance between what companies are willing to produce and what customers are willing to buy. Discover how prices that are too low result in a high demand for the game while setting prices too high will lower demand, causing lower attendance. Review an income statement to understand and improve profitability.

*For more information, go to **knowledgematters.com**.*

Artwork courtesy of Knowledge Matters, Inc.

COME ON DOWN, YOU'RE OUR NEXT CONTESTANT

In an age when attention spans are short and television programming is sometimes controversial, one daytime game show has remained incredibly popular with fans of all ages. *The Price Is Right* game show is taped at CBS Television City in Hollywood. Every morning long lines of people wait outside the studio, hoping to be asked to "Come on down!"

A Diverse Audience

The Price Is Right is truly a family tradition passed down from generation to generation. Many loyal fans of *The Price Is Right* developed a love affair with the show during their childhood while watching with their parents or grandparents. The show attracts a diverse market of millions of TV fans, ages 19 to 95. Whereas most game shows have contestants between the ages of 20 and 45, contestants on *The Price Is Right* are of all ages, races, and genders. Fans line up along Fairfax Avenue at 3 a.m., three days a week, most of the year, hoping to land one of the 325 spots in the studio audience. Hopeful contestants often come in intergenerational groups that schedule their vacations around tapings of the show. They appear at CBS studios wearing shirts that identify them by their town or family name.

Other local establishments also reap the benefits of the game show's popularity. The Farmer's Daughter Hotel across the street from the studio is a popular lodging establishment for hopeful contestants. At one time, desk clerks offered nightly tutorials to guests on how to improve their chances of being selected as members of the studio audience.

The Price Is Right is the longest-running game show in television history and had the longest-running game show host, Bob Barker. Drew Carey now hosts the successful show. Bob Barker once attributed the success of the show to its central theme—gauging inflation when guessing prices. Anyone who shops can play *The Price Is Right*.

Fans of the show can go online to request audience tickets or play the game on Facebook. Twitter, YouTube, Instagram, and Pinterest are other forms of social media that allow fans to keep up with the show. While other game shows come and go, *The Price Is Right* endures as a cultural touchstone for generations of American shoppers.

THINK CRITICALLY

1. Why has *The Price Is Right* remained popular over many decades?
2. What type of family value is associated with *The Price Is Right*?
3. What age groups make up the target market for *The Price Is Right*? What characteristics do they have in common?
4. Considering the target market for *The Price Is Right*, what types of commercials would likely be aired during the show? Explain.

MARKETING MANAGEMENT SERIES ROLE PLAY

The goal of television programming is to capture the greatest percentage of viewers possible. Television ratings determine which programs will stay and which ones will be canceled. The large number of college football bowl games has diluted the interest of many college football fans. The popularity of the teams and the significance of the game are factors that determine television success.

A lower-tier college bowl game is scheduled to air on the morning of January 1 immediately following *The Price Is Right*. The morning time slot is a drawback for television ratings, but no other games are scheduled to be broadcast on competing networks during 80 percent of the airtime. Television ratings for this game have been declining during the last three years. Two major football conferences have signed a five-year commitment to play in this game. Your marketing firm has been hired to increase the popularity of the game and the size of the television viewing audience.

Performance Indicators Evaluated

- Describe marketing functions and related activities.
- Identify market segmentation and explain how it relates to the marketing plan.
- Describe advertisements that will attract the attention of your target market.
- Develop action plans to encourage viewers of *The Price Is Right* to watch the bowl game.
- Evaluate the effectiveness of advertising.

You must develop a marketing plan and advertising campaign to promote the game and elevate it to the status of a major bowl game.

Consider the demographics of the television audience that normally tunes in on weekday mornings. Capture the attention of *The Price Is Right* viewers so that they stay tuned to the channel for the game.

THINK CRITICALLY

1. How have the number of bowl games affected the television ratings for the games?
2. Why are the scheduled date and time of the game important factors for ratings and promotions?
3. Why should television networks be aware of the programming scheduled around the game and on competing networks when making decisions?
4. How can promoters make an association between the game show and the bowl game to help pull in more viewers?

www.deca.org

9 SPORTS AND ENTERTAINMENT PROMOTION

9.1 Promoting Sports and Entertainment

9.2 Advertising and Sales Promotion

9.3 Publicity and Personal Selling

POINT YOUR BROWSER

ngl.cengage.com/sports4e

© Songquan Deng/Shutterstock.com

Winning Strategies

Samsung Electronics

A video for Samsung's Galaxy 11 technology had over 12 million views only three weeks after it was posted on YouTube. The four-minute, futuristic video was part of a "galactic-themed" series to promote Samsung's Galaxy mobile devices. Samsung Electronics is the world's largest smartphone provider.

The video series tells a story about a space alien's invasion of Earth. The only way to save the planet is for Earth's soccer stars to challenge aliens to a soccer match. Earth's "dream team" consists of 13 players who were drafted from around the world. The actors in the videos are actual top-ranked soccer players, led by one of the best soccer players in the world—Lionel Messi. Combined, the players have about 200 million followers on Facebook and Twitter. They were all under contract to post comments about the video series.

The story unfolded over the span of one year, with new video postings every few months. The series ended with the dream team playing the alien team. The video series was not a traditional commercial, but was considered branded content. All of the soccer players and actors were prominently shown using Galaxy devices in the videos. A Galaxy Gear "smartwatch," which can be used to make calls, record conversations, and shoot photographs and videos, was repeatedly featured.

Samsung's manager of sports marketing efforts, Hoon Kang, said, "Mobile technology is getting more complicated and can be very hard to understand sometimes. Through the football [soccer] videos, we want to show our key functionality and key technology in an emotional way."[1] Kang believes that showing Samsung devices in a dramatic setting connects with consumers more effectively than traditional ads do.

© iStockphoto.com/danlefeb

Think Critically

1. What do you think is the purpose of the video series?

2. What features make Samsung's videos more effective than traditional commercials?

9.1 Promoting Sports and Entertainment

The Essential Question

What are the purposes of promotion and what are its four elements?

Learning Objectives

LO 9.1-1   Describe the purposes of promotion.

LO 9.1-2   Summarize the significance of the four elements of promotion.

Key Terms

- media
- advertising
- sales promotion
- publicity
- personal selling

OPENING ACT

In recent years, Twitter has earned revenue of about $950 million from three basic advertising formats. The most frequently used format is the promoted tweet. An advertiser creates a tweet that looks like any other tweet. But the advertiser arranges to have the tweet sent only to certain users based on their Internet searches or tweets containing specific key words and interests. The advertiser pays Twitter when a user retweets the ad or marks it as a favorite.

Another ad format allows advertisers to pay Twitter a flat fee to be added to a list of the most popular subjects being discussed on the social media site. Using the third format, advertisers pay Twitter to have their ad appear on the top of the "new accounts to follow" list that Twitter suggests to each user. As Twitter grows, it is adding new advertising formats and partnerships. Twitter acquired MoPub, which places marketers' ads in mobile apps through a bidding process.

Cooperative Learning   Work with a group to brainstorm the kinds of products or services that would benefit from promotion through Twitter. Share your ideas with the class.

LO 9.1-1   THE PURPOSES OF PROMOTION

Promotion

Promotion is the process of making customers aware of a product, service, or event. The primary goal of promotion is to increase sales, both by winning new customers and by persuading existing customers to remain loyal. The best promotion communicates a message that generates interest from the consumer.

Promotional Goals

The main goal of promotion is to increase sales. Related goals include

- Increasing customer usage
- Maintaining customer loyalty

- Building a fan base
- Educating potential customers
- Overcoming the resistance of hesitant first-time buyers

Sporting event promoters often offer special prices for different groups. A promotion that offers half-price tickets to children who are accompanied by an adult increases adult attendance while also encouraging a younger fan base. For long-time supporters of a sports team, promoters might offer an upgrade in season tickets or discounted parking. Before spending money on a promotional campaign, the company must know exactly what it wants to accomplish and what market it wants to target. Once the target market has been identified, the company must use marketing information to determine the best media and message to reach that target market. **Media** are the channels of communication used to send a message to the target market.

Gaining New Fans—An Example

Broadway shows generally are promoted in local publications, through direct mail sent to theatergoers, in ads posted on taxis, and on websites such as Telecharge. The promotions target people who would be interested in the topic of the play. The promotion for the play *Bronx Bombers* about the New York Yankees targeted sports fans. The promotional efforts included

- Commercials shown on ESPN and the MLB Network
- Radio ads played on sports talk shows featuring John Sterling, the long-time play-by-play announcer for the Yankees
- Drink coasters found in New York sports bars
- Discount group ticket rates given to Little League teams
- Free tickets given to sports journalists and professional athletes

By all accounts the promotion was somewhat of a success. Sports journalists and professional athletes who had never attended a Broadway show before indicated they would attend more shows in the future.

INTERMISSION

What is the main goal of promotion?

LO 9.1-2 THE FOUR ELEMENTS OF PROMOTION

Promotion cannot overcome the drawbacks of a poor product that is overpriced. However, with the right mix of promotional elements, promotion can increase sales of a good product. The four elements of promotion are advertising, sales promotions, publicity, and personal selling.

Advertising

Advertising is a paid form of communication delivered to consumers by a product maker or seller. Effective advertising will catch the audience's

A radio sports announcer calling a baseball game describes the strikeout pitch by saying, "The pitcher painted the corner. Painting the corners is sponsored by Pro Painters." By doing so, the announcer is using a "drop-in," which is a type of quick ad embedded in the action.

attention and clearly explain the benefits of a product. It will also let consumers know where they may purchase the product. Advertising can take many forms, appear in almost any media, and reach millions of people.

Sales Promotions

A **sales promotion** is an additional incentive offered for a limited time to encourage consumers to buy a product. Examples include giveaways, coupons, items with the company's name printed on them, free samples of a product, and limited-time memberships to places such as health clubs. Sales promotions such as giveaways and free sample products target consumers. Other sales promotions may target vendors, such as the offer of a free display rack based on an agreement to sell a certain product.

Publicity

Unpaid media attention, whether negative or positive, about a business and its products, services, or events is **publicity**. Jeff Bezo, the CEO and founder of Amazon.com, scored a publicity jackpot when he was visited by CBS's Charlie Rose as part of a segment for the TV show *60 Minutes*. The news story was about Amazon's future plans to deliver customer purchases via drones. The timing of the segment—the eve of Cyber Monday (the Monday after Thanksgiving in the United States)—was also very beneficial to Amazon. Multiple news media picked up the story, and reporters discussed it all day long on the biggest online shopping day of the year.

Personal Selling

In-person, face-to-face communication between a seller and a customer is called **personal selling**. It can occur between a retail store salesperson and a customer or between a vendor and a business buyer, such as the representative of a sportswear manufacturer and the manager of a college bookstore. The advantage of personal selling is that the seller can immediately address any concerns that may be causing hesitation on the part of

JUDGMENT CALL

After graduating high school, Steven Rhodes served five years in the United States Marine Corp. and then applied to college with the hope of playing football. When Middle Tennessee State University was about to offer him a place on its team, the NCAA declared Rhodes ineligible to play college football because he played in a military recreational league. Prior NCAA rules had included an exception for players who had played in the military in organized morale-boosting activities. Along the way that rule was lost and was not included in current rules. Social media, sports talk shows, and even Senators and Congress members reacted negatively to the decision. After a firestorm of bad publicity, the NCAA decision was quickly reversed, and Rhodes was allowed to play. The NCAA indicated that there was no intent to deny eligibility to former service members.

Think Critically

Why would the NCAA be concerned about its image after unfairly penalizing a U.S. Marine? What action could the NCAA have taken to avoid the situation?

the buyer. A knowledgeable salesperson can offer information, demonstrate the product, make comparisons with a similar product, relay stories about personal experiences with the product, and answer any questions that may arise. Often, human interaction is needed to make the sale. Even if the sale is lost, customers are likely to return to the business for future sales if they are treated courteously and professionally.

How can personal selling help increase sales of a product?

INTERMISSION

List and explain the four elements of promotion.

ENCORE

Understand Marketing Concepts

Select the best answer for each question.

1. Promotion is
   a. the process of making customers aware of a product or service
   b. the exchange of a product or service for another item of value
   c. a deceptive practice
   d. part of product/service management

2. Which of the following is an example of publicity?
   a. offering a coupon for free popcorn at the movie theater
   b. being featured on the evening news
   c. buying advertising space in a newspaper
   d. helping a customer find an item in a sporting goods store

Think Critically

Answer the following questions as completely as possible.

3. Select one of the promotional goals and outline what steps you would take to fulfill that goal. (LO 9.1-1)

4. Think about a sales promotion that you were offered. Did it influence you to make a purchase? How could the experience have been improved without costing the company more money? (LO 9.1-2)

9.2 Advertising and Sales Promotion

The Essential Question

What are the components of effective advertising and sales promotion?

Learning Objectives

LO 9.2-1 Explain the components of effective advertising.

LO 9.2-2 Describe various types of sales promotions.

Key Terms

- copy
- product placement
- visual merchandising
- reach
- frequency
- native advertising
- consumer sales promotion
- trade sales promotion

OPENING ACT

The film *200 Cartas* (200 Letters) focuses on Puerto Ricans who live in New York and who frequently travel to Puerto Rico. The film is a family-friendly romantic comedy about a man trying to find a woman named Maria Sanchez, with whom he thinks he has fallen in love. He sends letters to all 200 women named Maria Sanchez living in Puerto Rico, in hopes of finding the right one. The film was financed in part by placing sponsors' products in scenes of the movie. One of the sponsors, Banco Popular, featured promotional ads of the film on their Automated Teller Machines (ATMs). Banco Popular also sponsored a float featuring the film in the national Puerto Rican Day parade in New York City. The parade is a popular way to target a Puerto Rican audience.

Cooperative Learning Work with a partner to research and discuss the ways that advertising for *200 Cartas* targeted customers. How might a film's producers know if the advertising is effective?

LO 9.2-1 ADVERTISING

Promotion

Advertising plays a strong role in a free-enterprise system. It promotes competition and, thus, innovation. Advertising makes customers aware of new products and services, which results in purchases. It also helps consumers make comparisons among alternatives, leading companies to make product improvements to beat the competition. Some companies spend millions or even billions of dollars advertising their products. Advertising is responsible for some of today's most successful brands.

Advertising is a common form of promotion used to introduce new products to the market. Successful products or services are fine-tuned to appeal to a specific market. Advertising focuses on the target market. The target audience for a TV show often can be determined by watching the advertisements. The term *highly sought after* is frequently used to describe the demographic attributes of customers that are desired by a business. Advertisements are designed to target that highly sought after demographic group—for instance, consumers ages 25 to 34.

Creative Attention Grabbers

Marketers must use their creative talent to choose the right message to convey to the target market. Marketers write **copy**, words to be spoken or printed in an ad, to convey their message. An effective ad generally has four components: Attraction, Interest, Desire, and Action (AIDA).

- **A**ttraction—the ad catches the attention of the intended consumer
- **I**nterest—the ad holds the interest of the consumer long enough to present the message
- **D**esire—the ad's message makes the consumer want the product
- **A**ction—the consumer is motivated to buy the product

Creative ads make a connection with the target audience. In a contest held at South by Southwest Music and Media Conference in Austin, Texas, unlikely sponsors converged to create a new advertising model. The retailer Target and Co.LABS, a technology blog published by *Fast Company* magazine, partnered to sponsor the Retail Accelerator contest. A $75,000 prize was offered for the development of a mobile app for shoppers. Seven finalists were awarded $10,000 each and given the chance to present their app to the judges. You typically won't find Target ads in *Fast Company* magazines or on Co.LABS blogs. However, Target's advertising goal was to gain access to the bright, young readers of *Fast Company*, who are generally savvier when it comes to technology, media, and design. The new advertising model was an attempt to overcome the public's increasing disinterest in traditional advertising and to interact with a specific target customer.

Interactive Advertising

Effective advertising will engage consumers and motivate them to take specific action. No matter which strategy is used, getting results is always a challenge. One method of engaging consumers is to use interactive digital communications to connect with them. Doritos brand chips has successfully used this type of advertising. Doritos is among the top ten Super Bowl advertisers because of its annual "Crash the Super Bowl" contest. The contest asks participants to create an ad that will air during the game, if selected as the winner. Consumers are encouraged to vote to help determine the winner, thus engaging them in the ad.

Product Placement

Product placement is the integration into a movie or television show of a product. It is a form of advertising that is a little more discreet than traditional ads. Sometimes a character will simply use the product and then place it in plain view for the audience to see. The camera may zoom in on the brand name of the product for an instant.

The Basics When the judges on *American Idol* are shown critiquing performances, a bright red Coca-Cola cup is in view in front of each judge. Whenever an actor on a TV show opens a laptop computer, viewers may see the iconic Apple computer logo. No one mentions the products by name, but they are embedded in the viewer's mind.

Product placement is not a new idea. In the 1920s, film studios and product producers bartered over the use of products in films. In 1950, a liquor company paid to have its product tossed overboard in the movie *The African Queen*. In the 1982 movie *E.T. the Extra-Terrestrial*, a loveable alien is coaxed out of hiding using Reese's Pieces.

Who Pays? There are a number of ways that product placement deals are negotiated, including the following:

- Fee basis
- Prominent display of brand name
- Fashions worn by cast
- Movie promotion in product advertising

Many products are placed in shows on a fee basis. A corporation will pay the film's or TV show's producers a fee for its product to be prominently placed on set.

In some cases, when very expensive products are needed as part of the story, the products may be provided in return for prominent display of the brand name. For example, in a film that needs a very expensive automobile, such as a Ferrari, the studio might barter for the use (and safe return) of the car.

Outfitting the cast in a movie offers another opportunity for product placement. In the 2013 film *Blue Jasmine*, the script called for actress Cate Blanchett to portray an Upper East Side, wealthy, New York socialite. She needed a very simple, but elegant high-end designer look. Hollywood costume designer Suzy Benzinger contacted Karl Lagerfeld, the creative head designer for French fashion house Chanel. Lagerfeld immediately sent the Chanel jacket that Benzinger requested. Blanchett, who won an Academy Award for her performance, wore the Chanel jacket frequently throughout the movie, exposing many moviegoers to Chanel's clothing line.

Product placement can be mutually beneficial. A company may agree to include movie promotion in its product advertising in exchange for placement of the product in the movie. Assuming the product and the movie appeal to the same market, both parties will gain from the partnership. Fast-food restaurants offer a good example of this. Animated movie characters often are turned into toys that are offered in kid-sized meals. The restaurant will promote the movie's characters in its advertising.

© Pavel L. Photo and Video/Shutterstock.com

How does product placement help fund movies or TV programming?

Visual Merchandising

In product placement and in retail stores, how products are displayed is important to the success of the promotion. **Visual merchandising** is the process of creating three-dimensional displays to promote products. Lights, sounds, smells, and tastes can all be part of visual merchandising. Catching consumers' attention through sensory experiences is a great way to motivate them to make a purchase. Visual merchandising has also taken on a new importance in the media. It is used to display products during *cast commercials*, which are ads delivered by actors from TV shows. A live commercial for the Toyota Highlander appeared during the *Hot in Cleveland* TV series featuring principal cast members Valerie Bertinelli and Betty White. Seeing a well-known actor use a product brings it to life.

Gauging Effectiveness

The effectiveness of an advertisement is measured in relation to its goal. The goal may be to increase sales by a specific percentage. To gauge the effectiveness, a business needs to know whether the ad is reaching the targeted demographic group. An ad's **reach** is the number of people in the target market expected to receive the message through the chosen medium (such as a TV commercial or magazine ad). A business also needs to know the **frequency**, or the number of times the targeted group has been exposed to the message. Nielsen helps companies measure an ad's effectiveness. It looks at data collected about ads viewed on TV or online in conjunction with data collected on U.S. credit card transactions. By combining the two types of data, Nielsen connects the ad to purchasing behavior—if credit card sales of the product have increased after the ad was introduced, a connection between the two can be made. Businesses can use this data to make adjustments to their advertising campaigns as needed.

Regulating Advertising

Regulation of advertising by state and federal laws is needed to protect consumers from deceptive practices. As stated on the Bureau of Consumer Protection's website, "under the law, claims in advertisements must be truthful, cannot be deceptive or unfair, and must be evidence-based."[2]

Federal Trade Commission (FTC)   The FTC oversees and regulates advertising at the national level in the United States. In addition to traditional advertising, the FTC monitors labeling, promotional emails, and telemarketing.

Some advertisements blur the line between news and advertising. **Native advertising** is online content created by a company that has the appearance of non-ad content, such as an editorial. For example, over-the-counter drugs that can be potentially harmful can be promoted in ads masquerading as news. Numerous native ads can be found on the Internet. They target very specific audiences but can be misleading when disguised as editorials or news. When they appear on social media sites, they can be shared, "liked," or commented on. The ad industry is opposed to labeling these types of online exposure as "advertisements." To better protect consumers, the FTC is working with the ad industry and consumer protection groups to develop rules about native ads. The FTC wants consumers to be

Why should children be protected from deceptive advertising?

able to clearly distinguish between an advertisement that is biased and a news article that is nonbiased. Consumer education is the key.

Media Regulations   There are several laws that apply specifically to advertising directed at children. The Federal Communications Commission (FCC) enforces rules about advertising on children's television programming. Commercials are limited to 10.5 minutes per hour on weekends and 12 minutes per hour on weekdays. The commercials must be distinctly different from the programming to protect young children who are vulnerable to commercial messages.

Associations   The American Association of Advertising Agencies (4As) is a national trade association. It helps regulate the advertising industry by monitoring industrywide advertising practices. Members of the 4As produce about 80 percent of the total ads placed by advertising agencies in the United States.[3]

Competition among advertising agencies helps keep advertising creative. But creativity should not step outside the boundaries of ethics. Unethical practices by agencies make the public skeptical of advertising and weaken the effectiveness of all ads. The 4As' Standards of Practice state that members will not create advertising that contains

- False or misleading statements or exaggerations, visual or verbal
- Testimonials that do not reflect the real opinion of the individual(s) involved
- Price claims that are misleading
- Claims insufficiently supported or that distort the true meaning of statements made by professional or scientific authorities
- Statements, suggestions, or pictures offensive to public decency or minority segments of the population.[4]

INTERMISSION

Name and explain three ways that product placement deals are negotiated.

LO 9.2-2   SALES PROMOTION

Promotion

Sales promotions are marketing efforts that offer the customer an additional incentive to buy a product or service. They are used for a limited time to motivate potential customers to act. Sales promotions can have an immediate, positive influence on sales, changing reluctant potential customers into buyers.

Consumer Sales Promotions

When a sales promotion is directed at the final consumer, it is called a **consumer sales promotion**. Consumer sales promotions can include

- Temporary price reductions, such as half-price ballgame tickets
- Price-pack deals, such as four ballgame tickets, drinks, and hot dogs packaged together at a special price
- Coupons offering a special price
- Special gifts, such as posters or team rally towels that are given out to the first 500 people entering the stadium
- Contests or games that offer prizes to customers
- Rebates that refund part of the purchase price of a product

There are many additional types of sales promotions that have proven to be an effective way to motivate consumers who like to feel that they are getting something for free or a good deal.

Trade Sales Promotions

When a sales promotion is directed at members of the distribution channel, it is called a **trade sales promotion**. Such promotions increase a retailer's enthusiasm for marketing a product. Trade sales promotions can include

- Trade allowances, which offer short-term discounts to distributors and retailers for selling or participating in the promotion of a product
- Trade contests, in which a retailer that sells the most of a product, such as a specific brand of tennis racquet, receives a reward

- Point-of-purchase displays, in which display materials are provided free to retailers to help them sell the merchandise
- In-store demonstrations performed by a product manufacturer representative to help increase store sales

Sometimes, trade sales promotions are used to get shelf space for products in a retail store, because space in a store is limited. The location of the product in a retail store can greatly affect sales and is also something that can be negotiated through trade sales promotion activities.

Employee Sales Promotions

Some companies want to differentiate themselves from competitors by offering the highest-quality service. To do this, the company focuses on training its employees and offering incentives. Cash and prize incentives may be awarded to employees who go above and beyond what is expected to serve and please customers. *Push money* is an extra commission paid to salespeople who sell or push particular products.

INTERMISSION

List and explain three types of sales promotions.

ENCORE

Understand Marketing Concepts

Select the best answer for each question.

1. The Federal Trade Commission is responsible for
   a. overseeing advertising regulations in the United States
   b. operating the American Association of Advertising
   c. protecting advertisers from fraudulent consumers
   d. all of the above

2. Which of the following is an example of a sales promotion?
   a. a limited-time discount
   b. sponsorship of a sports competition
   c. an email containing a coupon
   d. both a and c

Think Critically

Answer the following questions as completely as possible.

3. Compare and contrast advertising and product placement. What are the major differences in the two? How are the two alike? (LO 9.2-1)

4. Your company wants to provide a sales promotion item to 5,000 attendees at a professional baseball game. You must not spend more than $2 per item, including the cost of putting your company's name on the item. What would you choose and why? (LO 9.2-2)

9.3 Publicity and Personal Selling

The Essential Question

Why are publicity and personal selling effective forms of promotion?

Learning Objectives

LO 9.3-1 Distinguish between publicity and other types of promotion.

LO 9.3-2 Explain how to use personal selling in sports and entertainment.

Key Terms

- goodwill
- publicist
- grass-roots effort
- viral campaign
- public relations (PR)
- body language

OPENING ACT

Foursquare is a smartphone app that helps people find something entertaining to do. Its users "check in" while they are at a venue and receive specials or coupons. When Foursquare was first building its business, college students acted as unpaid salespeople. They were known as "ambassadors." The ambassadors encouraged other students to check in with friends when they were attending a basketball game or having pizza at a restaurant. The ambassadors also encouraged businesses and universities to create a presence on Foursquare, connecting them with over 45 million Foursquare users. The ambassadors were not paid, but they did receive valuable job experience.

As Foursquare has grown, it has moved away from using unpaid promoters to building a professional sales staff. Members of the sales staff focus on both small- and medium-sized businesses and major clients. They work across the United States and internationally, especially in Latin American markets.

Cooperative Learning Work with a team and develop a list of skills that Foursquare might be seeking in professional salespeople. Check the Foursquare website (or other similar websites) to see whether any sales positions are currently open. Use this information to help build your list of skills.

LO 9.3-1 PUBLICITY

Promotion

Publicity is free, but the message presented is not controlled by the business. It is controlled by the news or other media that are presenting the message. Positive publicity can be a good promotional tool, but negative publicity can be bad for business. Many people who do not watch weekly football tune in to the Super Bowl because of the publicity surrounding the event. They do not want to miss out on the excitement. Fans tweet and the news media write about the Super Bowl as soon as the game is over, resulting in even more publicity.

Goodwill

Publicity can be advantageous to a sports or entertainment business by creating **goodwill**—positive feelings about the business. The success of fund-raising charity events depends on the help of many people and businesses. A charity that is holding a marathon to raise money for a cause must inspire people to run in the event. Often, the runners must encourage others to pledge money. The charity also recruits businesses to make donations. In return for doing so, the businesses receive public acknowledgment of their gifts. The individuals who support the charity appreciate the businesses' support and, in turn, will likely patronize the businesses. On the other hand, if a prominent sports figure who is acting as a spokesperson for the event gets caught up in a scandal, the publicity can have a negative side effect for all involved.

How can publicity affect an athlete or sports team?

© CHEN WS/Shutterstock.com

Damage Control

When a sports figure is arrested, the information is printed in the newspaper, covered on TV, and posted and discussed on the Internet. The athlete's team cannot control the publicity that results from the player's arrest. The player and the team's **publicist**, the person responsible for maintaining relations with the public and news media, generally issue a statement. The statement attempts to provide *damage control* by refuting, justifying, or downplaying the stories in circulation and refocusing attention on more positive matters. If a business or individual tries to deny the obvious or to alter the facts, the matter may become even worse. It is much less damaging to admit a mistake and then move on to more positive news.

Grass-Roots Publicity

When an unknown person or event is propelled into the spotlight by fans, it is often referred to as a **grass-roots effort**. A number of films became very profitable through grass-roots efforts. Internet blogs have provided an effective and inexpensive way for fans to talk about movies they like. A **viral campaign** is a promotion in which a few online mentions produce millions of comments. Going viral can create a real buzz about a movie and propel it into a mega hit.

When a story goes viral, it does not mean that it contains accurate information. Organizations sometimes want to create the public image of a grass-roots effort when it doesn't actually exist. A fake grass-roots group, or *front group*, may imply it represents a movement when in fact it is serving a hidden sponsorship or corporate group. A front group may use deception, present false information, and prevent the public from knowing who is behind the efforts. People who forward a story on Twitter or Facebook without checking the accuracy of the information may unknowingly help promote a deceptive cause for a front group.

Image Is Everything

If you follow any major sports, you most likely chose your favorite teams and athletes based on past experiences and feelings of connection to the team or players and their image. Part of the reason that baseball, football, basketball, soccer, and ice hockey are popular sports is due to extensive promotional campaigns. **Public relations (PR)** is the arm of promotion that tries to create a favorable public opinion for an individual or organization. Public relations professionals work hard in the sports world to create positive public images of the game and the players.

A PR professional also works hard to develop positive relations with those working in the media, especially journalists. *Media relations* involves developing an authentic relationship with journalists through a proactive approach. A PR professional must be a reliable and trustworthy source of newsworthy information to a journalist.

Part of building positive media relations can include writing effective *press releases*, which contain newsworthy information that will be of interest to the public. To effectively manage media relations, the PR professional should know which publications and media outlets will be the most interested in covering the story. Most media are flooded with press releases that are competing for limited news time and space. To be effective, the information provided in a press release should have the following:

- An attention-grabbing headline and story
- An introductory paragraph that concisely states the most important points
- Information about the business
- A quote from a knowledgeable source
- Contact information

Creating an online press kit is also helpful to the media. The *press kit* can include the following items:

- More in-depth information about the business, its purpose, and its key players
- Photos or videos that pertain to the story
- Links to recent news coverage of the business

Creating an Image Public relations focuses on the future, with the intent of creating a positive image for a business. A comprehensive strategy for developing good PR involves defining the image the company desires. The company must then outline the steps needed to attain the image. A business may have a public relations department or may hire an outside public relations firm to help establish a good public image. A spokesperson will be selected to represent the business in the media. This spokesperson must know and understand the image desired. He or she must represent the company image in a professional manner, whether in writing or during interviews. The PR staff may even write corporate speeches that are to be delivered by high-ranking company officials.

COMMUNICATION CONNECTION

When a sports team wants to communicate information about a newly signed player, it may host a press conference, which is an event where members of the mass media are invited. The purpose is to draw attention to a story and gain positive publicity through coverage in newspapers and magazines and on blogs and TV. The story must be newsworthy. Newsworthy items are current, significant to a large number of people, impact the media audience, have an emotional appeal, or involve a prominent person or organization. The host issues a press release to announce the news. The press release does not provide the entire story, just enough information to entice journalists to attend the press conference. A spokesperson for the hosting organization will share the information and answer questions. A press kit is prepared for all attending journalists to provide additional information. The room should be prepared to hold attendees and camera crews, and the meeting should not last more than 30 to 45 minutes. A web conference can also be held, making attendance easy for journalists.

Write Now

Simulate a press conference that might be held by a local college that has just hired its first female soccer coach. Think of a catchy headline for the story. Develop all materials needed for the news conference, including a three-paragraph press release, press kit, and a list of media outlets whose journalists should be invited. Prepare a list of potential questions that the media might ask. Role-play the news conference with other class members.

Athletes and Their Public Image

There are many athletes who have managed to avoid the negative pitfalls of fame and fortune. Many donate time and money to causes and charities.

- NFL player Eli Manning and his wife, Abby, donated $1 million to the University of Mississippi for scholarships for students from low-income families.
- NBA legend Shaquille O'Neal gives back to the Boys and Girls Club, an organization that supported him as a youth. Each year since 1992, he has handed out toys and shoes to over 300 kids from the Boys and Girls Club of Venice, California. He also partners with Toys 'R Us to benefit the U.S. Marine's Toys for Tots Foundation.
- The Jackie Robinson Foundation honors the memory of baseball hall of famer Jackie Robinson by awarding four-year college scholarships to academically gifted minority students with financial need, enabling them to attend the college of their choice.

The positive image created by the generosity of famous athletes can benefit the sport and the charity. Good PR will focus on athletes' good deeds instead of their record-high salaries.

Game Day Image

The importance of a positive image extends beyond the individual athletes and the teams. Sports facilities need to maintain a reputation for excellent service, cleanliness, and safety. Fans are more likely to attend a sporting event if they believe they will be safe and comfortable.

Why is the image of a sports venue, such as Lambeau Field, just as important as the image of the team and its players?

They are also more likely to support their team when on the road in cities where fans are known for good sportsmanship. Hospitable fans are a bonus for team public relations.

Win or lose, the Green Bay Packers football team has a solid fan base. At any time, there are about 96,000 people on the waiting list for Packers' season tickets. The Packers are the only publically, community-owned NFL team in the league, and as such, the fans take great pride in supporting the team and caring for the stadium. Even in subzero temperatures, large numbers of fans always turn out to help remove snow from the field in preparation for a game. The Packers' Lambeau Field (shown above) is the oldest continually operating NFL stadium. A football team's stadium reflects the personality and image of the team and its fans. Lambeau Field has a positive image throughout the United States. It almost always ranks as one of the top five stadiums for having the "best fans." Packer fans love Lambeau Field and present a game day image to be admired.

INTERMISSION

How is publicity different from other types of promotion?

LO 9.3-2 PERSONAL SELLING

Promotion Recently, there has been much attention paid to using social media and the Internet to sell products, in which no personal interaction is required. Internet sales mostly consist of lower-cost, noncomplex items. Sales transactions that involve expensive or complex products generally require face-to-face interaction. *Personal selling* is, as the name suggests, a person-to-person communication between a salesperson and a potential customer. These transactions are usually more satisfying to both the buyer and seller because questions can be answered and information provided on the spot. People respond positively to personal interactions with salespeople who are knowledgeable, friendly, courteous, and truthful.

Face to Face

Personal selling is face to face. Sometimes the buyer makes the initial contact, and sometimes the seller starts the process. Personal selling often takes place in a retail setting, in which a salesperson works with a customer. However, personal selling can occur at a higher level, such as when the director of sales at one company makes direct contact with an executive at a major corporation to create a sales agreement. For example, if a sports team wants to obtain a sponsorship from a major corporation, personal selling will be involved. A food manufacturer may not have considered the benefits of sponsoring the local baseball team until the team's sales representatives present a proposal to the food manufacturer's executives.

Personal selling involves the delivery of information that is specifically designed for the customer. A great salesperson will take more time getting to know the customer than talking about the product for sale. Salespeople need to develop an understanding of the challenges faced by the customer. By being in close proximity to the customers, salespeople can read the customer's **body language**, or non-spoken signals. Body language is not an

TAKE A BOW *Alex and Cathy López Negrete*

Alex and Cathy López Negrete, founders of López Negrete Communications, started the full-service, Hispanic-owned marketing and advertising business in their home. One of their first clients was the Houston Rockets. Recently, they had annual billings of $193.5 million, over 200 employees, and many large impressive clients, including NBC Universal Motion Pictures Group.[5]

Alex López Negrete believes that marketers have begun to realize the growth potential that the Latino demographic offers businesses. His company is very aware of the cultural and linguistic distinctions of people from all over Latin America. According to López Negrete, his job is "to understand their culture and the insights that drive that customer." López Negrete helps clients maximize business with the Latino market.

Think Critically

What skills and knowledge do you think it takes to start an advertising agency and turn it into a multimillion-dollar business? What has helped make the López Negretes successful?

exact science. Facial expressions and the position of someone's body can provide insight into how he or she is receiving the message. If the customer is not reacting positively to the message, it can be adjusted. If the food manufacturer is not reacting positively to a request for sponsorship, the team's sales representatives can modify the message to make it more appealing, such as by offering sponsorship of a single game instead of the whole season.

The Power of Three

When trying to make a sale, the salesperson points out the benefits of the product or service. Recent research indicates that successful salespeople and advertisements offer consumers no more than three reasons to buy. Previously, it was thought that the more positive descriptors used in an ad or sales presentation, the better. However, marketing research has shown that while giving customers three reasons to buy persuades them, giving them more than three causes them to become distrustful and to develop a negative attitude about the product. In personal selling, salespeople must understand what works best to motivate customers to buy.

INTERMISSION

What is meant by personal selling?

ENCORE

Understand Marketing Concepts

Select the best answer for each question.

1. Which of the following examples would a public relations firm want to downplay?
   a. a Special Olympian throwing out the first ball at a baseball game
   b. media coverage about an athlete unjustly accused of taking drugs
   c. a professional athlete's record salary
   d. a charity event with proceeds going to a children's hospital

2. Personal selling provides
   a. direct contact between the customer and the salesperson
   b. delivery of information specifically for the customer
   c. an opportunity to adjust the offer to fit the customer
   d. all of the above

Think Critically

Answer the following questions as completely as possible.

3. Why is it difficult to control publicity? (LO 9.3-1)

4. What characteristics, knowledge, and skills do successful salespeople need? (LO 9.3-2)

Review Marketing Terms

Match the terms listed with the definitions.

1. Positive feelings about a business
2. The number of times the targeted customer is exposed to a message
3. A paid form of communication delivered to consumers by a product maker or seller
4. The process in which a product is integrated into a movie or television show
5. The person responsible for maintaining relations with the public and news media
6. The number of people in the target market expected to receive the message through the chosen medium
7. The arm of promotion that tries to create a favorable public opinion for an individual or organization
8. Unpaid media attention, whether negative or positive, about a business and its products, services, or events
9. A promotion in which a few online mentions produce millions of comments
10. Words to be spoken or printed in an ad
11. Promotion directed at the final consumer
12. Promotion directed at members of the distribution channel
13. Non-spoken signals between people
14. Channels of communication used to send a message to the target market.
15. When an unknown person or event is propelled into the spotlight by fans
16. Online content created by a company that has the appearance of non-ad content
17. Face-to-face communication between a seller and a customer
18. An additional incentive offered for a limited time to encourage consumers to buy a product
19. The process of creating three-dimensional displays to promote products

a. advertising
b. body language
c. consumer sales promotion
d. copy
e. frequency
f. goodwill
g. grass-roots effort
h. media
i. native advertising
j. personal selling
k. product placement
l. public relations (PR)
m. publicist
n. publicity
o. reach
p. sales promotion
q. trade sales promotion
r. viral campaign
s. visual merchandising

Review Marketing Concepts

Select the best answer for each of the following questions.

20. The major goal of promotion is to
    a. increase sales
    b. maintain customer loyalty
    c. educate potential customers
    d. all of the above

21. Examples of trade sales promotions include all of the following *except*

    a. a trade allowance

    b. a trade contest

    c. coupons

    d. point-of-purchase displays

22. Publicity is different from advertising because it

    a. is free

    b. cannot be controlled by the business or event

    c. can be positive or negative

    d. all of the above

23. Personal selling involves

    a. only transactions between businesses

    b. the disbursement of product knowledge

    c. online sales

    d. a scripted telephone conversation

24. Four components of an effective advertisement are

    a. creativity, reach, frequency, media

    b. personal selling, publicity, sales promotions, special offers

    c. attraction, interest, desire, action

    d. sports figures, Internet, newspapers, magazines

25. Public Relations (PR) focuses on

    a. creating a positive image

    b. developing advertisements

    c. providing discounts

    d. writing newsworthy articles

Think Critically

26. What factors influence the choice of advertising media? (LO 9.1-1)

27. Look at the promotions for your favorite professional sporting event. List the elements of promotion used and explain why you think each element was selected. How could promotions be improved to attract new fans to the sport? (LO 9.1-2)

28. Think of athletes who serve as public role models. What characteristics do these athletes have that contribute to their favorable image? How do they affect your perception of their sport? Now, think of athletes who have received negative publicity. What has contributed to their poor image? Have they been able to overcome it? How does negative media coverage affect your response to players and/or the sport in which they are involved? (LO 9.3-1)

29. Using the Internet, newspapers, or sports magazines, find and briefly describe three entertainment or sports examples where personal selling may have been used to make a sale. Why do you think personal selling was needed in these examples? (LO 9.3-2)

30. The FCC is considering tougher product placement regulations for shows that target audiences under the age of 15. Make a list of what you believe should be included in the regulations. (LO 9.2-1)

31. Think about the last time that you experienced personal selling, such as at a retail store. Write a paragraph about the experience. Include details about how you were treated. Were you given good information? Did you buy the product? Suggest how your experience could have been better. (LO 9.3-2)

32. Do you think salespeople should be given incentives to encourage them to increase sales? Should customers be made aware of the special incentives given to the salespeople? Do you think employee sales promotions help increase sales? (LO 9.2-2)

Make Academic Connections

33. **Marketing Math** A full-page, full-color ad placed in the Sunday comic section of a local newspaper costs $41,000. The comics have a loyal readership of about 2 million readers. The same ad placed in another section of the paper costs $12,000 and has about 1 million readers. What is the cost per reader of each ad? (LO 9.2-1)

34. **History** Assume you are employed by a promotion firm in the 1940s. Describe what changes are taking place in the media as they relate to advertising. How is the new media different and how will they affect the type of promotions you create? (LO 9.1-1)

35. **Technology** Explain the impact of technology on publicity and public relations in the sports and entertainment industries. (LO 9.3-1)

36. **Research** Your community has just opened a new, nostalgic drive-in movie theater. Conduct online research about drive-in movie theaters to help you prepare a billboard advertisement for this new entertainment venue. Describe a special sales promotion to increase attendance. (LO 9.2-2)

37. **Geography** Major League Soccer (MLS) has become increasingly popular in cities with populations of 100,000 to 400,000. Average attendance at games has been around 10,000. Choose a city where college football is played and is popular. Provide three good reasons for an MLS team to locate in this city. How would you use personal selling to convince the team to move to the city? (LO 9.3-2)

38. **Communication** Write a press release for a sports or entertainment business about an exciting upcoming event. In addition, create a press kit for the media, including an overview of what the business does and a photo related to the business. (LO 9.3-1)

39. **Ethics** Some people believe that product placement is a deceptive practice. List the pros and cons of product placement. Then write a paragraph explaining whether you believe product placement is misleading or deceptive. (LO 9.2-1)

40. **Communication** You have been asked to promote a popular band that is releasing a new album. The band has not had a top-selling album in three years. What types of promotions would you plan to help grow the band's fan base? (LO 9.1-1)

EXTRA INNINGS PROJECT

Your advertising company has been hired to help a television network find ways to use product placement in its television shows. The network is especially interested in targeting young people, ages 16 to 25. The network wants to attract advertisers that sell to this targeted age group.

Work with a group and complete the following activities.

1. Use information from the Nielsen website to research the television networks and television shows most watched by young people ages 16 to 25. Select one show in which to use product placement. Determine the average number of people in this age group who watch the show. Explain why you have selected this show.

2. Select three products that could be easily "placed" in the show. All of the products must be legal for use by the entire targeted age group and appropriate for family television viewing. Research the three selected products online and determine their manufacturers.

3. Create examples of how the three products could be placed in the show and describe which characters would be involved with their use.

4. Use all of this information to develop a written presentation to be given to the television network and then to the product manufacturers. Include ideas for coordinating promotion of the television show and the products.

VIRTUAL BUSINESS *Sports & Entertainment*

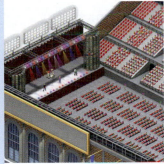

Use the *Promotion with Traditional Media* lesson to see how market research and different forms of traditional media work to promote events and increase attendance at a concert. The goal of promotion is to increase sales. Market research is conducted to determine which types of people will attend events. You will design marketing campaigns to reach specific target demographics. You also will analyze financial statements to see how promotion improves attendance and profitability.

*For more information, go to **knowledgematters.com**.*

Artwork courtesy of Knowledge Matters, Inc.

GETTING TO KNOW ALL ABOUT YOU

Advertisers want to be your new best friend. They want to know all your likes and dislikes, your favorite colors, and your favorite music. Your smartphone and Internet choices are helping them get to know you better. The better they know you, the better they can target ads specifically for you. In addition, advertisers want to send these ads to you on all of the devices you may be using, but it may cost you your privacy.

Following You

A few years ago, digital advertisers relied on "cookies" placed on your computer to monitor your Internet use. However, cookies are no longer useful to advertisers because of the addition of "cookie blockers" on personal computers. Cookies also do not work well with mobile apps and mobile browsers. So advertisers began looking for other ways to collect consumer data. Wireless phone service providers may be one answer. Verizon offers customers coupons as a way to gain their approval to share their data with advertisers.

Advertisers are also using Internet radio services, such as Pandora, to target listeners with customized ads. The ads are based on the type of music and the type of device that the listener is using. Advertisers believe that choice of music, movies, or books provides a glimpse of consumer preferences and political beliefs. Pandora uses song choices to target a listener with election campaign ads. Because

it has the listener's zip code, it can play political ads specific to that district. Listeners can pay an annual fee to opt out of receiving ads on the otherwise free Pandora service.

Because mobile app use is growing by as much as 115 percent each year, advertisers know this is a good way to reach consumers. Companies such as Flurry, a mobile measurement and advertising firm, embed software in mobile apps to help app developers track usage. Flurry can follow individuals on all of their Internet-connected devices—from their office computer to their phone to their home computer and tablet. Pinpointing individuals is so accurate that spouses using the same tablet can be shown different ads.

Few people realize how much of their information is available to advertisers. Technology providers agree that privacy is an important factor in the marketing industry. Advertisers must remain privacy-sensitive, or consumers will rebel.

Think Critically

1. What threats do you think loss of privacy present to people in the United States?
2. If you are not doing anything illegal, should you care that you are being tracked on the Internet?
3. Do you respond to ads on mobile devices? Why or why not?
4. What is the best way an advertiser could target ads to you? In other words, how can they reach you?

DESKTOP PUBLISHING EVENT

Many aspects of today's visual business publications require desktop publishing. This event challenges participants to demonstrate skills in the areas of desktop publishing, creativity, and decision making.

You have been hired by the CEO of Sun Life, an active adult community located in the southwestern part of the United States. Your job is to design the first two pages of a newsletter for residents and prospective residents.

An aging U.S. population has resulted in a higher demand for active adult communities for those ages 55 and older. These communities do not allow children, they charge a monthly homeowner's fee for amenities, and they are frequently located in warm climates with golf courses nearby. Clubhouses, swimming pools, tennis courts, wood working shops, and other amenities make the active adult communities attractive to an aging population.

You must research current active adult communities in the United States to gather ideas about the amenities, upcoming scheduled events, and trends of active adult communities.

Performance Indicators Evaluated

- Understand the changing needs of an aging population.
- Outline the major information to communicate to current and potential customers.
- Demonstrate critical thinking and problem-solving skills when creating the newsletter.
- Prioritize information to include in a desktop publishing newsletter.
- Describe the most effective newsletter layout for the active adult community.

You will work with a partner on this project. You may use any desktop publishing software to complete the project. Documents produced for this event must be prepared by the participants without help from the advisor or any other person. The finished product must be submitted in color. Copyright guidelines provided by FBLA must be followed. The final product should showcase your graphic and text creation skills. Layout creativity and appropriate use of fonts and type sizes are also important components in your final product.

Think Critically

1. Why are adult communities becoming increasingly popular?
2. What features of an adult community would be the best selling points?
3. Why is it important to highlight the golf courses and other activities offered in the adult community, taking into consideration monthly homeowner's fees?
4. How can the community newsletter be used to determine customers' top needs and wants?

www.fbla.org

10 PROMOTIONAL PLANNING

Photo courtesy of NuBoard Media Group

10.1 Promotional Events and the Event Triangle

10.2 Sponsorships and Endorsements

10.3 Promotional Plans

POINT YOUR BROWSER
ngl.cengage.com/sports4e

Winning Strategies

NuBoard Media

NuBoard Media Group reaches "Every Seat. Every Fan." The Florida-based sports marketing company provides interactive in-stadium and in-seat promotions for event sponsors.

The Tostitos Fiesta Bowl is sponsored by Frito-Lay. NuBoard activates Frito-Lay's sampling campaign every year at the bowl game. NuBoard Seat-Paks, containing samples of new chips and salsa flavors, are given to every fan in attendance. Imagine 70,000 branded, biodegradable Seat-Paks adhered to all of the seats in the stadium. During the game, fans have ample time to examine and, in some cases, consume the contents of the bag. Fans find call-to-action pieces in the Seat-Paks that engage them and their smart-phones throughout the game. For example, PA announcements might remind fans that they may win an iPod by scanning a quick response (QR) code located in their bags.

Photo courtesy of NuBoard Media Group

A much higher percentage of fans can recall the event sponsors featured on the Seat-Paks compared to those on traditional signage or other media. Most bags go home with the fans as souvenirs, keeping the message alive long after the game. The printed brand names on the bags receive additional buzz from tweets, online articles, and TV coverage surrounding the game. The sponsors receive measurable feedback from the fans. The high reach, frequency, and response of the consumers provide the data the sponsors need.

NuBoard founders James Allegro, his brother Frank Allegro, and Kevin Lilly acted on an idea for a creative, targeted, and measurable sports marketing opportunity that maximizes sponsorship branding. They turned a simple idea into a patented marketing bonanza.

Think Critically

1. What features make NuBoard's promotional media more effective than traditional media?

2. How could event sponsors use NuBoard's promotional media to make a stronger connection with people who are already their customers? What would you like to find in a Seat-Pak?

10.1 Promotional Events and the Event Triangle

The Essential Question

What impact does the event triangle have on the value of entertainment awards?

Learning Objectives

LO 10.1-1   Describe the components and exchanges of an event triangle.

LO 10.1-2   Explain the effects of media broadcasting on the event triangle.

LO 10.1-3   Explain the promotional value of entertainment awards.

Key Terms

- event triangle
- exchange
- booking agent
- trailer mash-up

OPENING ACT

As the music industry has struggled, its biggest event has taken on more importance than ever. The GRAMMY Awards bring together musicians, sponsors, and fans in a night of celebration. Both long-time greats and music newcomers receive recognition and invaluable publicity.

Beyoncé and Jay Z, two of the most famous and successful stars in the music industry, recently opened the GRAMMYs. During the event, less-recognized musicians were named best new artists. An independently recorded album, which had risen to the top of the charts through use of social media, was honored. The event sponsors received their reward in the form of 28.5 million viewers, according to Nielsen ratings.[1]

Cooperative Learning   Work with a group to discuss major entertainment or sports events that group members have attended or would like to attend. Select one event and outline the steps needed to produce it, the costs involved, and the sources of revenue. Discuss what businesses might be good sponsors for the event.

LO 10.1-1   THE RIGHT EVENT, FANS, AND SPONSORS

When a sports team plays a game, it is considered an event. A concert featuring a top musician is also an event. Sponsors pay the event producers to promote their products during the game or concert. The fans attend the game or concert. An **event triangle** is formed by the interaction of the event, the sponsors, and the fans. During this interaction, each group gives and takes one thing in return for another. The give-and-take between the event, the sponsors, and the fans is called an **exchange**.

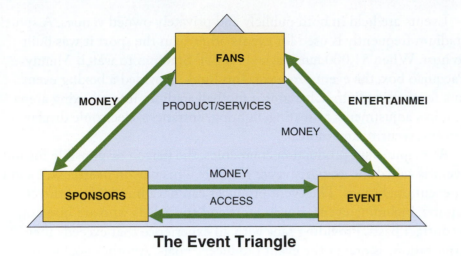

The Event Triangle

The Exchanges

As shown in the illustration above, an exchange takes place between each of the three groups of the event triangle.

- *The fans* pay money for tickets to the event and are rewarded with entertainment from the event. In return, the fans pay money to the sponsors and receive the sponsors' products or services during and/or after the event.
- *The event* receives money from the fans to provide the entertainment. The event receives money from the sponsors to provide access to the fans.
- *The sponsors* provide money to the event to receive access to the fans. The sponsors provide products and services and in return receive money from the fans during and/or after the event.

An event is considered successful if all three members of the event triangle benefit from and are satisfied with the exchanges.

Game and Event Operations

Marketing is the creation and maintenance of satisfying exchange relationships. Event marketing creates and maintains satisfying exchange relationships using an event as the medium. The event can be a concert or a sports game. Game and event production requires detailed coordination among the producers, venue, community, media, team, and others.

Game operations involve the extensive planning and implementation of every aspect that takes place in and around the sports venue, excluding the sports game itself. Game operations can cover parking, seating, player accommodations, scoreboard and message board operations, mascots, promotional giveaways and more. Halftime shows and other entertainment during a sporting event, such as tossing free T-shirts and other souvenirs to fans, are part of game operations. These activities are intended to make the game more entertaining and attractive to fans and sponsors. *Game attractiveness*, which influences attendance, is related to the current success of the team, star players, promotional activities, and venue amenities.

Events are held in both publicly and privately owned venues. A sports stadium frequently is used for events other than the sport it was built to host. When 51,000 fans packed AT&T Stadium to watch Manny Pacquiao box, the event producer, Top Rank, provided a boxing event in a football stadium. Changing a football stadium into a boxing arena requires adjustments to seating, lighting, entrances, electronic display screens, security, and more.

At major event production companies, the person responsible for the event is called the *executive event producer*. This person oversees all game or event operations. The event producer can have hundreds of direct reports, including event coordinators and specialists who are hired on a contract basis. Providing fans with an experience that exceeds their expectations is one of the event producer's goals. Another goal is to produce a perfectly executed event that convinces sponsors to be a part of future events.

INTERMISSION

Who are the members of the event triangle and what are their roles?

LO 10.1-2 MEDIA BROADCASTING

Each member of the event triangle is affected by the addition of media broadcasting. Broadcasting an event means the audio and video content will be distributed to a wide audience via television networks, the Internet, and/or radio.

What a Difference It Makes

If an event is predicted to have a large audience, such as a college or major professional sporting event, it will be broadcast. A minor league hockey game held in an event center probably would not be broadcast. Most entertainment events are recorded for future broadcasting.

The Event   A major event venue is equipped to handle the technical and staff requirements of all broadcast media. Some entertainment events bring their own broadcast equipment and staff. Other events contract with the venue for equipment and staff. Either way, the venue is prepared.

A firm that contracts with the venue on behalf of the performers is referred to as the **booking agent**. Once a contract for a concert or other event has been issued, the venue operations staff will review the facility requirements for the event. According to Scott Manley, Assistant General Manager of Toyota Center, home of the NBA Houston Rockets, about two weeks prior to the event, the event coordinators do the following:

- Reach out to the booking agent to confirm all requirements of the event
- Communicate with the venue staff to assign responsibilities
- Detail the event requirements, such as security
- Complete all precision pre-planning[2]

Events run like clockwork because of careful pre-planning. According to Chris Manley, Broadcast Services Engineer for the NBA Orlando Magic, the event producer writes a script that details exactly what will take place during every pause in a basketball game. The script describes what is shown on every LED board, sign, and banner on and off the court, as well as what is being heard through the audio feeds.

The Sponsors   As part of the negotiated contract, the venue and booking agents will agree on who will sponsor the event. However, the venue controls the final selection of businesses approved as sponsors. The venue will want to avoid a sponsor who is a direct competitor of the venue's naming rights sponsor. For example, Toyota Center would probably not approve another car manufacturer as the featured sponsor of an event. The sponsors will pay for access to the fans in attendance, as well as those watching a broadcast of the event.

Some sponsors work with the event promoter to set up all of their own marketing and promotional strategies. Others pay the venue's marketing department to develop and carry out the promotional ideas. The sponsors also determine the types of advertising they want to use before, during, and after an event. Options for in-venue advertising may include fixed or rotational signage, concourse signage, or backlit signs throughout the seating areas. Sponsors may also have in-game promotions, such as fan participation games or a T-shirt giveaway featuring the sponsor's brand.

The Fans   When a sporting event or concert is broadcast, the fans benefit. Sponsors attracted because of the broadcast may help offset the cost of tickets for fans. The price that fans pay for tickets may be less because of the financial exchange between the sponsors and the event. Additionally, fans assume a role in the broadcast. Cheering and clapping for the athletes or musicians becomes an integral part of the show. Fans viewing the broadcast will experience the excitement of the live audience. Interaction with fans motivates the athletes or celebrities to perform their best.

Super Bowls are sometimes quiet compared to regular-season football games. Super Bowls are played at neutral sites, and most tickets are sold to corporate accounts, not to the teams' fans. Even fantastic plays may not elicit the same roar that comes from energetic fans at a home-team stadium.

INTERMISSION

Describe some of the effects that broadcasting can have on an event.

LO 10.1-3   AWARDING THE BEST

Promotion   Annual entertainment awards shows on television compete for the attention of viewers. The "big four"—the Oscars for movies, the GRAMMYs for music, the Emmys for TV, and the Tonys for Broadway shows—overshadow all other awards shows and have a high marketing value. The MTV Video Music Awards, Screen Actors Guild Awards, and Country Music Association Awards are just a few of the other ceremonies, but they have a more limited marketing value.

Awards Influence Sales

Recognition by one's peers is a high level of honor in any industry. In the entertainment industry, recognition also brings money, praise, publicity, and greater potential for future success. Being nominated for an award can be as beneficial as winning one.

The Oscars   The most famous, sought-after, and prestigious of the entertainment awards is given by the Academy of Motion Picture Arts and Sciences. Approximately 6,000 artists and professionals who are members of the Academy determine the Oscar winners. An Oscar nomination usually brings lots of publicity to a movie studio, its director, and its stars. A nomination creates exciting media coverage and may greatly increase the box office numbers.

The Oscars are broadcast around the world in over 200 countries. The Academy extended ABC Network's broadcast rights to the Academy Awards through the year 2020, assuring it will be an ABC tradition for 45 consecutive years. In 1999 ABC moved the Awards from Monday night to Sunday night, which is the biggest TV-watching night of the week. Following the precedent set by the Super Bowl, the Oscars show is preceded by pre-event advertising meant to create a buzz. ABC recently charged about $1.9 million for each 30-second advertising slot during the Oscars.[3]

A "pre-show" that includes interviews of arriving stars is meant to entice viewers. Another promotion meant to create excitement is an Academy Awards' **trailer mash-up**, which combines the short ads, or trailers, for all of the award-nominated films into one short film that is posted online.

The GRAMMYs   The National Academy of Recording Arts and Sciences (NARAS) is an association of more than 12,000 singers, songwriters, musicians, producers, and other recording professionals. NARAS is internationally known for the annual GRAMMY Awards, in which top music recording artists are recognized. A committee chooses the nominees, and the final winners are selected by a vote of the membership. The awards include 30 fields of music, such as pop, country, and classical, and 82 subcategories.

The Emmys   Three sister branches of the same 12,000-member organization give out the Emmy Awards. The Academy of Television Arts & Sciences presents the Primetime Emmy for excellence in nighttime television. The National Academy of Television Arts & Sciences presents awards for daytime television, sports programming, newscasts, documentaries, and technology and engineering. With members from over 50 countries, the International Academy of Television Arts & Sciences presents awards for excellence in television programming produced outside the United States. The 2013 Emmys were the first to recognize programs produced by online streaming services and Spanish-language media.

The Tonys   The Tony Awards are given by the American Theatre Wing and The Broadway League to professionals in live theater for distinguished achievement on Broadway.

What is the promotional value of entertainment awards?

The Tony Awards also recognize regional theaters that have contributed to artistic achievement and growth in the industry. The ceremonies have been televised in the United States since 1967. The Tonys are more of a special-interest award than the Oscars or Emmys, because fewer people are able to attend the live theater productions. But in recent years, the use of popular celebrity hosts for the Tony Awards show has brought more attention to the Tonys, and attendance at Broadway shows is growing.

International Events

The Cannes International Film Festival has been held in Cannes, France, for more than 65 years. The purpose of the festival is to promote the film industry worldwide. Producers and sellers of films from throughout the world come together with purchasers of films at Cannes. Thousands of films are screened each year. Cannes Awards are presented for feature films, short films, and others. Winning a Cannes Award can be a bonus to the promotion of an otherwise unknown film.

INTERMISSION

Name the four major entertainment awards and explain their value to the industry.

ENCORE

Understand Marketing Concepts

Select the best answer for each question.

1. The members of the event triangle are
   a. Oscars, Emmys, Tonys
   b. TV, radio, Internet
   c. international awards, Cannes, Sundance
   d. events, sponsors, fans

2. Event coordinators are responsible for
   a. marketing
   b. detailed pre-planning
   c. post-event analysis
   d. all of the above

Think Critically

Answer the following questions as completely as possible.

3. Name the sponsors of a recent broadcast event. Explain why you think the businesses sponsored the event. (LO 10.1-1, LO 10.1-2)

4. If a movie, TV show, play, or song won one of the "big four" awards, would this influence your desire to see or hear it? Explain your answer. (LO 10.1-3)

10.2 Sponsorships and Endorsements

The Essential Question

What are the benefits of sponsorships and endorsements?

Learning Objectives

LO 10.2-1   Explain the benefits of sponsorship to the sponsor.

LO 10.2-2   Define endorsements and discuss their restrictions.

Key Terms

- sponsorship
- logo
- corporate sponsorship
- endorsement

OPENING ACT

Sportswear giants Nike, a U.S. company, and Puma and Adidas, both German companies, have battled each other to provide uniforms for professional sports teams all over the world. Professional sports teams offer opportunities to outbid competitors for the global retail, apparel, and product licensing business of the teams. The winner of the bidding wars has its name prominently displayed on the uniforms of famous athletes during games. Recently, England's Manchester United soccer team was expected to sign a ten-year uniform deal that would pay the team as much as £596m (more than $1 billion U.S. dollars) a year.[4] Lesser-known U.S. sportswear company Warrior Sports, a subsidiary of New Balance that provides shoes and apparel to the Boston Red Sox, was also making inroads in winning bids to provide uniforms and branded products to British soccer teams. Buying the rights to have its corporate brand seen weekly by millions of people can be a promotional bonanza for a sportswear business.

Cooperative Learning   With a partner, discuss the benefits of using professional teams' uniforms to promote a sportswear company. What information do you think a sponsoring company would need in order to determine how much to bid for the promotional opportunity?

LO 10.2-1   GAME DAY

Promotion   Part of a promotional plan involves associating a business or product with an event, such as the Olympics or a local charity event. **Sponsorship** occurs when an individual or business provides products, services, or financial support for a sports team or an event. The support provides a link in the mind of the consumers between the company, its product, and the team or event. This link makes it important for sponsors to carefully select teams and events that fit the image of the product and business.

Costs and Benefits of Sponsorship

Event producers or sports teams sell sponsorships to businesses to help pay for the costs of providing the event to fans and to keep ticket prices more affordable. The costs of sponsorships to the event producers include. Businesses purchase sponsorships to

- Costs for production of the event or game (venue rental, entertainment, staff)
- Costs of selling the sponsorship (salespeople, production of contracts)
- Costs of providing benefits to the sponsor (sponsor tickets, signage, VIP treatment and hospitality for sponsors, media promotion, publicity, production of press releases)

For sponsoring businesses, sponsorships can be a big expense, but they offer many benefits.

- Increase sales and profits
- Introduce a new product or service to a large audience
- Become associated with an event in which the audience is the target market
- Earn the goodwill of the audience by showing a commitment to the event
- Entertain clients or potential customers
- Serve as employee incentives
- Enhance the company's image and improve community relations
- Enter new markets or a niche market

United Airlines is the official airline of the United States Olympic Committee (USOC). It flies staff, athletes, and tons of equipment to USOC events, including the Olympics. United promotes its sponsorship in videos shown before the in-flight safety video on its flights. The videos show United employees helping Olympic athletes with transportation needs.

JUDGMENT CALL

After Taiwanese tennis player Hsieh Su-wei won the women's tennis doubles final at Wimbledon, she created a controversy. Hsieh's father indicated that a Chinese company had offered to sponsor her if she would renounce her Taiwanese citizenship and become a citizen of China. This hit a nerve with Taiwan, a small island off the coast of China. Taiwan has been in conflict with China since 1949 when the Republic of China Nationalists lost the civil war to the Communist Chinese. The leaders of the Nationalists fled from China to Taiwan. They have maintained a separate democratic government since that time. China continues to consider Taiwan a renegade province. Hsieh's "threat" to move to China was viewed by some as a ploy to attract more sponsors by putting her citizenship up for sale.

Think Critically

Is a sponsorship worth giving up an athlete's national citizenship? How is this different from an athlete who plays for another country during the Olympics or a city that pursues a professional football team from another city?

By Association

When businesses want to be associated with winning teams at the top of their game, the cost of sponsorships can be high. Companies in the same industry will often compete for sponsorships of the same teams.

Nike and Adidas continue their battle on and off the field of play. Adidas has the sponsorship contract with international soccer's FIFA until 2030, allowing only Adidas to sell official merchandise. Nike is the sponsor of Brazil's national soccer team, but Adidas soccer balls were used in the 2014 World Cup held in Brazil. Nike and all other unofficial brands were not allowed to run World Cup-themed ads. Of the 32 teams that qualified for the 2014 FIFA World Cup, 31 percent wore Nike-brand uniforms, including the U.S. team.[5]

Supporting Sports

A corporate **logo** is the graphic representation of a company's name. When displayed in the stadium of a football team, the logo provides financial support for the team and access to the fans by the corporation. Using the name of a product or business as part of the name of an event venue is a type of **corporate sponsorship**. For example, the San Diego Padres MLB team plays in Petco Park. In most cases, the owner of the venue owns the rights to sell sponsorships to generate revenue. Most sponsorship agreements are long term, lasting a number of years. The sponsoring corporation receives a substantial return on its investment by gaining access to fans and a positive association with the team.

INTERMISSION

What costs are involved with sponsorships?

LO 10.2-2   WHAT IS AN ENDORSEMENT?

The Federal Trade Commission (FTC) has the authority to regulate endorsements. The FTC defines an *endorsement* as "any advertising message that consumers are likely to believe reflects the opinions, beliefs, findings, or experiences of a party other than the sponsoring advertiser."[6] In other words, an **endorsement** is a well-known person's public expression of approval or support for a product or service. Endorsements are promotional tools—not a form of sponsorship.

The FTC also offers clarifying examples of what is and is not an endorsement. For example, a film critic's comments, if used by the filmmaker in an advertisement, are legally endorsements. The critic is a known and real person, and the critic's review is an opinion independent of any comments by the filmmaker. A commercial featuring two unidentified teenagers talking about a product is not an endorsement, because the teens are not known and they are acting as paid spokespersons for the company. However, a commercial for a brand of tires starring a well-known racecar driver is an endorsement because the public

- Knows the person is a professional driver
- Assumes the comments are personal opinion, whether or not that is actually stated
- Assumes the driver would not make the comment if he or she did not believe it

Similarly, an ad for golf balls in which a famous golfer is shown hitting the balls is considered an endorsement, even if the golfer does not speak.

In today's marketing environment, the most influential endorsements are made by friends and family. But celebrities and athletes are also influential, especially to young people. When celebrities tweet about products, they are subject to FTC regulations. The FTC's prohibition on unfair or deceptive acts or practices covers online advertising, marketing, and sales.

Legal Restrictions on Endorsements

What is said on behalf of an advertiser is commercial speech and can be regulated under the FTC Act, if it's deceptive. Commercial speech is not protected under the First Amendment. The FTC has several guidelines that must be met by the endorser and the sponsoring company.

1. The truthful opinions and beliefs of the endorser must be expressed in the endorsement.
2. Endorsers must have real experience with the product. If they haven't tried it, they can't talk about their experience with it.
3. The connection between the endorser and advertiser should be clearly revealed. If the endorser receives free products or is paid, this should be revealed to avoid being deceptive.
4. The endorsements may not contain any deceptive or misleading statements. The statements must be able to be substantiated by the advertiser.

Celebrity Endorsements

Celebrities and athletes frequently earn more from endorsements than in salaries or winnings. Lebron James and Tiger Woods have both signed some of the largest endorsement deals ever. For years, both athletes have ranked in the top ten for endorsement deal earnings. Nike has made some of the best-calculated but riskiest endorsement deals. Most Nike endorsement deals have paid off handsomely. Before Michael Jordan ever played a day in the NBA, Nike offered him a deal that included his own shoe. Jordan's shoes are still selling many years after he retired from the NBA. Celebrity endorsements have advantages and disadvantages and are often surrounded by controversy.

Alexander Tamargo/Getty Images

Why does the FTC regulate commercial speech involving celebrity endorsements?

Advantages   Celebrity advertising endorsements are advantageous to businesses in at least three ways.

1. Studies have proven that consumers will buy products endorsed by celebrities more often than products that are not endorsed. Fans and businesses like to be identified with a winning team or athlete.
2. Viewers and listeners are less likely to turn off a commercial featuring a celebrity than a commercial featuring a fictitious character.
3. Consumers tend to believe celebrities, especially those who are chosen for their good public image.

Disadvantages   Endorsements as a means of promotion have a few disadvantages. Celebrity endorsements are very expensive to the sponsoring company. In addition, a company sometimes regrets having been associated with an athlete who has legal problems. Alex Rodriguez (A-Rod) had some of baseball's highest-paying endorsement deals. He was reported to have made as much as $3.5 million a year in endorsements before his suspension from MLB for illegal drug use. The resulting scandal dried up A-Rod's brand value. Another risk occurs when celebrities endorse more than one product. If they endorse too many products, they risk losing credibility, meaning the sponsoring company may not get as much value from the celebrity's endorsement.

What a Business Seeks in an Endorser

When searching for a celebrity endorser, businesses look for someone who

- Has a positive, charismatic, trustworthy image
- Is familiar to most consumers
- Has a career in process (rather than being retired)
- Presents few risks
- Has a believable relationship with the product

Notice that speaking ability and personal appearance are not among the top requirements. Businesses believe that weaknesses in these areas can be remedied with voice coaches and wardrobe assistants.

In a recent year, football great Peyton Manning made about $12 million in endorsements for a wide array of products, including Papa John's Pizza, Gatorade, and Buick.

Do you believe a celebrity endorsement is worth millions of dollars to a company? Why or why not?

© bikerlondon/Shutterstock.com

According to Jordan Schlachter, Executive Vice President of Sports for The Marketing Arm, Peyton Manning is one of the most popular, trustworthy, well-known celebrities—not just athletes—in this country.[7] Add his three Super Bowl experiences to his great sense of humor and Manning has the formula to be a successful corporate salesman.

It's not easy for every professional athlete to win product endorsements. When J. J. Watt started his NFL career with the Houston Texans, he had all of the perfect characteristics of a national endorsement star. As a premier defense player with a record number of quarterback sacks, he became known for jumping up to swat down the other teams' passes. Watts also earned a good reputation for being well spoken and doing extensive charity work. Although he earned a number of endorsements on the regional and national levels, as a Houston Texan, he lacked the national spotlight that goes along with being part of a winning team. The prominence of the team can have a major influence on the types of endorsements earned by players.

INTERMISSION

What are the advantages and disadvantages of using celebrity endorsers?

ENCORE

Understand Marketing Concepts

Select the best answer for each question.

1. A sponsor does all of the following *except*
   a. helps pay for an event
   b. avoids entering new markets
   c. helps hold down the cost of ticket prices for fans
   d. wants to be identified with an event with the right target market

2. Which of these television ads would be an endorsement?
   a. an unknown actor playing the role of a professional who recommends the product
   b. a group of teens talking about a movie
   c. Peyton Manning eating Papa John's pizza
   d. all of the above

Think Critically

Answer the following questions as completely as possible.

3. What teams would you like to sponsor to promote your new women's sportswear line of clothing? Explain your choices. (LO 10.2-1)

4. To promote your new women's sportswear line, what female athlete would you ask to endorse the clothing and why? Explain possible advantages and disadvantages of the celebrity endorsement. (LO 10.2-2)

10.3 Promotional Plans

The Essential Question

What steps are taken to develop a promotional plan, and which current promotional trends might be a part of the plan?

Learning Objectives

LO 10.3-1 List steps in developing a promotional plan.

LO 10.3-2 Discuss recent promotional trends and ways to stay current.

Key Terms

- promotional plan
- gross rating points (GRP)
- cost-per-thousand (CPM)
- promotional mix
- quantitative measurement
- loyal users
- qualitative measurement
- experiential activations

OPENING ACT

The Super Bowl offers the largest mass-market advertising event in the United States. The 2014 Super Bowl was the first time a new kind of ad was used. Personalized messages were sent to fans based on their physical location. Smartphone users received messages announcing that Super Bowl merchandise was available on the fourth floor of Macy's Department store, located one block straight ahead. Fans who wanted to see the Vince Lombardi Trophy, which goes to the Super Bowl winning team, were told to take a right at the next corner. The information was sent via transmitters, called beacons, located in public areas, stores, and stadiums. Apple added the iBeacons to iPhone software updates. Users who downloaded a brand's app and gave permission received alerts whenever their phone was in range of a beacon.

Cooperative Learning   Work with a group and brainstorm ways for sports teams to use beacons to connect with fans. Make a list of the ideas to share with the class.

LO 10.3-1   PLANNING TO PROMOTE

Promotion Sports and entertainment promoters are facing a challenging and exciting future. Ways to make consumers aware of products and services continue to grow as new technology is developed. Marketers must have a plan to reach their target market.

Developing a Promotional Plan

A **promotional plan** is a written, detailed description of how the four elements of promotion—advertising, sales promotion, publicity, and personal selling—will be used. It is part of the overall marketing plan. It usually covers a year at a time and is reviewed and updated throughout the year. The development of the promotional plan includes the following steps:

1. Identify the target customers.
2. Set promotional goals.
3. Develop a promotional budget.
4. Select the promotional mix.
5. Measure the results.

Identify the Target Customers

Sports and entertainment businesses may have customers of varied ages and income. The promotional plan should identify which specific targeted group is the focus of each phase of the plan. This guides the selection of the media and the promotional mix.

Set Promotional Goals

Specific goals for each part of the promotional plan must be set. The goals should be measurable to help define a successful promotion. For example, a sports team's goal might be to increase the number of repeat season ticket holders for the following season by 10 percent. This goal can be easily measured.

Develop a Promotional Budget

The budget must be tied to the promotional goals. A common method of determining an overall promotional budget is to define the tasks needed to achieve the goals, estimate the costs of the tasks, and compare the costs to available funds.

Knowing which media will reach the target markets and how much it will cost is another step toward building the budget. The total *reach* of media is the number of people in the target market expected to receive an ad. The *frequency* is the number of times the targeted group is receiving the ad. Multiplying the reach by the frequency, expressed as a percentage, provides the estimated total potential audience, called the **gross rating points (GRP)**. The goal is to obtain the highest possible GRP at the lowest possible cost. The cost of the GRP can be used to develop the budget. The cost effectiveness of a specific media is evaluated based on the cost of each exposure to an ad divided by its reach in thousands, or the **cost-per-thousand (CPM)**. CPM is an abbreviation for *cost per mille* (pronounced mill), or thousand. (See the *Math in Marketing* feature on the next page to see how GRP and CPM are calculated.)

Select the Promotional Mix

The blending of the promotional elements of advertising, sales promotion, publicity, and personal selling make up the **promotional mix**. The promotional mix and the media used should be selected based on the targeted customers, the advertising campaign goals, and the budget. Advertising agencies use data about the target market to select the media. Some advertising agencies use high-speed, algorithmic software to sort data collected from targeted customers and then buy online ad space based on consumer patterns.

Marketing-Information Management

Measure the Results

Once a business has implemented a promotional plan, it needs feedback on how the plan is working. Sales data collected before, during, and after the promotional efforts will show changes in sales. If goals are not being met, then the promotional plan should be revised.

A **quantitative measurement** provides information in terms of numbers or percentages. A promotional goal might be to increase the market share

Google's advertising system is called Enhanced Campaigns. It allows advertisers to build a single ad campaign for all Internet-based devices. Prior advertising systems required a separate campaign for desktop computers, tablets, and smartphones. Google adapted its system to consumers' use of multiple devices to search and surf the Web.

MATH IN MARKETING

A company is trying to determine which TV promotional options might be the most valuable. A 30-second ad on station XYZ during the local news has a reach of 25 percent of the total targeted audience, or 1,500,250 viewers, and costs $35,000. A 30-second ad during a popular prime time show has a reach of 25 percent of the total targeted audience, or 5,650,000 viewers, and costs $148,000. Each ad is shown three times, and each time the reach is 25 percent of the targeted audience.

Do the Math

Determine the CPM for each of the ads. [*Hint:* CPM = Cost ÷ (Reach ÷ 1,000).] Which is the least-expensive ad per thousand viewers? Calculate the GRP for the ads. [*Hint:* GRP = Reach (%) × Frequency.] Why might the company consider the more-expensive ad?

of a product or service by 10 percent in one year. Data about the current market share can be compared to the market share at the end of the year to determine if the goal was met. A business might have 1.5 million mobile app **loyal users**, people who open an app at least three times in 30 days. If the business wants to increase that number to 3 million, a comparison between current data and new data provides a quantitative measurement. A **qualitative measurement** is subjective and depends on interpretation. It might assess the app user's opinion of the app's features.

A high percentage of consumers may indicate that they plan to try a new product because of a promotion. The quantitative measurement shows how many of them *actually* buy the product, which provides a more useful number. A combination of quantitative and qualitative measurements is useful in determining the success of a promotional plan.

INTERMISSION

Why is the promotional mix an important part of the promotional plan?

LO 10.3-2 PROMOTIONAL TRENDS

Technology has changed how and where products and services are promoted. Gaining the attention of potential customers and motivating them to act requires new and innovative marketing approaches. To stay current, marketers need to

- Be aware of changes taking place in the world, specifically those affecting the target market
- Read and listen to multiple sources of information on a consistent basis, including blogs, *The New York Times*, and *Advertising Age*

- Be open to the ideas and viewpoints of others
- Attend conferences or training opportunities with other professionals

The Super Ad Bowl

Early in February each year, a major advertising event takes place between plays at the Super Bowl. In recent years, about 30 to 35 companies spent approximately $133,333 per second to reach an audience of as many as 115 million people.[8]

You didn't have to be a football player to be a part of the action during a recent Super Bowl. Coca-Cola asked people to vote for an online match between three groups competing in a desert for a Coke on Game Day. Pepsi and Toyota used viewers' photos in their ads. Car manufacturer Audi let people choose the end of its Super Bowl ad, while Lincoln based its car ad on more than 6,000 tweets from fans.[9]

The use of young children, puppies, ponies, and patriotism to arouse emotion has been a trend in Super Bowl ads. Evoking emotion in viewers helps hold their attention and make a connection with them. WeatherTech of Bolingbrook, Illinois, which makes car floor mats and cargo liners, used its Super Bowl ad to emphasize that its products are made in America. The intent was to support manufacturing and jobs in the United States. David MacNeil, CEO of WeatherTech, said, "If my neighbor doesn't have a job, sooner or later I won't have a job either."[10]

The immediacy of viewers' reactions through social media has influenced the content of Super Bowl commercials. Advertisers are more likely to choose positive messages rather than controversial messages that might immediately result in a storm of negative social media comments.

Pre-Ads

Brief ads that give you a preview of the real ads are a way to build up suspense and make sure viewers watch a TV ad in the future. Treating the viewers to "inside" information about what is to come makes them feel special and a part of the action. It is also a way to get people to view the ad before it is released. Volkswagen was among the first to use this strategy

Using people as walking billboards is not a new idea in promotion, but earning your living that way may be. Jason Sadler, now Jason SurfrApp, started IWearYourShirt.com in 2009. The business offers funny photos and video campaigns featuring corporate T-shirts. Sadler has about 40,000 Twitter followers and more than 12,000 Facebook fans. He also appears in videos on YouTube, Ustream, and Flickr. The business has had more than 1,500 clients, including Nissan and Starbucks. More than once, Sadler has legally changed his last name after selling it for as much as $50,000.[11]

Think Critically

What companies might successfully use Sadler's business as part of their promotional mix. How could a company measure the results of using Sadler's ads?

successfully with its memorable ad that showed a pint-sized Darth Vader using "The Force" to start up a Volkswagen Passat.

Social Networking

The evolution of advertising on mobile devices is in an early stage, but social media will be an important part of the development. WhatsApp is a cross-platform mobile messaging app that uses the Internet to allow users to exchange messages without having to pay for short messaging service (SMS), commonly referred to as text messaging. WhatsApp has more than 400 million active users and does not use advertising, games, or gimmicks to support the service. WhatsApp promises to "never bother you with ads." WhatsApp is sending a trending message from users to marketers: Do not annoy or overwhelm people with advertisements. Facebook, which depends on ads for revenue, recently purchased WhatsApp for $19 billion.

With more apps under development, users will be able to interact with their mobile devices in new ways. This will be a growth area, but marketers must determine the best way to use this technology to attract customers.

Movie Promotions

Movies shown in theaters and on video generally are preceded by *trailers*, which are advertisements for other movies. Trailers are critical to attracting an audience. They are called trailers because they originally were shown after the feature movie, but marketers soon realized that the audience was leaving before the trailer was finished.

TAKE A BOW Brad Jacobs

As Executive Event Producer for Top Rank, a boxing promotions company, Brad Jacobs is a problem solver and crisis manager. He has produced over 800 events in more than 150 cities worldwide.[12] His planning and organizational skills are fine-tuned. He is admired for his strong sense of the realities of the boxing market. Jacobs produces events that keep fans coming back.

Jacobs began his career in sales for a professional soccer team and then moved to production of sporting and entertainment events. Jacobs uses a checklist of more than 400 items when producing a major boxing event. His professional-level communication and negotiation skills come into play when discussing rights fees, talent and broadcast agreements, venue locations, sponsorships, and promotions. The audience sees the results in perfectly executed, profitable events.

Think Critically

Why are communication and negotiation skills so important to an event producer? Why is detailed planning essential to the success of an event?

Film Buffs

Each month, Turner Classic Movie (TCM) cable channel has 62 million viewers between the ages of 18 and 49.[13] TCM earns about 30 cents per subscriber from cable system operators and generates $300 million a year in fees. TCM's promotional plan calls for interaction with *film buffs*, people who love movies. The interactions include a guided tour of New York City movie sites, an annual Hollywood film festival, and a TCM Classic ocean cruise. TCM will also be using other **experiential activations**—interactions with customers through festivals, tours, or licensed merchandise to retain satisfied customers.

A large number of advertisers offer Academy Awards-related experiences to consumers. *People* magazine held a sweepstakes to select 350 VIP subscribers and their guests to attend an all-day Oscar Fan Experience. It included bleacher seats on the Academy Awards red carpet and a viewing party at a nearby theater.

INTERMISSION

How can marketers stay current with promotional trends?

ENCORE

Understand Marketing Concepts

Select the best answer for each question.

1. Which of the following is *not* a quantitative measurement of a promotional activity?
   a. This year's sales increased 5 percent over last year's sales.
   b. Moviegoers interviewed said the movie trailer was entertaining.
   c. Four hundred season ticket holders bought five or more seats each.
   d. Product coupons were distributed to the 45,200 fans at the game.

2. The promotional mix is a blending of all of the following *except*
   a. advertising
   b. personal selling
   c. sales promotion
   d. quantitative measurements

Think Critically

Answer the following questions as completely as possible.

3. What promotional mix would you use to promote professional soccer to young people? (LO 10.3-1)

4. Think about how the promotion of products has changed over the years. What changes would you predict in the future? (LO 10.3-2)

Review Marketing Terms

Match the terms listed with the definitions.

1. Provides information in terms of numbers or percentages
2. Multiplying the reach by the frequency, expressed as a percentage
3. A written, detailed description of how the four elements of promotion will be used
4. The cost of each exposure to an ad divided by its reach in thousands
5. Occurs when an individual or business provides products, services, or financial support for a sports team or an event
6. The blending of the promotional elements of advertising, sales promotion, publicity, and personal selling
7. Provides information that is subjective and depends on interpretation
8. A well-known person's public expression of approval or support for a product or service
9. The give-and-take between the event, the sponsors, and the fans
10. A firm that contracts with the venue on behalf of the performers
11. Formed by the interaction of the event, the sponsors, and the fans
12. Combines short ads for the award-nominated films into one short film
13. People who open an app at least three times in thirty days
14. Interaction with customers to retain them as satisfied customers
15. The graphic representation of a company name
16. Using the name of a product or business as part of the name of an event venue or game

a. booking agent
b. corporate sponsorship
c. cost-per-thousand (CPM)
d. endorsement
e. event triangle
f. exchange
g. experiential activations
h. gross rating points (GRP)
i. logo
j. loyal users
k. promotional mix
l. promotional plan
m. qualitative measurement
n. quantitative measurement
o. sponsorship
p. trailer mash-up

Review Marketing Concepts

Select the best answer for each of the following questions.

17. Selecting the promotional mix
    a. should not take place until the promotional goals are set
    b. precedes the development of the promotional budget
    c. is the third step in promotional planning
    d. both b and c
18. According to FTC regulations, an endorser must
    a. have real experience with the product
    b. not make any deceptive or misleading statements
    c. express truthful opinions about the product
    d. all of the above

19. In an exchange, the sponsor
   a. pays the event for access to fans
   b. cannot use a logo
   c. provides all hospitality for fans
   d. pays for the fans' tickets
20. Emmys honor and promote the best
   a. movies
   b. music
   c. TV shows
   d. plays
21. Sponsorships are used to
   a. increase sales and profits
   b. introduce new products
   c. enhance a company's image
   d. all of the above
22. A promotional plan
   a. details the production staff needed
   b. determines the cost of a product
   c. details the promotional mix
   d. determines the amount of profit

Think Critically

23. Write a paragraph discussing the benefits versus the risks of a company using a controversial athlete to endorse its products. How could the company's promotional plan succeed? How could it fail? (LO 10.2-2)
24. Select an extreme sport that appeals to teenagers. You are the executive event producer of an upcoming event that will showcase this sport. As the event producer, you are responsible for choosing the game entertainment that will take place throughout the event. Describe the types of entertainment that you think will appeal to the sport's fan base. (LO 10.1-1)
25. Write a one-paragraph news release (publicity feature) about a popular brand of sports equipment. Remember that publicity is free. Then change the feature into an advertisement that you will pay a website to publish. Explain how the two promotions differ. (LO 10.3-1)
26. Make a list of the businesses that might want to sponsor the MTV Video Music Awards. Explain why you chose each business. (LO 10.1-3)
27. A local high school has an award-winning theater arts department. It has asked for help in promoting a play it is producing. Who are the members of the event triangle for this event? Who would be the best sponsors for this event and why? What media mix would you suggest be used to promote this event? (LO 10.1-1)

28. You have been hired by a university to find corporate sponsors for the women's golf team. The university hired a new coach last year and has recruited five strong players who have won several tournaments. What additional information would you need to help you select sponsors? Conduct research and make a preliminary list of corporations to consider. Explain why each business is on the list. (LO 10.2-1)

29. A local charity is having a fund-raiser concert at the city park. It has booked several popular bands and singers to perform. It can also pay a substantial amount to have the event broadcast on local TV and the Internet. Make a chart listing the benefits related to the event, the sponsors, and the fans if the event is broadcast. (LO 10.1-2)

Make Academic Connections

30. **Research** Use the Internet or other sources to research the changes made to the messaging service WhatsApp since it was purchased by Facebook. Has its no-ads policy changed? If yes, in what ways? Is the app still adding users or has it lost popularity? What has caused these changes? (LO 10.3-2)

31. **Marketing Math** Your bagel shop has just donated $500 to help build a neighborhood skateboarding park. In return for your donation, your shop's sign will hang in the park for one month. The skateboarders' association expects 1,000 people to see your sign. The average profit on a purchase at your shop is $0.96. How many customers will you need to make a profit of $500 to cover the donation? (LO 10.2-1)

32. **History** Conduct research to learn about the first Academy Awards event. What promotional mix might have been used to let the public know about the event? How is that mix different today? (LO 10.1-3)

33. **Technology** Conduct research to learn about online, invitation-only social networks. How do advertisers use them? How effective are they? (LO 10.3-2)

34. **Communication** Write letters to two local businesses asking the owners to sponsor one of the less-prominent sports at a local high school. Explain what the sport needs in the way of equipment, promotion, and professional advice. Propose an outline of objectives for the sponsorship. Be sure to tell the business owners what they will receive in return. (LO 10.2-1)

35. **Careers** A top quarterback whose team won a major college bowl game was drafted as a first-round pick by an NFL team that did not have many wins this past season. He currently has no endorsement contracts. What kinds of products or services should he consider endorsing? Which of his characteristics would be good to emphasize to the corporations who own the products? Should he accept every endorsement offer he receives? Why or why not? (LO 10.2-2)

36. **Problem Solving** Your advertising agency is representing a National Hockey League expansion team in Houston, Texas. Houston has a population of more than 2 million in the city and a metro area of about 6 million people. Prepare a two-minute PowerPoint presentation describing a game operations plan for the team. Explain what new trends in promotion you would use to increase game attractiveness for the fans and why. (LO 10.3-2)

EXTRA INNINGS PROJECT

You have been hired by a small, independent movie studio to develop a promotional plan for a new movie to be released in six months. The movie is about the life of Timothy Leif (T. J.) Oshie, who started playing for the St. Louis Blues National Hockey League team in 2008 and was a member of the 2014 Team USA Olympic Hockey Team. Oshie is a member of the Ojibwe people. The target audience for the movie is people ages 18 to 35. The movie will have a limited release in five theaters in each of the following cities: St. Louis, Seattle, New York, and Los Angeles. Your goal is to attract the target audience. You have a promotional budget of $500,000. If the movie gains momentum, additional funds will be spent on promotion, a wider release will be pushed, and you will make more money.

Work with a group and complete the following activities.

1. Research T. J. Oshie and assume that the most interesting points of his life will be covered in the movie. Explain what would attract the target audience.

2. Select the promotional mix to use for this movie. What combination of media would you use to let the target audience in the limited-release cities know about the movie? Make a chart that lists the media you would use in each location and the percent of the budget you would spend on that media and location.

3. Determine what message you would like to convey through the promotional plan to reach your target audience. How will you convince them to see the movie?

4. How will you determine whether the promotional plan was successful? At what point after the movie's opening in theaters will you know it deserves a wider release? If it does not justify a wider release, what would you recommend be done with the film to possibly generate some additional income?

VIRTUAL BUSINESS *Sports & Entertainment*

Use the *Sponsorships and Endorsements* lesson to understand how important corporate branding is for sports stadium signage. Sponsorships are a source of revenue for stadium owners. Negotiate pricing for different signage around the stadium and gain an understanding of why sponsorships work. At the end of the activity, you will be challenged to negotiate with multiple sponsors to achieve a specific target for sponsorship revenue.

For more information, go to **knowledgematters.com**.

Artwork courtesy of Knowledge Matters, Inc.

CHANGING NASCAR'S TARGET MARKET

The National Association for Stock Car Auto Racing (NASCAR) is the sanctioning body of NASCAR races. To remain a relevant sport into the future, NASCAR hired Kim Brink as Vice President of Marketing. Her job is to provide a new focus on youth and multicultural audiences and digital marketing.

In addition, NASCAR hired a new advertising agency, Ogilvy & Mather, known for its sophisticated work for big consumer brands such as American Express and IBM. The agency was given the task of developing a "new brand direction and a new creative platform"[14] for NASCAR.

New Fans

Studies have shown that the average NASCAR fan is a white (80 percent) male (60 percent),[15] who is employed full-time and married.[16] However, NASCAR has a higher share of female fans (40 percent) than many sports.[17]

As one of the largest spectator sports in the United States, NASCAR has an incredibly loyal fan base. NASCAR wants to maintain its current fan base while also attracting a new group of younger and multicultural fans. With the help of its new advertising agency, NASCAR implemented a Five-Year Industry Action Plan to help engage and excite existing fans, while creating new ones.

The first changes in the promotional plan were to include commercials in Spanish, online offerings like nascar.com, and the use of well-known NASCAR drivers in commercials.

Drivers also contacted fans and followers through social media and alerted them to watch the new commercials.

A few years ago, attorney Max Siegel became the first and only African-American president of a NASCAR franchise. His intent was to find new, more diverse drivers and fans. He also created a reality show with BET Networks to find the next female or minority driver.

In 2012 Viva La Raza Racing became the first Mexican-owned professional auto-racing team in NASCAR history. It intends to serve as a development program for young Latin American drivers.

NASCAR Mexico Toyota Series is a NASCAR series in Mexico. In 2014 it held a race in Phoenix, Arizona, as part of NASCAR's plan to attract the American Latino audience. It was a success and is scheduled to be an annual event.

In another attempt to grow the Latino audience, NASCAR worked with Univision, an American Spanish-language broadcast TV network, to put a racing-themed storyline into an existing show. A telenovela series about a female Latino driver, co-produced by Univision and NASCAR, debuted on Univision's website.

Think Critically

1. Why is NASCAR seeking additional Latino drivers? How does this fit into its overall marketing plan?
2. Are the promotional actions taken by NASCAR unusual? In what ways?
3. What could NASCAR do to increase the fan base of people ages 16 to 25?

GRAPHIC DESIGN PROMOTION EVENT

Computer-aided graphic design is frequently used to bring advertising campaigns and special promotions to life. The Graphic Design Promotion Event challenges participants to raise their computer skills to the next level.

Each contestant must select a theme to promote NASCAR to a diverse audience. Contestants must create a logo and a flyer based on this multicultural theme. The dimensions of the logo must not exceed 4″ × 4″, and the theme needs to be 25 characters or less, including spaces. Four originals of the flyer and logo must be produced at home or school. This graphic should not be professionally or commercially created or produced. All participants must submit four plastic sheet protectors (8½″ × 11″), each containing a flyer, a logo, and a Graphic Design Resource/Release Form. The final product may be black and white or color and printed on white paper.

Performance Indicators Evaluated
- Demonstrate knowledge of graphic design and rules for layout.
- Demonstrate effective use of color, lines, text, graphics, and shapes.
- Use principles of design, layout, and typography in graphic design.
- Apply technical skills to manipulate graphics, artwork, and images.
- Use appropriate artwork and design techniques to effectively illustrate a theme.
- Generate a promotional flyer for marketing purposes.
- Produce a graphic design promotion that has eye appeal and shows imagination, creativity, and originality.

All graphics must be computer generated. Public domain and contestant-prepared graphics may be used. No copyrighted items may be used in this contest. Although a work may be freely accessible on the Internet and contain no statement of copyright, copyright law provides that such works are protected. Contestants must assume that works are protected by copyright until they learn otherwise.

Think Critically
1. What are three examples of graphic design products that are used frequently in the business world?
2. Why is it important to carefully research information gathered on the Internet before using it in graphic design productions?
3. What does "copyrighted" mean?
4. How does graphic design enhance business publications?

www.bpa.org

SELLING SPORTS AND ENTERTAINMENT

© iStockphoto.com/JBryson

POINT YOUR BROWSER

ngl.cengage.com/sports4e

Winning Strategies

Country Stampede

Country music is popular throughout the world. Outdoor concerts provide an ideal setting for country music fans. The four-day, star-studded Country Stampede, held in Manhattan, Kansas, is a major outdoor country music festival that attracts the greatest country music stars and thousands of fans from all over the United States. As an added attraction, other events, such as craft shows, may be held in conjunction with the concerts.

Event planners are responsible for working out the logistics of the event, including parking, security, food, and restroom facilities. Because the event is outdoors, event planners must also have a plan for providing shelter in case of bad weather. Signing corporations and organizations to sponsor the event is also important. KICKER, a manufacturer of home, personal, and mobile audio products, is the main sponsor of Country Stampede. Other sponsors include Pepsi, DirecTV, Holiday Inn, and many other national and local businesses.

An elaborate website helps promote the event. Various ticket options are available, including VIP seating. Discounts are offered to those who purchase a four-day admission pass. Parking passes can also be purchased. Campsites are also available but sell out quickly.

Country Stampede is a classic example of how a small community can host a huge entertainment event with the help of sponsors, top performers, and the right mix of promotions.

© Digital Storm/Shutterstock.com

Think Critically

1. What types of pricing and promotional strategies does Country Stampede use to maximize attendance at the four-day event?

2. How might KICKER benefit from sponsoring Country Stampede?

11.1 The Sales Process

The Essential Question

What do salespeople need to know about their customers and products to close a sale?

Learning Objectives

LO 11.1-1   List the steps involved in the sales process.

LO 11.1-2   Discuss the management skills and knowledge necessary for successful salespeople.

Key Terms

- preapproach
- suggestion selling
- cold calling
- leads
- customer management

OPENING ACT

Every evening in homes around the country, the telephone rings with someone trying to sell insurance, credit offers, or time-share vacation properties. *Telemarketing*, a direct approach to selling by telephone, is often used by nonprofit organizations to solicit pledges for charities. Many Americans have grown weary of these sales pitches. Use of the National Do Not Call Registry, caller ID, and call blocking are a few strategies that consumers use to eliminate the frustration associated with telemarketing. While telemarketing is annoying to many individuals, the success rate for this form of selling gives companies and nonprofit organizations the incentive to continue the practice.

Cooperative Learning   Work with a partner to identify negative examples of telemarketing. Why have consumers become extremely cautious when dealing with telemarketers?

LO 11.1-1   SELLING SPORTS AND ENTERTAINMENT

Selling   *Selling* is direct, personal communication with prospective customers in order to assess and satisfy their needs with appropriate products and services. Sports and entertainment industries depend on salespeople who can effectively communicate product and service information to consumers. The salesperson becomes the link between the customer and the business, with many customers seeing the salesperson *as* the business. *Personal selling* is one of the four elements of promotion. The sales process creates awareness and the desire to purchase on the part of the consumer.

The Sales Process

People who have strong sales skills are in high demand and are well paid for their abilities. Whether or not a sale is made often comes down to the salesperson. Effective selling can be organized into six steps.

1. **Preapproach** During the **preapproach**, the salesperson learns everything possible about the products and services offered, the target market, and the competition. Salespeople must be knowledgeable about what they are selling and understand the wants and needs of target customers.

2. **Approach** This step is the first contact with the customer to gain the customer's attention and interest. The salesperson should have a plan for what to say when speaking with a customer, but the plan should be flexible. It is important that the salesperson listen carefully to the customer to determine the customer's needs and wants. The salesperson should strive to create a favorable first impression on which to establish and build an ongoing business–customer relationship.

3. **Demonstration** During the demonstration, the salesperson enthusiastically presents the product in a way that addresses the needs of the customer. The product's features and benefits should be highlighted. If all is going well, the salesperson may even ask the customer to make a purchase at this point.

4. **Answering Questions** At this step, a customer may voice objections to the product or service or have questions and concerns. These responses generally mean the customer is considering the purchase. Providing additional information to counter the objections may resolve the customer's concerns.

5. **Closing the Sale** During this stage, the customer makes the decision to buy. Actions to help the customer reach this final decision may include offering a discount or an incentive gift for buying today. This is also the time to suggest additional items to increase customer satisfaction and the amount of the sale. **Suggestion selling** occurs when the salesperson asks customers if they want to purchase related products. Consider the last time you were at a movie theater or an amusement park. The concession worker probably suggested that you upsize your meal or add another snack item. The amusement park associate may have suggested a multiday pass or a VIP ticket for added benefits and value.

6. **Follow-Up** The continued success of a salesperson (and the business) is based on establishing long-term relationships with customers. The salesperson can strengthen these relationships by following up with customers. Follow-up occurs when the salesperson contacts customers to ensure they are satisfied with their recent purchases and to determine additional needs. Valuable feedback can be obtained, resulting in improved services for future customers.

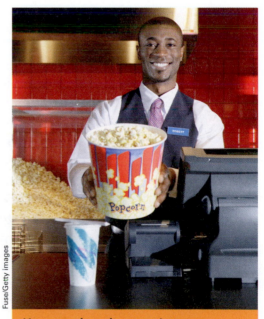

Fuse/Getty images

How can the sales associate use suggestion selling in this situation?

When Is Personal Selling Appropriate?

The advantage of personal selling is that the seller has the opportunity to address any concerns that may be causing hesitation on the part of the consumer. A knowledgeable seller can offer information, demonstrate the product, make comparisons with similar products, tell stories about personal experiences with the product, and answer any questions that may arise. Personal selling is effective for

- Expensive, complex products
- Markets with a few large customers
- Unfamiliar, unique products
- Customers in a limited area
- Complicated, long decision-making processes
- Customers who expect personal attention and help with the decision-making process

Salespeople involved with personal selling benefit from the feedback received from customers, enabling sellers to improve future sales strategies. Feedback may include the customer's level of satisfaction and his or her suggestions for making the sales process better for the buyer.

Disadvantages to a business of personal selling include the high cost and time commitment per salesperson and the required skills and training.

INTERMISSION

Explain why personal selling is necessary when selling expensive items, such as an exotic vacation.

MATH IN MARKETING

Tourism is the number one or number two industry for most states. Michigan is no exception. The award-winning Pure Michigan advertising campaign attracted 3.8 million out-of-state visitors to the Great Lakes state in a recent year. For every dollar spent on the Pure Michigan campaign, the state has earned $4.10 in tax revenue.[1]

The Pure Michigan tourism website had 8.8 million visitors in one year. Click-throughs from the site to other Michigan tourism industry sites totaled 5.3 million for the year.[2] Facebook, Twitter, Google+, Instagram, Pinterest, and YouTube are active social media outlets that play an important role in promoting Michigan business and tourism.

Do the Math

If the current return on investment continues, how much revenue can the state of Michigan expect if it spends $13 million on its Pure Michigan campaign? What percentage of the visitors to the Pure Michigan tourism website clicked through to other Michigan tourism sites? How does the Pure Michigan website address the six steps of the selling process?

LO 11.1-2 MANAGEMENT SKILLS AND KNOWLEDGE FOR SUCCESS

Selling Salespeople must effectively manage themselves, customers, and information. They must be motivated individuals who use time effectively. Emotional and physical stability are important attributes for those dealing with the public. Continuing education and personal development help salespeople keep up to date in their profession.

Successful salespeople must understand three things: the product/service they are selling, their customers, and the competition.

Time Out Most customers will respond that they are "just looking" if a sales associate simply asks if they need help. Instead, sales associates should use the approach (the second step in the sales process) as an opportunity to introduce themselves, point out new products and special offers, and let customers know they are available to assist should questions arise.

Know the Product

Salespeople must have thorough knowledge of the products or services they are selling. Successful salespeople are familiar with all parts of the marketing mix—product, distribution, price, and promotion. Sources of product information for salespeople include fact sheets and product manuals. Salespeople often receive special training to help them learn about new products and sales strategies. They must effectively communicate product information, including benefits and unique features, to customers. To maintain credibility with their customers, salespeople must clearly understand the products or services they sell.

Know the Customer

It is important that salespeople know their customers. They must carefully determine customer needs in order to present the most appropriate products to meet those needs. **Cold calling** involves contacting potential customers at random without researching the customers' needs first. Marketing-oriented businesses normally do not depend on cold calling. They gather **leads**, or information and data on prospective customers who have shown interest in the product or service and/or meet the definition of the target market.

© dotshock/Shutterstock.com

How does having product knowledge help a salesperson close a sale?

Riddell manufactures football helmets. Top sales leads for Riddell include high school, college, and professional sports programs. Riddell must network with football coaches to maximize sales. Research is conducted to determine who needs the product, what resources they have available to purchase the product, and what authority they have to make the purchase. Riddell must also conduct research to improve its product in order to reduce the number of serious football injuries—a top priority for its customers.

Understand Customer Decisions   Most customers use a five-step decision-making process for purchases. The steps include the following:

1. Recognize a need for a product or service.
2. Search for information about the alternative products or services available.
3. Evaluate all of the options to see which one best meets needs.
4. Reach a decision and buy the product or service.
5. Evaluate the purchase decision to determine if it is satisfactory.

Salespeople can assist customers through this process by helping them define their needs, showing them alternative products or services, explaining the features and benefits, making the sale, and following up to ensure satisfaction.

Manage Customer Information   Building a customer base and carefully scheduling time spent with customers is called **customer management**. Spending too much time with one customer may result in lost opportunities and lost sales with other customers. Salespeople must collect and manage information about customers. Once a customer base is established, salespeople are challenged to develop an effective record-keeping system that enables them to maintain customer information and gain a better understanding of their customers. The database should include birthdays, product preferences, and additional demographic information that enables the salesperson to better serve the customers. Those customers who receive thank-you notes or birthday cards from the salesperson appreciate the specialized attention.

Know the Competition

Customers who want to purchase running shoes or the latest electronic device for entertainment will have many options at different prices. Many purchases are made electronically instead of buying at the store. Salespeople must meet the needs of traditional and high-tech customers.

Why is it important for a salesperson to remember customers' personal information, such as birthdays?

© iStockphoto.com/Thomas_EyeDesign

Successful sales depend on understanding the competition and the products and services they sell. Consumers want to buy the most satisfying products for the best price. Salespeople must be able to explain the differences between their products and competitors' products and offer solid evidence why their products are the better choice to meet customer needs.

INTERMISSION

List three things successful salespeople must understand.

ENCORE

Understand Marketing Concepts

Select the best answer for each question.

1. At which stage of the sales process might suggestion selling be used?
   a. approach
   b. demonstration
   c. closing the sale
   d. follow-up

2. Personal selling is appropriate for
   a. expensive items
   b. complex products that need explanation
   c. markets with a few large customers
   d. all of the above

Think Critically

Answer the following questions as completely as possible.

3. You are the ticket manager for a professional football team that only won two games the past season. List the steps you will follow to sell season tickets for the team's games next year. (LO 11.1-1)

4. Many successful salespeople at clothing stores maintain personal information records on their customers. The information collected includes sizes, style preferences, spending habits, and birthdays. Consider how you would use this information to communicate with customers and increase sales for a sports or entertainment business. Write an example of what you might communicate to a customer. (LO 11.1-2)

5. Why is it important that successful salespeople know the competition? (LO 11.1-2)

11.2 Ticket Sales

The Essential Question

How can fans buy tickets for sports and entertainment events?

Learning Objectives

LO 11.2-1 Explain the difference between ticket brokers and ticket scalpers.

LO 11.2-2 Describe the ticket economy and strategies for getting highly sought-after tickets.

Key Terms

- ticket brokers
- ticket scalpers

OPENING ACT

Your favorite college football team has made it to the Fiesta Bowl being held in your city. You are a dedicated fan who follows all of the games on TV, and you would like to attend the Fiesta Bowl. This may be your only chance to get to see your favorite team play live, since the team is located in another state. The only problem is that you do not have tickets.

Your cousin who attends the college attempted to get one of the 2,000 student tickets that were made available through a lottery. Unfortunately, his numbers were not drawn. However, you are determined to go to the game. Your cousin is coming to town for the game, and you and he plan to arrive early at the Fiesta Bowl in hopes that someone will be selling tickets outside of the stadium. You have saved your money and are willing to pay a premium price for the tickets. Your parents suggest you look into the state's laws regarding ticket scalping. Your friends recommend looking for tickets on auction sites such as eBay.

Cooperative Learning Working in a group, discuss why you should research state laws regarding ticket scalping? Why might you check the Internet for tickets? How can you protect yourself if you purchase tickets online?

LO 11.2-1 HIGH PRICES FOR POPULAR ENTERTAINMENT

In recent years, the prices charged for tickets to a major football game, such as Alabama versus Texas A&M, have been as high as $705 to $770 each. New York Yankees fans can expect to pay from $50 to $500 per seat to see their team in action. Popular music concerts also carry a high price tag. Ticket prices to see country singer Taylor Swift in concert range from $258 to $1,358 apiece. Tickets for popular Broadway shows, such *Book of Mormon*, can sell for more than $480.

Ticket Brokers

Selling

Ticket brokers are registered businesses that legally buy and resell tickets to a variety of entertainment events and guarantee ticket authenticity. Many of the ticket transactions occur online, making it essential for consumers to research the ticket brokers before sharing their credit card information to make purchases. Reputable ticket brokers should be members of the National Association of Ticket Brokers and the Better Business Bureau.

Major ticket brokers offer a wide variety of tickets, often selling them for more than their face value. The Denver Broncos faced the Seattle Seahawks in Super Bowl XLVIII. Ticket prices charged by brokers for the 2014 Super Bowl ranged from $2,505 to $4,063.62.[3] The average purchase price for a recent World Series game ticket on the resale market was $1,979.[4]

Ticket brokers operate businesses that depend on contracts with people and venues. Some brokers have contracts to obtain the best tickets before they go on sale. These transactions are unethical and unfair, and in some cases, illegal. Unscrupulous ticket brokers often try to monopolize the market by paying substantial bribes to people who have control over the supply of tickets, including box-office employees, managers of concert venues, promoters, and ticket agents.

Ticketmaster, the global-event ticketing leader and one of the world's top ten e-commerce sites, uses various strategies to help fans fight back against unscrupulous ticket brokers. For example, it offers presales to musical artists' fan club members. The fan club members have a special password that gives them a chance to buy premium seats several days before tickets are available to the general public. Ticketmaster's latest strategy allows fans to resell their tickets on the Ticketmaster website. Although "resale" tickets are offered for more than face value, buying them through the Ticketmaster website adds a layer of security and protection against counterfeit tickets. In return, Ticketmaster gets a portion of the sale.

The Big Ten is one of the top basketball conferences in the nation. Many of the league's coaches communicate with their teams' fans through social media. Several of the coaches have more than 20,000 Twitter followers. One of the more popular coaches on Twitter is Nebraska's head basketball coach, Tim Miles. He gained over 47,000 Twitter followers after only two years on the job.[5]

The University of Nebraska has always been recognized as a football powerhouse. However, Coach Miles stirred up excitement for Nebraska basketball. Tickets for the new 15,000-seat Pinnacle Bank Arena were sold out for Miles' second season, when the team lost only one home game. Coach Miles successfully uses social media to engage fans and build excitement on and off the basketball court.

Think Critically

Why are an increasing number of coaches becoming actively involved in social media? How can social media be used to sell tickets?

Ticket Scalpers

Ticket scalpers sell tickets to major sporting and entertainment events, often outside the venue on the day of the event, for inflated prices. Receiving $300 for a ticket that cost $55 provides a high rate of return, but it comes with the risk of being arrested for an illegal transaction. Ticket scalping is against the law in many states. Undercover police often arrest scalpers selling tickets outside stadiums and arenas.

Scalpers get tickets the same way legitimate fans do, but they know how to "work the system" to get the best seats, which they resell for up to ten times their face value. Consumers join fan clubs for the opportunity to buy the best concert tickets. Ticket scalpers also join the fan clubs of top artists, buy large quantities of the best seats, and resell those tickets for highly inflated prices. The odds were stacked against fans who wanted to purchase good seats for affordable prices to a recent Eric Church concert, because up to 75 percent of the floor seats had been sold to professional ticket scalpers. Fans had to pay $150 for a ticket with a face value of $40.

Baltimore has an anti-scalping ordinance that allows no fees over 50 cents to be attached to the sale of sports and entertainment tickets. Ticketmaster is contracted by many sports and music venues to sell tickets to events. Although a legitimate ticket seller, Ticketmaster charges additional service fees much higher than 50 cents when consumers purchase tickets. A Baltimore lawsuit against this excessive service fee practice indicated that Ticketmaster took in $1 billion in surcharges on worldwide ticket sales of $8 billion in the year the lawsuit was filed.

Opportunistic scalpers frequently post counterfeit tickets for sale on websites such as Craigslist. The tickets are advertised for great prices, and the sellers ask buyers to bring cash for the tickets to a certain location. Savvy consumers conduct thorough research before buying tickets through channels such as Craigslist.

TKTS Booths

When visiting New York City, tourists can purchase tickets to Broadway shows and other theater events at discounts ranging from 25 to 50 percent at three TKTS booths located in Times Square, downtown Brooklyn, and the South Street Seaport. These discount ticket booths are operated by the Theatre Development Fund. Tourists discover that waiting in long ticket lines at TKTS booths can save them a lot of money when attending the most popular Broadway shows and other theater events.

Ticket Frenzy

Sports and music fans often get caught up in the heat of the moment and rationalize that what may be a "once-in-a-lifetime" event is worth a high price tag. Games between large rival schools and concerts for top performers sell out in a few hours. Hundreds of fans may form lines the night before tickets actually go on sale. Successful college football programs like the Nebraska Cornhuskers have experienced

Why are tickets to entertainment events offered through more than one source?

© Stuart Monk/Shutterstock.com

consecutive sold-out home games for more than 40 years. Waiting lists of people wanting to purchase Nebraska tickets are long. Having season tickets to powerhouse teams is a status symbol for some people. The fans own the Greenbay Packers' NFL team. When a season ticket holder passes away, family members anxiously await the reading of the will to see who inherits the highly desired tickets. The Super Bowl and NCAA College Football Playoff games are sold out even before the professional and college football seasons begin.

College athletes receive complimentary tickets for family and friends to attend their games. The NCAA prohibits athletes from selling these tickets. Selling the complimentary tickets is classified as an NCAA infraction that will result in trouble for the university and the athlete.

INTERMISSION

Explain why ticket scalping is illegal in some states.

LO 11.2-2   THE TICKET ECONOMY

Channel Management Buying tickets to sports and entertainment events has become very easy. Ticketmaster controls the sale of tickets for most venues in the country. Concert tickets usually go on sale at 10 a.m. on Fridays. The telephone, mobile apps, and the Internet provide consumers with the tools to purchase tickets the second they go on sale. The greatest volume of online sales happens in the first hour.

Ticketmaster sells seats for more than 12,000 clients through telephone operators, its website, and ticket outlets located in retail stores and box offices. A little more than 70 percent of its $9 billion annual ticket sales are sold over the Internet. Ticket sales are rapidly shifting to mobile devices, recently doubling to almost 14 percent of total ticket sales.[6]

Ticketmaster has a huge database of fans. When fans try to buy tickets online for popular concerts, they are competing against ticket scalpers who have no intention of attending the events. In addition, the corporate sponsors of major events claim a large number of tickets, making even fewer tickets available to average consumers through normal outlets.

Work the System

Ticketmaster suggests the following strategies to obtain highly sought-after tickets to entertainment events.

1. Buy over the Internet or via a mobile app. Your odds of getting good seats are much better than if you are twentieth in line at a ticket outlet. Look for notices of special presales on fan club websites.
2. To save time, set up an account with your billing information on the website before the on-sale date so you are ready to go.
3. Log on to the site a few minutes early, preferably with a high-speed Internet connection. Hit your refresh button every few seconds so you are connected the instant the sales lines become open. Having a friend work the phone or a second computer at the same time doubles your chances of obtaining tickets.
4. If the concert sells out, check the website again in a few days. Additional dates may be added to the tour.

5. Try again on the day before the show, or even on the afternoon of the show. Artists and sponsors may give back tickets that they had reserved. Sometimes those extras are available only at the venue's box office, so it is worth stopping by the venue on the day of the show as well.

Landing Super Bowl Tickets

Attending the Super Bowl may be only a dream if you are not wealthy, lucky, or a celebrity. The majority of tickets are allotted to the two participating teams, and to a lesser extent through the other NFL teams. Remaining tickets for the general public are made available through a ticket lottery. To participate in the lottery, you must submit, by certified or registered mail, a request with your name, address, telephone number, and email address to the NFL Super Bowl ticket lottery office. Only 500 names are selected from some 30,000 entries. Winners receive the option to purchase two tickets at face value (about $500 each). The 500 pairs of tickets made available through the lottery represented slightly more than one percent of the 82,500 tickets distributed for a recent Super Bowl.

Other options for obtaining Super Bowl tickets include overpriced hotel packages from NFL-approved tour operators or independent travel agents. Ticket brokers are another source for obtaining Super Bowl tickets.

The National Association of Ticket Brokers has established a code of standards and ethics for all member brokers to follow. It requires that members support Super Bowl ticket orders with a 200 percent guarantee. If for any reason a broker fails to deliver promised tickets, a refund equivalent to 200 percent of the purchase price is due to the buyer.

Beware of Scams

The FBI receives annual reports of fraudulent sales for Super Bowl tickets. A common scam involves tickets advertised on well-known online auction and classified ad websites. Buyers are instructed to use a wire transfer payment service to send money to secure the tickets. In some cases, the buyers are instructed to wire the money overseas under the pretense that the seller is out of the United States for work reasons or vacation and therefore

JUDGMENT CALL

Justin has two tickets for a big college football game that pits the number one team against the number two team. Justin paid $130 for the pair of tickets. The game is sold out, and avid fans are offering up to $750 per ticket. Justin believes that a free-enterprise system allows him to sell the tickets for $1,500 since the demand for the tickets is so high.

Think Critically

Can Justin sell the pair of tickets for $1,500 in most states? Should the free-enterprise concept prevail in this situation? Explain your answers.

cannot use the tickets. Once the payment is received, the seller stops all contact, and the tickets never arrive. Consumers should never send cash payments or use wire transfer services to pay for tickets.

Movie Theaters Aim for High-Def Sports

 For those fans who can't get tickets to a game or concert, they may be able to head to their local movie theater instead. Movie venues are now hosting entertainment events in addition to motion pictures. Live concerts, plays, operas, and sporting events are being presented at movie theaters at a time when attendance for traditional movies is flat. Movie theaters are adding huge screens with 3D capability, multiple screens within one theater, restaurants, and better food to attract more customers.

INTERMISSION

How has the Internet changed the way sports and entertainment tickets are sold?

ENCORE

Understand Marketing Concepts

Select the best answer for each question.

1. Ticket brokers
   a. work in an illegal profession
   b. are the same as ticket scalpers
   c. obtain the best tickets to sporting events
   d. only sell tickets through the Internet

2. Ticket scalpers
   a. sell tickets to major entertainment events
   b. sell tickets for more than their face value
   c. may be arrested for illegal activity in many states
   d. all of the above

Think Critically

Answer the following questions as completely as possible.

3. What is the role of a ticket broker when selling tickets for the Super Bowl? (LO 11.2-1)

4. List four ways to effectively "work the system" to obtain tickets to popular sports and entertainment events. (LO 11.2-2)

5. Explain how movie theaters can connect with fans of major sports and entertainment events to increase theater attendance. (LO 11.2-2)

11.3 Group and Corporate Sales

The Essential Question

How do corporations outside of the sports and entertainment industries use sports and entertainment events for business purposes?

Learning Objectives

LO 11.3-1 Explain sales strategies for attracting groups to sports and entertainment venues.

LO 11.3-2 Describe how corporations use sports and entertainment to motivate employees and impress clients.

Key Terms

- group packages
- luxury boxes
- club seats

OPENING ACT

Department stores and other retailers have effectively used incentives, such as coupons worth 10 to 20 percent off of future purchases, to increase repeat visits of customers. Sports and entertainment businesses also use special promotions to increase attendance at events. At some events, free or discounted admission is offered to fans who bring canned goods for the local food bank. This promotion not only increases attendance but also gives the events a favorable image in the community. Corporate and local business sponsors may host a free cookout for attendees at a sports or entertainment event. A season-long raffle for a new car may be an incentive that keeps fans returning game after game.

Cooperative Learning With a partner, develop three promotional strategies to attract more people to sports events at your school. Explain how you will carry out the strategies.

LO 11.3-1 FILLING THE STANDS

Sports and entertainment events must compete for consumers' discretionary dollars. Marketers for sports and entertainment are constantly searching for ways to attract more people to events.

Appealing to Groups

Major League Baseball teams have many home games during the long baseball season. Baseball games that are scheduled during weekdays are less likely to sell out than games on weekends. Special group and corporate promotions are used to fill the stands. Special promotions are offered to church groups, senior citizens, schools, Boy Scouts, Girl Scouts, Little League baseball teams, and student organizations to sell tickets during slow periods. **Group packages** are

What promotions can be used to fill stadiums with fans?

promotions that give special ticket prices to members of a group when tickets are purchased in large quantities, such as 15 or more. Free transportation may even be offered to senior citizens to motivate them to attend. Frequently, the groups are recognized during the game over the public announcement system or on the big video screen.

Special group rates not only fill stadiums, ballparks, and arenas, but they also solidify current and future customer bases. Sometimes additional entertainment, such as live music or fireworks, is added during breaks or immediately after an event to appeal to special groups.

Special Privileges

Major universities entertain wealthy alumni and other individuals who contribute money to athletic departments and scholarship funds. Being a substantial contributor to an athletic department may have special perks, such as preferred seating at sports events. Access to tickets for successful college programs is often easier for contributors. Large contributions may be rewarded with season tickets and possibly suites. The largest contributors may even have a suite or practice field named in their honor.

INTERMISSION

Explain how group packages can help fill sports and entertainment venues.

LO 11.3-2   CORPORATE PERKS

Corporations understand the importance of teamwork and employee bonding. Social outings can strengthen the cohesiveness of company teams. Corporate groups may have a picnic followed by an evening at a professional sporting event. Corporations can take advantage of group packages offered by sports and entertainment venues. These events allow employees to interact socially outside of the office setting.

Corporate employees may be rewarded for meeting sales quotas or reaching other corporate goals. Many times the reward for high performance is tickets to highly popular sporting events. Corporate executives

Disneyland and Disney World have mastered upselling at the exits for its most popular attractions. *Upselling* is a sales strategy used to sell related products. Adventure and safari gear are sold at the end of the Adventureland ride. Disney guests can purchase Star Wars souvenirs outside of Space Mountain and the Jedi Training Academy. Disney's successful upselling strategy is based on having the merchandise at the right place at the right time.

often entertain clients and visiting colleagues at sports and entertainment events, and they want to impress them with the best seats available.

Special Seating

Special seating has become a lucrative income source for professional sports teams. **Luxury boxes** (or luxury suites) are lavish rooms inside stadiums and arenas that allow corporate executives and some wealthy private individuals to entertain clients and friends while watching the events. The suites are high in the stands, near the press-box level, and are usually equipped with closed-circuit television for close-ups of the action. Luxury boxes continue to increase in demand, contributing to an extraordinary growth in sports venue construction. Every facility built within the last 20 years has luxury suites, and most of the older stadiums have been remodeled to add them. Even college stadiums are adding suites.

Sales of luxury boxes have become a valuable source of additional revenue. Major college football stadiums have luxury skyboxes that seat 8 to 50 fans

TAKE A BOW Gary Krueger

One hot summer in 1992, four former Texas A&M golfers had the idea to start a golf ball retrieval company. What began as a hobby for Gary Krueger and his college friends (including an experiment with washing salvaged golf balls in home laundry machines) quickly evolved into a niche business with room for sizable growth.

Gary Krueger and his partners opened PG Professional Golf. The company initially created its supply network by retrieving golf balls from murky golf course ponds across the nation. Fast forward 20 years and the company now staffs over 100 employees, has retrieval contracts with over 2,000 courses in 42 states, and ships over 40 million golf balls each year to mass merchants, sporting goods retailers, and golf retailers around the globe. Recognized as industry leaders, PG Professional Golf focuses on providing excellent quality golf balls at unbeatable prices. Its Reload™ Recycled Golf Ball is currently the number one selling recycled golf ball brand in the world. Gary Krueger determined that the best sales outlets for his company's recycled golf balls included retail giants like Walmart and Academy Sports + Outdoors. Golf enthusiasts can also order the golf balls online.

Original founders Gary Krueger and David Jones continue to grow PG Professional Golf from its headquarters in Sugar Land, Texas. They estimate that they have 40 percent market share. They now also sell new golf balls, tees, gloves, and other accessories.

Think Critically

Why is it wise for PG Professional Golf to sell its products in large national retail stores and online? Why is recycling a good selling strategy?

and cost between $8,000 and $80,000 per season. Red Bull Arena, a New Jersey soccer venue, requires customers to sign multiyear leases for its 30 sky-boxes, each seating 17 to 22 fans and costing $65,000 to $75,000 per year.[7]

Club seats are premium stadium seats usually located outdoors that provide a source of high revenue. Club seats can vary by venue but are usually cushioned and roomy, provide a good view of the action, and are located one level below the luxury boxes. Club-level seating often comes with added benefits, such as special admission to indoor areas of the stadium. These areas are air-conditioned and allow access to special restaurants, merchandise stands, and lounge areas not available to regular ticket holders.

INTERMISSION

Why are luxury boxes at sports venues popular among corporations?

ENCORE

Understand Marketing Concepts
Select the best answer for each question.

1. Sports and entertainment marketers try to appeal to groups by offering
   a. special ticket prices on large quantities of tickets
   b. live entertainment or fireworks after the event
   c. access to luxury boxes in return for contributions
   d. all of the above

2. Club seats
   a. are located in lavish rooms inside stadiums and arenas
   b. are located at the press-box level of an arena
   c. often come with added benefits, such as access to exclusive restaurants, merchandise stands, and lounge areas
   d. are available only to members of corporate clubs

Think Critically
Answer the following questions as completely as possible.

3. You are the alumni director for a major university. Write a letter to a wealthy alumni, inviting him or her to be your guest at the upcoming homecoming game. You are hoping your guest will be inspired by the visit to make a sizable donation to the athletic department. (LO 11.3-1)

4. If you were the human resources director for a major corporation, what types of activities outside of work would you recommend to company team leaders and why? (LO 11.3-2)

CHAPTER ASSESSMENT

Review Marketing Concepts

Match the terms listed with the definitions.

1. The sales process step in which the salesperson learns everything possible about the products and services offered, the target market, and the competition
2. Registered businesses that legally buy and resell tickets to a variety of entertainment events and guarantee ticket authenticity
3. Building a customer base and carefully scheduling time spent with customers
4. Promotions that give special ticket prices to members of a group when tickets are purchased in large quantities
5. Premium stadium seats that are usually located outdoors and provide a source of high revenue
6. Contacting potential customers at random without researching the customers' needs first
7. Information and data gathered on prospective customers who have shown interest in the product or service and/or meet the definition of the target market
8. Those who sell tickets to major sporting and entertainment events for inflated prices
9. Lavish rooms inside stadiums and arenas that allow corporate executives and some wealthy private individuals to entertain clients and friends while watching sports and entertainment events
10. Asking customers if they want to purchase related products

a. club seats
b. cold calling
c. customer management
d. group packages
e. leads
f. luxury boxes
g. preapproach
h. suggestion selling
i. ticket brokers
j. ticket scalpers

Review Marketing Concepts

Select the best answer for each of the following questions.

11. For most purchases, the majority of consumers go through a decision-making process that includes all of the following steps *except*
    a. reach a decision and buy the product
    b. recognize a need for a product
    c. know the competition
    d. evaluate alternative products
12. Customer management includes
    a. carefully scheduling time spent with customers
    b. developing an effective record-keeping system of customer data
    c. using aggressive tactics to push customers into a decision to buy
    d. both a and b

13. The National Association of Ticket Brokers has a code of standards and ethics requiring members to support Super Bowl ticket orders with a(n) _____ percent guarantee.
   - a. 100
   - b. 80
   - c. 200
   - d. 150
14. Club seats at sporting events
   - a. are premium seats
   - b. are frequently purchased by corporations
   - c. have added benefits for fans
   - d. all of the above
15. Prospective customers who have shown interest in the product or service are called
   - a. closers
   - b. leads
   - c. cold calls
   - d. repeats

Think Critically

16. You are the president of a celebrity's fan club. What kind of customer management strategies could you use to stay in touch with fans? What form(s) of social media will you incorporate? (LO 11.1-2)
17. You have been given permission to set up a booth to sell merchandise at the Country Stampede in Manhattan, Kansas. Use the Internet to research this entertainment event. What will you sell at your booth? Why? (LO 11.1-1)
18. Research your favorite sports team's stadium or arena. How many fans does it hold? Does it offer club seating and luxury boxes? If so, how much does it charge for these types of seats? Does it offer group ticket sales? Write a one-page report on your findings. Include recommendations for additional seating and group sales promotions. (LO 11.3-2)
19. You work at a sporting goods store. A customer has shown interest in purchasing a pair of running shoes. Describe how you will use the sales process to try to make the sale. (LO 11.1-1)
20. A major amusement park wants to increase the sale of two-day passes, season passes, and family ticket packs. Who are the target markets for each category of tickets? How can suggestion selling be used to increase ticket sales? (LO 11.1-2)
21. A major university wants to sell more tickets to its men's basketball games. Its new basketball arena holds 14,000 people. Last year, the average attendance at the games was 6,500. A new coach, outstanding recruits, and early wins this season are sparking student and alumni enthusiasm. What types of promotions and sales strategies would you suggest to ensure seats are filled at the games this season? (LO 11.3-1)

Make Academic Connections

22. **Math** The face value of a ticket to the Final Four championship game is $65. You purchase a ticket from a ticket broker for $100. What percentage of profit has the ticket broker earned from this transaction? (LO 11.2-1)

23. **Ethics** You work for the MLB stadium in your city. Sparked by fan complaints, you would like to discourage ticket scalping. What strategies would you suggest to ensure fans have a fair chance of buying tickets at their face value? How could you work with the police department to prevent ticket scalping? (LO 11.2-1)

24. **Research** Use the Internet to research group packages for youth organizations for sports and entertainment events. What kind of groups qualify for these packages? What is offered in these packages? (LO 11.3-1)

25. **Communication** Successful retailers have taught sales associates to avoid the "no thanks, just looking" response from customers by creating conversations that spark customer interest. The bookstore at a major university campus has an excellent sporting goods department, but sales have not been satisfactory. Outline an approach for sales associates to follow in order to spark customers' interest in sporting goods. (LO 11.1-1)

26. **Communication** You have been hired as a marketer for a friend's hotel located in rural America, where farming is the major industry. The busiest season for the hotel is the fall, when guests enjoy hayrides, campfires, and visits to the pumpkin patch. The kids enjoy the Halloween haunted house. Your goal is to increase sales during other times of the year. The closest nearby community has many antique shops, a farmers' market, and three outstanding restaurants. The location has an average snowfall of 50 inches during the winter. Your friend also has a Christmas tree field that will be ready for harvesting next year. During the summer, the nearby lake offers great fishing. Outline a strategy to increase group or corporate sales for the hotel during the winter, spring, and summer. (LO 11.1-2)

27. **History** Conduct research to learn about the history of movie theaters. Find out the latest trends that movie theaters are using to attract more customers. Also find out what prices are being charged to see today's movies compared to the cost of admission to the earliest movies. Prepare an electronic presentation that covers the history of the movie theater industry. Make sure that your presentation includes all of the latest developments for the industry. (LO 11.2-2)

28. **Geography** Select four different sports products that are suited for different types of geography. Thoroughly describe each of the products and the type of geography where each product would be sold. Describe the sales strategies to sell each of the four items. (LO 11.1-1)

EXTRA INNINGS PROJECT

Post-prom parties have become popular in recent years. The parties are often held on school property. Typically, students have to arrive by a certain time and cannot be readmitted if they leave before the party has ended.

Successful post-prom parties require lots of planning. Themes, decorations, activities, music, food, prizes, and sponsors are some of the considerations. Party rules should also be set and made clear to all who attend.

You are in charge of the post-prom party at your high school. The party will be held at the school and will run from 12 a.m. to 5 a.m. as a way to keep students entertained and safe. The key to success for the post-prom party is to acquire sponsorships from local businesses and parents. You must sell the party to juniors and seniors.

Work with a group and complete the following activities.

1. What will you do to get a better idea of student entertainment needs? What types of social media should be used to collect information from students?
2. What activities will you include during the five-hour event to keep students entertained?
3. What is your sales strategy for getting business and parent sponsors for the event?
4. Create an advertisement and promotional incentives to increase attendance of juniors and seniors at the post-prom party.
5. Why is this event beneficial to the community and school?
6. Why is it a good idea to get parents involved with the event?
7. What businesses would make good local sponsors for this event? Explain your choices.

CASE STUDY

SELLING THE BENEFITS OF A CITY AND ITS VENUE

College and professional sports are economy boosters for their host cities. The stream of revenue to the local economy generated by excited fans comes from the sale of tickets, hotel room rentals, car rentals, restaurant meals served, gasoline sales, parking fees, and vendor sales. The sales become even greater when a team is winning.

Cities such as Lincoln, Nebraska; Columbus, Ohio; Tallahassee, Florida; and Baton Rouge, Louisiana count on the revenue generated by sell-out crowds during the college football season. Stadiums that hold from 82,000 to 102,000 fans provide an economic windfall for the college communities where they are located.

Some fans of professional sports teams, such as the Chicago Cubs and Green Bay Packers, are loyal no matter how well their team is performing. These faithful fans provide a steady flow of revenue to the sports program and surrounding communities.

College World Series Wars?

Cities that host major sporting events understand the financial benefits. Omaha, Nebraska, appreciates the millions of dollars poured into the city during the annual College World Series. Zesto's, a popular fast-food restaurant, has truckloads of food rolling in each day to meet the demands of customers from all over the United States.

The event has been voted the Best Annual Local Event and ranks as the third-most important state tourist attraction, according to a survey conducted by Omaha Magazine. The revenue from this two-week event has attracted the attention of other cities, such as Oklahoma City, that would like the opportunity to host the event in the future. Economic experts estimate that the College World Series generates more than $40 million for the Omaha economy. It is no wonder that other cities would like to host this event.

Omaha tore down Rosenblatt Stadium, the former home of the College World Series, to build the new $131-million TD Ameritrade Park Omaha that has 24,505 seats. Omaha must continue to demonstrate top-notch hospitality so that the College World Series event planners continue to choose Omaha as its host city.

Think Critically

1. Why is it important for Omaha to continue hosting the College World Series? Consider both financial and nonfinancial benefits.
2. What are some of the greatest sources of revenue for cities that are home to popular college and professional sports teams?
3. How can hosting a major event like the College World Series help a city develop a national image? Explain your answer.
4. List ten good food items for vendors to sell at the College World Series.

HOSPITALITY AND TOURISM PROFESSIONAL SELLING EVENT

This individual event provides an opportunity for participants to demonstrate knowledge and skills needed for a career in sales. Participants will organize and deliver a sales presentation for one or more products and/or services. Key features for the professional selling event include new products, services, and the target market customers (prospects).

The participant must research the company he or she represents and the products/services to be presented. The participant will also research the business/organization to which the product/service will be presented. Finally, the participant will present the products/services to meet the needs of the customer (prospect).

A major U.S. city wants to host a future Super Bowl. The city leaders have instructed you to develop a program to train workers in all aspects of the hospitality industry (hotel concierges, restaurant servers, taxi drivers, car rental associates, airport personnel, and others) to be more customer-service oriented. They have also asked you to design the itinerary for the visiting Super Bowl selection committee. The itinerary should include activities that create a positive image of the city.

The city has two international airports and ample hotel rooms and restaurants to accommodate a major event like the Super Bowl. The city's mass transportation system is also adequate to handle the needs of a Super Bowl.

You have a meeting scheduled with the marketing director for the city's travel bureau to discuss your training plan, itinerary for the Super Bowl selection committee, and the associated costs of implementing the training. You will have 15 minutes to deliver your sales presentation. The judge has 5 minutes to ask questions about your presentation. You may use appropriate visual aids listed by the DECA guidelines for the presentation.

Performance Indicators Evaluated

- Demonstrate critical thinking and problem-solving skills.
- Illustrate creativity and innovation.
- Demonstrate communication skills.
- Explain the role of customer service as a component of selling relationships.
- Describe factors used to position products/services (as related to the itinerary).

Think Critically

1. Why should cities be concerned about the hospitality skills of those working in local businesses?
2. What key hospitality workers can make or break tourists' image of a city?
3. Give two examples of how hospitality skills can be improved.
4. What activities should be included in the meeting with the Super Bowl selection committee? Explain your answer.

www.deca.org

THE MARKETING GAME PLAN

© Maxim Blinkov/Shutterstock.com

POINT YOUR BROWSER

ngl.cengage.com/sports4e

Winning Strategies

Vivendi

Vivendi is a leading multinational mass media company headquartered in Paris, France. It provides products and services across a number of industries, including film, music, video game, and telecommunications. Vivendi has reported income in excess of €29 billion (roughly $40.3 billion in U.S. dollars) and has more than 58,000 employees worldwide. In the content and media area, Vivendi operates Universal Music Group (UMG), one of the world's leading music companies.

© Maxx-Studio/Shutterstock.com

UMG discovers and develops recording artists and songwriters and markets their music across all formats and platforms. Worldwide, UMG holds leading market positions in recorded music, music publishing, and merchandising. UMG has a roster of hundreds of artists covering all types of music. Notable UMG artists include Selena Gomez, Nicki Minaj, and Robin Thicke. UMG's music labels include Capitol Records, DECCA, Def Jam Recordings, EMI Records, Motown Records, and Virgin Records.

In the United States, sales, marketing, and distribution of UMG products in all formats, including digital, physical, streaming, subscription, and mobile, are handled by Universal Music Group Distribution. UMG seeks opportunities to continue to lead the music industry through the discovery and development of new talent and the use of new platforms/technologies for distribution. In addition, UMG plans an expansion of artist- and music-branded lines of merchandise sold through multiple sales points, including online, through fashion retailers, and at live performances.

Think Critically

1. Why do you think Vivendi offers such a wide array of products and services?

2. What strategies would you suggest to UMG to keep its catalog of music talent fresh?

3. What does UMG need to know about competing music businesses?

12.1 Mapping Strategies

The Essential Question

Why is marketing planning important, and what information is needed to begin planning?

Learning Objectives

LO 12.1-1 Explain the importance of marketing planning.

LO 12.1-2 Determine the information needed to begin marketing planning.

Key Terms

- marketing plan
- situational analysis
- marketing strategy
- SWOT analysis
- marketing intelligence

OPENING ACT

The New York Times writer Howard Beck stated that the Houston Rockets' front office had a "bold, creative vision, and the conviction to carry it out—qualities that are not found in every front office."[1] The compliments were based on the actions taken by the Houston Rockets to carry out their plan to pursue a championship. The strategy was to acquire talent, trade that talent, and package new talent with draft picks to acquire new, better talent, ending with star players who could win. Having a winning team and a shot at a championship is at the heart of the Rockets' multiyear marketing plan. Their goal is to keep loyal fans and attract new fans and sponsors.

Cooperative Learning In a group, discuss the difference in marketing planning for a team with a winning record as opposed to one with a losing record. Which of the seven core standards of marketing (see Chapter 1) are most affected for a winning team as opposed to a losing team?

LO 12.1-1 KNOW WHERE YOU ARE HEADED

Coaches develop game plans detailing the approach to use to achieve the goal—winning the game. Marketing managers develop a **marketing plan**, which is a precisely written document that describes a company's situational analysis, marketing strategy, and implementation plan for meeting company objectives.

- **Situational Analysis**—An in-depth look at the current conditions of the business, the competition, and the target customer.
- **Marketing Strategy**—An idea for achieving marketing objectives that can be put into action.
- Implementation Plan—The process of putting plans into action by carrying out strategies, assigning responsibilities, and establishing timelines.

The marketing plan is a component of the overall business plan. Marketing plans are generally created annually for the upcoming year.

How can mapping out a plan improve marketing?

A Sense of Direction

When a family decides to go on vacation, family members could all jump into the car and drive around for a day or two, stopping at sites along the way. Another option is to spend time planning before the vacation begins. Having a plan is more efficient because it makes better use of your time and money.

English author Lewis Carroll once said, "If you don't know where you are going, any road will get you there." Without a marketing plan, a business can wander down many roads, wasting its resources—time and money. Successful businesses want to be sure they are headed in the right direction. The time spent planning is like setting up a navigational system for marketing. Successful marketers want to know

- Where they are
- Where they need to be
- How to get there

The written marketing plan, like the family vacation plan, can be flexible. It can be changed if circumstances change. The plan gives the business a sense of direction. It should be shared with employees to ensure they know the current circumstances of the business, where the business is headed, and the steps that must be taken to reach the company's goals.

INTERMISSION

What kinds of information does a marketing plan provide?

LO 12.1-2 WHAT YOU NEED TO KNOW

Marketing-Information Management
To begin developing a marketing plan, an organization needs information about its current business conditions, the competition it faces, and its existing and potential customers. A good place to start is with a SWOT analysis.

Sports marketing plans should focus on building a fan base. Fans identify with teams and pay to promote the teams by purchasing and wearing team-branded clothing. Fans also have positive feelings about products from team sponsors. Marketing plans should include strategies that satisfy fans' desire to be a part of a team's community.

SWOT Analysis

As part of a situational analysis, many companies will conduct a **SWOT analysis**—an examination of the business's strengths, weaknesses, opportunities, and threats.

- **S**trengths are the characteristics of a business or product that give it an advantage over others, such as a superstar player.
- **W**eaknesses are the characteristics of a business or product that place it at a disadvantage relative to others, such as a poor location.
- **O**pportunities are external factors that a business could use to its advantage, such as changing demographics in the region.
- **T**hreats are external factors that could cause trouble for the business or product, such as a weak economy.

Strengths and weaknesses are generally determined by looking at the past and current conditions of the business. Focusing on the customers and competition can help identify opportunities and threats. Businesses can use the information gathered to develop marketing plan objectives.

The Customers The products or services provided by a business are designed to meet the needs of a specific group of people. The product must match what the customers want at a price they are willing and able to pay. The targeted customers can be similar in age, gender, income, education, and/or occupation, or they can be a mix of demographics. They can also share common psychographics, such as lifestyles or values. Or, they may be a geographic group who live in the same country, city, or neighborhood. The demographics will help you visualize the customer. The psychographics will help you get to know the person that you visualize. The geographic information will tell you where to find them.

Some marketing research divides people into groups based on their available resources, such as income or education. People with low levels of resources are thought to be cautious and do not like change. People with

COMMUNICATION CONNECTION

The 1994 movie *The Shawshank Redemption* is the story of a wrongly convicted man's 19 years in prison. The movie brought in only $18 million at the box office but was nominated for seven Academy Awards, winning none. During its post-Oscars re-release, it grossed an additional $10 million. From that point until recent times, the strength of the movie has never wavered, first as a home video and then as a cable TV favorite. It has been rated for years, by users of imdb.com, as the best movie of all time. About 80,000 tourists a year visit the closed prison and town where the movie was filmed.

Write Now

Choose a movie that you think is great but did not do well at the box office. Make a list of the reasons you like the movie. Then list the demographic characteristics of potential viewers. Write at least two paragraphs about creative ways to promote a re-release of the movie to potential viewers.

high levels of resources tend to be curious and independent leaders. Most people fall somewhere between the two groups. Using the information collected through research, a business can direct its marketing efforts on the customers who have the characteristics the business is targeting.

The Competition Studying the competition helps a business get a sense of its place in the market. Information gathered about competitors is referred to as **marketing intelligence**. Competitor information can be collected by searching the Internet, listening to customers, attending trade shows, and monitoring social media.

Through research a business must identify threats posed by competitors. If competitors are known for low prices, trying to compete with them on price may only result in lower revenues. If the business cannot beat or match competitors' prices, it will need to look for opportunities to compete in other ways. To justify a higher price, the business can provide a higher-quality product or offer more value in other ways, such as by providing better service, a more convenient location, or a better selection.

What are the benefits of using a SWOT analysis in the early stages of marketing planning?

Understand Marketing Concepts

Select the best answer for each question.

1. Marketing plans
   a. are a study of the sales process
   b. include an analysis, strategies, and an implementation plan
   c. explore consulting services
   d. focus on the design of new products

2. To find information about the competition, marketers can
   a. use the Internet
   b. attend trade shows
   c. talk with customers
   d. do all of the above

Think Critically

Answer the following questions as completely as possible.

3. Why is information about the current state of the business important for planning? (LO 12.1-1)

4. Your target customer is someone who likes innovative, leading-edge products. What else do you need to know about the customer to develop a marketing plan? (LO 12.1-2)

12.2 Sports and Entertainment Strategies

The Essential Question

How do strategies help fulfill marketing objectives?

Learning Objectives

LO 12.2-1   Describe the importance of marketing objectives and strategies.

LO 12.2-2   Explain how the design of a sports property can be used as a marketing strategy.

LO 12.2-3   Identify entertainment marketing strategies.

Key Terms

- SMART objectives
- strategic thinking
- tactics
- applied research
- interpretation
- anthology series

OPENING ACT

In his book, *RG3 The Promise*, author Dave Sheinin gives credit to Robert Griffin III's parents for raising Griffin to be someone who leads by example. As the team's quarterback, Griffin helped bring the Baylor University Bears football team from a bottom-level team to one of national prominence. He brought enough interest to the game to support construction of a new football stadium on campus. The Bears had previously used an off-campus stadium.

The new riverfront stadium was part of the university's marketing planning to offer fans a unique experience. One of the first steps of designing and building the stadium was a fan survey and feasibility study. The response was overwhelmingly positive in support of a new on-campus stadium. Fan-friendly features were incorporated into the design to help generate high attendance.

Cooperative Learning   Discuss with a group how a winning team can use a new stadium to attract additional fans. Why do the features offered in the stadium make a difference to fans? What features would you like to see added to a new stadium?

LO 12.2-1   OBJECTIVES AND STRATEGIES

The purpose of marketing is to create a satisfactory exchange between the business providing the product or service and the consumer. With this purpose in mind, marketers develop specific objectives that define the results the business aims to achieve. Once the specific objectives are determined, it is time to develop the marketing strategy, an idea for achieving marketing objectives that can be put into action.

Developing Objectives

As part of marketing planning, a business must decide what the objectives are for the business. Objectives are more concrete than goals. Marketing objectives, as with all objectives, should be written in a way that makes them **SMART objectives**, which are specific, measurable, attainable, relevant, and timely, as described below.

- **S**—Specific. Objectives are specific and answer "What?" "Why?" and "How?" An objective to increase attendance by 10 percent is more specific than an objective to simply "improve attendance."
- **M**—Measurable. Objectives include a quantifiable way to measure whether they have been accomplished. For example, attendance numbers can be compared to previous seasons.
- **A**—Attainable. Objectives are stated as outcomes that can realistically be achieved. Increasing attendance by 10 percent may be realistic, while adding 100 million new fans is not.
- **R**—Relevant. Objectives pertain to the mission of the business, which is generally to make a profit. Increasing attendance by 10 percent will increase revenues proportionately through ticket sales, concession sales, and merchandise sales.
- **T**—Timely. Objectives have a start date and completion date. Objectives should be reviewed at least every three months to evaluate their progress.

SMART objectives could cover a period of time from a few months to a year. While the timeline to meet the objectives set for a professional sports team may cover a year, the timeline for a Broadway play may be shorter. An objective for a new Broadway play could be to "boost box office sales by 15 percent over the first month's attendance during the second and third month of the play's run." This objective is specific, measurable, potentially attainable, relevant, and timely.

Creating Strategies

Market Planning

Marketers must use **strategic thinking**, which is the process of finding unique, innovative ways to reach an objective.

The marketers for a new Broadway play must first determine the demographics of the target audience. Then they need to identify the most important aspects of the play that will appeal to this group. Next, marketers will come up with ideas on how to communicate with members of the target audience and convince them to spend their time and money attending the play. These ideas become the marketing strategies.

With so many forms of entertainment in New York City, capturing the attention of a target group requires creativity. Seeking nomination of a play for a Tony Award is one possible marketing strategy. Marketing research conducted by The Broadway League shows that 21 percent of respondents cited a Tony Award nomination as a reason they attended a particular show. The research also shows that tourists purchase approximately 63 percent of all Broadway tickets, and 47 percent buy their tickets online. This is helpful information in developing marketing strategies.

Staying in touch with customers is an important way to keep them loyal. Because people are constantly bombarded with emails and social media hype, mail sent through the U.S. Postal Service may be a cost-effective marketing strategy to get the attention of a specific target market.

In marketing, what is the difference between strategies and tactics?

Implementing Tactics

With an objective and strategy in mind, marketers must decide on the **tactics**, or the actions taken to implement the strategy. A tactic that could be used to get a Broadway play nominated for a Tony Award might be to open the play in April right before the cutoff date for the Tony Awards nominations. This will ensure that the play is fresh in the minds of the theater professionals who make up the nominating committee. It will also allow a good play to stay open during tourist season, which begins in June. A tactic to draw crowds to a play is to hire well-known movie or TV stars to act in the play. For example, Jim Parsons, famous for TV's *The Big Bang Theory,* has starred in Broadway plays.

Being unique is a tactic used to distinguish a business's product or service from the competition. However, it's important to target the right market. This tactic works well for companies that sell technology products because their target market includes consumers who like to be on the leading edge. Using unique advertising methods is another tactic that may help set apart a business from its competition. Tactics play an important role in marketing plans and thus require careful thought.

Write a SMART marketing objective for a movie theater in your area.

LO 12.2-2 SPORTS MARKETING STRATEGIES

Attracting fans to buy tickets to games and motivating them to buy related merchandise to generate a profit is generally the purpose behind both professional and collegiate sports. Sports teams without fans cease to exist. Developing the right marketing strategies and tactics to get fans in the seats is a challenge for all teams.

The Right Strategy Makes a Difference

Market Planning Sports teams work hard to win over fans. When the first Major League Soccer team, The Wizards, took to the field in Kansas City, the marketing strategy consisted of tapping into the families who were involved with youth soccer and finding ways to attract them to the games. New tactics, such as free pony rides, were tried each week to attract families, but attendance at games remained consistently low. The Kansas City team was eventually sold. The new owners immediately developed an innovative marketing plan that focused on young professionals who are serious soccer fans, instead of families with kids. Their tactics included changing the team's name, colors, logo, and uniform; interacting with the team's supporters' club; connecting with fans via social media; and building a new stadium. Sporting Park Stadium was designed for soccer and is the heart of Sporting Kansas City's new marketing plan. The fans have responded positively, resulting in many sellout games.

Fans Rule

Sports properties are often the heart of a marketing plan and the financial plan of a sports team. For fans of the Green Bay Packers, there is no thrill like attending a game at Lambeau Field. Fans' excitement starts as they enter the famed stadium and continues throughout the game. Win or lose, Green Bay fans are loyal and enthusiastic. Such is not the case for the MLB's Tampa Bay Rays. Locked into a lease with the city to remain at Tropicana Field until 2027, they are having problems attracting enough fans to maintain their payroll. Although the Rays are extremely effective at managing their trades and spending money, the old, outdated stadium is located in an isolated neighborhood across the bay from Tampa. Even when the Rays are having a winning season, they often are ranked at the bottom of the MLB teams for attendance. The Rays must develop strategies to resolve their stadium and attendance problems.

Applied Research   When marketers want to know what fans think about building a new stadium, they can use applied research to answer the question. **Applied research** focuses on solving a specific problem. In marketing it often is used to aid in the development of new or improved products. **Interpretation** is the explanation of research data in a way that makes it meaningful and informative. Before the Baylor University Bears could build a new stadium on campus, they conducted a fan survey and feasibility study. According to the stadium website, the survey produced the following results.[2]

Of the general population survey respondents

- 89 percent indicated a positive attitude towards a new on-campus stadium
- 54 percent would attend more games in a new on-campus stadium

Of the student survey respondents

- 87 percent believed a new on-campus stadium would enhance their Baylor experience
- 79 percent would attend more games in a new on-campus stadium

Who benefits from construction of a sports stadium?

The stadium plans received high praise from many people. David Ubben on ESPN.com called the location "A gorgeous riverside venue… that will make Baylor Stadium a must-see venue in the Big 12 and really, the college football world."[3] The City of Waco, Texas, provided $35 million in Tax Increment Financing (TIF) Zone funds for infrastructure around the stadium. The balance of the funds for the $260 million project was provided through donations and funding from the private university. The stadium is a big part of the Baylor University marketing plan.

INTERMISSION

How do teams use sports stadiums as part of their marketing strategy?

LO 12.2-3 ENTERTAINMENT MARKETING STRATEGIES

The entertainment industry uses many different kinds of marketing strategies to connect to the target market. Marketing strategies help create exposure for businesses and individuals in the entertainment world. To stay competitive, marketers must stay up to date with the latest marketing strategies and tactics that will ensure success.

Making the Move

There was a point in time when Broadway stage performers considered acting in a movie as a step down for their career. Acting on TV was the lowest-level platform for an actor. But today, actors move seamlessly between the Broadway stage, movies, and TV. These transitions from one platform to another are being transformed into effective marketing strategies. HBO's series *True Detective* is an **anthology series**, which is a TV series that has a different cast, setting, and story line each season. The first eight episodes of the series starred Matthew McConaughey, an Academy-Award winning actor, and Woody Harrelson, an Academy-Award nominated actor—both strong movie stars at the height of their careers. A strategy of using very popular movie stars to act in a TV series is mutually beneficial to both the program producers and the stars. When using this strategy, care must be taken not to overexpose a star by having him or her appear in too many ads, TV shows, plays, or movies at the same time.

YouTube Music and Videos

When YouTube and its corporate parent, Google, created the YouTube Music Awards, their objective was long-term brand perception. Although awards voted on by fans were handed out, they took a backseat to the show itself. The online music awards show was streamed live on the Internet. It provided YouTube an opportunity to turn brand perception into advertising sales. It increased YouTube's standing with fans as a go-to music media. In recent years, YouTube has ranked in the top ten most popular brands in the United States and is one of the largest music search engines in the world. YouTube is expected to introduce a subscription music service to allow customers to use their mobile devices to watch music videos or listen to music. Some music labels block their content from mobile devices, but YouTube is expected to gain the licenses needed to legally offer the content.

YouTube is probably best known for offering short videos. When Jimmy Fallon took over NBC's *The Tonight Show*, clips from the show were uploaded daily to YouTube as a marketing tactic to attract an audience. The clips were posted at the same time the show was on the air. One clip entitled "Ew!" featured a teen girl party sketch with Fallon, Will Ferrell, and First Lady Michelle Obama. *The Tonight Show*'s ratings with viewers aged

The feedback available from social media makes it a valuable marketing tool. Most sites sell the information collected about users to the sites' advertisers. When Twitter opened its performance analytics to the public for free, anyone could see how many faves, retweets, and replies someone else had received. The dashboard graphics used to display the data show the actual reach and the number of people clicking on tweeted links.

Posting a new tweet can be scheduled based on when members of the target audience are most likely to check their mobile devices or log on to Twitter. The social media consultant company Social Caffeine created an infographic that lists the best and worst times to post to Twitter and other major social networks. The times are based on the number of people using the media at specific hours of the day. Social Caffeine suggests that you can maximize the reach of your posts on Twitter by posting Monday through Friday between 1:00 p.m. and 3:00 p.m. It recommends to avoid posting after 3:00 p.m. on Friday.

Think Critically

Why might certain groups of people be on social media sites at specific times? How could marketers of an entertainment event use this information to implement a strategy?

18 to 49 skyrocketed, exceeding the ratings of any other show with that demographic in its time slot.

Hashtag That

 A hashtag is a word or phrase prefixed with the number sign (#) that is used on social media sites to identify topics of interest.

Hashtags can be distracting when overused, but they can speed up searches for related comments in social media. Marketers can interact with consumers and get their input by following hashtagged comments. As the release of each movie in the series *The Hunger Games* approached, fans used #HungerGames to discuss the characters and content. Tweets related to #HungerGames peaked at over 3 million a day. The Twitter Oscars Index is a social media platform that tracks comments about Academy Award nominees. The index may not be able to predict the winner, but it shows what the fans are discussing.

INTERMISSION

List and describe three strategies that can be used as part of an entertainment marketing plan.

ENCORE

Understand Marketing Concepts

Select the best answer for each question.

1. Tactics are
   a. the study of the sales process
   b. the actions taken to implement a strategy
   c. the study of competitors
   d. strategies for success

2. Applied research is
   a. gathered from all points of customer contact
   b. conducted to solve a specific problem
   c. a channel management element
   d. none of the above

Think Critically

Answer the following questions as completely as possible.

3. Think of two radio stations in your area. How do they differentiate themselves from each other? What are their strategies and tactics? (LO 12.2-1)

4. Look up information about a sports stadium where you have been or would like to go. Does the team use features of the facility as part of its marketing strategy? What about the facility appeals to fans? (LO 12.2-2)

12.3 Detailing the Plan

The Essential Question

What are the major components of a marketing plan, and why is positioning an important part of the plan?

Learning Objectives

LO 12.3-1 Describe how a marketing position is developed.

LO 12.3-2 List and describe the components of a marketing plan.

Key Terms

- product portfolio
- nonprice competition
- positioning statement
- executive summary
- mission statement
- project matrix

OPENING ACT

Today's golf industry faces many challenges. The decline in core golfers—those who play 18 holes of golf at least eight times each year—is the greatest challenge. This trend is a result of the high fees associated with the sport, the time required to play and practice, and changing cultural dynamics.

Innovative golf courses are addressing the challenges with creative marketing planning. Strategies that reach golfers through social media, even when they are not playing, help keep them involved with the game. Short golf courses, with less than the standard 18 holes, are being offered as a way to shorten the playing time. Some courses entice young golfers by charging them low prices or allowing them to play at no charge when accompanied by a paying adult. Alternative forms of golf are offered as a way to attract new players. Footgolf involves kicking a soccer ball into a larger-than-normal golf hole. Basketgolf involves tossing Frisbees into baskets located throughout the golf course. These and other alternatives are making a positive difference.

Cooperative Learning   Work with a team and discuss strategies for attracting new and younger players to golf. What could be done to get you to become a core golfer?

LO 12.3-1   OCCUPYING A POSITION

Product/Service Management

Based on its mission, a business produces products and services that will differentiate it from the competition. Generally, the products are marketed to a target group of customers rather than a broad group, or mass market. All of the products a company has available for customers at any one time make up the company's **product portfolio**.

Standing Out in the Crowd

A company's product portfolio can *directly* compete with the same or similar types of products or services offered by another business. The New York Jets and the New York Giants football teams are in direct competition for fans and sponsors. A company can also *indirectly* compete with other companies that offer products in a different product category but that satisfy

How can a sports team distinguish itself from other teams and sports?

similar customer needs. For example, the New York Giants *indirectly* compete with the New York Knicks basketball team.

Because most consumers have limited funds to spend on sports and entertainment purchases, pricing is also a point of competition. Fans are willing to pay premium prices when they have the funds available and believe the product or service is unique or of superior quality. If a regular seat at the Jets' game costs twice as much as the same seat at the Giants' game, some fans might rethink their loyalty. The cost of a ticket to see the Knicks is less of a factor because they are indirect competitors.

When a business decides to emphasize other factors in the marketing mix besides price, it is using **nonprice competition**. Technological innovations, product features, customer service, or unique advertisements are all nonprice ways to make the product portfolio stand out.

A marketing plan clearly identifies what differentiates a product or service from the competition and makes it stand out in the minds of consumers. The specific description of the unique qualities of a product's marketing mix is called the **positioning statement**. Small companies may not be able to compete with national companies on price, but they can excel in other areas, such as customer service. Some national customer service call centers have a frustrating series of automated choices (press 1 for billing, press 2 to make a payment. . .). They put customers on hold for extended periods of time, often referring them to a company website to resolve issues. To distinguish itself from the competition, a small company could have knowledgeable, well-spoken customer service representatives who promptly answer the phone or are readily available to chat on the website. A small company's positioning may fill a niche market that a large company cannot serve efficiently. If the needs of a specific niche market are not being fully met by the competition, an opportunity exists that can be defined in the company's positioning statement.

Major League Baseball (MLB), the National Football League (NFL), the National Basketball Association (NBA), and the National Hockey League (NHL) are indirect competitors. In a recent year, the average price of a nonpremium seat was as follows:[4]
MLB – $27.73
NBA – $50.99
NHL – $61.01
NFL – $78.38
Pricing is less of a consideration when comparing indirect competition.

INTERMISSION

How does a positioning statement help a business differentiate itself from the competition?

12.3-2   THE MARKETING PLAN

The marketing plan is a formal document that details and defines how the business will address the core marketing standards. It is a part of the overall business plan and is shared with all employees, as well as current or potential investors. If an organization moves its focus away from its customers, it loses the customers' business. The current and future needs of customers should act as a guide in developing the marketing plan.

Components of a Marketing Plan

The major components of a marketing plan are determined by the specific needs of the organization and the products or services to be marketed. Businesses use a variety of formats, but most plans cover comparable topics. The main body of the marketing plan can generally be divided into three major segments—the situational analysis, marketing strategy, and implementation. These main segments are preceded by an executive summary.

Executive Summary   The **executive summary** is placed at the front of the marketing plan to present a short, concise restatement of its contents. The executive summary is a very important part of the marketing plan because some people may read only this section. By factually presenting bits of the total report, the executive summary should entice people, such as potential investors, to read the rest of the report.

JUDGMENT CALL

Major League Soccer (MLS) in the United States faced a dilemma. While trying to attract new fans and keep loyal fans, the MLS wanted to tone down the offensive chants used by some fans. The teams' marketing plans incorporated behavioral psychology and motivational tactics to discourage off-color taunts. Some teams have gone as far as offering official supporter groups a financial reward for every game in which they hold down distasteful chants. Some fan groups took offense at being "bribed" to control their behavior. Other fan groups accepted the challenge and the financial reward.

The league was concerned that bad behavior on the part of current fans could discourage potential new fans from bringing their families and young children to the games. Additionally, the MLS was set to renew the league's national broadcast contracts. National broadcasters will not tolerate offensive language heard in the background of broadcast games.

Think Critically

How can a sport's reputation of offensive fan behavior be harmful? What would you suggest be done to keep the fans' excitement within acceptable norms?

Situational Analysis

The situational analysis section includes the mission statement and information about the current conditions of the business.

- **The Mission Statement** The nature of the business and the reason that the company exists are described in the **mission statement**.
- **Analysis** This section contains information obtained from the SWOT analysis, including data about direct and indirect competitors. Opportunities for fulfilling unmet needs in the market are identified. The marketing information provides background and support for the strategies described in the next section.

Marketing Strategies

The strategies section describes the target market and the marketing mix—product or service, price, distribution, and promotion. Financing and risk management plans are also discussed. The positioning statement can be included at the end of this section.

- **The Target Customers** This section describes the potential and current customers (the target market), their needs and wants, what motivates them to buy, and how to acquire and retain their loyalty.

- **Product/Service** The product or service is planned and designed based on the needs of the target market and the opportunities that are identified in the situational analysis.

- **Price** Marketers must analyze various price points. The price must be set where revenues will be maximized to cover all costs and provide a profit. The following pricing questions must be addressed:
  - What is the best price for the product or service?
  - How much will it cost the organization to provide the product or service to customers?
  - How much are customers willing to pay?
  - How many customers will buy the product or service at this price?
  - Would a lower price increase the customer base and revenue?

- **Distribution** This section describes how the product or service will be made available to customers. It also examines how place utility (access to the product) can be improved.
- **Promotion** This part of the plan describes how the organization will use advertising, publicity, personal selling, and sales promotion to position the product or service in the minds of customers. It incorporates the details developed in the promotional plan (see Lesson 10.3), including a description of the media to be used. It explains how the promotional strategies will help the organization meet its objectives.
- **Financing** Expected costs and expected revenues must be fully disclosed in the marketing plan. Questions to be answered include the following:
  - How much will it cost to produce or deliver the product?
  - What is the estimated revenue from the product?
  - What costs are involved in marketing the product?
  - How long will it take to make a profit?

Answers to these questions may show a need for the organization to borrow funds or obtain additional investments. Plans for repaying loans are also included in this section.

- **Risk Management** There are risks, such as potential legal liabilities, involved with marketing any new product. In this part of the marketing plan, the possible risks and strategies for minimizing them are outlined. Handling weaknesses and threats as identified in the SWOT analysis is also addressed in this section.
- **Positioning Statement** The specifics of how the product is unique and will satisfy the target market are clearly stated in this section.

Implementation

The implementation section describes how the marketing plan will be put into action. It includes tasks to be completed, assignments of responsibility, a timeline for completing tasks, communication procedures to be followed, sales strategies to be used, and guidelines for review and evaluation of the plan.

- **Tasks** The tasks that must be completed to implement the marketing plan are detailed in this section. The tactics for carrying out the strategies are also described here.
- **Assignments of Responsibility** The plan must specify who is responsible for carrying out each task. Without clear ownership of a task, there will be duplication of effort, or worse, no effort at all. Team members might assume that others are responsible for completing a task. Clear organization and assignment will enable the work to be accomplished in an effective and efficient manner.
- **Timeline** Due dates for the tasks are established to ensure that they are started and completed on time. Missed deadlines can be costly to a business. If an ad that was scheduled to be shown during the Super Bowl is not completed on time, it can have a

© Monkey Business Images/Shutterstock.com

What are the benefits of assigning a task to a specific person?

negative effect on the overall marketing plan. When establishing a timeline, start with the date the plan needs to be completed and work backwards to the start date of the plan. If the deadline for getting the ad to the TV network is two weeks prior to the Super Bowl, set the completion date three weeks prior to allow some flexibility. Specify what needs to be accomplished and in what sequence. Set a scheduled date for the action to begin and for each stage of the plan to be completed.

A timeline can be in the form of a project matrix. A chart displaying the tasks, groups or individuals responsible for completion of the tasks, and the due dates or timelines is called a **project matrix**. For example, if an organization is going to promote a new product at an NFL game in September, a simple version of the project matrix may look like the chart on the next page. The real project timeline would be much more detailed. For this promotion to be completed in September, it needs to start in March.

Project Matrix				
Tasks	Responsibility	Mar	July	Sept
Strategies	Marketing	→		
Tactics	Marketing	→		
Production	Operations		→	
Distribution	Marketing		→	
Implementation	Marketing			→

- **Internal Communication Systems** It is desirable that all areas of the organization buy into the plan. Communication systems must be in place to ensure that all key members of the organization have a chance to review and communicate their feedback. When all departments are involved in the planning process, they will have a better understanding of the objectives and be more cooperative in implementing the plan.

Selling

- **Selling** The marketing plan must outline how direct sales, such as ticket and related merchandise sales, will be handled. All potential customer interactions that could lead to sales opportunities should be identified.

TAKE A BOW   Mariah Carey

Mariah Carey, whose mother is of white Irish heritage and father is of African-American and Venezuelan heritage, was born on Long Island, New York. She has been successful in multiple genres, including pop, hip hop, soul, and rhythm and blues. By performing in concerts and tours around the world, Carey has maintained popularity across many cultures.

When Carey was the guest vocalist with the New York Philharmonic, she had recently injured her shoulder. But that didn't stop her from being fashionable—she wore a series of sparkling, fur and feather-draped slings that matched each of her dresses. The performance was during a benefit for hurricane relief held in Central Park in New York City and was in coordination with the MLB's All-Star Game at Citi Field. More than 60,000 tickets were distributed, and the MLB donated $1 million to the relief efforts. This charity event is only one of many performed by Carey throughout her career. The marketing plan for the event was detailed and precise, but flexible enough to accommodate Carey's injury.

Think Critically

Name one possible marketing strategy for a charity performance supporting relief efforts that will have an MLB connection. Describe a few of the tasks and timelines, assuming the concert is held in July.

- **Review and Evaluation** The marketing plan should include mileposts at which point the organization can measure progress to ensure the plan is on track. At this stage, the organization can also determine if adjustments to the plan are needed. The final results should be reviewed for use in future planning.

Look to the Future

An organization must consider where its business is going and what the next steps will be for staying ahead of the competition. Because products and services fall in and out of favor with consumers, it is important to be prepared. Organizations should identify the next product or service to offer while the current one is still selling well. Over time, changes will occur, such as changes in the economy, new technology, new products, or new competitors. Marketing plans likely will need to be revised frequently. By looking to the future, organizations can ensure their plan will lead to success.

Why must the marketing plan include time for review and evaluation?

Understand Marketing Concepts

Select the best answer for each question.

1. Customer service can be
   a. used to level the playing field between large and small businesses
   b. too expensive to implement
   c. automated to eliminate the need for live representatives
   d. a legal problem

2. The major components of a marketing plan include
   a. situational analysis
   b. marketing strategies
   c. implementation
   d. all of the above

Think Critically

Answer the following questions as completely as possible.

3. If you want to distinguish your sporting goods company from the competition, what are three ways to accomplish this objective? What are the pros and cons of each? (LO 12.3-1)

4. When setting a timeline, why would you start at the target completion date of a marketing plan and work backwards? How would this help in planning? (LO 12.3-2)

CHAPTER ASSESSMENT

Review Marketing Concepts

Match the terms listed with the definitions.

a. anthology series
b. applied research
c. executive summary
d. interpretation
e. marketing intelligence
f. marketing plan
g. marketing strategy
h. mission statement
i. nonprice competition
j. positioning statement
k. product portfolio
l. project matrix
m. situational analysis
n. SMART objectives
o. strategic thinking
p. SWOT analysis
q. tactics

1. An idea for achieving marketing objectives that can be put into action
2. A TV series that has a different cast, setting, and story line each season
3. Information gathered about competitors
4. A specific description of the unique qualities of a product's marketing mix
5. All of the products a company has available for customers
6. Describes the nature of the business and the reason it exists
7. A precisely written document that describes a company's situational analysis, marketing strategies, and implementation plan
8. Actions taken to implement strategies
9. A chart displaying the tasks, responsible parties, and timelines of a plan
10. An examination of a business's strengths, weaknesses, opportunities, and threats
11. The process of finding unique, innovative ways to reach an objective
12. Competition focused on marketing mix elements other than price
13. An in-depth look at the current conditions of the business, the competition, and the target customers
14. Objectives that are specific, measurable, attainable, relevant, and timely
15. Research that focuses on solving a specific problem
16. An explanation of research data in a way that makes it meaningful and informative
17. A short, concise restatement of the marketing plan

Review Marketing Concepts

Select the best answer for each of the following questions.

18. The major components of a marketing plan can be divided into
    a. emails, websites, and text messages
    b. introduction, main section, and ending
    c. the situational analysis, marketing strategy, and implementation
    d. advertisements, copy, and photographs
19. The implementation section of the marketing plan will contain
    a. timelines
    b. assignments of responsibility
    c. tasks to be completed
    d. all of the above

20. A product portfolio is
    a. the research completed on a product
    b. a pricing strategy
    c. all of the products a company has available for customers at any one time
    d. all of the above
21. A competitor who sells the same or a similar product is
    a. not a concern in marketing planning
    b. an indirect competitor
    c. a direct competitor
    d. none of the above

Think Critically

22. Why do successful marketers focus on how a product's characteristics are unique from competing products? Provide an example of a sports or entertainment product or service and specify how it is unique from its competition. (LO 12.3-1)
23. You are a salesperson for a sportswear company that sells to Little League teams. What would you do to gather marketing intelligence about your competition? What would you want to know? (LO 12.1-2)
24. You want to increase sales of your music. You know that 5,000 people visited your website. From those 5,000 visits, you sold only 75 downloads. What else do you need to know and how would you use the information to increase sales? (LO 12.1-2)
25. You own and operate a roller rink. You actively promote your business and special events on the company website and through social media sites. Describe a way you can incorporate YouTube as part of your marketing strategy. How can you use hashtags in your social media marketing campaign? (LO 12.2-3)
26. What does it mean to "make a product stand out in the minds of consumers"? Why is it important to do so? (LO 12.3-1)
27. If the competition already has a large share of the market, how can you differentiate your product or service to grow your business? (LO 12.2-1)
28. Assume you are the marketer of a sporting event. What information would you need to gather for the pricing section of the marketing plan? Explain how and where you would obtain the information. (LO 12.3-2)
29. Your city of 2 million people does not have a professional men's soccer team. To be considered, a city must agree to have a soccer stadium built within two years after the team starts playing. You want to make sure that the facility will appeal to the fan base, who are adults aged 21 to 35. What steps would you take to determine features to include in the stadium plans? (LO 12.2-2)

Make Academic Connections

30. Marketing Math A movie theater has 24 screens. Half of the screening rooms seat 150 people, and the remainder seat 250 people. Each screen shows a movie three times a day, seven days a week. How many movie screenings are there in one week? The theater has been selling tickets at about 75 percent of capacity and would like to increase the daily ticket sales by 5 percent. How many additional tickets will have to be sold to reach the goal? (LO 12.3-2)

31. Communication Write a one-page summary of information about the last sports or entertainment event you attended or would like to have attended. Include information a competitor would want to know about the event. What media was used to promote the event? How did you buy your ticket and how much did you pay? What was done really well at the event? What could have been done better? (LO 12.1-2)

32. History Use the Internet or library to research the history of a current collegiate or professional sports facility. How and when was it built? What role does it play in the marketing strategy of the team that uses it? Does it have or need luxury suites? Are any changes needed or planned for the facility? (LO 12.2-2)

33. Marketing Math Based on its marketing plans, your DECA chapter had 100 nonrefundable T-shirts printed at a cost of $5.50 each. There were 25 shirts of each size (XL, L, M, S). The school let the club have a sales table at a school event. The club sold the shirts at $15.00 each, which also covered the 6 percent sales tax the club had to pay on the sales. If the club sold 6 XL, 25 L, 25 M, and 10 S, how much total profit did the DECA chapter make? How many shirts were left over that couldn't be sold? How much profit could the club have made if all the shirts had sold? What can the club do to improve its future marketing planning? (LO 12.1-2)

34. Ethics Some research has shown that repeated exposure to graphically violent scenes in movies or other media may be linked to actual violent or anti-social behavior. Other research has shown that children who are exposed to media violence become desensitized and may lack sympathy for victims of violence. What marketing strategies could be used to assure that children have limited exposure to movies or other media that contain violence? Discuss the ethical obligation the entertainment industry has to limit the exposure of children to violence. (LO 12.2-3)

35. Geography Using the Internet, find a map on which you can locate the baseball stadiums used in the three most recent MLB World Series. Read available information about the stadiums. Select one of the stadiums and make a chart listing information about it. Include characteristics such as when the stadium was originally built, the games and other events held in the stadium (excluding World Series games), the capacity of the stadium, and any special features used to attract fans to the stadium. How would you attract fans to attend games or events at this stadium? (LO 12.2-2)

EXTRA INNINGS PROJECT

A sports drink company wants your marketing firm to select a sport for it to sponsor, research the target market, and prepare a marketing plan. The company prefers to sponsor an up-and-coming sport or extreme sport that is gaining popularity. The company wants consumers to see its product as fresh, exciting, invigorating, young, and daring. After performing its own SWOT analysis, the company has determined the following:

- Strengths—Its product is a refreshing and healthy drink, sweetened with cane sugar.
- Weaknesses—The company holds only 25 percent of the market, cannot compete on price, and is not well known.
- Opportunities—Research has shown that most people like the taste of the company's product better than the competitors' brands, which are sweetened with high fructose corn syrup.
- Threats—The competitors are sponsoring popular sports teams in several states.

Work with a group and complete the following activities.

1. Use the Internet to find a nontraditional sport that the company can sponsor. It can be a team or an individual sport. Determine what features of this sport can be associated with the product's characteristics.
2. What are the demographics of the sport's fans, including age range, gender, income, and education? Also research psychographic (lifestyle) data about the fans. Explain why these fans should be the target market.
3. What strategies will you use to communicate with the target customers? What tactics will you use to implement your strategies?
4. Prepare a project matrix based on starting the sponsorship at the beginning of the next full season of the sport.
5. Prepare the marketing plan and present it to the class as you would the client. Use multimedia presentation software or other visual aids. Include an executive summary of the main points.

VIRTUAL BUSINESS *Sports & Entertainment*

Use the *Ingress and Egress* lesson to determine ways fans get into a stadium. Both ingress and egress are vital to a positive customer or fan experience. Calculate attendance and estimate parking and satellite transportation that will be required. Learn how to factor in appropriate staffing for an event.

Observe the difference between a well-staffed and poorly staffed event. You will be challenged to manage ingress for a football game—getting fans into the stadium on time, with no complaints, and within budget.

For more information, go to **knowledgematters.com**.

Artwork courtesy of Knowledge Matters, Inc.

AMAZÔNIA—A NEW STADIUM

When the Fédération Internationale de Football Association (FIFA) awarded Brazil the 2014 FIFA World Cup, it was the second time that the international men's soccer tournament had been played in Brazil. The previous occurrence was in 1950. As the host of the FIFA World Cup, Brazil hosted the 32 national teams that advanced through three years of qualification competitions.

Hosting the World

Twelve cities in Brazil hosted a total of 64 World Cup matches in either new or redeveloped stadiums during the 2014 World Cup. Maracanã Stadium is an open-air stadium in Rio de Janeiro, Brazil. It was opened in 1950 to host the FIFA World Cup. Major renovations were completed so that it could be used during the 2014 World Cup and for the opening and closing ceremonies of the 2016 Summer Olympics.

One of the newly constructed World Cup stadiums, the Arena Amazônia, was built in Manaus, Brazil. Founded in 1669, Manaus is a city of about 2 million residents and the capital of the state of Amazonas in northern Brazil. It is located where two rivers meet to form the Amazon River in the middle of the Amazon Rainforest.

Manaus has not had a top-division soccer team, and critics of the stadium were not in favor of its construction. The stadium has a capacity of over 42,000. Critics questioned how the stadium would be used after the World Cup. Four of the World Cup games, including the United States against Portugal, were played in the Arena Amazônia in Manaus.

Supporters of bringing the World Cup to Manaus highlighted multiple purposes for the stadium. Beyond having an "if we build it, they will come" attitude, supporters believe the stadium offers opportunities for Manaus. Manaus's economy, which includes electronics, chemical and oil companies, and a Free Economic Zone that is a significant industrial hub, is strong and growing. Thus, there is thriving potential for other events to be held at the stadium. Manaus is also the starting and/or returning point for tourists exploring the Amazon region. Tourists can be attracted to attend a special event held in the stadium at the beginning or end of their Amazon journeys.

Think Critically

1. What information would you need before developing a marketing plan for the Arena Amazônia?
2. Who would be your target market for events at the arena? What types of events would you plan?
3. What marketing strategies would you propose to make effective use of the arena?
4. What tactics would you use to help attract supporters for the arena?

TRAVEL AND TOURISM TEAM DECISION-MAKING EVENT

The 2016 Summer Olympics in Rio de Janeiro, Brazil, had some U.S. tourists hesitant to attend the games because of the city's reputation for high crime rates.

Brazil is the most-visited country on the continent of South America, and Rio de Janeiro (Rio) is one of the world's most popular destinations. Rio is the second-largest city in the country. The beautiful beaches, including Copacabana and Ipanema, are major attractions.

The city is often identified with the 125-foot-high statue "Christ the Redeemer" located on top of Corcovado Mountain within the city limits of Rio. The peak can be reached by a 20-minute train ride and a climb up 222 steps. For those not wanting to make the climb, elevators and escalators also take visitors to the observation deck at the foot of the statue. More than 300,000 visitors visit the statue each year.

No trip to Rio is complete without a cable car ride to Sugarloaf Mountain, which rises straight from the water's edge at the entrance to Guanabara Bay. Its name is derived from its resemblance to a refined sugar block used in the 19th century. The cable car ride provides a 360° breathtaking view of the surrounding city and gleaming bay areas.

Your public relations team has been hired to develop a marketing plan for Rio de Janeiro to ease the concern of international travelers to the Summer Olympics. U.S. tourists must feel that they will be safe attending the 2016 Olympic Games. Your presentation must include all of the extra measures that the Brazilian government will take to assure the safety of international guests.

Performance Indicators Evaluated

- Explain the nature of effective communication.
- Explain communication channels used in public relations activities.
- Explain the concept of marketing strategies.
- Explain the role of promotion as a marketing function.
- Explain the nature of positive customer relations.

Think Critically

1. Why should a SWOT analysis be conducted for Rio de Janeiro?
2. What can officials in a country with a negative crime record do to convince tourists that they will be safe?
3. What are some SMART objectives for this plan?
4. What types of communication would you use to attract guests to the Summer Olympics?

www.deca.org

SPORTS AND ENTERTAINMENT LEGAL ISSUES

© Orange Line Media/Shutterstock.com

POINT YOUR BROWSER

ngl.cengage.com/sports4e

Winning Strategies

IMG—Licensing Sports

IMG Worldwide is a global sports, fashion, and media business with many divisions that oversee the production of merchandise, services, and events related to sports. IMG is owned by William Morris Endeavor, a Hollywood talent agency. The IMG Academy NFL Combine/Draft Training Program is used by college players to participate in position-specific training in preparation for the NFL draft. Another of its divisions is IMG College and its affiliate Collegiate Licensing Company (CLC). CLC has marketing rights to nearly 200 of the nation's colleges and universities as well as bowl games, the Heisman Trophy, and the NCAA. This is nearly 80 percent of the more than $4.6 billion retail market for collegiate licensed merchandise.

CLC sees its focus as connecting college fans to their favorite college brands. It assists colleges in managing their merchandise production to assure quality, availability, and selection of products for college fans. CLC also works to develop brands, protect brand integrity, and grow revenue for the colleges. It finds and negotiates with qualified licensees, activates retail channels, and brings together partners for promotional opportunities.

© Black Russian Studio/Shutterstock.com

Think Critically

1. Why would a college want to legally protect its team's sports-related merchandise?

2. What do you think a college should do if it discovers that unauthorized jerseys with its team's name and logo are being sold online?

13.1 Laws

The Essential Question

How are the governing bodies of sports involved with athletes and in the fair use of a sports teams' brand?

Learning Objectives

LO 13.1-1   Discuss the role of governing bodies in the sports industry.

LO 13.1-2   Distinguish between copyright laws, licensing, and fair use.

Key Terms

- copyright
- intellectual property
- patent
- royalty
- public domain
- fair use
- parody
- time-shifting
- broadcast flags

OPENING ACT

Television contracts, sponsorships, wealthy boosters, and bowl games provide millions of dollars of revenue to college teams. Despite this, college athletes are classified as unpaid amateur athletes. They are given college scholarships, food, and housing as a condition of playing for a university's team. The scholarships provide thousands of dollars toward the players' educations but do not cover the full cost of attending college.

The National Collegiate Athletic Association (NCAA) previously prevented college athletes from receiving wages that would help cover their additional living expenses. Phil Hughes, associate director for student services at Kansas State University, refuses to use the term "amateurs" or even student-athletes. "My job is to protect The Entertainment Product. My job is to make sure The Entertainment Product goes to class,"[1] Hughes told Mark Yost, author of *Varsity Green: A Behind the Scenes Look at Culture and Corruption in College Athletics*. In a recent turnaround, however, the NCAA voted to allow colleges in the top five conferences to pay players' cost-of-attendance (living) expenses not covered by an athletic scholarship. Many colleges, outside the top five, will not be able to afford to pay players.

Cooperative Learning   Work with a group to determine the current status of the pay-for-play issue. How might this affect universities with small athletic budgets?

LO 13.1-1   GOVERNING SPORTS

Product/Service Management   Imagine the chaos each week if there were no written, pre-agreed-upon rules for professional football games. Teams might try to agree on rules just before the start of the game. The game might look more like rugby than U.S. football. The fans might go home in disgust. TV coverage would never happen. To prevent this type of disorder, the governing bodies of all well-known sports leagues agree upon the rules well in advance of the season. The members of the leagues agree to abide by the rules and accept the benefits of orderly play.

Why are governing bodies needed in sports?

International Sports Associations

International sports federations are nongovernmental governing bodies for specific sports. They are made up of representatives from the national sports associations in individual countries. They develop the rules for their sport, set standards of fair play, organize world-level competitions, and promote their sport. The International Olympic Committee recognizes the national federations for individual sports that conform to the Olympic Charter and permits them to participate in the Olympic Games.

The Fédération Internationale de Football Association (FIFA) is the worldwide governing body of soccer. It has 209 national associations as members. As one of the largest sports associations in the world, FIFA promotes the sport and supports it financially and logistically.

U.S. Professional Sports Leagues

Professional football, baseball, basketball, and hockey are the most popular sports in the United States. Soccer is a rising star. Each sport has its own league that sets the rules for play and regulates the teams' spending.

In Major League Baseball (MLB), the large-market teams dominate the game. The New York Yankees were recently valued at about $1.7 billion, while the Pittsburgh Pirates were valued at $304 million.[2] The popularity of professional baseball in the United States seems to be stable, but not growing. The gap between the top- and bottom-value teams tends to make the winners predictable. If the baseball teams do not remain competitive, fan interest may decline.

U.S. Soccer is the governing body for all forms of soccer in the United States, including the National Women's Soccer League. Major League Soccer (MLS) was founded in the United States in 1993. It has grown from 10 teams to 19 teams with 3 more teams planning to join the league soon. MLS games have average attendance that exceeds games played in the National Basketball Association and National Hockey League. MLS operates as a single entity in which teams are centrally owned by the league. Each team has an investor-operator that is a league shareholder.

JUDGMENT CALL

Japanese baseball player Sadaharu Oh played for the Yomiuri Giants for his entire 22-year professional career. He holds the world's career home run record with 868 home runs. He held the single season record of 55 home runs from 1964 until it was finally broken in 2013 by Wladimir Balentien from Curaçao. Two other players, American Tuffy Rhodes and Venezuelan Alex Cabrera, tied Oh's season record, but both finished with exactly 55 homers while playing in Japan. The two ties were not a coincidence. In both games, Oh was the manager of the opposing team. Oh was held in such great esteem in Japan that other teams repeatedly walked the two batters. One coach reportedly threatened a pitcher with a $1,000 fine for any pitches thrown to the two batters' strike zones. No Japanese team wanted to be the team that allowed Oh's record to be broken.[3]

Think Critically

How do you think fans feel when baseball players are walked intentionally? Should teams be allowed to control the game in this manner? Why or why not?

U.S. Amateur and Collegiate Sports Leagues

Governing bodies also exist in amateur and college sports. U.S. Soccer created the Development Academy in 2007 to develop young soccer players. Most of the academy teams are associated with a professional MLS team. Boys who participate in the academies are not allowed to play on their high school teams, but girls can play for both at the same time. The academies are considered the top tier of play, above high school teams. Colleges scout the academies and offer scholarships to top players.

The National Collegiate Athletic Association (NCAA) develops the rules for competition among college athletes. The NCAA also organizes national championships. The governance structure consists of legislative bodies and committees made up of volunteers from the member colleges and universities that govern each division.

The NCAA was forced to consider significant changes to its rules by the wealthiest, highest-profile universities. Schools in the Atlantic Coast, Big Ten, Big 12, Pac-12, and Southeastern Conferences form the upper tier of the Football Bowl Subdivision. They wanted to provide more benefits, such as enhanced scholarships, to college athletes, primarily football players. They also wanted to use their extensive resources as they wished. In the past, the 65 schools in the wealthiest conferences were outvoted by the more than 350 other member schools. The wealthy schools threatened to break away from the NCAA if the changes were not permitted. In 2014 the NCAA Board of Directors voted 16-2 to allow the wealthiest schools to set their own rules.

The NCAA has exclusive rights to audio and video footage for all NCAA championships and events. It controls the use of all game highlights. News organizations have limited use of the highlights and can air them only after the broadcast of the game has ended.

LO 13.1-2   WHO HAS THE RIGHTS?

Protecting players, celebrities, musicians, team owners, producers, promoters, and investors is the purpose of most of the laws governing sports and entertainment. Laws are also designed to encourage and protect competition and increase the safety of consumers, viewers, and fans.

Musicians, athletes, and artists make money by selling their product, which happens to be their work and their image (brand). Their work and brand are protected by copyright law and is theirs alone to sell. A **copyright** legally protects the unique work of the originator from use by others without permission. When pricing their product, artists and athletes must take copyrights into consideration. For example, the price of a music download includes not only the costs to make the download available, but also an amount to pay the writer and performer of the music.

The unique works of writers, artists, and musicians that are protected under copyright law are often referred to as **intellectual property**. Before 1978, works were copyrighted for 28 years. Expiring copyrights could be renewed for 67 more years, for a total of 95 years. Since 1978, works may be copyrighted for the lifetime of the artist plus 70 years.

Many types of works can be copyrighted. Some common copyrighted items are books, songs, and computer programs. In order for a work to be copyrighted, it must be fixed and original. *Fixed* means that the work must be recorded on a permanent medium, such as written or printed on paper or digitally recorded on a disc. Material available over the Internet is also protected by copyright law.

© Everett Collection/Shutterstock.com

How do copyright laws affect musicians?

Inventors of products may want to obtain a **patent**, which is a property right that excludes others from making, using, offering for sale, or selling the invention. For example, if a sports apparel manufacturer, such as Nike or Under Armour, creates a product that offers unique benefits not previously available on the market, it may want to get a patent to protect its invention from use by others.

International Protection

Channel Management   U.S. copyright laws are meant to protect creative, original work. They are not enforceable in other countries, except those where the United States is part of an international copyright convention. The United States and China have had battles over the piracy (theft) of copyrighted intellectual property such as movies and music. "In China, pirated content is faster, cheaper, and easier to acquire than legal content," according to a *USA TODAY* article.[4] In the United

Why is it harmful when foreign countries do not abide by international copyright agreements involving piracy of movies or music?

Ownership of original work is often the subject of court cases. When artists, musicians, or authors create work that is done "for hire," they do not own the work. The business entity that hired them owns the work. The legendary artist Jack Kirby helped create the comic book characters Spider-Man, Iron Man, and the Incredible Hulk. When his estate sued for the rights to these comic book legends, a U.S. Circuit Court of Appeals ruled that Kirby was hired by Marvel Comics, who owns the rights to the work.

States, revenue for movies is generated through ticket sales and transmission (broadcast) rights. In China, online video sites that offer pirated, free-to-watch content earn revenue through paid advertising, but none of the revenue goes to the rights holder. According to a study commissioned by NBCUniversal, "online piracy in North America, Europe, and Asia has risen 160 percent in two years and consumes 24 percent of Internet bandwidth in those regions."[5]

The revenue from pirated music, films, and software in Russia is estimated to be more than $4 billion, well above the revenue earned legally in the Russian marketplace. Russia is currently the world's second-largest distributor of pirated music, behind only China. In Russia, some piracy has been justified as "promotion" of the work, which supposedly benefits the owner of the content.

Piracy can consume the majority of revenue and threaten the existence of businesses in the sports and entertainment industries. The piracy of films has reached a point in which it is affecting the number of studio and independent films released each year. The revenue generated by selling film rights to foreign movie distributors has almost ceased to exist because of piracy. The film industry was hoping for support from Internet service providers such as Google. It wanted Google and others to agree to place restrictions on the Internet services provided to suspected copyright infringers. An attorney for Google called such voluntary restriction a threat to free speech.

Fair Use

Owners of a copyright have the exclusive right to reproduce, sell, perform, or display the work. For the life of a copyright, the owner must give permission for the work to be used in any significant way, and there is usually a fee involved. A **royalty** is the payment for the use of copyrighted work. After a copyright expires, the work moves into the **public domain**, or the realm in which the originator's work can be used by anyone without cost or permission. Before a work becomes public domain, **fair use** allows limited creative uses of music, literature, movies, and more without asking permission or making payment. The Copyright Act lists four conditions under which it is fair to use copyrighted material.

- *If the work has been transformed, such as in a* **parody***, which is a humorous imitation of the original work.* Comedians such as Jon Stewart often use clips of actual newscasts to poke fun at headline stories. This is a fair use of the clips.
- *If the work is factual, rather than creative, and is used to educate and inform the public.* For example, limited use of factual material from the biography of a historical figure is considered fair use.
- *If the use is for private, noncommercial purposes and will not impact the market value of the copyrighted material.* **Time-shifting***,* which is the recording of a television show for private viewing later, is fair use.
- *If only a small amount of the original work is used.* Although there is no exact limit on the quantity of work that can be used, the use of a small portion of copyrighted material may be considered fair use under certain circumstances.

Licensing

Product/Service Management Licensing of trademarks and brands is a contractual agreement between the owner (the *licensor*) and another business (the *licensee*). The licensor grants the licensee the rights to use the brand or trademark in return for payment (royalty).

Sports and entertainment entities license their brands to businesses that have expertise in manufacturing and marketing clothing, toys, or other items for retail sales. The licensor benefits from increased brand awareness. Disney's intellectual property includes images of its famous cartoon characters. Having a licensing agreement with Disney for use of its images can

COMMUNICATION CONNECTION

Some people have trouble telling the difference between a fact, an opinion, and a fabrication. If someone else tells you, "That movie was selected by the Academy of Motion Picture Arts and Sciences as the best movie of the year," you can find a reliable source to see if that is factual. If someone says, "That movie is the best movie of the year," it is his or her opinion. Information written about actors frequently contains fabrications that are meant to stir up emotions. Slandering, or making false statements that can damage someone's reputation, can result in a lawsuit. Instead of spreading inaccurate information that can be harmful, be smart and check information for factual content.

Write Now

Write two paragraphs about a television or movie actor whose work you do not like. Write the first paragraph using factual information that you have gathered from reliable, credible sources. Ask the school librarian to approve the sources for your facts. Write a second paragraph and include only your opinion of the actor, but no misinformation or slander.

provide marketing benefits to a company and its products. The products can also sell for higher prices than similar items without the images or with unknown characters.

The NFL owns the rights to its brands and logos, including the NFL shield; the words "Super Bowl" and "Pro Bowl"; and all NFL team names, nicknames, colors, symbols, emblems, helmet designs and uniform designs. Only the manufacturers of a product, not the distributors, are considered for NFL licensing. The manufacturers must be able to generate enough sales to meet the minimum royalty fee of about $100,000 per year. Each year U.S. federal customs agents seize millions of dollars' worth of counterfeit NFL clothing and other merchandise.

Although licensing offers many advantages, there are some disadvantages. If an athlete or entertainer loses popularity or a sports team suffers a losing season, the licensee could lose money due to lower sales. If the licensee produces poor quality products, this could damage the reputation of the licensor. Also, by signing a licensing agreement, the licensor is relinquishing control of the marketing mix.

The Broadcast Flag Rule

Channel Management The United States Court of Appeals for the District of Columbia ruled against the Federal Communications Commission (FCC) in 2005, striking down the broadcast flag rule. Digital bits, called **broadcast flags**, can be embedded in digital programming to prevent programs from being recorded and redistributed. The overturned FCC rule required HDTV sets built after June 2005 to restrict viewers' ability to record broadcasts flagged by the program provider. Program providers wanted the rule, stating they were protecting programs from copyright infringement. The federal court ruled that the FCC could not regulate equipment, only communications. Every few years, major television networks renew their call to have the ruling reinstated and to add the use of broadcast flags into pending U.S. federal laws.

Why did U.S. Courts rule against broadcast flags that restrict TV recording and redistribution?

© iStockphoto.com/mgturner

Legal Listening

Channel Management In the United States, when music is played on the radio, the radio station is required to pay only the songwriter and publisher, not the performer of the recording. For many years, musicians have campaigned for a law that would require payment of royalties to performers. Royalties are paid to performers for online streams, but not radio plays. Clear Channel is an exception and is the first radio network to pay performers when their music plays on its airwaves and web streams.

The entertainment industry has a growing concern about new technology that makes it easy for consumers to make quality duplicates of audio and video performances. The Recording Industry Association of America

(RIAA) regards the Russian social networking site vKontakte as one of the worst sites in the world when it comes to unlicensed copyright works. Many such sites exist around the world. While the RIAA battles against illegal downloads, the technical revolution of the music industry continues. Fans' hunger for free content is, in some cases, starving the artists.

Prior to iTunes, the RIAA offered downloadable music with many restrictions. Limits included the number of times the music could be transferred to a CD and the number of days the CD could be used. The restrictions were so burdensome that few people bought the products and many continued to download music illegally. Consumer-oriented companies like Apple Computer forced the music industry to rethink its distribution channels and find ways to satisfy customers while protecting profits. RIAA has recognized the emergence of the streaming music model as a positive force for the industry. Paid subscription services are one of the fastest-growing digital formats. Streaming services contribute about 21 percent of the music industry's revenue.[6]

INTERMISSION

List some advantages and disadvantages of licensing.

ENCORE

Understand Marketing Concepts

Select the best answer for each question.

1. The legal issue of greatest concern to artists in the music industry is
    a. cartels
    b. copyright protection
    c. new laws regulating commerce
    d. broadcast flags

2. The main reason the National Football League (NFL) seizes and destroys counterfeit sportswear is because
    a. it does not sell well
    b. it is illegal merchandise
    c. it is low-quality merchandise
    d. the sizes and colors are wrong

Think Critically

Answer the following questions as completely as possible.

3. What roles do the governing bodies of sports play in keeping the games on a level playing field? (LO 13.1-1)

4. Explain reasons for copyright laws as they relate to the intellectual property of celebrities and musicians. Why is this protection needed? (LO 13.1-2)

13.2 Labor Unions

The Essential Question

How do labor relations affect the sports and entertainment industries?

Learning Objectives

LO 13.2-1 Investigate the role of labor unions in sports and entertainment.

LO 13.2-2 Describe the financial and public relations effects of strikes on sports and entertainment.

Key Terms

- labor union
- strike
- collective bargaining
- collective bargaining agreement
- salary cap
- lockout

OPENING ACT

The College Athletes Players Association (CAPA) petitioned the regional National Labor Relations Board (NLRB) to recognize Northwestern University football players as employees of the university. The regional NLRB ruled that the players were employees of the university who could form a union and bargain for benefits. The ruling was based on a number of things, including the fact that players spent as many as 50 hours per week on football—more time than they spent on their education. The NLRB concluded that the students were recruited for their athletic ability—not their academics—and players' scholarships can be revoked if they do not follow the rules. In order to form the union, a majority of the players who had signed the original petition had to vote to do so. The NLRB ruling would impact only private colleges and universities. State college and university employees are covered by state labor laws, not the NLRB.

As of this writing, Northwestern University appealed the regional ruling to the NLRB national office in Washington, D.C. If the regional ruling is upheld and Northwestern refuses to bargain with the union, the case could be sent to a federal appeals court, and possibly the U.S. Supreme Court.

Cooperative Learning With a group, discuss the current unionization status of college athletes. Can they legally form a labor union? How will this impact their relationships with universities?

LO 13.2-1 ORGANIZED LABOR

A **labor union** is an organization of workers formed to advance the rights and interests of its members. Both professional sports and the entertainment industries have members represented by unions. Since the early 1950s, athletes in major professional sports have organized themselves into labor unions called *players' associations*. Entertainers have multiple labor unions for different categories of workers, such as the Actors' Equity Association that represents live theatrical performers.

Players and Performers United

The television and movie industries are both highly unionized. Unions get their power from their members who agree to abide by the decisions of the group and to strike in support of those decisions if necessary. A **strike** is a work stoppage caused by the voluntary, temporary refusal of the employees to work. Strikes usually take place when negotiations between employees and employers have come to a dead-end. The right to strike is guaranteed in U.S. federal law. Bringing the workplace to a halt can cause economic damage to both the employees and employers.

Each sports team has a collective bargaining agreement with the players' association. **Collective bargaining** occurs when a group of employees join together as a single unit to negotiate with employers. In the late 1950s, the NFL Players Association (NFLPA) started with modest requests, such as a minimum $5,000 annual salary, $50 for each preseason game, an allowance for uniforms, equipment provided by the league, medical insurance, and an ongoing salary for injured players. Lawsuits were threatened before the owners reluctantly responded to each series of requests. Over the next 40 years, the NFLPA battled with the owners in and out of court and formally became a union representing the players.

Collective Bargaining Agreements

The players' associations and the entertainment industry unions negotiate an employment contract with the owners or management called a **collective bargaining agreement** (CBA). The CBA covers all players in the league or members of the union. It generally includes a minimum salary (and may include a maximum salary); working conditions; contract lengths; and rules under which teams, studios, or networks will operate. CBAs govern the employment relationships between the players and the leagues or the entertainment workers and the production companies.

Attorneys for the team owners usually negotiate with the associations' executive director or attorneys. Each side must know all of the laws that govern collective bargaining and have a strategy for the negotiations that will take place. The people who are selected to conduct the actual contract negotiations must be skilled communicators. Their goals are to avoid work stoppages and achieve the objectives they have outlined for the new contract.

Players usually want higher salaries, a higher percentage of the revenues from the games, and increased benefits for retired players. Owners want to limit their monetary commitment to protect the financial standing of their team. Salaries are a significant operating expense of sports teams. When salary demands exceed a team's ability to make a profit, the team must find other ways to finance the business, including raising the price of tickets. Ultimately, the increased costs are passed along to the fans.

Topping the Salary

Most professional sports leagues, with the exception of baseball, have salary caps. A **salary cap** is the maximum amount that a team can spend on players' salaries. The purpose of a salary cap is to help keep the teams competitive. Otherwise, the teams with the most money would attract the best players. Eventually, one team would dominate the sport. There would

The strike of the Writers Guild of America (WGA) in late 2007 caused substantial losses in employment, wages, retail sales, and personal income. The three-month strike paralyzed the entertainment industry, shutting down movie and television production. The major points of disagreement were centered around compensation to writers for media downloads and streaming of TV programs and feature films.

be no suspense about which team would win, and fans' interest would fade. Salary caps also protect the owners' profits.

Major League Soccer has a salary cap. However, some situations are allowed in which a player's salary does not count against the salary cap. To retain a key soccer player instead of losing him to a higher-paying team, the player can be designated as a "core player." Salaries of core players do not count against the cap.

INTERMISSION

How do players' salaries affect the finances of professional teams?

LO 13.2-2   LABOR RELATIONS

Labor and management must compromise if a business is to succeed. Employees and employers need each other. In both the sports and entertainment industries, pleasing fans is the number one consideration. Without fan support, neither of these industries would survive.

Big Money versus Big Players

Between contract negotiations, when the relationship between the owners and the players is going well, the sports commissioner and the head of the players' union often appear together at media events. They seem to be friendly and cooperative. But when negotiations fail, the conflict becomes public and everyone loses. Conflicts generally arise over the following:

- How the revenue will be split between the owners and the players
- How players' health and safety will be protected
- How retired players will be treated
- How new players will be selected and compensated

Who benefits when players and owners reach an agreement?

The average career of an NFL athlete is only 3.2 years. Major league football players generally do not make enough money in that time to support them financially for the rest of their lives. The players' associations attempt to assist with career transition programs and benefits, such as health care for former players.

The NFL Players Association and the league owners reached a ten-year collective bargaining agreement in July 2011. The agreement ended a 136-day **lockout**, a period of time during which the owners keep the players from using the team facilities and shut down league operations. For the players, the lockout meant there were no training camps, no visits to team doctors, no workouts in team facilities, and no communications with coaches. By reaching the agreement, the NFL avoided shortening or canceling the NFL season. The major components of the NFL collective bargaining agreement's revenue split are shown in the following table.

Revenue Component	Players' Percentage	Owners' Percentage
League media	55%	45%
Licensed products	45%	55%
Local club revenue	40%	60%
Total revenue	48.5% to 46.5%*	51.5% to 53.5%*

*Varies by year over ten years.

The agreement runs through the 2020 season and the 2021 draft. A ten-year agreement adds a layer of stability. Knowing the costs of the game for the ten-year period allows owners (and cities) to confidently invest in players, coaches, and stadiums.

Picking Up the Pieces

By avoiding a shortened or canceled sports season, both owners and players emerge as clear winners. When professional games do not take place, everyone loses. In addition to loss of earnings for the team and players, other damage includes loss of revenue for sponsors, advertisers, concession sellers, ushers, maintenance crews, and businesses and destinations surrounding the stadium or arena.

In 2012 the National Hockey League (NHL) season was shortened from 82 to 48 games. An entire NHL season was lost because of a player lockout in 2004. The 2011–12 NBA season was shortened from 82 to 66 games due to a lockout. The negative image that results when wealthy owners and players refuse to find common ground often angers fans.

Winning Back the Fans

Promotion When strikes or lockouts occur, players and owners hope that fans will forget the controversy surrounding the sport and return to the games once the strike ends. After shortened or lost seasons, both the league and the media work hard to bring back fans and sponsors by using special promotions and coverage. Sometimes the league gives away tickets and provides promotional prizes to increase attendance. After a long period of inactivity, the quality of play may suffer, causing fans' interest to sink even lower. In addition, some fans may have turned to other sports or types of entertainment during the strike. It could take a number of years for the game to regain its popularity.

Entertainment Labor

Celebrities do not always make huge amounts of money for starring in movies or plays. In the past, studios often employed actors under long-term, low-paying contracts. Lew Wasserman was a powerful agent in the early days of Hollywood who is credited with changing that system.

The Screen Actors Guild (SAG) and the American Federation of Television and Radio Artists (AFTRA) have collective bargaining agreements that regulate the levels of compensation, benefits, and working conditions for actors. SAG and AFTRA collectively bargain through a joint board. Members believe that they receive better compensation and working conditions because of the unions' power.

Stagehands in New York City are members of Local One of the International Alliance of Theatrical Stage Employees. Recently, they were earning an average of $310,000 per year. In some cases, they were earning more than the onstage talent. Local One has strength because of its members' hard-to-replace technical skills. However, Local One is viewed by some as driving up arts organizations' costs and ticket prices. Nonprofit groups, such as the New York Metropolitan Opera, depend on season ticket holders for revenue. Threats of canceled performances due to a strike can damage a group like the Opera. The Opera has a tight budget, which is dependent upon the revenue generated by performances. Recently, Carnegie Hall's season-opening orchestra concert was canceled by a Local One strike. Such actions by the union are not looked on favorably by fans.

INTERMISSION

How do strikes and lockouts financially affect the sports and entertainment industries?

ENCORE

Understand Marketing Concepts
Select the best answer for each question.

1. An NFL collective bargaining agreement defines how to
   a. split revenue between owners and players
   b. keep teams with big markets from dominating teams in smaller markets
   c. make soccer a strong competitor to football
   d. both a and b

2. The purpose of salary caps in sports is to
   a. protect owners' profits
   b. hold down players' salaries
   c. keep teams more competitive
   d. all of the above

Think Critically
Answer the following questions as completely as possible.

3. How are fans partly responsible for the high income of owners and players? Can players' salaries ever be reduced? Is there really a ceiling for players' salaries? Explain your answers in two paragraphs. (LO 13.2-1)

4. How can disputes between management and labor be settled? Do fans play a role in professional sports disputes? Explain. (LO 13.2-2)

13.3 Agents and Contracts

The Essential Question

What roles do agents, handlers, and advisers play in an athlete's personal and professional life?

Learning Objectives

LO 13.3-1   Identify the roles of athlete agents, handlers, and advisers.

LO 13.3-2   Describe contract law.

Key Terms

- agent
- handler
- adviser
- contract
- agent contract
- noncompete clause

In 2006 Vince Young was selected by the Tennessee Titans in the NFL draft. Although once called "in-Vince-able," by the end of 2010, he suffered from injuries and was released by the Titans. Over the next four seasons, he was hired and cut by four additional teams. Young was reported to have earned $34 million in salary and $30 million in endorsement deals. In 2012 Young filed lawsuits against lender Pro Player Funding LLC. He claimed that the company misled him into signing loan documents for $1.8 million at 20 percent interest. He also filed lawsuits against his former agent and financial adviser, accusing them of mishandling his money. In January 2014 Young filed for Chapter 11 bankruptcy.

Brandon Brooks, an offensive lineman for the Houston Texans, spent an off-season working as an intern at a bank. He plans to use pro football as a springboard to the rest of his life. He also entered into a Master's of Science in Finance program, taking a college class one night a week during the football season.

The NFL is doing its part to help players be more financially responsible. It holds the NFL Rookie Symposium each year. As part of the Total Wellness portion of this 2½-day event, NFL players are given guidance in setting and reaching financial goals.

Cooperative Learning   Work with a group and research the current status of Vince Young and Brandon Brooks. What could Vince Young have done differently to avoid his current circumstances? What are the ways Brandon Brooks is assuming responsibility for his own future?

LO 13.3-1   SHOW ME THE MONEY

An **agent** is the legal representative of an athlete or celebrity. The athlete or celebrity pays the agent to manage his or her career, including negotiating contracts with a team, filmmaker, or concert producer. An agent will also negotiate contracts for endorsement opportunities.

All but about 10 of the 50 U.S. states have adopted the Uniform Athlete Agents Act (UAAA) as a way to bring more uniformity to the laws that apply to agents who represent athletes. The intent of the UAAA is to protect student-athletes, as well as the universities, that are sometimes penalized for problems caused by unethical agents. It requires potential athlete agents to complete an application, pay fees, and sometimes pass an examination to practice as an agent. The exam covers an understanding of the rules and laws governing player-agent relations. The state issues a certificate of registration to the individual agents who comply with the law.

Legally Speaking

Most agents for big-name celebrities are either attorneys, accountants, or both. The complexity of contracts requires knowledge of laws as well as negotiation skills. The agent is paid a percentage of the celebrity's negotiated earnings. Agents can be credited—or blamed—for the high salaries of top celebrities and athletes.

With strategic help from a sports agency, a player's position in the professional team draft can be improved. An agent can place the player in contact with trainers and make sure the teams and the media receive the right message about the player. Being selected in the first rounds of the player draft can provide the player with bargaining power to increase his or her salary and bonuses. Quality agents have taken players who were not expected to be drafted and propelled them into first-round draft picks.

Athlete agents must be very careful to follow federal and state laws regarding the management of athletes. Additionally, they must follow NCAA and other college-level rules and regulations for athletes coming out of the college sports programs. Many states and most leagues require agents to be registered with the league. For example, all contract advisers to NFL players are fully regulated by the NFL Players Association (NFLPA) and cannot do business without NFLPA certification and approval.

Handlers

Young celebrities and many professional athletes are suddenly propelled into wealth and fame. Their coaches and trainers work with them to develop their talent, but many athletes and celebrities need help navigating their

© iStockphoto.com/mediaphotos

How can handlers help young professional athletes succeed?

When agents are negotiating endorsement deals for athletes, a clause or provision for social media interaction and posts about the endorsed product will be included. The more followers and social media activity of the athlete, the more money it will cost the company to contract for the athlete's service.

An effective agent will make sure the athlete is educated about the proper use of social media, such as what not to tweet or post online. When mistakes are made, they can spread quickly and uncontrollably because of the instant nature of social media. NFL team executives follow potential players on social media to determine if they will be a good fit for the team. Careless actions on social media are likely to translate to other poor choices while representing the team. Agents must be well versed in social media etiquette and management to provide the critical advice needed by high-profile clients.

Think Critically

What impacts can social media have on the financial success of an athlete? Why should both student and professional athletes avoid making blunders on social media sites?

personal lives. When they misbehave, they damage their own brand and potential future earnings. Most of them need the assistance of professionals if they are to avoid a life filled with financial and legal problems.

An athlete's image can affect the success of a sponsor's product. Many sponsors hire a **handler**, or someone who manages an athlete's life off the field. Handlers often serve as a parental figure. Some handlers are employed to act as a full-time mentor, companion, and off-court coach. Preventing problems is in the best financial and legal interests of both the athlete and the sponsors whose products the athlete is endorsing. Neither the sponsoring company nor the athlete can afford negative publicity.

Advisers

Few people would know the best way to manage their money if they suddenly won the Mega Millions lottery. Most athletes who step into a top draft position are in a similar situation. They need experienced financial advisers who have accounting and legal credentials that make them experts. In most cases, an **adviser** is a financial and business counselor, not a behavioral monitor. Agents refer players only to those financial advisers who are registered with the league and have completed training provided by the league.

Athletes' professional careers can be relatively short-lived, so their high, short-term earnings must be invested wisely for the future. Under the guidance of Nike's Howard White, Michael Jordan became the nation's richest athlete and spokesperson. White is credited with the long-standing partnership between Jordan and Nike, which started in 1984 and continues today. Advisers who act in this capacity work to keep the athlete and sponsor together for the benefit of both.

INTERMISSION

What are some of the responsibilities of a sports agent?

LO 13.3-2 LEGAL AGREEMENTS

When celebrities and athletes agree to perform, they expect to be paid and receive other benefits. Most athletes and celebrities do not have experience negotiating and dealing with the legalities involved in contracts, so they rely on their agents to determine what should be put in writing.

Contracts That Bind

A **contract** is an agreement enforceable by law that details the transactions of business between two or more people. It is best to put contracts in writing. Anyone involved in the marketing of sports or entertainment must become familiar with contract law. A contract should be worded to avoid multiple interpretations. Examples of contracts in sports and entertainment are player/performer contracts, sponsorships, broadcast rights, concessions/vendor agreements, and facilities contracts. An **agent contract** is an agreement in which an athlete or celebrity allows a person or agency to act as a representative in marketing his or her ability and name.

In many states, a written contract between an agent and a student-athlete hoping to enter professional sports must state the fees and percentages to be paid to the agent. Now that the five largest NCAA football conferences have been granted self-governance rights, the interaction between college athletes and agents will change. Players will be permitted to have more contact with agents, who can offer them professional advice.

TAKE A BOW *Kristen Kuliga*

Kristen Kuliga was one of the first women to represent NFL players as an agent. As the Principal and founder of K Sports & Entertainment, she is considered the leading female sports agent in the United States. Kuliga was the first woman to negotiate a starting NFL quarterback's contract, obtaining a $33 million, six-year contract for Doug Flutie with the San Diego Chargers in 2001.

After graduating from the University of Massachusetts at Amherst, she earned a degree at the Suffolk University Law School. Before founding her own company, she worked as a general counsel for Altus Marketing & Management LLC, where she handled the Events and Athletes divisions. Out of about 1,000 NFL agents, Kuliga is one of only about 30 women certified by the NFL Players Association as a contract adviser. She now handles contracts for a number of NFL players and has negotiated endorsement contracts with Nike, ESPN, and others.

Think Critically

Why is it harder for women to succeed in male-dominated businesses? Why do you think Kristen Kuliga has been successful?

Contracts are enforceable by law when they involve a promise in exchange for something of value. For example, salaries are paid to professional athletes in exchange for the promise that they will play for the team. Promising someone a gift is not a contract, since nothing of value is received in return. The law firm of Steinberg & Moorad, made famous in the movie *Jerry Maguire*, at one point had a third partner named David Dunn. The partners had a contract with each other that included a non-compete clause. A **noncompete clause** is a provision in a contract that prohibits a person from working in a competing business for a specific period of time. Two years after signing a five-year contract, Dunn left the firm and opened Athletes First, taking 50 NFL clients with him. Steinberg and Moorad successfully sued Dunn for violating the noncompete terms of the contract and were awarded $44.66 million in damages.

INTERMISSION

Whom do contracts protect?

ENCORE

Understand Marketing Concepts
Select the best answer for each question.

1. An agent for a professional athlete serves the role of
   a. legal representative
   b. companion
   c. trainer
   d. supervisor

2. A contract
   a. should be in writing
   b. details the agreement between two or more parties
   c. is enforceable by law
   d. all of the above

Think Critically
Answer the following questions as completely as possible.

3. Think about athletes who are financially successful after their sports careers have ended. Then think about athletes who end up in financial trouble after having made millions of dollars. Describe reasons for the different outcomes. (LO 12.3-1)

4. Why are most athlete agents also lawyers? Why are knowledge of law and negotiation skills both important for this job? (LO 13.3-2)

CHAPTER ASSESSMENT

Review Marketing Terms

Match the terms listed with the definitions.

1. The legal representative of an athlete or celebrity
2. Legally protects the unique work of the originator from use by others without permission
3. Maximum amount that a team can spend on players' salaries
4. An employment contract negotiated between a labor union and owners/management
5. Payment for the use of copyrighted work
6. An agreement enforceable by law that details the transactions of business between two or more people
7. Occurs when a group of employees join together as a single unit to negotiate with employers
8. The unique works of writers, artists, and musicians that are protected under copyright law
9. An agreement in which an athlete allows a person or agency to represent the athlete in marketing his or her ability and name
10. Someone who manages an athlete's life off the field
11. A work stoppage caused by the voluntary, temporary refusal of the employees to work
12. The recording of a television show for private viewing later
13. Allows limited creative use of music, literature, movies, and more without asking permission or making payment
14. The realm in which a work can be used by anyone without cost or permission
15. A financial and business counselor
16. Digital bits embedded in digital programming to prevent programs from being recorded and redistributed
17. A period of time during which the owners keep players from using the team facilities and shut down league operations
18. A provision in a contract that prohibits a person from working in a competing business for a specific period of time
19. A humorous imitation of an original work
20. An organization of workers formed to advance the rights and interests of its members
21. A property right that excludes others from making, using, offering for sale, or selling an invention

a. adviser
b. agent
c. agent contract
d. broadcast flags
e. collective bargaining
f. collective bargaining agreement
g. contract
h. copyright
i. fair use
j. handler
k. intellectual property
l. labor union
m. lockout
n. noncompete clause
o. parody
p. patent
q. public domain
r. royalty
s. salary cap
t. strike
u. time-shifting

Review Marketing Concepts

Select the best answer for each of the following questions.

22. A lockout means that players cannot
    a. use team facilities
    b. go to team doctors
    c. communicate with coaches
    d. do any of the above

23. A players' union
    a. has collective bargaining rights
    b. is an illegal cartel
    c. negotiates based on what is best for the fans
    d. does not negotiate with the league's owners

24. Which of the following is an example of collective bargaining?
    a. owners decide what to pay players
    b. salaries are set by agreement between players and owners
    c. agents negotiate with big name players
    d. an actor demands high pay

25. Items may be copyrighted for the lifetime of the artist plus _____ years.
    a. 50
    b. 60
    c. 70
    d. 80

Think Critically

26. What is your opinion of the statement, "Success in business requires a partnership between labor and management"? What does the statement mean? Is it a true statement? Why or why not? (LO 13.2-2)

27. If you were advising a young athlete who has just signed with a professional team for a multiyear, multimillion-dollar contract, what would your advice include? How can the athlete maximize his athletic skill and health, manage his personal life, and turn his financial assets into long-lasting financial security? (LO 13.3-1)

28. What personal characteristics, knowledge, education, and skills should an athlete want in an agent? (LO 13.3-1)

29. Many people have negative opinions of labor unions. They believe that they drive up the costs of the product, whether it is a car or a football game. Make a list of the positive things the players' associations have accomplished for professional athletes. (LO 13.2-1)

30. Research the requirements of contract law in your state. Summarize the elements that must be included in a contract to make it legally enforceable. (LO 13.3-2)

31. Governing bodies for sports face a tough job in setting rules for the sport, protecting the athletes, promoting the sport, pleasing the owners or members of the association, and keeping the interest of the fans. Sometimes all of the different groups come into conflict. The athletes may need protection from dangerous situations, such as blows to the head, but steps to change the game may lessen the excitement for fans. Write a paragraph explaining what you believe should be the priorities of sports governing bodies and why. (LO 13.1-1)

32. Salary caps are agreed on by a sports league. A wealthy team owner wants to hire the best players and pay them more than other teams can pay. Why would league rules prevent the owner from doing this? Whom do the rules benefit and why? (LO 13.2-1)

Make Academic Connections

33. **Social Studies** Organized labor had success in the early part of the twentieth century in improving salaries and working conditions for employees. Since that time, the power and effectiveness of U.S. unions have gone up and down. Are sports and entertainment unions different from other labor unions? Why are they so strong when other unions seem to be in decline? (LO 13.2-1)

34. **Problem Solving** Write a promotional plan for a sports team to use in the first two weeks after a lengthy strike or lockout in which many games were canceled. Include ideas for advertising, publicity, sales promotion, and personal selling. Your plan has two goals: Bring back angry fans and increase the number of new fans. (LO 13.2-2)

35. **Government** Use the Internet or other sources to determine the current status of the broadcast flag rule. Is there current or pending legislation that would limit the rights of viewers to record television broadcasts for their personal use? Write a paragraph about the current status. Then write another paragraph that includes your opinion of the use of broadcast flags. (LO 13.1-2)

36. **Business Law** Use the Internet to research the purpose of contracts. Write a two-page summary about the types of contracts related to sports and entertainment. Be sure to cite your sources. (LO 13.3-2)

37. **Technology** The Internet has made it easier for people to make illegal copies of music and movies. Research legal alternatives that will give you access to music and movies online. Create a chart called "The Top Five Legal Ways to Get Music and Movies on the Internet." Criteria may include price, selection, and user-friendliness of the website. (LO 13.1-2)

38. **Marketing Math** A stadium has 8,000 "cheap seats" that sell for $8 each per game. The team would like to raise the price to $10 each but isn't sure that fans would be willing to pay the higher price. It has decided to look for other sources of revenue. How much money does the team need to earn from other sources to make up for the loss of selling tickets at $8 versus $10? For example, how many jerseys would it need to sell per game if it increased the profit earned on each jersey from $2.50 to $5.00? Suggest three other ways to increase revenues. (LO 13.2-2)

EXTRA INNINGS PROJECT

Major League Baseball fans, owners, and players all have a strong opinion regarding the need for salary caps. Some think a salary cap would improve the game. Others think it would destroy baseball. Another group thinks it would just bog the game down with rules and deadlines. Currently the wealthiest teams are able to offer the highest salaries to the best players, leaving other teams unable to match the top salaries. If one teams always wins, fans might lose interest. Two major reasons to consider a salary cap are to improve competition and to improve the profits for owners by holding down the cost of labor.

A salary cap can be a hard cap or a soft cap. A hard cap is an amount that cannot be exceeded for any reason. A soft cap generally means there are reasons that the amount can be exceeded. The National Football League has a salary floor that is the minimum amount that teams can spend on salaries. Major League Baseball has a luxury tax cap based on an amount determined each year to be the maximum payroll for a team. An MLB team that exceeds the cap pays a penalty (22.5 to 50 percent) on the excess amount. The MLB cap limit for 2015 to 2016 is $189 million. Five teams paid the luxury tax between 2003 and 2013. The New York Yankees have paid the luxury tax each of those years.

You have been hired by Major League Baseball (MLB) to research the pros and cons of adding a salary cap to MLB teams. Your salary is being paid by both the league and the players' association, so you are open to listening to both sides. You are being asked to decide whether or not a salary cap should be implemented and to defend your decision.

Using the Internet, work with a group and complete the following activities.

1. What is the history behind the lack of a salary cap in MLB? Does the MLB have a problem with the competitive balance between teams? Are owners having a problem making a profit?
2. Why do other sports leagues have salary caps?
3. Which MLB teams would be affected the most by implementation of a salary cap? How would they be affected?
4. How would salary caps affect individual players? How might the decision affect fans? Is there a relationship between players' salaries and ticket prices?
5. Choose a position on the issue of salary caps and defend your position to the class.

Do You Have Rights to Your Avatar?

The NCAA has all student-athletes sign a variety of forms each year. Form 05-3a states the following: "You authorize the NCAA [or third party acting on behalf of the NCAA (e.g., host institution, conference, or local organizing committee)] to use your name or picture to generally promote NCAA championships or other NCAA events, activities, or programs."

The NCAA licensed the rights to create video football game avatars to Electronic Arts (EA) Sports and Collegiate Licensing Company (CLC). Ed O'Bannon, who played basketball for a University of California, Los Angeles (UCLA) Bruins championship team, filed an antitrust lawsuit against the NCAA, EA, and CLC. O'Bannon's UCLA jersey number and physical attributes were very apparent in the video game. EA and CLC settled out of court, agreeing to a $40 million settlement for using the images of former athletes in the video games. EA, whose last published game in the series was NCAA Football 14, stopped producing a college football video game with NCAA player likenesses. O'Bannon and others believe that the NCAA benefited by licensing rights to athletes' images years after they had left the NCAA team, generating hundreds of millions of dollars for the NCAA and the universities.

O'Bannon wanted to find a way to provide more compensation for student-athletes. In addition to receiving their university education, he believed college athletes should be paid for playing. The NCAA stopped selling individual player jerseys online after being criticized for not allowing players to sell their jerseys or autographs. The NCAA used the concept of amateurism as its defense, while at the same time turning collegiate sports into big business.

The conflict between the NCAA and amateur athletes is made more difficult by the limited number of college sports teams that are actually profitable. According to data compiled by *USA TODAY Sports*, only about "23 of 228 athletics departments at NCAA Division I public schools generate enough money on their own to cover their expenses."[7]

Revenues are generated from media rights contracts, ticket sales, and donations.

Think Critically

1. Why would current or former college athletes object to the use of their likenesses in a video game?
2. What will likely happen to the price of game tickets if colleges have to share the revenue with players?
3. Do you think there is a need for NCAA's Form 05-3a? Why or why not?
4. Besides giving college athletes partial scholarships or paying them as employees, what are some other alternative ways to operate student-athlete programs?

EXTEMPORANEOUS SPEECH EVENT

The best public speakers are capable of producing an interesting speech in a limited amount of time. Frequently, these individuals are called on to speak at business and social events without much time to prepare their presentations. The extemporaneous speech event requires participants to arrange, organize, and effectively present information without prior knowledge of the selected topic.

You will draw two different sports and entertainment marketing topics from which you will select one topic for the development of an extemporaneous speech. Possible topics include:

- Ethics in Sports
- Safety Issues at Large Sports and Entertainment Events
- Elements for a Successful Concert
- Paying College Athletes
- Attracting the Olympics to a Major City
- Performance-Enhancing Drugs
- The Cost of Winning
- The Role of Good Sports Agents

You will have ten minutes to develop your topic. You will be allowed to write notes on cards provided by the event coordinator, but no other materials or previously prepared notes will be allowed into the preparation or presentation room with you. You will not be allowed to communicate with your teacher/adviser during the ten-minute preparation time.

The length of the speech should be no less than three minutes and no more than five minutes. You will speak before a panel of judges and a timekeeper. No audience will be allowed to observe the speech. Flashcards will be used to make contestants aware when there are two minutes remaining and when there is one minute remaining during the speaking time.

Performance Indicators Evaluated
- Demonstrate effective communication skills.
- Demonstrate skills in developing a speech that includes an introduction, body, and conclusion.
- Use appropriate tempo and pitch.
- Utilize nonverbal gestures as appropriate.
- Achieve the purpose of the speech.

Think Critically

1. Why is extemporaneous speaking a valuable skill in the business world?
2. Why are issues related to amateur, college, and professional sports also business issues?
3. Why is the introduction to the speech important?
4. Why should the conclusion of the speech be related to the introduction?

www.bpa.org

14 BUSINESS OWNERSHIP AND LEADERSHIP

© Ikonoklast Fotografie/Shutterstock.com

POINT YOUR BROWSER

ngl.cengage.com/sports4e

Winning Strategies

From Yellow Pages to Facebook

Katherine Cheng-Arif was a college-educated housewife who wanted the challenge of operating her own business. She and her husband, Rahyab Arif, created Houston Event Planning (HEP), a full-service event planning company. In 2007 they designed and built Signature Manor.

Image courtesy of Katherine Cheng-Arif

Signature Manor is an event venue with ballroom space that can serve up to 1,200 people. Signature Manor provides the perfect setting for weddings, anniversaries, corporate events, and birthday parties. Katherine has the creative ability to make the client's dream event come true.

In 2003, before social media, Houston Event Planning relied on the *Yellow Pages* and word of mouth as its primary marketing tools. The bigger the ad in the *Yellow Pages*, the more attention it received. Today, at the height of the social media and search engine optimization (SEO) boom, a well-designed website that is easy to navigate plays an important role in the success of HEP. In addition, Katherine uses Facebook to find target markets for her company. Key search words that she uses on Facebook include "engaged" and "married" for those in the 24 to 36 age group. She also uses Twitter to search for tweets about weddings and engagements.

Katherine's business received a big boost when the YouTube video "Greatest Father Daughter Dance Medley Ever," which was one of HEP's events, went viral after it aired on NBC's *Today Show*.

Katherine attributes her success as an event planner to using social media, following digital marketing trends, and providing excellent service that customers want. The Better Business Bureau named Houston Event Planning the "Winner of Distinction" for 2011.

Think Critically

1. Why should companies keep up to date with the latest technology trends?

2. How have technology and social media made it easier for businesses to locate prospective target markets?

14.1 Entrepreneurship

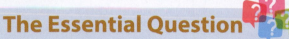

The Essential Question

Why is a business plan important to the success of entrepreneurs?

Learning Objectives

LO 14.1-1 Define entrepreneur and describe characteristics of successful entrepreneurs.

LO 14.1-2 List and describe the key elements of a business plan.

Key Terms

- entrepreneurs
- business plan
- sole proprietorship
- partnership
- corporation

OPENING ACT

According to a study by the Small Business Administration, many startup companies fail within the first five years of operation. Some of the top reasons for failure are: starting a business for the wrong reason, poor management skills, and insufficient capital. Other reasons include lack of planning, over-expansion, a bad location, and little or no web presence. Business owners who overcome these obstacles, however, find entrepreneurship very rewarding in the long run.

Cooperative Learning With a partner, discuss what entrepreneurs can do to avoid failure of a new business within the first five years of operation.

LO 14.1-1 THE IMPORTANCE OF ENTREPRENEURS

Entrepreneurs are individuals who take the risk of starting, owning, and operating a business. These ambitious individuals identify unmet consumer needs and wants in the marketplace and supply products and services in hopes of making a profit. Individuals become entrepreneurs for different reasons. Most entrepreneurs start their own business to pursue a personal dream. Some people choose to leave the fast-paced corporate environment to become their own boss. Working in a corporate setting provides individuals with valuable information about consumer demand and opportunities for new products and services. Every ambitious entrepreneur believes that he or she has a profitable idea.

Impact of Entrepreneurs

There are many opportunities for small businesses in the sports and entertainment industries. Sports and entertainment venues will frequently subcontract jobs to entrepreneurs who specialize in marketing, sales, promotions, security, maintenance, concessions, and so forth.

Many people believe that powerful corporations employ the majority of the U.S. working force. However, over 70 percent of all U.S. businesses are owned and operated by sole owners. The Small Business Administration defines a small business as an enterprise having fewer than 500 employees. More than 28 million small businesses contribute billions of dollars every year to the U.S. economy. Over 22 million small business owners are self-employed with no additional payroll or employees.

Why are small businesses, such as companies that provide maintenance services, important to the U.S. economy?

These businesses are referred to as *nonemployers*. More than 50 percent of the working population (over 150 million people) are employed by a small business. Small businesses have generated over 65 percent of the new jobs over the past 20 years and employ more workers than all of the country's large corporations combined.[1]

Many large corporations started as small entrepreneurial ventures. Nike was started by Philip Knight and Bill Bowerman as a small business. Riddell also started as a small company before it became a major athletic equipment manufacturer. The movie industry has advanced from motion pictures shown in theaters and drive-ins to digital formats viewed on computers, i-Pads, and other mobile devices. Each new phase started as a small entrepreneurial venture that grew rapidly.

What It Takes to Be an Entrepreneur

Entrepreneurs are independent, self-confident individuals who possess the determination and commitment necessary for success. They are goal-oriented people who set high standards for themselves and their businesses. Frequently, entrepreneurs are called upon to think and act quickly—timing is important when making business decisions. Entrepreneurs must be willing to work long hours—most new business owners work up to 70 hours each week. In addition, entrepreneurs must be good communicators who can express their thoughts to a variety of people, including investors, suppliers, and customers.

Goal Setting   Entrepreneurs must set both financial and nonfinancial goals to measure the success of their business. They must have strong money management skills or at least have help and advice from those who do. Financial goals set by entrepreneurs must be realistic. Some entrepreneurs get caught up in the excitement of a great idea for a new product or service. They overestimate projected revenues while failing to fully account for expenses, resulting in unrealistic financial projections. It usually takes up to three years for new businesses to begin showing a profit. Entrepreneurs must plan for those first few lean years and save money to survive until they start making a profit. Initially, nonfinancial goals may be easier to achieve than financial goals. Nonfinancial goals may include ways to achieve personal satisfaction or serve a community need.

Communication Skills   Successful entrepreneurs must have effective communication skills. Business communications must be accurate, positive, and persuasive. The language used should be clear and concise.

Much business communication takes place over the telephone. When communicating by phone, individuals should speak clearly in a cheerful and polite tone. Two successful strategies include making notes beforehand about topics to be covered and taking notes during the conversation.

Written communication is also common, whether it be by letter, email, or social media. When writing a business letter, there can be no errors. Although emails may not be as formal as business letters, they require careful preparation and should be proofread for errors. Email messages should be brief because long emails often go unread.

Entrepreneurs will also have important meetings with customers, lenders, investors, and suppliers. "You only get one chance to make a positive first impression." This is a common saying that applies in business. Good rules for a successful meeting include speaking clearly, not appearing rushed or anxious to be somewhere else, listening, and taking good notes. Listening is a fine art that most people need to improve. Focusing attention on what the other person is saying allows you to gain a better understanding of the situation. Good listening includes asking questions to clarify what you have heard.

INTERMISSION

List five characteristics and skills required to be a successful entrepreneur.

LO 14.1-2   THE BUSINESS PLAN

Statistics show that over half of new businesses fail within the first five years due to lack of research and inadequate financial resources. To avoid these pitfalls, entrepreneurs should prepare a business plan. A **business plan** is a formal, written document that provides the details for a proposed new business. The business plan establishes a framework for the business and serves as a tool for managing it in the short and long term.

The business plan also serves as a tool for securing financing from lenders and investors. *Stakeholders* in a business, including investors, lenders, and suppliers, want to know that the entrepreneur has done his or her homework to develop a solid plan for running a successful business.

Even the best-laid plans have to be changed sometimes. The business plan may require adjustments for various reasons, such as changing economic conditions and consumer preferences.

There are many opportunities for those wanting to start their own business. In a recent year, popular small business startups included computer technology companies, beauty/nail salons, auto repair shops, dry cleaners, and landscaping services.

Key Elements of the Business Plan

The key elements of the business plan are the executive summary, business description, marketing plan, business structure and operations, financial forecast, and schedule, which are discussed below.

Introductory Elements

The most successful business plans begin with a well-written *executive summary*. The executive summary briefly describes the entrepreneur's business idea. It should spark the interest of prospective stakeholders. Most investors will decide whether it is worthwhile to read the rest of the business plan based on what they read in the executive summary. The executive summary is followed by the *business description*. This includes the history and background of the business idea, short- and long-term goals for the business, and the products and services that will be offered by the business. Stakeholders particularly want to know what makes the new business's product offerings unique.

The Marketing Plan

Another important part of the business plan is the *marketing plan*. It addresses the seven core marketing standards and financing. Market research provides a description of the target market, the market size, an analysis of the competition, and estimated market share. Planned marketing strategies and pricing strategies are also outlined. Promotional strategies describe the promotional mix (advertising, sales promotion, publicity, and personal selling) to be used by the business.

Structure and Operations

The *business structure* must be specified in the business plan. Will it be a **sole proprietorship**, which is owned and operated by one person? Or, will it be a **partnership**, where two or more individuals sign an agreement to own and operate a business together? A partnership agreement states who is responsible for each aspect of the business and how profits and losses will be split. A **corporation** is a form of business in which ownership is represented by shares of stock. In corporations, the owners (also called *stockholders*) may or may not be directly involved in the business's day-to-day operations. Company officers, who are elected by a board of directors, run the business.

JUDGMENT CALL

Businesses face risks every day. The "baseball rule" is a legal standard that protects teams from being sued over fan injuries caused by events on the baseball field, court, or rink. A fan attending a Kansas City Royals game was struck in the eye by a hot dog thrown by Sluggerrr, the mascot for the team. The fan had two surgeries after suffering a detached retina. He sued the Royals for damages. The court's initial ruling, which favored the Royals, stated that spectators are subject to unavoidable risk during games. The ruling has been appealed, and now the Missouri Supreme Court must decide whether the "baseball rule" comes into play in this situation.

Think Critically

Because businesses face risk, many business owners address it in the business plan. Assume you are a judge on the Missouri Supreme Court, how would you rule in this situation? Explain why.

The business plan should also describe *operations management*. Human resources are a business's most valuable asset. To show that the business will be run by competent people, the business plan should include descriptions of the roles of key managers and staff members along with their backgrounds and experiences.

Forecast and Schedule   Prospective stakeholders will also want to see a *financial forecast*. This section of the business plan shows current and projected financial statements. It is important to show that all business expenses have been anticipated and that projected revenues are realistic.

Finally, the business plan must include a *schedule* that sets specific milestones and deadlines for the business to meet. Evaluation periods should also be planned to help determine whether objectives are being met and whether adjustments need to be made to the business plan.

INTERMISSION

List seven key elements of a good business plan and explain why each is important.

ENCORE

Understand Marketing Concepts

Select the best answer for each question.

1. The executive summary of the business plan
   a. is usually the last element of the business plan
   b. must grab a prospective stakeholder's interest
   c. briefly describes the entrepreneur's ideas
   d. both b and c

2. Over half of new businesses fail
   a. within five years
   b. because of a lack of research
   c. because of inadequate financial resources
   d. all of the above

Think Critically

Answer the following questions as completely as possible.

3. What is the advantage of working for another company before becoming an entrepreneur? (LO 14.1-1)

4. Write a paragraph that describes five characteristics you possess that would help you to be a successful entrepreneur. (LO 14.1-1)

5. You are proposing to build a drive-in movie theater in your community. Provide brief examples of what you will include in each section of your business plan. (LO 14.1-2)

14.2 Managing Human Resources

The Essential Question

How do the four functions of a human resources department help attract and retain good employees?

Learning Objectives

LO 14.2-1   Explain the need for human resources.

LO 14.2-2   List and describe the four functions of human resources departments.

Key Terms

- human resources
- job analysis
- probationary period
- salary
- fringe benefits
- cafeteria plan

OPENING ACT

Each year, *Fortune* magazine releases its list of "100 Best Companies to Work For." Companies that consistently make the list have excellent human resources practices. Qualities important to employees include a healthy workplace, performance-linked bonuses, a fair evaluation system, and opportunities for open discussion and feedback. Google has received the top ranking four times because of the employee benefits it provides. Google employees enjoy free food, onsite recreational activities, profit sharing, and comprehensive health care, including onsite wellness centers. In a recent year, Google provided employees with 100,000 hours of free massages.

Cooperative Learning   Working in groups, make a list of unique benefits a company can offer its employees to help it receive top ranking as an employer.

LO 14.2-1   THE IMPORTANCE OF HUMAN RESOURCES MANAGEMENT

Human resources (HR) are the employees who work for an organization. Sports and entertainment businesses cannot function without people. The success of any business is based on the competence and professionalism of its employees. The management of human resources is one of the most important responsibilities within an organization. Medium- to large-size businesses normally have a human resources department. The human resources department may have a manager and other staff to carry out human resources duties. Owners of small businesses usually manage human resources without a separate specialized department.

The Society for Human Resource Management has reported that employers are increasingly relying on social networking sites to recruit employees. LinkedIn is the most popular tool for employers, while Facebook is the second most popular social media recruitment tool.

While enthusiasm is high for using social media as a recruitment tool, employers are hesitant about using it as a screening device. Human resource managers are concerned that the use of social media to recruit employees will expose their organizations to lawsuits.

Job applicants may accuse potential employers of discrimination based on information gathered from social media sites that employers should not have when making hiring decisions, such as a person's race, ethnicity, age, or disability status.

Think Critically

How has social media provided human resource directors with more tools for recruiting employees? Why should applicants be concerned about discrimination when social media is used in hiring decisions?

Attracting and Keeping the Best

Human resources departments hire employees to fulfill all of the employee positions within a company. The job market in the sports and entertainment industry is highly competitive, with many applicants applying for each opening. Individuals who desire to work in these fields often must start out by learning and working in unpaid internships. Positions generally require ambitious individuals who are willing to work nights and weekends. Each applicant is unique with different talents, knowledge, skills, and motivations. It is the function of the human resources department to match the right person to the job. Responsibilities of the HR department include the following:

- Identify employee needs of the organization
- Attract and maintain an adequate supply of employees to fill needs
- Match abilities and interests with specific jobs
- Provide training and development to prepare employees for their jobs and improve their skills as jobs change
- Develop plans to compensate employees for their work
- Protect the health and well-being of employees
- Maintain a satisfying work environment

INTERMISSION

Why is the human resources department so important for an organization?

LO 14.2-2 FOUR FUNCTIONS OF HUMAN RESOURCES DEPARTMENTS

An athletic department at a major university may have an athletic director who earns more than $1 million per year, a successful football coach earning more than $5 million per year, a basketball coach earning more than $2 million per year, and other coaches whose salaries total $10 million per year. The organization also has managers for ticket sales, finance, promotion, recruitment, facilities, equipment, and other aspects of the sports industry. Companies that book and organize concerts hire individuals to manage contracts, bookings, ticket sales, facilities, security, and all other details to ensure the event is successful. It is the responsibility of the human resources department to help find, keep, and manage the right people serving in all of these positions.

The responsibilities of human resources departments can be divided into four major functions: planning and staffing, performance management, compensation and benefits, and employee relations.

Planning and Staffing

The planning process involves examining the company's current and future personnel needs and performing job analysis. **Job analysis** is the study of a specific job to identify the duties and skill requirements of the job. Once companies determine personnel needs, the recruitment process begins. Job placement involves locating candidates who have the identified skills necessary for the job, narrowing down the choices, and hiring the best candidates. Job candidates may be found through college placement offices, by networking with professionals at other organizations in the industry, through postings on Internet career sites and social media sites, and by placing job ads in major news publications. For some positions, candidates are first required to participate in unpaid internships to show their level of interest and skills. The pool of individuals working as interns then serves as the source for finding the best candidates for open paid positions.

Permanent, Part-Time, Temporary, or Outsourced? Part of job analysis is determining whether the position needs to be permanent, part-time, temporary, or outsourced.

There are many Americans over the age of 65 who want to continue working, yet less than 20 percent are currently employed. It takes individuals who are 55 and older several months longer than their younger peers to find a job. Employers are hiring younger workers who they think are more tech and digitally savvy.[2]

What positions at sporting events may be filled by temporary employees?

© Martin Smith/Shutterstock.com

Permanent employees are hired as long-term employees with no pre-determined time limit. These individuals are expected to provide long-term satisfactory performance. In a sports organization, ticket managers, athletic directors, facility directors, and coaches are all permanent employees who are expected to perform at high levels. The performance of coaches is based upon winning records, which makes their employment more unstable than other permanent employees. Universities and professional sports teams are known to fire coaches who do not meet winning expectations. Some coaches' contracts are bought out in order to hire a new coach.

Part-time workers may be in permanent ongoing jobs, but they work less than 30 hours per week. *Temporary employees* may be hired for a short time to complete a specific task. For example, temporary employees are hired to set up and tear down tents and bleachers for entertainment events. Individuals who take tickets at college football games, parking lot attendants, and workers at a three-week rodeo are other examples of temporary employees.

Part of planning is determining which jobs may best be *outsourced*, or subcontracted, to other businesses that will provide the service. A company may use outsourcing instead of hiring full-time, part-time, or temporary employees to do the job. Jobs that need to be performed for only a limited time and that may be handled more efficiently by a business with expertise in a particular field or function may fall into this category.

What is the purpose of a resume?

The Application Process   Individuals who are qualified and interested in applying for sports and entertainment positions must have a professional *resume* that lists their qualifications and experience. An *application letter* (or *cover letter*) should accompany the resume. It is the first document read by the human resources department or hiring manager. The letter should describe how the job candidate can meet the employer's needs. Prospective employers will eliminate resumes and letters of application that are poorly written and have errors. From a large pool of applications, a few individuals will be chosen as the most promising candidates and invited for interviews. The most qualified candidate will be offered the job. While the human resources department helps find and screen candidates, department managers and supervisors may make the final hiring decision. The human resources department must ensure that all federal equal opportunity employment laws are followed throughout the application process.

Performance Management

After employees are hired, the human resources department is in charge of arranging training for them. Frequently, new employees are paired with experienced workers to learn about the organization and their personal responsibilities. Some new employees have a **probationary period**, or a test period of a few months to determine whether they can fulfill the needs of the organization. Employees who do not meet company expectations during the probationary period will not be offered permanent employment.

Performance evaluations are used by organizations to determine whether employees meet quality and quantity standards and whether they are completing their work efficiently. Evaluations may come from supervisors and coworkers, but the human resources department works to ensure that performance reviews take place and that all employees are evaluated fairly using the same process and standards.

Compensation and Benefits

Various compensation plans are available for employees. The human resources department is responsible for researching compensation plans offered by other organizations in the industry and recommending competitive packages to help attract and keep quality employees.

A **salary** is a specified amount paid annually for a job regardless of the number of hours worked. Salaries are usually offered to executives, managers, and others in professional positions. Other employees work for an hourly wage. Part-time workers are usually paid an hourly wage and are not eligible for employee benefits. Employers invest less money in part-time workers, making them an attractive option to meet labor needs. Hourly wage earners who work beyond 40 hours in a workweek are required by law to be given overtime pay of 1.5 times their normal hourly wage. Other types of employee compensation plans are described below.

Commission	Employees are paid a percentage of their sales
Piecework pay	Employees are compensated for each unit produced or action performed
Incentive pay	Employees are compensated based on the quantity and quality of work completed
Base-plus-incentive pay	Employees receive a combination of a salary plus bonus or commission for achieving beyond an established level of productivity
Profit sharing	Employees are rewarded with a portion of the company's profits

Full-time employees usually receive some type of benefits. **Fringe benefits** are extra incentives to employees beyond salary and wages. They may include health and dental insurance, eye care, life insurance, paid vacations, paid sick time, retirement savings plans, profit-sharing plans, and employee discounts. Some companies offer a **cafeteria plan**, which is a benefit plan whereby employees pick and choose from various benefit options to best meet their needs. Fringe benefits, on average, add a value of between 20 and 40 percent of employees' salaries or wages, making them an important consideration for job seekers.

The *Affordable Health Care Act* requires employers with more than 50 employees to provide health insurance for all employees. Currently,

96 percent of U.S. businesses have fewer than 50 employees. Businesses that opt out of paying health insurance for employees must pay a penalty to the federal government based on the number of employees. Businesses have to make calculated financial decisions about providing health insurance.

Employee Relations

The human resources department has certain responsibilities to the employees of the company. It must provide a workplace orientation to new employees. This involves explaining company rules and policies. If conflict arises between employees or with supervisors, the human resources department should help resolve the problem fairly. Finally, the human resources department must look out for the best interests of the employees by making sure that fair employment practices are followed, discrimination is not tolerated, and working conditions are safe.

INTERMISSION

What is job analysis and why is it important?

ENCORE

Understand Marketing Concepts

Select the best answer for each question.

1. A cafeteria plan
   a. provides on-site lunches as a fringe benefit to employees
   b. sets the same fringe benefits for all employees in a company
   c. pays a higher salary instead of fringe benefits
   d. allows employees to select from various options of fringe benefits

2. Which of the following is *not* a fringe benefit?
   a. health insurance
   b. overtime pay
   c. paid vacation
   d. employee discounts

Think Critically

Answer the following questions as completely as possible.

3. What are some of the responsibilities of the human resources department? (LO 14.2-1)

4. List and briefly explain the four main functions of a human resources department. (LO 14.2-2)

5. Use the Internet to look up the job description for an athletic director. Write a job analysis for this position at a major university. (LO 14.2-2)

14.3 Workplace Skills

The Essential Question

What interpersonal, leadership, and communication traits are necessary for success?

Learning Objectives

LO 14.3-1   Identify effective interpersonal skills.

LO 14.3-2   Describe effective team-building skills.

LO 14.3-3   Explain how to give an effective oral presentation.

Key Terms

- interpersonal skills
- cohesion
- feedback
- reflection
- clarification
- autocratic leader
- democratic leader
- laissez-faire leader

OPENING ACT

Why do some college graduates get numerous interviews but no job offers? Some of the top reasons for not getting a job offer include not being qualified, lacking enthusiasm, failing to establish your worth with a prospective employer, not having clear goals, having a poor personal appearance, bad mouthing previous employers, not being prepared for the interview, lacking interpersonal skills, and failing to sell yourself. On a daily basis, half of all job seekers are active on social networking sites. An increasing number of prospective employers are utilizing those networking sites to make hiring decisions. Twitter, LinkedIn, Facebook, and Google+ allow employers to learn more about you than what is included in your resume, cover letter, and interview. Unfortunately, negative social media participation by college graduates is becoming another reason job offers might be scarce.

Cooperative Learning   With a partner, identify why it is important to carefully consider your social media participation. How might personal information posted on social media sites turn off prospective employers?

LO 14.3-1   INTERPERSONAL SKILLS

In the workplace, interpersonal skills are highly valued. **Interpersonal skills** are an individual's character traits that allow him or her to effectively interact and work with other people. Many workers struggle to achieve results due to a lack of interpersonal skills rather than a lack of technical skills. Employees often must work as part of a team. Thus, organizations seek employees who possess solid interpersonal skills because they have the ability to get along with others to successfully complete the job.

Effective Interpersonal Skills for Team Members

In today's workplace, teamwork is often necessary to achieve goals. Successful interaction within a group requires a clear objective that is understood by all team members. There are several benefits to teams. Generally, the problem-solving process is quicker. Also the various experiences and backgrounds of the team members result in more creative and innovative ideas and solutions. Overall, teamwork improves productivity. However, team members must cooperate and collaborate in order for the team to be effective.

A wide array of personalities, opinions, and backgrounds among team members can lead to conflict when determining how to meet goals. Interpersonal skills can mean the difference between success and failure. Team members must have the ability to value different opinions and to negotiate the best strategies to accomplish goals.

Some important interpersonal skills for team members include

- Listening to what others are saying
- Voicing opinions clearly
- Giving and receiving constructive criticism
- Putting the needs of the team before oneself

Successful work teams depend on **cohesion**, which is the act or state of working, uniting, or sticking together. Work teams that do not have cohesion result in a loss of time and money for companies. Members of cohesive teams share trust. Because team members must be able to rely on each other to get the job done, trust is an essential element.

Communication Is the Key to Team Success

The number one key to success for teams is effective communication. There must be a clear two-way communication process between the sender and receiver of messages. When communication breaks down, the team dissolves.

The senders and receivers of messages must show a mutual respect and willingness to listen to one another. **Feedback** is the receiver's response to the sender's message. Feedback may include reflection and clarification.

COMMUNICATION CONNECTION

Some individuals believe that the world of social media, text messaging, and email has resulted in the decline of interpersonal skills. Most teens choose texting over using the telephone. Texting and other social networking channels of communication may lead to poor grammar (such as incomplete sentences and misspelled words) and an increased use of slang. Colleges and employers are looking for candidates who still possess strong communication skills.

Write Now

You are applying for an internship position at Disney World in Orlando. Conduct research to determine the best style for an application letter. Look up the address for the Disney World Human Resources Department and compose a well-written application letter.

Reflection involves paraphrasing, or restating, what the speaker has said to demonstrate your understanding. It does not involve asking questions. If the listener does not understand the message, he or she may ask for **clarification**, which involves offering back an interpretation of the meaning of the message, as understood by the listener, and then asking questions to make things clearer. The sender of a message should use the feedback to determine if the listener's understanding is correct or if any areas of confusion need to be resolved.

Communication can be verbal or nonverbal. *Nonverbal communication* includes body language, facial expressions, gestures, and postures. Individuals with good interpersonal skills use nonverbal communication cues, such as facial expressions, eye contact, and nodding, to indicate that they are actively listening. Nonverbal communication often has more impact than verbal communication. If the verbal response is positive while the nonverbal cues are negative, the receiver is likely to give the nonverbal cues more weight.

The timing and place of communication are also very important. Approaching a coworker about an important strategic decision five minutes before leaving the office for the weekend will not prove to be productive. Communication will also lose its effectiveness in a noisy, busy place that has numerous distractions and a lack of privacy.

In the workplace, communication often takes place in the form of meetings. Successful meetings have a purpose or objective. All meeting participants should be provided an agenda in advance. The agenda should clearly spell out what is to be covered in the meeting so participants can prepare and successfully contribute to the meeting. Meetings should have a set beginning and ending time. All team members should be given the opportunity to express themselves and ask questions during meetings.

Effective Interpersonal Skills for Team Leaders

Interpersonal skills are essential for those employees in leadership roles. Successful teams are not possible without good leadership. Leaders must have a vision of where they want to go (the overall objective) and understand how to motivate others to help them get there.

Good leaders know how to utilize team members' knowledge and skills in order to solve problems and accomplish tasks. They assign roles to the team members and clearly state the responsibilities of the roles. Leaders provide the guidance and support needed to help all team members work to their fullest potential.

Leadership Traits Leaders come in all shapes and sizes, but effective leaders are known to have certain traits. Most leaders have captivating personalities that appeal to others. They are good communicators who are knowledgeable and persuasive. They are able to motivate and inspire team members. Integrity is another key characteristic for leaders. Team members must be able to put their trust and confidence in their leader. Leaders are also good at planning, setting goals, and strategizing. Finally, leaders are good at giving credit to other people for their contributions to the team.

Leadership Styles Throughout your career, you will likely encounter different leadership styles. Good leaders will adapt their leadership style to the abilities and needs of the group with which they are working. Three common styles of leadership include autocratic, democratic, and laissez-faire. An **autocratic leader** is a take-charge person who does not seek the input of team members. This type of leader can make decisions quickly because he or she does not seek advice from team members. Most employees do not enjoy working for an autocratic leader because the environment is closely controlled and discourages creativity. A **democratic leader** involves team members in the decision-making process. Democratic leaders use brainstorming as a way for employees to express their ideas. A **laissez-faire leader** offers little or no guidance to team members and leaves the decision making to them. These leaders believe that the talents of team members will surface, allowing them to ultimately accomplish the task.

INTERMISSION

What interpersonal skills do team members need for success?

LO 14.3-2 TEAM BUILDING AND EVALUATION

Because teams play an important role in the success of a company, it is essential to ensure that they function properly. Using a team-building process and evaluating a team's effectiveness help prevent failure and provide opportunities for success and improvement.

Stages of Team Building

Teams go through five distinct stages from the time they are formed to accomplish goals. The five stages of team building include forming, storming, norming, performing, and adjourning.

How are the team-building stages similar for a sports team and a work team?

© Corepics VOF/Shutterstock.com

Forming   During the forming stage, the team is created. Because team members may not yet know each other, they may be hesitant to voice their opinions. At this stage, the team relies on the leader to provide direction and keep order in the group. Ground rules are established for the way the team will communicate and function.

Storming   During the storming stage, personality differences among members become evident. Conflict and disagreement are common. Group members may compete for position within the team. Members brainstorm ideas and try to reach agreement. At this stage, team leaders should encourage open discussion and participation by all team members.

Norming   Conflicts and differences are resolved during the norming stage, and the team works in unity. Team members' roles become well defined. The team is now focused on the task at hand. During this stage, team leaders should help clarify team roles and objectives.

Performing   Teams increase their level of productivity during the performing stage. There is an emphasis on problem solving. Team members are committed to the team's mission and work together to meet objectives. The leader provides help and guidance as needed to help team members accomplish their tasks.

Adjourning   During the adjourning stage, tasks are completed to bring things to a closure and disband the team. Upon completion of the task, team leaders should take the time to recognize the team's achievements.

 Companies are using scavenger hunts to build stronger teams within the organization. Team members are challenged to work together to find answers to questions and riddles at different locations—all while competing against other work teams.

Measuring Team Results

A team's performance should be measured to determine its effectiveness. Evaluations are based on many things, including whether all goals were accomplished on time and within budget. Teams may be evaluated on how well members worked together as a group, their strategic ability, and their overall contribution to the company. Team members should also be evaluated individually. Their performance might be measured by their participation in team meetings, their communication skills, and their ability to complete tasks correctly and efficiently.

Giving Recognition

When a team has performed well, it should receive recognition, or a thank-you for a job well done. Recognition serves as a valuable motivator and can increase company loyalty. It helps build self-esteem and confidence that leads to better performance. Companies may also acknowledge individual team members who perform exceptionally well. Perhaps a team member offered a solution to a particularly challenging problem, made processes more efficient, learned new skills and shared them with others, or took on extra tasks.

Recognition can take on many forms. It can be as simple as a handwritten thank-you note or a company-wide announcement. Teams may be recognized with a plaque that is displayed for all company employees to see. Rewards are a part of some recognition programs. Rewards may

Why is it important to recognize employees for their work?

include a special outing or event for the team. Some teams may be deserving of a bonus if their efforts have resulted in increased sales.

Rewards for individual team members can be personalized, such as a gift card of the employee's choosing. Or the employee can be rewarded with tickets to a movie or sporting event. For greater accomplishments, rewards could include free trips or cash bonuses. All of these rewards go a long way in building employee loyalty.

Team members should be involved in defining and planning a company's recognition program. There should be a clear link between team performance and recognition or rewards. Management must clearly communicate what actions will be recognized. Successful recognition programs build pride in individual and team accomplishments, resulting in higher levels of performance. They can even result in lower employee turnover rates.

INTERMISSION

Which of the five stages of team building is the most productive and why?

LO 14.3-3   SUCCESSFUL PRESENTATIONS

Giving presentations to communicate a message to a group of people is common in the workplace. Successful presentations require planning. The presenter must learn about the audience and understand the purpose of the presentation. Research must be conducted to learn more about the topic. Although being prepared is a key factor in delivering a successful presentation, the presenter's personality, words, gestures, visual aids, and interpersonal skills also have an impact on the presentation.

Know Your Audience

Prior to preparing your presentation, you must consider who your audience members will be. What do they already know about the topic and what else do they want to learn about it? What expertise do you have that they need? Why are they coming to hear you speak? This information will help you structure your presentation and avoid presenting content that is too difficult or complex for the audience.

Determine the Purpose

There must be a reason for a presentation. Once you consider your audience's needs, determine the goal of your presentation. Write the main point that you wish to convey as a single sentence. You may have several side points that feed into the main point, but begin by focusing on the main point. Next decide on objectives. What do you want your audience to know or do at the end of your presentation? Objectives should be specific and reasonable. They provide direction and focus as you prepare your presentation.

Conduct Research

Even if you are an expert on the topic being presented, you most likely will need to do some research to find quotes and recent statistics that back up your statements. Care should be taken that your resources are objective (factual) and reliable. It is also important that the information used as a source is current. Because change is constant, information quickly becomes outdated, especially when it involves technology.

Evaluating the Reliability of Resources   Resources used to prepare presentations must be credible (trustworthy). The source is only as credible as the author's credentials (experience) and the reputation of a publication or organization. Before choosing a source for your presentation, you should determine if the author has the qualifications that make him or her an expert on the topic. Credible authors often have articles published in scholarly and professional publications.

The Internet provides a vast amount of information. Unlike similar information found in newspapers, magazines, or television broadcasts, information on the Internet is not checked for accuracy or quality. Almost anyone can publish whatever he or she wishes on the Web. Before using Internet sources, it is more important than ever to determine if the author is a credible source for the topic. Also determine the purpose of the source. Is it to inform, teach, enlighten, persuade, or sell a product? If the purpose is to persuade or to sell, the source may not be objective. Objective sources present facts, not opinions. Reliable and credible sources contain information that can be verified through other means of research, such as company, government, or university sources.

Choose Your Visual Aids

Visuals can capture an audience's attention and leave a more lasting impression than just words alone. Multimedia presentation software, such as PowerPoint, and other visual aids should be used to enhance a presentation. "Keep it simple" is a good strategy to follow when producing visual presentations. PowerPoint slides should not be too wordy—short, bulleted items are easier to read. Cartoons, pictures, and charts can also be used to support the statements being made. Because the attention span of most people is very short, you are challenged to present a lively, interesting speech. Visual aids can help you accomplish this.

Practice and Present

Effective presentations require practice. Record yourself and watch it or practice in front of a mirror. Be sure to time yourself, especially if there is a time limit for the presentation. Preparing an outline ahead of time will help keep you focused and ensure you cover all topics.

Make an opening statement at the start of the presentation. The statement should introduce the topic in a way that grabs the audience's attention and gets them focused. It could be in the form of a question that

TAKE A BOW Jase Kaser

Jase Kaser comes from an entrepreneurial background. His family owns Kaser MotorSports, which sells racing fuels and owns a dirt track racing team. Kaser jumped into the family business at an early age when he began racing mini sprint cars at the age of nine. He now races dirt late model cars. Kaser has won numerous awards throughout his racing career. He now successfully juggles car racing and school, as he works toward a degree in mechanical engineering at the University of Nebraska.

Although the main focus at Kaser MotorSports is winning races and championships, a lot of time is devoted to business and advertising. To be successful in the car racing industry, sponsorships are essential. Just like other forms of motorsports, dirt late model race teams rely on the financial support of sponsors in order to race at the highest level possible.

Kaser views sponsorships as partnerships that benefit Kaser Motor-Sports and the sponsors. Product sponsors are those businesses that are involved in the racing industry, such as companies that produce parts used in racecars. Typically, product sponsors will offer a discount on products that the race team purchases from them throughout the year, or they will provide a set amount of parts at the beginning of the year for free. In return, the sponsor receives product recognition within the racing industry. So the sponsorships are a win-win for both businesses. Kaser and the other team members at Kaser MotorSports know the importance of making good business decisions. It keeps their business on track to succeed.

Think Critically

How is car racing similar to operating a successful business? What factors do you think have contributed to the success of Jase Kaser and Kaser MotorSports?

gets the audience thinking. Reciting a famous quote, telling a humorous story, or discussing current events are other good ways to start the presentation. The first 30 seconds of your presentation will make a positive or negative impression and set the tone with your audience.

During the presentation, make eye contact with your audience. Be aware of your voice, including volume, speed, clarity, and pronunciation. Show enthusiasm and energy. Depending on the type of presentation, you may want to use audience participation, which can add entertainment value. As a closing, you should summarize the main points. If you want audience members to take some kind of action, state it clearly. Finally, allow time for audience members to ask questions. It is a good idea to anticipate questions and prepare answers in advance.

INTERMISSION

What steps are involved in giving a successful presentation?

ENCORE

Understand Marketing Concepts
Select the best answer for each question.

1. All of the following are important interpersonal skills for team members except
   a. voicing your thoughts clearly
   b. listening to what others are saying
   c. making autocratic decisions
   d. giving and receiving constructive criticism

2. Brainstorming likely takes place during which of the following team-building stages?
   a. forming
   b. performing
   c. norming
   d. storming

Think Critically
Answer the following questions as completely as possible.

3. Think of a team or group in which you have participated. Was the team leader effective? Describe the interpersonal skills that made him or her effective (or ineffective). (LO 14.3-1)

4. Why is it important to measure team results? How can team results be linked to a recognition program? (LO 14.3-2)

5. You have been asked to make a short presentation at the beginning of a student awards banquet. How might you start the speech to catch the audience's attention? (LO 14.3-3)

CHAPTER ASSESSMENT

Review Marketing Terms

Match the terms listed with the definitions.

1. The employees who work for an organization
2. A business owned and operated by one person
3. A leader who offers little or no guidance to team members
4. A form of business in which ownership is represented by shares of stock
5. Individuals who take the risk of starting, owning, and operating a business
6. A formal, written document that provides the details for a proposed new business
7. The study of a specific job to identify the duties and skill requirements of the job
8. A specified amount paid annually for a job regardless of the number of hours worked
9. Character traits that allow a person to effectively interact and work with other people
10. A test period of a few months to determine whether a new employee will fulfill the needs of the organization
11. Benefit plan in which employees pick and choose benefit options to best meet their needs
12. The act or state of working, uniting, or sticking together
13. Involves paraphrasing, or restating, what the speaker has said to demonstrate understanding
14. A leader who is a take-charge person and who does not seek the input of team members
15. The receiver's response to the sender's message
16. A business owned and operated by two or more individuals who have signed an agreement
17. Extra incentives to employees beyond salary and wages
18. A leader who involves team members in the decision-making process
19. Offering back to the speaker an interpretation of the meaning of a message, as understood by the listener, and asking questions

a. autocratic leader
b. business plan
c. cafeteria plan
d. clarification
e. cohesion
f. corporation
g. democratic leader
h. entrepreneurs
i. feedback
j. fringe benefits
k. human resources
l. interpersonal skills
m. job analysis
n. laissez-faire leader
o. partnership
p. probationary period
q. reflection
r. salary
s. sole proprietorship

Review Marketing Concepts

Select the best answer for each of the following questions.

20. A form of pay for which employees receive a percentage of their sales is called
   - a. piecework
   - b. commission
   - c. bonus
   - d. salary

21. Fringe benefits
   - a. add value of between 20 and 40 percent of employees' salaries
   - b. are required by law to be paid by employers
   - c. are a major consideration for job applicants
   - d. both a and c

22. Some new employees are given a(n) _____ to determine if they can fulfill the needs of the job.
   - a. internship period
   - b. probationary period
   - c. mentor period
   - d. nonpaid observation period

23. Leaders should seek responses in the form of _____ from team members.
   - a. fringe benefits
   - b. commissions
   - c. feedback
   - d. cohesion

24. Internet resources are
   - a. checked for accuracy
   - b. not always reliable
   - c. always credible
   - d. not widely available

25. In a business plan, the business description follows the executive summary and includes all of the following *except*
   - a. the history and background of the business idea
   - b. short- and long-term goals for the business
   - c. products and services that will be offered by the business
   - d. the promotional mix

26. Companies give employees recognition
   - a. to build pride in individual and team accomplishments
   - b. to encourage high performance
   - c. to reduce employee turnover rates
   - d. all of the above

Think Critically

27. Why are communication skills so important to the success of entrepreneurs? (LO 14.1-1)

28. Explain the purpose of a business plan. Why do you think it is important for entrepreneurs to prepare a business plan? (LO 14.1-2)

29. Interview five to ten people who have full-time jobs with benefits. Find out what fringe benefits they receive. Create a two-column table. In the first column, list ten benefits. In the second column, explain why the benefit is important. (LO 14.2-2)

30. Make a list of interpersonal skills important for team members. Check off the skills that you possess. For those skills that you do not possess, write a strategy to acquire them. (LO 14.3-1)

31. Create a list titled "How to Give Effective Presentations." Include ten tips that will help make presentations more successful. (LO 14.3-3)

Make Academic Connections

32. Research Use the Internet or library to locate information about entrepreneurs. Write a one-page paper about a successful entrepreneur in sports and entertainment. List five characteristics that have made him or her successful. (LO 14.1-1)

33. Ethics You are an entrepreneur who owns and operates a medium-sized sporting goods business. Your human resources director has brought up some concerns about the hiring practices of one of your department managers. Although he interviews a diverse group of qualified candidates, he seems to hire only men. At performance review time, the department manager usually recommends lower raises for the female employees even though they receive positive customer feedback. The department manager is a top performer, but his attitude seems to indicate that women are not qualified to work in the sporting goods industry. Describe how you would handle this situation. (LO 14.2-2)

34. Math An employer has 60 employees who each earn $20 per hour. This year the 60 employees have worked a total of 150,000 hours during the 52-week year. How much will the employer have to pay the employees? How much of the amount is for overtime pay? Is the employer required to provide his employees with affordable health care? Explain your answer. (LO 14.2-2)

35. Technology How has technology enhanced modern-day presentations? What types of technology are available for use by speakers? How can technology make presentations more meaningful? (LO 14.1-3)

36. Communication Assume you are an entrepreneur wishing to create a special sports or entertainment event, such as an art festival. Write the executive summary of a business plan to catch the attention of potential sponsors for your event. Briefly outline the remaining six elements of your business plan. (LO 14.1-2)

EXTRA INNINGS PROJECT

An important function of human resources is to fill all open employee positions within a company. As a job candidate, it is your responsibility to research job openings and companies, communicate with the companies (HR departments) to get an interview, and then follow up after the interview. Individuals seeking employment should prepare a career portfolio that includes a resume, an application letter, and a list of references. The employment portfolio should be updated continuously.

Complete the following activities to create your career portfolio.

1. Use the Internet to determine the latest styles of resumes. Choose the style that best suits your needs and prepare your resume.

2. Determine four people that you can use as references. The best references are those people who have known you for more than a year and who can provide information about your skills, character, and achievements. Ask the individuals for permission to use them as a reference. Prepare a reference sheet that includes names, relationship with the selected references, addresses, telephone numbers, and email addresses of your references.

3. Use the Internet to search for a job in sports and entertainment. Prepare an application letter for the selected job.

4. Create a list to help you prepare for your job interview. The list should include things to do before, during, and after the interview. Also create a list of questions that you can ask during the interview.

5. Many companies now want an electronic resume from applicants. Conduct research to determine what to include in an electronic resume and prepare your own.

VIRTUAL BUSINESS *Sports & Entertainment*

Use the *Stadium Staffing* lesson to understand two key positions within a stadium—ushers and security. The success of any business is based on the competence and professionalism of its employees. Sports and entertainment businesses cannot function without qualified staff members. The management of people (human resources) is one of the most important responsibilities within an organization. Observe what can occur at a concert and football game when there is not adequate staffing. You will be challenged to properly staff a concert with ushers and security so that fans do not seat-hop (move to better seats) and no crowd injuries occur.

*For more information, go to **knowledgematters.com**.*

Artwork courtesy of Knowledge Matters, Inc.

BULLYING IN THE WORKPLACE

Hazing is the practice of playing unpleasant tricks on someone or forcing someone to do unpleasant things as initiation into a group. Hazing can take place at fraternities, college campuses, the workplace, and even within the National Football League (NFL). Many justify hazing by calling it a long-held tradition. But this excuse will not hold up in a court of law.

Richie Incognito was suspended by the Miami Dolphins over allegations of harassment of teammate Jonathan Martin. Incognito allegedly sent offensive texts to Martin and created a hostile work environment. Some people believe that the NFL locker room is a macho, all-male environment where crudeness is acceptable. Any player who shows resistance could be hazed. Veteran players on NFL teams have always had initiation rituals for rookies. Some rituals include forcing rookies to carry the veterans' football pads and other gear and making the rookies take veterans out for expensive meals. Other rookies have been forced to get their heads shaved or to sing in front of the entire team.

Bullying is the process of intimidating somebody weaker or in a more vulnerable situation. It can range from yelling at a person to spreading untrue rumors about him or her. More subtle examples of bullying are excluding coworkers (or teammates) from important meetings or social outings. Individuals participate in bullying to express their superiority. When businesses and sports agencies do not take actions to correct bullying, the unethical behavior continues.

According to the Workplace Bullying Institute, behaviors that represent workplace bullying may include verbal abuse, work interference, and offensive conduct or behavior that is harmful to the health of the person(s) being bullied. Victims of workplace bullying can suffer from physical and mental health issues.

Concerned Employers

Businesses are concerned about bullying in the workplace because it can lead to legal consequences for the "bully" and the business. Verbal and physical threats and assaults by employees can result in legal action against the employer. In addition, workplace bullying that leads to a hostile work environment can affect the work performance of the victim and other employees. Employers must stress that they will not tolerate bullying behaviors and that bullies will be punished, and possibly fired.

Think Critically

1. Does any form of hazing or bullying take place in your school? What can be done to stop bullying?
2. Do you believe the Incognito/Martin situation is a case of bullying? Why or why not? What can organizations like the NFL do to stop bullying?
3. Do you think businesses should be held legally responsible for a bully's actions? Why or why not?
4. Why do you think some individuals participate in bullying activities?

PUBLIC SPEAKING I EVENT

Speaking with others and giving public speeches is an important part of a marketer's and business owner's job. This event gives FBLA members the opportunity to demonstrate leadership through effective speaking skills. The topic for your speech is "Leadership Strategies for Business Owners." Your speech should describe how business owners can encourage employees to work toward the mission of the company. Explain the importance of motivating individual employees as well as teams in the workplace. You also have been asked to explain the value of employee recognition programs and describe how to determine what rewards have the greatest positive impacts on employee performance.

Your business speech should be four minutes in length and must be developed from one or more of the nine FBLA-PBL goals found on the FBLA website. Five points will be deducted for any time under 3:31 or over 4:29 minutes. You may use notes or note cards when delivering the speech, but no visual aids may be used.

Each participant's speech must be the result of the participant's own efforts. Facts and working data may be secured from any source. Speeches must be well organized, contain factual statements, and be written in an acceptable business style.

Performance Indicators Evaluated

- Understand the importance of leadership strategies.
- Describe the leadership role on a team.
- Explain the cost of high employee turnover rates.
- Explain how recognition and reward programs are related to employee performance.
- Describe strategies to maintain high employee morale.

Think Critically

1. What leadership strategies are effective within the workplace?
2. Why should employee turnover rates be a major concern for organizations?
3. How can an employee recognition program be used to increase employee morale?
4. What type of employee recognition would encourage fewer sick days taken by employees?
5. What types of employee rewards will make the greatest positive impact on recipients? Explain your answer.

www.fbla.org

15

SCORING A CAREER

© DmitriMaruta/Shutterstock.com

POINT YOUR BROWSER
ngl.cengage.com/sports4e

Winning Strategies

How about a Three-Peat?

It's a great feeling when you have a winning year, whether it's in business or sports. It's even better when you can string together two successful years back to back. In today's business climate, two successful years in a row is very solid. So, as coined by former NBA coach Pat Riley, how can an organization go for the "three-peat"? It must find the winning strategy. It starts with the players on your team. It is important to find the right people to fill each position. And great players need the leadership of a good coach.

Image courtesy of Mark Krieschen

Mark Krieschen is Vice President and Market Manager for Cox Media Group in Houston, Texas. Cox Media operates radio stations, owns newspapers, and provides cable TV advertising services throughout the United States. Despite intense competition and a shaky economy, Krieschen led Cox Media to huge back-to-back wins.

Krieschen believes in surrounding himself with highly talented people. When it comes to annual business planning, Krieschen conducts a complete review of business operations. Then in his role as the leader, he works with his team to develop specific strategies to meet and exceed company/team goals and objectives.

Think Critically

1. How important are leaders like Mark Krieschen to the success of a business?

2. Explain the important role that team members play in reaching company goals.

15.1 Choosing and Preparing for a Career

The Essential Question

What are the characteristics and skills needed for success in a sports and entertainment marketing career?

Learning Objectives

LO 15.1-1   Describe the variety of careers available in sports and entertainment marketing.

LO 15.1-2   Explain the skills needed and ways to prepare for a career in sports and entertainment marketing.

Key Terms

- *Occupational Outlook Handbook*
- public relations specialist
- internship
- marketing manager
- jargon

OPENING ACT

You may be a good athlete or someone who enjoys watching and following sports. Maybe you enjoy the exciting world of the performing arts. Because of your interests, you are considering a career in sports and entertainment marketing. In addition to professions that deal directly with athletes and performers, there is a wide range of careers indirectly linked to sports and entertainment. Before deciding on a career, you will need to explore the possibilities.

Cooperative Learning   Working in a group, brainstorm various ways you can learn about career possibilities related to sports and entertainment. Select your best five source ideas and share them with the rest of the class.

LO 15.1-1   A WIDE WORLD OF CAREERS

The fields of professional sports and entertainment continue to expand. Many sports- and entertainment-related careers are available. Some of the most interesting and exciting careers can be found in sports and entertainment marketing. In the sports industry, jobs range from careers with college, amateur, and professional sports teams to positions in sports-related businesses, such as sports apparel and equipment manufacturers and retailers. In the entertainment industry, marketing careers range from public relations specialists to celebrity agents. Even farmers who grow the sod for football stadiums are indirectly involved in the sports industry. Owners of charter buses that take people to concerts are indirectly involved in the entertainment industry. So it is very likely that you can find a career in the sports and entertainment industry that appeals to you.

What are some jobs that are indirectly related to sports and entertainment?

Two Roads to Success

Marketers divide sports marketing opportunities into two general categories—management activities and technical services. Management activities include the following:

- Designing marketing campaigns for clients
- Overseeing marketing activities
- Matching clients with sponsoring organizations
- Preparing contracts
- Evaluating marketing activities to ensure goals have been met

Technical services related to marketing involve different aspects of media, such as graphics, photography, and website and video production.

Marketing Jobs

The *Occupational Outlook Handbook (OOH),* a publication of the Bureau of Labor Statistics, provides an overview of jobs and careers in different fields, including marketing. According to the handbook, which is also available online, opportunities for marketers, advertisers, and public relations specialists are expected to grow through the year 2022.

Broadway plays and live opera performances are attracting record audiences. At the same time, symphonies, orchestras, and dance groups struggle to attract audiences. Trends in the sports and entertainment industries are followed carefully. Increases in attendance at games, concerts, and other events naturally lead to a rise in the number of sports and entertainment marketers and public relations specialists needed.

Public Relations Specialist An individual hired to build and maintain positive relationships between his or her employer and the public is called a **public relations specialist**. Public relations (PR) specialists' responsibilities include keeping the media and public aware of the

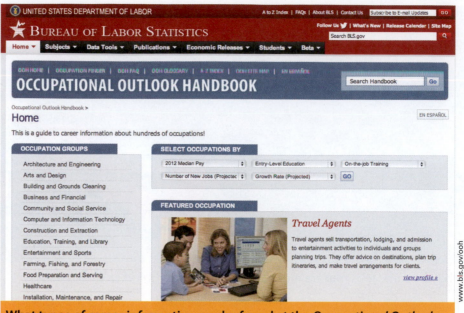

www.bls.gov/ooh

What types of career information can be found at the *Occupational Outlook Handbook (OOH)* website?

company or person they represent. In the entertainment business, PR specialists might include actors' agents and studio press agents. In the sports industry, PR specialists include spokespersons who communicate to the media on behalf of the teams. Understanding the attitudes and concerns of their employers, the public, and various other community and business groups is a vital part of the PR specialist's job. To improve communications, PR specialists establish and maintain cooperative relationships with representatives from these groups as well as with the media.

The average workweek of public relations specialists is 40 or more hours, which can easily increase, with or without pay. Flexibility with daily schedules and a willingness to travel are necessary. The best opportunities for PR specialists are in large cities where more entertainment and sports venues exist. Most employers prefer a candidate with a bachelor's degree combined with work experience. Participation in college internship programs can qualify as the desired work experience. An **internship** is a hands-on learning experience at a real work site. A general background in marketing, advertising, or public relations in any field can be transformed into a career as a PR specialist in sports and entertainment.

Marketing Managers The person who drives the creative development of the company's messages about its products is called the **marketing manager**. However, the marketing manager position may have many different titles, such as Marketing Director, Creative Director, Brand Manager, and many others. Generally, the person in this position is responsible for developing marketing strategies to help the company reach its goals. Other common tasks include creating advertising and promotional plans, developing sales presentations, and planning market research. Marketing managers must have good communication and organization skills to manage many projects and people at the same time.

A bachelor's degree in marketing or communications is usually required for marketing manager positions. Some companies require a graduate degree and several years of work experience. A marketing manager is not an entry-level position in most companies. Those working in lower-level marketing positions are usually promoted to marketing managers.

Other Marketing Avenues *Promotions managers* plan and coordinate activities to attract fans to sports and entertainment events. They also sign sponsors to help finance events. At professional and college football and basketball games, the promotions manager plans half-time performances, contests, and other activities to ensure that fans enjoy their experience.

Agents that represent athletes and celebrities negotiate contracts and endorsement deals. *Directors of corporate sales* work to establish partnerships with businesses for sponsorship of sports and entertainment events. For a sports team, directors of corporate sales are also responsible for selling luxury skyboxes. *Ticket operations directors* are responsible for filling stadium and arena seats. *Market researchers* conduct surveys to gather information about sports and entertainment trends and statistics.

Many smaller sports and entertainment businesses hire marketing firms to perform marketing activities for them. You may serve in any one of the above positions while working in a marketing firm that serves other businesses.

Books and Lecture Series Sports and entertainment provide excellent storylines for popular books written by former coaches and players and celebrities. To fans, these books are inspirational and motivational. The popularity of these books requires the work of many people. When writing their books, the authors work with publishers. Editors help them plan and develop their story ideas while being mindful of the target audience for the book. Art designers create the covers. The marketing team plans promotions and promotional tours. Book reviewers provide critiques of the book to the media. In addition to these careers, there are a number of others that play a role in the success of these books.

Compensation for Marketing Positions

The pay for sports and entertainment marketing positions varies greatly, depending on the size and type of employer. An entry-level sports marketing manager working for a professional team may earn $40,000 annually. The average annual salary for a sports marketing manager is $60,000. Salaries for ticket managers for professional sports teams average more than $50,000 per year. The recent average salary for producers and directors of motion pictures, television shows, live theater, and other performing arts productions was $71,350 per year.[1] Marketers with prominent roles in professional sports or entertainment organizations can earn $130,000 or more per year.

INTERMISSION

Describe five careers related to sports and entertainment marketing.

LO 15.1-2　GETTING THERE FROM HERE

Breaking into sports and entertainment marketing is not always easy. But there is room for people who are willing to prepare themselves, take advantage of internships and other opportunities, work hard, and continue their education.

Narrow Your Choices

As is true with landing any job, getting a position in sports or entertainment marketing is a matter of marketing yourself. The first step is planning the product—you. To do this, you must know what you want to do and what it takes to be able to do it. Research and gather information about the jobs that exist in your areas of interest to help you decide whether that sort of work is for you. Knowing about the companies that provide those jobs is also helpful. The Internet offers a vast amount of information about companies and careers. Other sources of information include the following:

- People you know or people already in the business
- Company annual reports
- Business directories, such as *Standard & Poor's Register of Corporations, Directors and Executives*
- College placement offices
- Recent news articles and trade publications

Why are good communication skills necessary for marketers?

Once you have narrowed down your career choice, determine the educational background, skills, and experience required for your desired position and set out to acquire them.

Skill Requirements

Marketers generally have certain characteristics and skills that help them succeed on the job. They are creative and enthusiastic. They are also good at solving problems, remaining calm under pressure, and adapting to changes. Some of the top skills required of marketers are communications, interpersonal, time management, and technical skills.

Communications skills (writing and speaking) are critical in marketing-related jobs. Interpersonal skills are not far behind. The abilities to meet people, talk with them in a relaxed manner, and speak confidently and persuasively, both one-on-one and in a group setting, are essential marketing skills. Time management is another important skill for successful marketers. It involves establishing a plan to help you manage your time more effectively. Prioritizing tasks helps marketers stay on schedule and meet deadlines.

Technical skills involving computers and the Internet are also crucial in today's workplace, especially in the field of marketing. On a typical day, marketers may use the Internet to conduct research, a database program to help track and analyze customer information, a graphics design program to create an advertisement, and social media to promote products.

One of the largest career areas in sports and entertainment marketing is media. Under this broad umbrella, you will find four focus areas—print, radio, television, and the Internet. Even if you do not intend to work directly in the technical aspects of these media, you will need to communicate with those who do. Sports and entertainment marketers must have some knowledge of each area to effectively work as part of a team.

The Internet, radio, TV, and print media each have their own **jargon**, or language that relates to a specific area and that makes communication more concise. Future sports and entertainment marketers that have internships can learn marketing and media jargon, giving them a solid foundation on which to build a career.

Professionalism and Work Ethics

Professionalism is a highly desired trait by organizations. Because competition is strong in the sports and entertainment industry, individuals who expect to succeed must demonstrate a high level of professionalism. Traits associated with professionalism include maturity, punctuality, reliability, and honesty, as well as a positive attitude. Work ethics go hand in hand with professionalism. A good work ethic is characterized by drive, persistence, and hard work.

Math in Marketing

You have just graduated from college with a degree in sports marketing. While in college, you participated in two internships. These internships helped you acquire a job. You have been hired by the New York Jets for an entry-level marketing position. Your salary is $40,000 per year. While you are excited about your new job, you are also concerned about your living expenses in New York. Conduct research to determine the cost of living in New York City. Then prepare a monthly budget based on your salary. Make sure to include fixed expenses (such as rent, insurance, and other monthly fixed costs) and variable expenses (such as food, clothing, and entertainment), in your budget.

Do the Math

Based on your annual salary, what is your monthly salary? What are your fixed expenses and how much do they total? What are your variable expenses and how much do they total? Will your salary cover all expenses? If not, which expenses can you eliminate or reduce? Given the high cost of living in New York, do you think accepting this position is wise? Why or why not?

Amy, a high school student in Dallas, knew she wanted to work with the Dallas Cowboys in some capacity. She wrote letters, filled out applications, and followed up with phone calls to check the status of her requests. Although she was requesting only part-time work or even an unpaid internship, she was not interviewed. The Cowboys hired only college students. After more letters, calls, and a visit to the human resources department, she was finally asked, "Can you come in for a few hours each week during the summer?" At first, the work merely involved answering the phone and sorting mail. But Amy handled it with such enthusiasm and efficiency that her supervisor took notice. Soon she was handling more demanding work. She was asked to return during summer vacations while in college. Her basic skills, professionalism, work ethic, and desire to succeed opened the door for her. Amy came to be recognized as a team player.

INTERMISSION

What are some of the top skills needed in marketing careers?

ENCORE

Understand Marketing Concepts
Select the best answer for each question.

1. Which of the following is *not* an aspect of sports and entertainment marketing?
   a. matching clients with sponsors
   b. overseeing marketing projects
   c. teaching new employees basic writing skills
   d. working with media

2. Which of the following skills is important to the success of a sports and entertainment marketing career?
   a. problem-solving skills
   b. interpersonal skills
   c. communications skills
   d. all of the above

Think Critically
Answer the following questions as completely as possible.

3. Imagine that you can enter the world of sports and entertainment as a marketer. What type of position would you choose? What appeals to you about this job? What are some of the things you would enjoy doing? (LO 15.1-1)

4. Conduct research to learn about the productivity of the average worker. How does this relate to time management? (LO 15.1-2)

15.2 Student Professional Organizations

The Essential Question

Why is it important to become actively involved in a professional organization?

Learning Objectives

LO 15.2-1 List and describe three national student professional organizations.

LO 15.2-2 Explain the benefits of involvement in student professional organizations.

Key Terms

- professional organizations
- networking
- student professional organizations

OPENING ACT

Every year, thousands of students' lives are positively affected by active membership in student professional organizations. These organizations offer opportunities for social, career, and leadership development, as well as community service. Students learn how to develop strategies and make important career decisions for the future as they compete at the local and state levels in business-related events. The ultimate goal is to qualify for participation in the national conferences. There, students will mingle and compete in challenging tests and role-plays with top students from around the nation. These conferences offer a great opportunity for students to form valuable professional networks. The national leadership conferences are filled with young business leaders who hold promising futures.

Cooperative Learning Work with a partner to research a student professional organization at your school. List the benefits of becoming an active member of this organization.

LO 15.2-1 THE VALUE OF NETWORKING

There is some truth to the statement "it's not what you know, but who you know." The knowledge you gain from your education is valuable, and getting to know people who work in your career field is a way to expand your education. **Professional organizations** are associations for professionals in the same or similar industries formed for the purposes of continuing education and networking. **Networking** is the process of developing contacts with other individuals, groups, or organizations for the benefit of career development. Networking through professional organizations allows you to keep up to date with the latest industry trends. It is also a way to learn about business opportunities and job openings in your field.

Get Involved Early

High school and college students should focus on earning high grades. Involvement in professional organizations and internships is also valuable. Participation in these organizations looks great on a resume. Students should become actively involved in extracurricular activities related to their majors. Involvement with community organizations is also beneficial. All of these activities create networking opportunities.

When you start your job search, there will be many more candidates than open positions for the best entry-level sports and entertainment marketing jobs. Thus, job seekers need to have a competitive edge. Active involvement and visibility in student professional organizations can provide the edge needed. Local, state, and national student organizations provide students with the skills that are highly desired by employers.

Student professional organizations are associations for students that foster leadership, civic consciousness, career training, and social responsibility. Three excellent student professional organizations are DECA, Future Business Leaders of America (FBLA), and Business Professionals of America (BPA). All three organizations offer professional development conferences and healthy competition that can teach students how to succeed in a free-enterprise economy.

DECA

DECA was established nearly 70 years ago as an association of students, teachers, and administrators. It sought to improve education and career opportunities for students with interests in marketing, management, finance, entrepreneurship, and hospitality. It began with a few hundred students in 22 states. DECA now has both a High School Division, with more than 190,000 members in 3,500 high schools, and a Collegiate Division, with over 15,000 members in 200 colleges. DECA chapters can be found in all 50 states, as well as the District of Columbia, Canada, China, Germany, Guam, Hong Kong, Korea, Mexico, and Puerto Rico.

© DECA Inc.

How do organizations like DECA build character for young people?

DECA Objectives   The mission of DECA has largely remained the same since its beginnings: to prepare emerging leaders and entrepreneurs for careers in marketing, finance, hospitality and management in high schools and colleges around the globe. DECA's major objective is to strengthen marketing and management skills. In addition, special attention is given to building technical, basic scholastic (reading, writing, and math), communication, human relations, and other employable skills. Programs and activities offered by DECA are tailored to the career interests of students. They help students develop confidence and self-esteem, experience leadership, and practice community service. DECA also places an emphasis on economics and free enterprise. DECA is committed to supporting marketing education and increasing and maintaining business and education partnerships.

Activities and Services   Training conferences, publications, and competitive events are sponsored by DECA to enhance students' learning experiences. Regional leadership conferences in the fall provide officer and leadership training. During the summer, DECA officers from several states visit Capitol Hill to inform government leaders about marketing education and leadership development. The ultimate goal is to gain the understanding and support of federal government leaders. Professional meetings offered by national DECA include the Sports & Entertainment Marketing Conference, the Innovations and Entrepreneurship Conference, and the New York Experience. These meetings provide participants with valuable information and professional networks.

DECA Networks   Professional business leaders throughout the United States understand the value of DECA. Many of today's business leaders were involved with DECA as student members. They have continued their support as adults, taking on the roles of judges, mentors, and internship sponsors. Friends, acquaintances, and business contacts gained through DECA membership become a strong professional network that contributes to the personal and professional success of DECA members. DECA has had an impact on the lives of more than 10 million students. More than 70 percent of students surveyed at a recent international DECA conference indicated that their college decision was influenced by membership in DECA. National DECA gives out more than $300,000 in scholarships each year.

How do students benefit from the support of professional business leaders?

Professional student organizations like DECA have publications to keep members and advisers current on the latest news and events. *DECA Direct* is the official professional publication for DECA. Members and other interested parties can also access the latest DECA information through *DECA Direct* online.

FBLA

Future Business Leaders of America (FBLA) is a nonprofit educational association of students preparing for careers in business and business-related fields. The mission of FBLA is to bring business and education together in a positive working relationship through innovative leadership and career development programs. FBLA has four divisions, including

- FBLA–High School. The first high school FBLA chapter was in Tennessee in 1942.
- FBLA–Middle Level. The Middle Level Division was added in 1994.
- Phi Beta Lambda (PBL) for college and university students. The first collegiate chapter was formed in Iowa in 1958.
- Professional Division for business people, educators, and parents who support the goals of FBLA. The Professional Division was added in 1979.

High school membership in FBLA is greater than 215,000, and Phi Beta Lambda has over 11,000 college members. FBLA–Middle Level (grades 5–9) has more than 20,000 members, creating student interest for involvement in high school FBLA. The Professional Division has more than 3,000 members. FBLA is the largest business career student organization in the world.

The FBLA National Leadership Conference is a four-day event for the top FBLA students. They compete and share ideas for shaping future careers. The Institute for Leaders is a two-day conference for state and local officers, advisers, and members. The leadership and career-skills training, with special emphasis on entrepreneurship and communication, provides students with valuable experiences that provide lifelong benefits. National Fall Leadership Conferences are held throughout the United States to guide and provide motivation for the upcoming year. Publications produced by FBLA, including *Tomorrow's*

© luminaimages/Shutterstock.com

What lifelong benefits may result from involvement in student professional organizations?

Business Leader, provide fresh ideas for success and network-building opportunities for members.

BPA

Business Professionals of America (BPA) is a third student organization with around 43,000 members in more than 2,300 chapters in 23 states. The mission of BPA is to contribute to the preparation of a world-class workforce through the advancement of leadership, citizenship, and academic and technological skills. BPA fosters pride in the United States and its free-enterprise business system.

Students join BPA to take advantage of a wide range of professional development opportunities. Programs offered by BPA include the Workplace Skills Assessment Program and the National Internship Program. At the BPA National Leadership Conference, participants assess workplace skills, develop leadership skills, test for software certification, elect national officers, and socialize while competing in 72 competitive events. BPA produces a web magazine called *The Wire* that offers BPA-related articles as well as articles on professional development and trends.

Corporate Support

DECA, FBLA, and BPA enjoy the support and/or endorsement of major corporations, departments of education, and professional education organizations. This support is valuable for students seeking employment and internships. Corporations know what skills future employees need and can help plan and integrate the necessary training.

INTERMISSION

Name three benefits of student professional organizations.

JUDGMENT CALL

Colleges and businesses are looking for candidates who not only earn high grades but also become actively involved in professional organizations and internships. Well-rounded individuals are more valuable to universities and companies.

Many students pay membership dues to professional organizations just to be able to add extracurricular activities to their resumes. After they pay their dues, these individuals do not attend meetings and conferences. They do not take advantage of leadership and networking opportunities offered by the professional organizations. Professional organizations at high schools and colleges offer individuals great opportunities for leadership development and social interaction. The elected leaders of professional organizations have the responsibility to develop a program that actively involves all members.

Think Critically

What is the ethical issue in this case? What can officers of extracurricular professional organizations do to increase the involvement of members? Should attendance at meetings by all members be required?

LO 15.2-2   GETTING THE MOST FROM YOUR MEMBERSHIP

Joining a student professional organization is a good step toward leadership development. Benefits of membership greatly increase with active involvement. You can practice your communication skills through participation in organization meetings, programs, and competitive events. Networking opportunities are available to members who make a point of getting to know other members and sponsors. Responsibilities of members in a student professional organization include the following:

- Contributing meaningful ideas at meetings
- Volunteering for community service projects
- Networking with other members and business leaders
- Preparing for successful careers in the free-enterprise system

Leadership

One of the most important ingredients for a successful career is leadership. The ability to motivate and guide others to accomplish organizational goals is a highly valued skill among employers. You will have opportunities to develop leadership skills when you become involved in professional student organizations. Leadership skills are further developed when you volunteer for student organization committees and run for office in your local chapter, or even state and national offices. Meeting the challenges that go hand in hand with leadership roles will foster the confidence and social skills needed to improve your professional image. Membership in professional organizations and active leadership roles catch the attention of potential employers.

© racorn/Shutterstock.com

In what ways do student professional organizations foster leadership development?

Professional Memberships after Landing the Career

Involvement in professional organizations does not end after you graduate from high school or college. Whatever your career after graduation, there is likely a professional organization associated with that career or industry that can foster your professional growth. Business leaders often take active roles in their communities, churches, and professional organizations. As a young professional, getting involved in various community and professional organizations expands your network, improves your skills, and provides valuable learning experiences. Participation in these organizations also allows you to get a broader perspective of the real world and avoid the tunnel vision that can occur when focusing on your day-to-day responsibilities.

INTERMISSION

Why is it important for individuals to remain actively involved in community and professional organizations throughout their careers?

ENCORE

Understand Marketing Concepts

Select the best answer for each question.

1. Professional organizations
   a. provide valuable networking opportunities
   b. keep individuals up to date on current trends in their field of work
   c. enhance leadership skills
   d. do all of the above

2. Involvement in professional organizations
   a. is not as important as high grades in school
   b. is still important after landing a career
   c. does not provide long-term benefits
   d. is becoming less important

Think Critically

Answer the following questions as completely as possible.

3. Create a PowerPoint presentation that explains the importance of networking for high school students. This presentation should give students a good reason for joining professional organizations at school. (LO 15.2-1)

4. Design a brochure to advertise one of the three professional organizations discussed in the lesson. The brochure should explain the value of active involvement. (LO 15.2-2)

15.3 Continued Professional Development

The Essential Question

Why is professional development important throughout your career?

Learning Objectives

LO 15.3-1   Explain the need for continuous professional development.

LO 15.3-2   Give examples of professional development opportunities.

Key Terms

- professional development
- mentor

OPENING ACT

ADMIT ONE
289147

Large professional organizations look for convention centers that can accommodate their meeting needs. The Orange County Convention Center (OCCC) in Orlando, Florida, is an ideal venue for large conferences. More than 2.5 million square feet of meeting space makes it possible to host multiple large meetings simultaneously. The Orange County Convention Center, which is located in the heart of Downtown Orlando only 15 minutes from the airport, has won several awards, including the Prime Site Facilities & Top Destinations Award based on the attractiveness of the facility, marketability, customer service, high-tech meeting spaces, and customer satisfaction rating. Two 92,000-square-feet general assembly areas, 74 meeting rooms, 235 breakout rooms, and 113,000 surrounding hotel rooms make the Orange County Convention Center a perfect choice for the International DECA Conference, which has more than 18,000 attendees. Orlando is a prime location for business and entertainment with nearby theme parks, beaches, and shopping.

Cooperative Learning   In a group, discuss how the location of a conference can affect its success. Then select a good city for a national conference to accommodate 10,000 attendees. Give ten reasons why this city would be a good location for the conference.

LO 15.3-1   CONTINUING EDUCATION CONFERENCES

Professionals in all career fields are challenged to stay at the top of their game to remain competitive. They must continually update their skills, knowledge, and networks. Individuals in sports and entertainment marketing work in fast-paced industries that require professional development and continuing education. **Professional development** includes all meetings, courses, seminars, and networking opportunities that enhance an individual's knowledge and performance in his or her career area. Regional

What is the purpose of professional development conferences?

and national conferences present opportunities to keep up to date with the trends in sports and entertainment marketing. Continuing education conferences are often hosted by professional organizations. Businesses that sell goods and services related to sports and entertainment marketing may sponsor the conferences. Sports conferences associated with the National Collegiate Athletic Association (NCAA) are held after the completion of the season for each sport. The conferences provide a great way to wrap up the season and discuss issues related to the next season.

Costs

The registration fees for continuing education and professional development conferences can be very expensive. Usually, conferences are held at nice hotels and convention centers located in desirable cities. Motivational speakers are scheduled by conference planners in order to increase the appeal of the conference and boost attendance. Top coaches and athletes, for example, may charge from $10,000 to more than $50,000 for a one-hour motivational speech. Conference registration fees may be as high as $1,500 to cover all of the costs of a top-rate conference.

In addition to conference registration, the cost of travel and lodging can also be expensive. Sports and entertainment marketing organizations often pay for their employees to attend professional development conferences that will enhance or improve their skills.

Topics

Conference participants who are asked to make presentations at professional conferences should take advantage of the opportunity. The invitation means that the profession recognizes the individual as a leader with valuable experience and information to share with others. Topics covered at a professional development conference may include the latest industry trends, new products and services, and new rules and regulations. Although the knowledge gained at these conferences is beneficial, individuals frequently rank camaraderie and professional networking as the top advantages for attending conferences.

One out of ten young job seekers has not been offered a job due to his or her social media profile. This statistic is based on a recent study from the market analyst firm, One Device Research. What individuals post on their Facebook page or their Twitter accounts can prevent them from getting hired. Eight percent of people between the ages 16 and 24 were not offered jobs as a result of their social media postings. For individuals between the ages of 25 and 34, five percent were denied jobs due to their personal social media accounts.

Unfortunately, 70 percent of the young people surveyed stated that they were not concerned that their social media activity could have a negative impact on their career opportunities.[2]

Think Critically

How can social media be your greatest friend and greatest enemy when searching for a job?

Getting Away

Professional development conferences can last from one-half day to an entire week. National conferences are frequently held in cities noted for tourism. These cities provide convention participants opportunities to golf or enjoy other activities and attractions when meetings are not taking place. Cities chosen to host professional meetings typically have a convention center, plenty of hotel rooms, a good airport, public transportation, and numerous restaurants and entertainment venues. Orlando, Florida, for example, has a huge convention center, an international airport, numerous hotels, theme parks, golf courses, and many other attractions. These features along with Florida's mild weather make it an ideal selection for professional meetings. Getting participants away from the usual work environment helps them to focus on new ideas with a fresh perspective.

Why is continuing education important for all career fields?

LO 15.3-2   BOOT CAMPS AND ACADEMIES

Today's marketplace is going through many changes. Organizations face increased competition as they battle to gain market share. They depend on qualified employees to help them win the battle. Those working in the sports and entertainment industries must be well equipped with the right skills and knowledge to help their organizations succeed.

The AMA Marketing Boot Camp

The American Marketing Association (AMA) Marketing Boot Camps, which are part of AMA's Corporate Training, are highly interactive programs led by an experienced AMA instructor. The Boot Camps are especially useful for marketers who are new to the profession. Individuals who have recently acquired positions requiring marketing, sales, management, advertising, promotion, brand building, and pricing skills will benefit from the meaningful learning experiences provided. Participants will leave with relevant and immediately usable marketing skills. Major topics covered include the following:

- Branding
- Marketing research
- Social media
- Strategic research planning
- Content marketing
- Email marketing
- Integrated marketing communications
- Search engine optimization (SEO)

NCAA Men's Coaches Academy

The sports industry is a billion-dollar industry in the United States. A successful sports program can be very profitable for colleges and universities. Whether or not a team performs well is often because of the coach. It is the coach's responsibility to lead his or her team to victory. Coaching programs help prepare coaches to perform on the job.

The National Collegiate Athletic Association (NCAA) and National Football League (NFL) Coaches Academy is a program that gives participants the opportunity to gain a better understanding of football coaching careers. The NCAA and NFL work together in an effort to provide active and former players, as well as current intercollegiate coaches, a perspective on what it takes to be an effective coach at the collegiate and professional levels. Overall objectives of the Coaches Academy include the following:

© Herbert Kratky/Shutterstock.com

What is the advantage of having an experienced coach mentor a new coach?

- Gaining a better understanding of how behavioral styles and personal values impact the effectiveness of an offensive or defensive coordinator
- Acquiring information on personal growth and development that will be beneficial in becoming an offensive or defensive coordinator
- Learning a realistic view of the role of an offensive, defensive, or special team's coordinator in collegiate athletics
- Examining the possibility of pursuing a career as an offensive or defensive coordinator
- Networking with football coaching professionals from NCAA member institutions[3]

To help coaches succeed, the NCAA and NFL Coaches Academy provides education and training on many topics. Participants learn about communicating with other campus leaders, the importance of building the right culture for the overall success of student-athletes, budget management, coaching strategies, and other aspects of coaching at the collegiate football level.

TAKE A BOW Mike Pede

Since the days of "Phi Slama Jama" (the nickname of the University of Houston Cougars men's basketball teams in the mid-1980s), Mike Pede has been a devoted Cougar fan. While attending UH, Pede served as Shasta, the university's mascot. He started the push-up tradition for every point scored.

Following graduation from UH's Conrad N. Hilton College of Hotel and Restaurant Management, Pede worked in several positions at UH Athletics. He then moved on to Rice University, where he served as assistant and associate Athletic Director (AD) for 13 years. In 2007 Pede entered private business, co-owning a minor league baseball team for two years. He also served as Director of Sales for Live Nation, which handles concert promotions and venue operations, and was a partner at GameDay Consultants, an advertising and sports marketing agency. Pede rejoined his alma mater in 2010, serving as President and CEO of the University of Houston Alumni Association. Pede's career in the sports and entertainment industry has taken many twists and turns. Along the way, he has been able to build an extensive network of contacts in the industry. In addition, Pede's vast work experience helped him develop the skills and knowledge needed to succeed. Using his skills has enabled him to lead the UH Alumni Association to an exciting new level.

Think Critically

What do you think has contributed to Mike Pede's success? How did his career path help him attain his current position?

The Best Never Stop Growing Professionally

Professionals in all career fields understand the value of continuing education. Professional development comes through a wide range of opportunities. Some individuals stay at the top of their profession by networking with the best people in the field. A **mentor** is an experienced professional who willingly acts as a role model and provides guidance, encouragement, and training for individuals. Many professional organizations have quarterly newsletters and websites that allow individuals to keep current on the latest trends in their profession. The American Marketing Association created Virtual Xchange® Events, which are highly interactive, free online conferences featuring leading names in marketing who discuss a variety of today's most trending topics. Many professional organizations and universities offer professional development courses. The courses allow individuals to learn about the latest topics and to network with other individuals in their career field.

 Mentoring .org estimates that 15 million young people in the United States could benefit from having mentors. Benefits of mentoring include networking, tutoring, and guidance in developing a roadmap for future success. The number of mentoring relationships has grown from 300,000 to 4.5 million since Mentoring.org began more than 20 years ago.[4]

INTERMISSION

How can employees increase their value to their employers?

ENCORE

Understand Marketing Concepts

Select the best answer for each question.

1. Professional development
   a. is a lifelong process
   b. is not necessary for all careers
   c. has become less important
   d. all of the above

2. Mentors
   a. are paid for their services as experienced professionals
   b. are good role models
   c. are assigned to all new employees
   d. both a and b

Think Critically

Answer the following questions as completely as possible.

3. Think about the career that you have chosen. Give two examples of professional development opportunities and reasons for participating in these programs. (LO 15.3-1)

4. If you could choose any professional in your chosen career field as a mentor, who would you choose and why? Write two paragraphs explaining your answer. (LO 15.3-2)

Review Marketing Concepts

Match the terms listed with the definitions.

1. Language that relates to a specific area and that makes communication more concise
2. An individual hired to build and maintain positive relationships between his or her employer and the public
3. The person who drives the creative development of the company's messages about its products
4. Associations for students that foster leadership, civic consciousness, career training, and social responsibility
5. The process of developing contacts with other individuals, groups, or organizations for the benefit of career development
6. A publication of the Bureau of Labor Statistics that provides an overview of jobs and careers in different fields
7. Associations for professionals in the same or similar industries formed for the purposes of continuing education and networking
8. Meetings, courses, seminars, and networking opportunities that enhance an individual's knowledge and performance in his or her career area
9. An experienced professional who willingly acts as a role model and provides guidance, encouragement, and training for individuals
10. A hands-on learning experience at a real work site

a. internship
b. jargon
c. marketing manager
d. mentor
e. networking
f. *Occupational Outlook Handbook*
g. professional development
h. professional organizations
i. public relations specialist
j. student professional organizations

Review Marketing Concepts

Select the best answer for each of the following questions.

11. Members of student professional organizations can develop leadership skills by
    a. volunteering for committees
    b. serving as an officer
    c. participating in role-plays and other competitive events
    d. all of the above
12. Which of the following statements is *not* true regarding the field of sports and entertainment marketing?
    a. Opportunities for marketers are on the rise.
    b. Participation in internship programs is not important.
    c. The best opportunities for public relations specialists are in large cities.
    d. Strong communication skills are critical for marketers.

13. Personal characteristics that can help marketers succeed include which of the following?
    a. Enthusiasm
    b. Creativity
    c. Flexibility
    d. all of the above
14. Individuals in charge of coordinating activities to attract fans to sports and entertainment events are
    a. promotions managers
    b. public relations specialists
    c. marketing managers
    d. sports information specialists
15. Which of the following is *not* associated with professional development?
    a. networking
    b. attending conferences
    c. working with a mentor
    d. joining the labor union

Think Critically

16. Write a letter to incoming freshmen in your school encouraging them to join a nationally recognized student professional organization offered at your school. Make sure to emphasize the importance of active participation, networking, and leadership opportunities. (LO 15.2-1)
17. Write a job description for a position with a sports marketing firm. The job description should include education, internship or work experience, and skill requirements. (LO 15.1-1)
18. Use the *Occupational Outlook Handbook* to research a sports and entertainment marketing career that interests you. What is the outlook for this career field? What is the salary? What are the job duties? What are the education and skill requirements? (LO 15.1-1)
19. Research DECA, FBLA, or BPA to find out what makes membership in these organizations attractive to employers. Write a list of five advantages that members in these organizations have over the competition when applying for a job. (LO 15.2-1)

Make Academic Connections

20. **Math** Sports agents are often paid a commission (percentage) of the negotiated contract for their clients. One successful sports agent has negotiated contracts for five popular professional athletes. The salaries negotiated are $2.5 million, $12 million, $7.5 million, $1.8 million, and $500,000. How much will the agent earn from these successful negotiations if the agent's commission is 5 percent? (LO 15.1-1)

21. **Communications** Displaying professionalism in the workplace can help you succeed in your chosen career. Write a one-page paper explaining what "professionalism" means to you. (LO 15.1-2)

22. **Problem Solving** You are the director of a successful sports marketing firm. You realize the value to your employees of attending a professional development conference. Currently your firm has 20 employees who would benefit from this conference. The company budget can cover expenses for only eight people to attend the conference. How will you select who will attend the conference? How can the other 12 individuals learn the latest industry trends without attending the conference? (LO 15.3-1)

23. **Geography** Where would be a good location to host a conference for the Big Ten athletic directors? Why? Where would be a good location to host a conference for the Southeastern (SEC) athletic directors? Why? (LO 15.3-1)

24. **Math** You are in charge of organizing a national conference. You must negotiate prices for hotels, the convention center, and meals during the conference. You are planning to serve 850 people during the awards luncheon. Each meal will cost $28 plus 24 percent for tax and gratuity. How much will each individual meal actually cost? What will be the *total* cost of the awards luncheon? If attendance reaches 1,000, you will receive an 8 percent discount on the $28 price. What will be the *total* cost of the awards luncheon with the discount if 1,000 people attend? (LO 15.3-1)

25. **History** The role of athletic directors has changed dramatically with Title IX, sponsorships, conference realignments, growing budgets, facility construction, and increased competitive pressure. Write a one-page report explaining how the role has changed for athletic directors at major universities. (LO 15.1-1)

26. **Government** Federal, state, and local government agencies have been criticized for spending taxpayers' money to attend professional development conferences. Conduct research to learn about a government conference attended by federal, state, or local officials. Write a one-page report about it. What was the purpose of the conference? Who were the speakers? What were the costs? Do you think the conference was worthwhile? Why should taxpayers be concerned about these conferences? (LO 15.3-1)

27. **Research** Conduct research about internships with an entertainment organization, such as Disney or Universal Studios, and a professional sports team. Describe the process to apply for the internship, duties required of interns, and the value associated with participating in an internship. (LO 15.1-2)

28. **Communications** Mentors are commonly used in the workplace. They provide guidance and training and are a good resource for less experienced workers. Mentors can also be useful in a school setting. Develop a mentoring program for your school. Create a presentation that you will give to student council. Describe the benefits of a mentoring program and explain how it will operate. (LO 15.3-2)

EXTRA INNINGS PROJECT

Select a city to host a four-day conference for a national student organization such as DECA. Assume that 14,000 people will attend the conference. It will require a large convention center and seating capacity for the general and split sessions. You must hire entertainment for the opening session. The general sessions are noted for using high-tech electronics and music-coordinated events. The conference must have a large exhibit hall for more than 100 companies, schools, and other vendors to set up booths.

Work with a group and complete the following activities.

1. Use the Internet to research the details for a major national convention such as DECA.

2. How much does a popular singer or entertainer charge for a one-hour performance at an opening event? List five possible entertainment options and the cost for each one.

3. List five cities that would be good choices to host this conference. Create a table to compare the following:
    (a) number of hotel rooms
    (b) square feet of space at the convention center
    (c) airport capacity
    (d) other modes of public transportation
    (e) entertainment and tourist attractions appealing to high school students
   Then select one of the cities and prepare a tri-fold brochure to advertise your conference and the highlights of the city where it will be held.

4. Prepare a PowerPoint presentation that includes important facts about the conference. Use music and images to create excitement about the conference and the host city.

VIRTUAL BUSINESS *Sports & Entertainment*

Use the *Sports & Entertainment Mogul* lesson to apply everything you've learned in this course. Your goal is to make a $5 million profit during a season. Find and book bands, configure a winning team, and control all aspects of the stadium and a season of events. This activity will help you understand all of the variables involved in successfully managing a stadium. Forecast attendance, set pricing and manage ticket sales, promote events, find sponsorships, analyze event reports, and more. You have up to ten seasons (attempts) to make your goal. Good luck!

*For more information, go to **knowledgematters.com**.*

WHAT IT TAKES TO BE A BRAND MANAGER IN SPORTS AND ENTERTAINMENT MARKETING

Many aspiring marketers dream of working for a major corporation like Coca-Cola, Nike, Southwest Airlines, or the Marriott Corporation. Each of these corporations has spent time and money on brand strategies. Brand association is important in a world that offers a vast number of choices to consumers. A brand is more than a name. The brand represents a company's quality, reliability, and leadership in an industry.

Nike understands the importance of providing an excellent product endorsed by experts in the field. Nike has received endorsements from top athletes in every sport, including Cristiano Ronaldo, Maria Sharapova, LeBron James, Tiger Woods, Derek Jeter, and Michael Jordan. Although celebrity endorsements are effective, companies cannot rely on them solely to sell products. Today's consumers are more sophisticated and better educated than previous generations. Successful companies like Nike anticipate what consumers want and provide a product or service that is better than consumers' expectations.

Do You Have What It Takes?

Nike's brand managers are expected to provide strategic leadership when developing marketing plans. To identify "influencers" and keep current with the latest market trends, a brand manager travels to major sports and entertainment events, works closely with consumer groups, and interacts with the company's various marketing teams.

Strong communication skills are necessary to lead the development of strategic marketing plans. The brand manager establishes measurable business objectives, executes the marketing plan, and monitors the results to ensure excellence.

The brand manager position requires a minimum of a bachelor's degree in marketing, business, or a related field. Experience in advertising, social media, and digital marketing are preferred. In addition, Nike looks for brand managers who can develop innovative and creative ways to reach consumers. A challenging responsibility of the position is to develop and lead marketing plans that utilize talent (celebrities) to enhance brand initiatives and events.

Think Critically

1. Why is the brand so important when marketing a product? What do consumers associate with a brand?
2. Why is it important for the brand manager to be able to connect with consumers?
3. What are the education requirements to become a brand manager for a major company?
4. Why do you think the Nike brand manager would be required to travel to sports and entertainment events throughout the world?

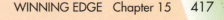 DECA WinningEdge

BUYING AND MERCHANDISING OPERATIONS RESEARCH EVENT

You (alone or with one or two partners) are to assume the role of a consultant for the athletic department of a major university noted for its successful football program. Universities are becoming increasingly concerned about the decline in the number of students who are purchasing season tickets for home games.

The university for which you are consulting is proud of its sold-out attendance record for home games, held since 1967. But like other major universities, it is also experiencing a decrease in ticket sales among college students. The number of students purchasing season football tickets has decreased from 20,000 to 12,000 in four years. Officials from the athletic department are concerned that the sold-out attendance record for home football games may be in jeopardy.

You must conduct research to find out reasons for the decrease in student season ticket sales for home football games. You must also determine what types of game experiences will bring more students back to home football games. The athletic department wants an improved marketing strategy to sell more season football tickets to students.

Performance Indicators Evaluated
- Select an actual university that has declining student season football ticket sales.
- Define a research study.
- Conduct a research study.
- Analyze the results of a research study.
- Propose a marketing strategy from the results of a research study.

All participants must present their marketing plan, including research findings, to the judges and respond to their questions. The body of the written plan must be limited to 30 numbered pages, including the appendix and excluding the title page and table of contents. Participants are responsible for bringing all visual aids to the event. The oral presentation may be a maximum of 15 minutes in length. The first 10 minutes will include an explanation and description of the project followed by 5 minutes for the judges' questions.

Think Critically

1. Other than attendance records, why else should universities be concerned that students aren't attending football games?
2. What groups should be surveyed to ensure you meet the goals of this research project?
3. What types of research can be used to gather the necessary information for this project?
4. What types of questions should you ask students to gather the information wanted by the university?

www.deca.org

CHAPTER 1

1. American Marketing Association, accessed October 15, 2013, http://www.marketingpower.com/AboutAMA/Pages/DefinitionofMarketing.aspx.
2. "What it costs for a family of four to attend an MLB game," *Milwaukee-Wisconsin Journal Sentinel*, accessed October 15, 2013, http://www.jsonline.com/sports/etc/rank--file-ed9djas-201365781.html.
3. "What's good for Daytona International Speedway is good for Volusia County," *Headline Surfer*, accessed November 19, 2013, http://headlinesurfer.com/content/411883-whats-good-daytona-international-speedway-good-volusia-county.
4. NASCAR Racing Statistics, accessed November 19, 2013, http://www.statisticbrain.com/nascar-racing-statistics/.
5. "Infographics: Social Media Stats 2013," Digital Buzz Blog, accessed November 14, 2013, http://www.digitalbuzzblog.com/infographic-social-media-stats-2013/.
6. Brian Warner, "The Highest Paid College Basketball Coaches," *Celebrity Net Worth*, March 27, 2013, accessed October 17, 2013, http://www.celebritynetworth.com/articles/entertainment-articles/the-highest-paid-college-basketball-coaches.
7. National Collegiate Athletic Association, accessed November 21, 2013, http://www.ncaa.org/wps/wcm/connect/public/ncaa/finances/revenue.
8. "NCAA Finances," *USA TODAY*, accessed November 21, 2013, http://www.usatoday.com/sports/college/schools/finances/.

CHAPTER 2

1. "Approximately how much money is spent each year marketing food products to children?" Extension: America's Research-based Learning Network, March 16, 2010, accessed November 16, 2013, http://www.extension.org/pages/42692/approximately-how-much-money-is-spent-each-year-marketing-food-products-to-children#.Un_vY6jnbcs.
2. Scott Bowles, "Movie ticket prices jump to all-time high," *USA TODAY*, July 23, 2013, accessed April 21, 2014, http://www.usatoday.com/story/life/movies/2013/07/23/movie-ticket-prices-nato/2577199/.

3. "The World's Highest-Paid Athletes," *Forbes*, values calculated June 2013, http://www.forbes.com/athletes/list.
4. "Big Ten Team Tix," BTN Big Ten Network, accessed November 16, 2013, http://bigten.teamtix.com/content/home?host=b1g.
5. Darren Rovell, "Texas leads in merchandise royalties," ESPN.com, August 12, 2013, accessed April 21, 2014, http://espn.go.com/college-football/story/_/id/9560094/texas-longhorns-again-top-merchandise-sales-list.
6. "Football Continues to Be America's Favorite Sport; the Gap with Baseball Narrows Slightly This Year," Harris Interactive, January 17, 2013, accessed December 21, 2013, http://www.harrisinteractive.com/NewsRoom/HarrisPolls/tabid/447/ctl/ReadCustom%20Default/mid/1508/ArticleId/1136/Default.aspx.
7. "Adidas History," Fashion, accessed November 16, 2013, http://fashiongear.fibre2fashion.com/brand-story/adidas/history.asp.

CHAPTER 3

1. Alexandra Cheney, "On the Horizon: Ron Howard Drove 'Rush' Fundraising," *The Wall Street Journal,* August 25, 2013, B5.
2. "Sports Industry Overview," accessed November 2, 2013, http://www.plunkettresearch.com/sports-recreation-leisure-market-research/industry-statistics.
3. "Kickstarter: The Best of 2012," accessed November 5, 2013, http://www.kickstarter.com/hello.
4. Stephen Battaglio and Michael Schneider, "TV's Highest Paid Stars: What They Earn," *TV Guide*, August 20, 2013, accessed November 3, 2013, http://www.tvguide.com/News/TV-Highest-Paid-Stars-1069334.aspx.
5. Eamon Murphy, "Price of Victory: Phil Mickelson Hit With 61% Tax Bite on UK Winnings," July 22, 2013, accessed November 5, 2013, http://www.dailyfinance.com/on/price-of-victory-phil-mickelson-hit-with-61-tax-bite-on-uk-win/.
6. Brooks Barnes, "Trying to Spice a Recipe for Cinematic Popcorn," *The New York Times,* July 30, 2013, accessed November 6, 2013, http://www.nytimes.com/2013/07/31/business/media/with-elysium-sony-hopes-to-break-a-string-of-failures.html?pagewanted=all&_r=0.

7. David Waldstein, "A Most Likable Yankee Spends His Goodbye Tour Saying Hello," *The New York Times,* July 16, 2013, A1.

8. Waldstein, "A Most Likable Yankee Spends His Goodbye Tour Saying Hello," B12.

9. Peter May, "Patriots Store Takes Back Unwanted Hernandez Jerseys," *The New York Times,* July 7, 2013, sec Sports 5.

10. Stephen Bronars, "Does the NFL Have a Crime Problem?" December 9, 2012, accessed November 5, 2013, http://sbronars.wordpress.com/2012/12/09/does-the-nfl-have-a-crime-problem/.

CHAPTER 4

1. Brad Jacobs, Top Rank, telephone interview with Dotty Oelkers, April 20, 2012.

2. Artem Zagorodnov, "Planning for Economic Success in Sochi after the 2014 Olympics," Special Russian Advertising Feature, *The New York Times*, October 16, 2013, 5.

3. "Tim Hughes Elected Chairman of Little League International Board of Directors," Little League, accessed November 15, 2013, http://www.littleleague.org/media/llnewsarchive/05_2004/04hugheselected.htm.

4. Kevin Baxter, "If Mexico fails to get to World Cup, backers could lose $600 million," *Los Angeles Times,* October 15, 2013, accessed November 15, 2013, http://www.latimes.com/sports/sportsnow/la-sp-sn-world-cup-failure-mexico-20131015,0,1505046.story#axzz2iHLj5k00.

5. Special Russian Advertising Feature, *The New York Times*, October 16, 2013.

6. Michelle Kung, "Odd Couple: China Meets Hollywood," *The Wall Street Journal,* April 17, 2012, A1, A12.

7. Edward Wong, "Filmmaker Giving Voice to Acts of Rage in Today's China," *The New York Times,* September 14, 2013, A5.

8. Edward Wong, "Drama Behind Film Awaits Climax," *The New York Times,* November 23, 2013, C1–2.

9. Michael Cieply, "China Wants Its Movies to Be Big in the U.S., Too," *The New York Times,* November 7, 2013, B10.

10. Scott Bowles, "Clear 'Instructions' point to the power of Latino audience," *USA TODAY,* September 25, 2013, D1-2.

11. Juliet Macur, "Antidoping Lab's Flaws Put Olympics in a Bind," *The New York Times,* November 16, 2013, B9–B12.

12. "Title IX Myths and Facts," Women's Sports Foundation, accessed December 1, 2013, http://www.womenssportsfoundation.org/en/home/advocate/title-ix-and-issues/what-is-title-ix/title-ix-myths-and-facts.

13. Naila-Jean Meyers, "The Breakthrough of 1973," *The New York Times,* August 26, 2013, F10.

14. Kurt Badenhausen, "Maria Sharapova Tops List of The World's Highest-Paid Female Athletes," *Forbes*, August 5, 2013, accessed December 1, 2013, www.forbes.com.

15. "Our Mission," World Travel and Tourism Council, accessed November 18, 2013, http://www.wttc.org/our-mission/.

16. The New Orleans Super Bowl Host Committee and The University of New Orleans Division of Business Economic Research, *2013 Super Bowl Visitor Study & Economic Impact (Super Bowl XLVII)*, April 2013, 3, 6.

17. "What is Ecotourism?" The International Ecotourism Society, accessed November 18, 2013, http://www.ecotourism.org/what-is-ecotourism.

18. Susan and Simon Veness, telephone interview with Dotty Oelkers, November 21, 2013.

19. "Fast Facts About Orlando," Orlando Convention and Visitors Bureau, accessed November 15, 2013, http://media.visitorlando.com/press-kits/orlando-overview-and-facts/fast-facts/.

20. "The Organisation—Mission & Statutes," FIFA, accessed November 18, 2013, http://www.fifa.com/aboutfifa/organisation/mission.html.

CHAPTER 5

1. Patrick Healy, "Dialing Up a Hit? Influence Over Musical Is in the Crowd's Hands," *The New York Times,* June 26, 2013, A1, A20.

2. Healy, "Dialing Up a Hit? Influence Over Musical Is in the Crowd's Hands," A20.

3. Ian Urbina, "I Flirt and Tweet. Follow Me at #Socialbot," August 10, 2013, *The New York Times,* accessed November 24, 2013, http://www.nytimes.com/2013/08/11/sunday-review/i-flirt-and-tweet-follow-me-at-socialbot.html?_r=0.

4. *State of the Global Workplace: Employee Engagement Insights for Business Leaders Worldwide,* Gallup, *2013, 50.*

5. "You are what you watch: The importance of engaging TV shows to ad success," Nielsen, September 12, 2013, accessed November 24, 2013, http://nielsen.com/us/en/newswire/2013/you-are-what-you-watch--the-importance-of-engaging-tv-shows-to-a.html.

6. William G. Zikmund and Barry J. Babin, *Exploring Marketing Research, 10*th edition (Mason, Ohio: Cengage, 2010*) 112.*

7. BrainyQuote, accessed November 15, 2013, http://www.brainyquote.com/quotes/quotes/j/jackwelch173305.html.

8. Bill Carter, "Where Have All the Viewers Gone?" *The New York Times,* April 23, 2012, B1.

9. Bruce Nash, "Analysis: The Numbers Bankability Index Under the Covers," Nash Information Services, accessed November 20, 2013, http://www.the-numbers.com/news/8658.

CHAPTER 6

1. "Celebrity Profile: Ellen DeGeneres," Examiner.com, May 24, 2009, accessed November 3, 2013, http://www.examiner.com/article/celebrity-charity-profile-ellen-degeneres.

2. Tony Manfred, "20 Golfers Who Make More Money Endorsing Products Than Playing Golf," *Business Insider*, accessed November 3, 2013, http://www.businessinsider.com.au/highest-paid-golfers-endorsements-2013-1#yani-tseng-35-million-off-the-course-1.

3. Jeremy Crabtree, "Changes to Texting Rules on Table," ESPN College Football, October 8, 2013, accessed April 30, 2014, http://espn.go.com/college-football/story/_/id/9794026/unlimited-texting-coming-back-college-football-recruiting.

4. "NCAA Finances," *USA TODAY*, accessed March 21, 2014, http://www.usatoday.com/sports/college/schools/finances/.

5. Rachel Cohen and Ralph D. Russo, "Paying College Athletes: Not If but How," *The Huffington Post*, January 6, 2013, accessed November 6, 2013, http://www.huffingtonpost.com/2013/01/07/paying-college-athletes_n_2424429.html.

6. Zach Gorwitz, "Money Madness: Why and How College Athletes Should Be Paid," *Duke Political Review*, October 1, 2013, accessed April 30, 2014, http://dukepoliticalreview.org/money-madness-why-and-how-ncaa-athletes-should-be-paid/.

7. "High Cost of Youth Sports," *The Huffington Post*, June 21, 2013, accessed February 17, 2014, http://www.huffingtonpost.com/visualnewscom/high-cost-of-youth-sports_b_3469012.html#.

8. Matthew Emmons, "Highest Paid College Football Coaches—2013," AZCentral, November 6, 2013, accessed November 10, 2013, http://www.azcentral.com/sports/colleges/free/20131106highest-paid-college-football-coaches-2013.html.

9. "From High School to Pro—How Many Will Go," Georgia Career Information Center, accessed November 17, 2013, http://freedom.mysdhc.org/guidance/information/From%20High%20School%20to%20Pro%20Statistics.pdf.

10. "WNBA Salaries for the 2013 Season," Examiner.com, accessed November 21, 2013, http://www.examiner.com/article/wnba-salaries-for-the-2013-season.

11. "NBA Player Salaries—2013–2014," ESPN.com, accessed December 6, 2013, http://espn.go.com/nba/salaries.

12. Alan Black, "New Poll Shows Soccer's Popularity on the Upswing," SFGate, accessed November 30, 2013, http://blog.sfgate.com/soccer/2012/03/06/new-poll-shows-soccers-popularity-on-the-upswing/.

13. "Youth Sports Statistics," Michigan State Survey, accessed November 30, 2013, http://statisticbrain.comyouth-spots-statistics.

14. Ben Lingenfelter, "How Do Different Age Groups Use Facebook," eHow, accessed November 17, 2013, http://www.ehow.com/info_12033172_different-age-groups-use-facebook.html.

15. Dorothy Pomerantz, "The World's Most Powerful Celebrities," *Forbes*, June 26, 2013, accessed March 21, 2014, http://www.forbes.com/profile/maria-sharapova.

CHAPTER 7

1. "DreamWorks plans Netflix TV shows," *Houston Chronicle,* June 18, 2013, B7.

2. Bill Carter, "Bold Play by CBS Fortifies Broadcasters," *The New York Times,* September 7, 2013, B1-2.

3. Claire Cain Miller, "Addicted to Apps," *The New York Times,* August 25, 2013, SR3.

4. Nick Wingfield, "The Only Games in Town," *The New York Times,* September 30, 2013, B1, B3.

5. Allan Kozinn, "A Pay-What-You-Can Music Model," *The New York Times,* August 21, 2013, C1.

6. *Katy Perry: Part of Me*, Box Office Mojo, accessed March 4, 2014, http://boxofficemojo.com/movies/?id=katyperry.htm.

7. Bill Carter, "NBC Says It Will Put on a Show, Again," *The New York Times,* December 10, 2013, C1.

8. Carter, "NBC Says It Will Put on a Show, Again," C6.

9. Dale Russakoff, "Old Age in America, by the Numbers," *The New York Times,* July 21, 2010, accessed December 6, 2013, http://newoldage.blogs.nytimes.com/2010/07/21/aging-in-america-how-its-changing/?_r=0.

10. "2013 Sports, Fitness and Leisure Activities Topline Participation Report – New Release!!," Sports & Fitness Industry Association, http://www.sfia.org/reports/301_2013-SPORTS%2C-FITNESS-AND-LEISURE-ACTIVITIES-TOPLINE-PARTICIPATION-REPORT----NEW-RELEASE!!

11. Paul Myerberg, "Six ways to watch BCS title game," *USA Today*, December 19, 2013, 3C.
12. Sandomir, James Andrew Miller, and Steve Eder, "To Protect Its Empire, ESPN Stays on Offense," *The New York Times*, August 27, 2013, A1.
13. "Most Popular Sports in the World," Most Popular Sports, accessed January 16, 2013, http://mostpopularsports.net/in-the-world.
14. Charles V. Bagli, "Giants and Jets, Super Bowl Hosts, Have Already Been Richly Rewarded," *The New York Times,* November 29, 2013, A30.
15. Davis Barron, "Howard to Rockets unlikely to get carriage dispute settled," *The Houston Chronicle,* July 19, 2013, C4.
16. Richie Parker, "Richie Parker: Drive," interview by Tom Rinaldi, ESPN2 *SportsCenter*, July 21, 2013.

CHAPTER 8

1. "Redbox Fun Facts," Redbox Media Center, accessed November 17, 2013, http://www.redbox.com/facts.
2. Brad Tuttle, "Kid Rock's $20 Concert Ticket Plan: Good for Fans, Bad for Scalpers," *Time*, June 26, 2013, accessed April 20, 2014, http://business.time.com/2013/06/26/kid-rocks-20-concert-ticket-plan-good-for-fans-bad-for-scalpers/.
3. Doug Farrar, "Trading for Tim Tebow was a mistake, former Jets GM Tannenbaum says," January 17, 2014, accessed April 20, 2014, http://nfl.si.com/2014/01/17/tim-tebow-jets-trade-mistake-mike-tannenbaum/.
4. "How Much Does Social Media Marketing Cost?" The Content Factory, accessed April 20, 2014, http://www.contentfac.com/how-much-does-social-media-marketing-cost/.

CHAPTER 9

1. Andrew Adam Newman, "Samsung's Video Campaign Pits Earth's Soccer Stars vs. Aliens," *The New York Times*, December 19, 2013, B6.
2. "Advertising and Marketing," Bureau of Consumer Protection, accessed January 11, 2013, http://business.ftc.gov/advertising-and-marketing.
3. "About the Association," American Association of Advertising Agencies, accessed January 12, 2014, http://www.aaaa.org/about/association/Pages/default.aspx.
4. "Standards of Practice," American Association of Advertising Agencies, updated June 7, 2011, accessed January 12, 2014, http://www.aaaa.org/about/association/Pages/standardsofpractice.aspx.

5. Katherine Feser, "Agency true to Hispanic roots," *Houston Chronicle*, October 28, 2013, B6.

CHAPTER 10

1. Bill Keveney, "Grammy TV ratings remain solid for CBS," *USA TODAY,* January 27, 2014, accessed January 28, 2014, http://www.usatoday.com/story/life/tv/2014/01/27/grammy-tv-ratings-on-cbs-rise-slightly-from-2013/4939973/.
2. Scott Manley, Toyota Center, Houston, Texas, phone interview with Dotty Oelkers, January 30, 2014.
3. "30 Second Ad Rates for the 2014 Academy Awards," Media Buying, Ocean Media, posted November 14, 2013, accessed January 31, 2014, http://www.oceanmediainc.com/media-agency-blog/30-ad-rates-2014-academy-awards/.
4. Kyle Stock, "Is Manchester United Worth $1 Billion to Nike?" *Bloomberg Businessweek*, March 11, 2014, accessed May 7, 2014, http://www.businessweek.com/articles/2014-03-11/is-manchester-united-worth-1-billion-to-nike.
5. Rochi Palacios, "2014 FIFA World Cup: A Brand Love Affair," Football Marketing, January 8, 2014, accessed February 1, 2014, http://www.football-marketing.com/2014/01/08/2014-fifa-world-cup-a-brand-love-affair/.
6. "Guides Concerning the Use of Endorsements and Testimonials in Advertising," Federal Trade Commission, 16 CFR Part 255, accessed February 1, 2014, http://www.ftc.gov/sites/default/files/attachments/press-releases/ftc-publishes-final-guides-governing-endorsements-testimonials/091005revisedendorsementguides.pdf.
7. Erik Brady and Brent Schrotenboer, "From QB to pitchman, what you see is what you get with Peyton Manning," *USA TODAY*, January 31, 2014, 1C, 6C.
8. Stuart Elliott, "High Stakes for Agencies, and Products, at Super Bowl," *The New York Times*, January 31, 2014, B6.
9. Mae Anderson, "Adver-Teasers: Super Bowl Viewers Get Peek at Ads," AP, posted January 29, 2013, accessed February 2, 2014, http://bigstory.ap.org/article/super-bowl-advertisers-tease-viewers-0.
10. Elliott, "High Stakes," B6.
11. Elizabeth Olson, "I'll Be Your Billboard," *The New York Times,* January 26, 2014, BU8.
12. Brad Jacobs, Top Rank, telephone interview with Dotty Oelkers, April 20, 2012.
13. Stuart Elliott, "TCM Moves to Lure Film Buffs Out of Their Living Rooms," *The New York Times,* August 22, 2013, B4.

14. Stuart Elliott, "Nascar Drivers Speak Up, Aiming to Attract New Fans," *The New York Times,* February 19, 2013, B6.

15. "NASCAR Racing Statistics, Statistic Brain, updated January 14, 2014, accessed May 20, 2014, http://www.statisticbrain.com/nascar-racing-statistics/.

16. "Loyal NASCAR Fans Please Stand Up," Performance Research, accessed February 18, 2014, http://performanceresearch.com/nascar-racestat.htm.

17. Tori Petry, "NASCAR Not Just for the Boys," ESPNW. Today, August 20, 2012, accessed February 18, 2014, http://espn.go.com/espnw/news-commentary/article/8284577/espnw-nascar-not-just-boys.

CHAPTER 11

1. Michelle Begnoche, "Pure Michigan Campaign Results in $1.1 Billion in Visitor Spending in 2012," Pure Michigan, April 15, 2013, accessed January 10, 2014, http://www.michigan.org/pressreleases/pure-michigan-campaign-results-in/.

2. Michelle Begnoche, "Streak Continues: michigan.org Most Visited State Tourism Website for Sixth Year in a Row," Pure Michigan, January 17, 2013, accessed May 2, 2014, http://www.michigan.org/pressreleases/streak-continues-michigan-org-most-visited-state-tourism-website-for-sixth-year-in-a-row.

3. Darren Heitner, "Broncos vs. Seahawks Super Bowl Tickets Becoming More Affordable by the Day," *Forbes,* January 25, 2014, accessed May 4, 2014, http://www.forbes.com/sites/darrenheitner/2014/01/25/broncos-vs-seahawks-super-bowl-tickets-becoming-more-affordable-by-the-day/.

4. Darren Rovell, "Record prices for Game 6 tickets," ESPN.com, October 30, 2013, accessed January 10, 2014, http://espn.go.com/boston/mlb/story/_/id/9897792/2013-world-series-record-sale-prices-boston-red-sox-tickets-fenway-park-game-6-vs-st-louis-cardinals.

5. Roger Kuznia, "College basketball Twitter coach rankings: Tim Miles the standout of Big Ten," *Sporting News*, August 19, 2013, accessed May 2, 2014, http://www.sportingnews.com/ncaa-basketball/story/2013-08-19college-basketball-twitter-rankings-2013-tim-miles-tom-crean-social-media.

6. Live Nation Entertainment 2013 Annual Report, accessed May 2, 2014, http://investors.livenationentertainment.com/files/doc_financials/2013/2013 Annual Report.pdf.

7. Red Bull Arena Tickets, accessed May 2, 2014, http://www.redbullarena.us/tickets/.

CHAPTER 12

1. Howard Beck, "For Rockets, Every Move Was a Step Forward," *New York Times,* July 11, 2013, B11.

2. "McLane Stadium: Stadium Facts," *Baylor-Stadium.com*, accessed February 24, 2014, http://www.baylor-stadium.com/stadium-facts/.

3. David Ubben, "New Baylor stadium? Say 'Thanks, RG3,' Big 12 Blog, March 14, 2012, accessed May 24, 2014, http://espn.go.com/blog/big12/post/_/id/46848/new-baylor-stadium-say-thanks-rg3.

4. "MLB ticket prices up 2.7 percent," Associated Press, *ESPN.com,* updated April 1, 2013, accessed February 28, 2014, http://espn.go.com/mlb/story/_/id/9121457/mlb-ticket-prices-see-steepest-hike-2009.

CHAPTER 13

1. Mark Yost, "Varsity Green: A Behind the Scenes Look at Culture and Corruption in College Athletics" (Stanford University Press, 2010), 13.

2. *The U.S. Professional Sports Market & Franchise Value Report 2012*, W.R. Hambrecht + Co., 28.

3. Hiroko Tabuchi and Joshua Hunt, "Deference to a Revered Record in Japan Is Going, Going …," *The New York Times,* September 5, 2013, A1, A3.

4. "China video sites confident public will pay for content," *USA TODAY,* January 14, 2014, accessed June 4, 2014, http://www.usatoday.com/story/tech/personal/2014/01/14/china-piracy-illegal-download-copyright/4471237/.

5. Michael Cieply, "Hollywood's Antipiracy Efforts Add New Voice," *The New York Times,* March 31, 2014, B1-2.

6. Joshua P. Friedlander, *News and Notes on 2013 RIAA Music Industry Shipment and Revenue Statistics*, RIAA, accessed March 20, 2014, http://76.74.24.142/2463566A-FF96-E0CA-2766-72779A364D01.pdf.

7. Steve Berkowitz, Jodi Upton, and Erik Brady, "Most NCAA Division I athletic departments take subsidies," *USA TODAY,* July 1, 2013, accessed June 5, 2014, http://www.usatoday.com/story/sports/college/2013/05/07/ncaa-finances-subsidies/2142443/.

CHAPTER 14

1. Jason Nazar, "16 Surprising Statistics About Small Businesses," *Forbes*, September 9, 2013, accessed June 13, 2014, http://www.forbes.com/sites/jasonnazar/2013/09/09/16-surprising-statistics-about-small-businesses/.

2. Helaine Olen, "Discrimination Against the Old? Even the Old Do It," *The New York Times*, March 24, 2014, accessed June 17, 2014, http://www.nytimes.com/2014/03/25/your-money/discriminate-against-the-old-even-the-old-do-it.html/.

CHAPTER 15

1. Bureau of Labor Statistics, *Occupational Outlook Handbook*, accessed June 19, 2014, http://www.bls.gov/ooh/.

2. Erik Sherman, "1 In 10 Young Job Hunters Rejected Because of Their Social Media," AOL Jobs, accessed June 19, 2014, http://jobs.aol.com/articles/2013/06/04/applicants-rejected-social-media-on-device-research.

3. NCAA.com, accessed June 29, 2014, http://www.ncaa.org/about/resources/leadership-development-programs-and-resources/ncaa-and-nfl-coaches-academy.

4. Mentor National Mentoring Partnership, accessed June 19, 2014, http://www.mentoring.org/about_mentor/.

Glossary

A

Advertising a paid form of communication delivered to consumers by a product maker or seller (p. 237)

Adviser a financial and business counselor, not a behavioral monitor (p. 353)

Agent the legal representative of an athlete or celebrity (p. 351)

Agent contract an agreement in which an athlete or celebrity allows a person or agency to act as a representative in marketing his or her ability and name (p. 354)

Algorithm a detailed set of instructions on how to sort data (p. 136)

Amphitheaters oval-shaped outdoor theaters with tiered seating around a central staging area (p. 181)

Analytics the process of using computer programming and incorporating statistics to organize data into meaningful patterns (p. 136)

Anthology series a TV series that has a different cast, setting, and story line each season (p. 320)

Applied research focuses on solving a specific problem (p. 319)

Art-house movies typically independent films that are outside the commercial mainstream of blockbuster films and draw smaller audiences (p. 193)

Autocratic leader a take-charge person who does not seek the input of team members (p. 378)

B

Bait and switch occurs when a product that is advertised at a low price is "out of stock," so the salesperson tries to sell customers a higher-priced alternative (p. 215)

Balance sheet a statement that shows the company's assets (items of value, including cash, property, and equipment) and its liabilities (amounts owed for purchases made on credit and loans) at a specific point in time (p. 74)

Benefits derived the value people believe they receive from a product or service (p. 40)

Big data the extraordinary amount of data that is being collected and stored for marketing purposes (p. 139)

Blue-chip athletes high-prospect athletes who have exceptional athletic ability and who demonstrate good character and leadership qualities on and off the field (p. 156)

Body language non-spoken signals (p. 252)

Booking agent a firm that contracts with the venue on behalf of the performers (p. 264)

Box office income from ticket sales (p. 103)

Brand the name, symbol, logo, word, or design (or a combination of these elements) that identifies a product, service, or company (p. 153)

Breakeven point minimum sales required to cover all of the expenses of organizing, promoting, and running the event (p. 37)

Broadband high-speed Internet service (p. 187)

Broadcast flags digital bits that can be embedded in digital programming to prevent programs from being recorded and redistributed (p. 344)

Budget a detailed projection of financial performance for a specific time period (p. 73)

Business cycle refers to the ups and downs of the economy; also known as the economic cycle (p. 222)

Business plan a formal, written document that provides the details for a proposed new business (p. 366)

C

Cable bundle a group of TV channels sold as a package for one monthly price by TV subscription services (p. 196)

Cafeteria plan a benefit plan in which employees pick and choose from various benefit options to best meet their needs (p. 373)

Capital a company's wealth in the form of money or property (p. 73)

Cart-reminder email an email reminding a customer of his or her incomplete purchase left in an online shopping cart (p. 141)

Cartel an organization of independent businesses formed to control production, pricing, and marketing of a product (p. 199)

Censorship the act of altering or editing media that is considered objectionable (p. 100)

Channels of distribution include all of the businesses through which products or services pass on the way to the consumer (p. 179)

Clarification offering back an interpretation of the meaning of the message, as understood by the listener, and then asking questions to make things clearer (p. 377)

Client-side researchers in-house staff researchers who also work with external research agencies (p. 127)

Club seats premium stadium seats usually located outdoors that provide a source of high revenue (p. 303)

Cohesion the act or state of working, uniting, or sticking together (p. 376)

Cohort a group of people who share certain characteristics (p. 140)

Cold calling involves contacting potential customers at random without researching the customers' needs first (p. 291)

Collective bargaining occurs when a group of employees join together as a single unit to negotiate with employers (p. 347)

Collective bargaining agreement when the players' associations and the entertainment industry unions negotiate an employment contract with the owners or management (p. 347)

Comparative advantage the capability to produce products or services more efficiently and economically than the competition (p. 40)

Consumer sales promotion when a sales promotion is directed at the final consumer (p. 245)

Contingency planning the preparation for an unexpected emergency (p. 78)

Contract an agreement enforceable by law that details the transactions of business between two or more people (p. 354)

Convergence analytics the process of organizing data from multiple sources into usable information (p. 139)

Copy words to be spoken or printed in an ad, to convey their message (p. 241)

Copyright legally protects the unique work of the originator from use by others without permission (p. 341)

Corporate sponsorship using the name of a product or business as part of the name of an event venue (p. 270)

Corporation a form of business in which ownership is represented by shares of stock (p. 367)

Cost-per-thousand (CPM) when the cost effectiveness of a specific media is evaluated based on the cost of each exposure to an ad divided by its reach in thousands (p. 275)

Culture the shared history, beliefs, customs, and traditions of a group of people that distinguishes them from another group (p. 107)

Customer management building a customer base and carefully scheduling time spent with customers (p. 293)

Customer service gap the difference between customer expectations and the service that is actually received (p. 53)

Customer's lifetime value a calculation of the estimated profit the business will earn from the customer (p. 139)

D

Data-driven decisions decisions based on data and analysis rather than experience and intuition (p. 140)

Data interpretation finding meaning in data (p. 136)

Data mining using technology to "dig up" data (p. 138)

Democratic leader a leader who involves team members in the decision-making process (p. 378)

Demographics shared characteristics of a group, such as age, marital status, gender, ethnic background, income level, and education level (p. 13)

Differentiation when a product is customized to appeal to different markets (p. 103)

Direct economic impact the total amount of new spending resulting from an event or attraction (p. 113)

Discretionary income the amount of money individuals have available to spend after paying for the necessities of life and other fixed expenses, such as housing and car payments (p. 6)

Disruptive technologies new technologies that change existing forms of communication channels (p. 184)

Distribution the locations and methods used to make products available to customers (p. 5)

E

Economic impact the effect produced by decisions that are made by consumers and businesses (p. 68)

Economic market all of the consumers who will purchase a product or service (p. 39)

Economic utility the amount of satisfaction a person receives from the consumption of a particular product or service (p. 69)

Economics the study of how goods and services are produced, distributed, and consumed (p. 68)

Ecotourism responsible travel to natural areas that conserves the environment and improves the well-being of local people (p. 114)

Emotional purchases when consumers spend with little thought during emotional highs or lows (p. 41)

Endorsement a well-known person's public expression of approval or support for a product or service (p. 270)

Entertainment some type of performance that people are willing to spend their money and spare time watching (p. 20)

Entertainment marketing influencing how people choose to spend their time and money on entertainment (p. 20)

Entrepreneurs individuals who take the risk of starting, owning, and operating a business (p. 364)

Equilibrium the point at which the supply and demand curves intersect (p. 212)

Ethical dilemma when one has to choose between two equal moral principles (p. 81)

Ethics a system for deciding between right and wrong in a reasoned and impartial manner (p. 81)

Event triangle formed by the interaction of the event, the sponsors, and the fans (p. 262)

Exchange the give-and-take between the event, the sponsors, and the fans (p. 262)

Executive summary placed at the front of the marketing plan to present a short, concise restatement of its contents (p. 325)

Experiential activations interactions with customers through festivals, tours, or licensed merchandise to retain satisfied customers (p. 279)

F

Fair use allows limited creative uses of music, literature, movies, and more without asking permission or making payment (p. 343)

Feedback the receiver's response to the sender's message (p. 376)

Focus groups a panel of people who answer market research questions related to their observations or opinions about a product or service (p. 136)

Forecast a report that predicts the expenses to be incurred and the revenues to be earned (p. 72)

Frequency the number of times the targeted group has been exposed to the message (p. 243)

Frequency table a table that shows how often each numerical value, response, item, or range of numbers in a set of data occurs (p. 136)

Fringe benefits incentives received in addition to a base salary (pp. 159, 373)

G

Gender equity when opportunities for men and women are roughly equal (p. 96)

Globalization the international economic relationships resulting from the integration of the world's markets (p. 103)

Goodwill positive feelings about the business (p. 248)

Grass-roots effort when an unknown person or event is propelled into the spotlight by fans (p. 248)

Gross impression the number of times per advertisement, game, or show that a product or service is associated with an athlete, team, or entertainer (p. 15)

Gross rating points (GRP) multiplying the reach by the frequency, expressed as a percentage, provides the estimated total potential audience (p. 275)

Group packages promotions that give special ticket prices to members of a group when tickets are purchased in large quantities (p. 300)

H

Handler someone who manages an athlete's life off the field (p. 353)

Hard data statistics gathered through valid research (p. 129)

Human resources the employees who work for an organization (p. 369)

I

Income statement a statement that shows all revenues received and all expenses incurred over a specific period of time (p. 73)

In-concert movie contains film of actual concert performances (p. 191)

Indirect economic impact determined by the multiplier effect, which is the portion of the money spent by visitors on local goods and services that is in turn spent by local employers and employees and re-circulated in the area (p. 113)

Inflation occurs when prices for goods and services rise faster than consumer income (p. 223)

Integrity a strong, voluntary adherence to honesty and morality; often linked to ethical behavior (p. 83)

Intellectual property the unique works of writers, artists, and musicians that are protected under copyright law (p. 341)

Intermediaries the businesses, or channel members, involved in making the product or service available (p. 179)

International marketing marketing a product in another country (p. 102)

International Olympic Committee (IOC) the governing authority of the Olympic Movement, which includes all of the National Olympic Committees (NOC), the International Sports Federations, Organizing Committees for the Olympic Games, athletes, sponsors, and broadcasting partners (p. 95)

Internship a hands-on learning experience at a real work site (p. 394)

Interpersonal skills an individual's character traits that allow him or her to effectively interact and work with other people (p. 375)

Interpretation the explanation of research data in a way that makes it meaningful and informative (p. 319)

J

Jargon language that relates to a specific area and that makes communication more concise (p. 397)

Job analysis the study of a specific job to identify the duties and skill requirements of the job (p. 371)

Joint venture an agreement between two or more companies to work together on a business project (p. 100)

L

Labor union an organization of workers formed to advance the rights and interests of its members (p. 346)

Laissez-faire leader a leader who offers little or no guidance to team members and leaves the decision making to them (p. 378)

Law of demand when the price goes up, demand goes down; when the price goes down, demand goes up (p. 211)

Law of supply when the price goes up, the supply produced goes up; when the price goes down, the supply produced goes down (p. 212)

Leads information and data on prospective customers who have shown interest in the product or service and/or meet the definition of the target market (p. 291)

League agreement controls the marketing mix and governs the distribution of professional sports games, including the locations of the teams and the number of teams allowed in the league (p. 199)

Liable being held legally responsible for damages and possibly medical costs and other losses suffered by the injured person (p. 77)

Licensed brand a well-known name and/or symbol established by one company and sold for use by another company to promote its products (p. 154)

Lockout a period of time during which the owners keep the players from using the team facilities and shut down league operations (p. 348)

Logistics the process of planning, organizing, and managing the distribution of products and services (p. 180)

Logo the graphic representation of a company's name (p. 270)

Loss occurs when not enough revenue is made to cover expenses (p. 68)

Loss-leader pricing involves reducing the price of a product below the store's cost to create more customer traffic (p. 219)

Loyal users people who open an app at least three times in 30 days (p. 276)

Luxury boxes (luxury suites) lavish rooms inside stadiums and arenas that allow corporate executives and some wealthy private individuals to entertain clients and friends while watching the events (p. 302)

M

Market research information that is specifically focused on a single target market (p. 132)

Market segment a group of consumers within a larger market who share one or more characteristics (p. 46)

Market share the percentage of total sales of a product or service that a company expects to capture in relation to its competitors (p. 50)

Marketing the creation and maintenance of satisfying exchange relationships (p. 4)

Marketing concept keeping the focus on satisfying customer needs; requires maintaining important relationships with customers (p. 35)

Marketing-information system a set of procedures and methods used to systematically collect, analyze, distribute, and store information needed by business managers to make decisions, including decisions about how to please customers (p. 126)

Marketing intelligence information gathered about competitors (p. 315)

Marketing manager The person who drives the creative development of the company's messages about its products (p. 394)

Marketing mix describes how a business blends the four marketing elements of product, distribution, price, and promotion (p. 5)

Marketing plan a precisely written document that describes a company's situational analysis, marketing strategy, and implementation plan for meeting company objectives (p. 312)

Marketing research a process designed to provide solutions to marketing problems through the use of a scientific problem-solving system (p. 127)

Marketing strategy an idea for achieving marketing objectives that can be put into action (p. 312)

Markup the amount that is added to the cost of a product or service to cover operating expenses and to allow for a profit (p. 216)

Mass marketing an attempt to appeal to a large, general group of consumers (p. 47)

Mass media a term used to describe a method of distributing an event to a large volume of people—the masses (p. 181)

Media the channels of communication used to send a message to the target market (p. 237)

Mentor an experienced professional who willingly acts as a role model and provides guidance, encouragement, and training for individuals (p. 411)

Mission statement the nature of the business and the reason that the company exists (p. 326)

Multichannel video programming distributor a cable or satellite distributor (p. 201)

Multigenerationalism satisfying the needs of several generations of a family (p. 116)

N

Native advertising online content created by a company that has the appearance of non-ad content, such as an editorial (p. 243)

NCAA a voluntary organization through which the nation's colleges and universities govern their athletics programs (p. 157)

Networking the process of developing contacts with other individuals, groups, or organizations for the benefit of career development (p. 399)

Niche travel recreational travel or tours planned around a special interest (p. 114)

Noncompete clause a provision in a contract that prohibits a person from working in a competing business for a specific period of time (p. 355)

Nonprice competition when a business decides to emphasize other factors in the marketing mix besides price (p. 324)

Nonrevenue sports those sports that are funded by schools but do not provide a return on investment (p. 196)

O

Occupational Outlook Handbook a publication of the Bureau of Labor Statistics that provides an overview of jobs and careers in different fields, including marketing (p. 393)

Operating expenses all of the costs associated with running a business in addition to the cost of the merchandise (p. 216)

Opportunity cost value of the next best alternative that you pass up when making a choice (p. 37)

P

Parody a humorous imitation of the original work (p. 343)

Partnership when two or more individuals sign an agreement to own and operate a business together (p. 367)

Patent a property right that excludes others from making, using, offering for sale, or selling the invention (p. 341)

Patronage purchases purchases based on consumer loyalty to a particular brand or product (p. 41)

Penetration price strategy uses low pricing to help capture a large market share early (p. 164)

Personal selling in-person, face-to-face communication between a seller and a customer (p. 238)

Piracy the theft of copyrighted material (p. 100)

Platforms types of delivery systems (p. 192)

Podcasts a way of distributing multimedia files over the Internet for later playback (p. 188)

Polyglots people who speak many languages (p. 103)

Positioning a strategy used by a company to differentiate its products or services from its competitors' products or services (p. 167)

Positioning statement the specific description of the unique qualities of a product's marketing mix (p. 324)

Preapproach the first step in the sales process whereby the salesperson learns everything possible about the products and services offered, the target market, and the competition (p. 289)

Predictive search a feature that reviews your private data to provide you with answers to questions it predicts you might ask (p. 186)

Price the amount that customers pay for products (p. 5)

Price discrimination occurs when an individual, group, or business is charged a higher price than others purchasing the same product or service (p. 215)

Price fixing occurs when related businesses conspire to charge high prices (p. 214)

Price lines distinct categories of merchandise based on price, quality, and features (p. 218)

Price points the range of prices charged for a category of merchandise (p. 134)

Prime time the block of time during the middle of the evening when the largest number of viewers is watching (p. 108)

Principles the rules and codes of conduct on which ethical behavior is based (p. 83)

Probationary period a test period of a few months to determine whether an employee can fulfill the needs of the organization (p. 373)

Product what a business offers customers to satisfy needs (p. 5)

Product enhancements features added to the basic product to satisfy additional needs and wants with a single purchase (p. 151)

Product extensions items offered in addition to the product to make it more attractive to the target market (p. 151)

Product life cycle four stages of a product including introduction, growth, maturity, and decline (p. 163)

Product line a group of similar products with slight variations to satisfy the different needs of consumers (p. 152)

Product mix a new product's final form and its total assorted features, including the brand name, the various products offered under the brand, and the packaging (p. 150)

Product placement the integration into a movie or television show of a product (p. 241)

Product portfolio all of the products a company has available for customers at any one time (p. 323)

Productivity rate at which companies produce goods or services in relation to the amount of materials and number of employees utilized (p. 36)

Professional development includes all meetings, courses, seminars, and networking opportunities that enhance an individual's knowledge and performance in his or her career area (p. 406)

Professional organizations associations for professionals in the same or similar industries formed for the purposes of continuing education and networking (p. 399)

Profit the amount of money remaining from income after all expenses are paid (p. 67)

Profit motive when a company makes decisions on how to use resources in ways that result in the greatest profit (p. 67)

Project matrix a chart displaying the tasks, groups or individuals responsible for completion of the tasks, and the due dates or timelines (p. 327)

Promotion ways to make customers aware of products and encourage them to buy (p. 5)

Promotional mix the blending of the promotional elements of advertising, sales promotion, publicity, and personal selling (p. 275)

Promotional plan a written, detailed description of how the four elements of promotion—advertising, sales promotion, publicity, and personal selling—will be used (p. 274)

Public domain the realm in which the originator's work can be used by anyone without cost or permission (p. 342)

Public relations (PR) the arm of promotion that tries to create a favorable public opinion for an individual or organization (p. 249)

Public relations specialist An individual hired to build and maintain positive relationships between his or her employer and the public (p. 393)

Publicist the person responsible for maintaining relations with the public and news media (p. 248)

Publicity Unpaid media attention, whether negative or positive, about a business and its products, services, or events (p. 238)

Q

Qualitative measurement a method used to measure results that is subjective and depends on interpretation (p. 276)

Quantitative measurement a method used to measure results that provides information in terms of numbers or percentages (p. 275)

R

Ratings the number of viewers a program attracts (p. 22)

Rational purchases when consumers recognize needs and wants, assess their priorities and budget, conduct research, compare alternatives, and then make purchases based on careful thought and sound reasoning (p. 41)

Reach the number of people in the target market expected to receive the message through the chosen medium (such as a TV commercial or magazine ad) (p. 243)

Reflection paraphrasing, or restating, what the speaker has said to demonstrate your understanding (p. 377)

Return on investment calculates the business's return as a percentage of the money invested (p. 71)

Revenue stream an activity that will produce money (p. 67)

Risk the possibility of financial gain or loss or personal injury (p. 75)

Risk assessment a step-by-step process by which knowledgeable safety and security staff identify and prepare to manage risks (p. 80)

Risk management preventing, reducing, or lessening the negative impacts of risk (p. 77)

Royalty the payment for the use of copyrighted work (p. 342)

S

Salary a specified amount paid annually for a job regardless of the number of hours worked (p. 373)

Salary cap a maximum amount that a team can spend on players' salaries (p. 347)

Sales promotion an additional incentive offered for a limited time to encourage consumers to buy a product (p. 238)

Sample a small number of people representative of the large group (p. 133)

Scarcity occurs when there is a limited amount of resources needed to produce and distribute goods and services (pp. 68, 212)

Shopping cart abandoners people who start to make an online purchase, but leave the website without completing it (p. 141)

Shoulder period a period of moderate demand (p. 224)

Situational analysis an in-depth look at the current conditions of the business, the competition, and the target customer (p. 312)

Skimming price strategy introduces new products at a very high price (p. 164)

SMART objectives specific, measurable, attainable, relevant, and timely objectives (p. 317)

Soft data data based on an educated guess (p. 129)

Sole proprietorship a business that is owned and operated by one person (p. 367)

Sponsorship occurs when an individual or business provides products, services, or financial support for a sports team or an event (p. 268)

Sports marketing using sports to market products (p. 13)

Strategic thinking the process of finding unique, innovative ways to reach an objective (p. 317)

Strike a work stoppage caused by the voluntary, temporary refusal of the employees to work (p. 347)

Student professional organizations associations for students that foster leadership, civic consciousness, career training, and social responsibility (p. 400)

Suggestion selling occurs when the salesperson asks customers if they want to purchase related products (p. 289)

SWOT analysis an examination of the business's strengths, weaknesses, opportunities, and threats (p. 314)

Syndicated research when research is conducted by an independent company and then offered for sale to all businesses in the industry (p. 127)

T

Tactics the actions taken to implement the strategy (p. 318)

Target market a specific group of consumers a business wants to reach (p. 46)

Ticket brokers registered businesses that legally buy and resell tickets to a variety of entertainment events and guarantee ticket authenticity (p. 295)

Ticket scalpers individuals who sell tickets to major sporting and entertainment events, often outside the venue on the day of the event, for inflated prices (p. 296)

Time-shifting the recording of a television show for private viewing later (p. 343)

Trade sales promotion when a sales promotion is directed at members of the distribution channel (p. 245)

Trademark the legal protection of words and symbols used by a company (p. 153)

Trailer mash-up combines the short ads, or trailers, for all of the award-nominated films into one short film that is posted online (p. 266)

V

Values-based culture a culture that communicates values through high performance and excellent customer service (p. 54)

Venture capital financing provided to start a company in return for owning part of the company (p. 72)

Venue the facility where an event is held (p. 181)

Viral campaign a promotion in which a few online mentions produce millions of comments (p. 248)

Visual merchandising the process of creating three-dimensional displays to promote products (p. 243)

W

Wide release involves distributing a movie nationally to a thousand or more theaters at the same time (p. 193)